David M. Wrobel / Michael C. Steiner

Editors

Many Wests

Place,
Culture, &
Regional
Identity

University Press of Kansas

Published by the University Press of Kansas (Lawrence,
Kansas 66049), which was organized by the Kansas Board
of Regents and is operated and funded by Emporia State
University, Fort Hays State University, Kansas State University,
Pittsburg State University, the University of Kansas, and
Wichita State University

Library of Congress Cataloging-in-Publication Data

Many wests : place, culture, & regional identity / edited by
   David M. Wrobel and Michael C. Steiner.
       p. cm.
   Includes index.
   ISBN 0-7006-0861-3 (cloth). — ISBN 0-7006-0862-1 (pbk.)
      1. Regionalism—West (U.S.) 2. West (U.S.)—Geography.
   3. West (U.S.)—Social life and customs. I. Steiner,
   Michael (Michael C.) II. Wrobel, David M.
   F595.3.M36   1997
   978—dc21   97-23019

British Library Cataloguing in Publication Data is available.

Printed in the United States of America

10 9 8 7 6 5 4 3 2 1

The paper used in this publication meets the minimum
requirements of the American National Standard for
Permanence of Paper for Printed Library Materials Z39.48–1984.

Many Wests

As the frontier disappeared like a mirage on the desert

and the mist of early speculation and fancy cleared,

it was soon discovered that there were many Wests

within the West.

—Carey McWilliams, "Myths of the West"

New England is pretty much of a piece. The South is

essentially of a piece. The Middle West is there from

the eastern edge of Indiana ... clear to the Missouri. ...

But the West is several different regions. ... all so different

in their history and ethnic compositions, that I think

trying to make a unanimous culture out of them would

be a hopeless job. It would be like wrapping five

watermelons.

—Wallace Stegner, "On Western History and Historians"

Contents

Preface

In conceptualizing and co-editing this book of essays about regional identity in the West's many places, we have incurred numerous debts. First, we must thank the staff of the University Press of Kansas for their enduring patience and enthusiasm. Cynthia Miller, former editor at Kansas, provided great encouragement for the project when it was in its embryonic stages. Michael Briggs then carried the torch for *Many Wests* until Nancy Scott was hired and took over responsibility for the volume. Nancy provided incisive criticism and vigorous encouragement over a long period. We are indebted to all three of our Kansas editors.

Our institutions (California State University, Fullerton, for Michael and Widener University for David) generously supplied funding for the volume. The California Studies Seminar at the University of California, Berkeley, became a forum for airing some of our key themes in the spring of 1997, as did the Humanities Colloquium at Widener University in the fall of 1996. Our respective departments of American Studies and History/Humanities furnished unfailing academic support. The Huntington Library in San Marino, California, has also been a strong presence in the history of *Many Wests*. The two of us first met at the Huntington in the summer of 1990, and we developed the final structure of the book there in the summer of 1996.

Many colleagues and scholars of regionalism—including Charles Alexander, Allan Axelrad, Peter Blodgett, Kathleen Conzen, David Emmons, James Grossman, Robert Hine, Wayne Hobson, Frederick Hoxie, Wilbur Jacobs, Karen Lystra, Yi-Fu Tuan, and Leila Zenderland—carefully listened to and generously encouraged our keen interest in western regional diversity. For their enduring patience and emotional support we are forever thankful to Lucy Lefren Steiner and Rebecca J. Wrobel.

The value of any anthology rests on the strength of its contributors. We feel immensely fortunate to have worked so closely with thirteen accomplished and imaginative regional scholars from American studies, geography, history, and literature who wrote so effectively about the many configurations of western land and life. Every contributor exhibited great buoyancy and good humor in responding to our suggestions, and this made our work much easier.

As co-editors we are also indebted to each other. *Many Wests* has been a collaborative effort from start to finish, and we have equally shared all of the conceptual and editorial responsibilities during the three full years devoted to this project. Through countless telephone conversations, faxes, letters, and discussions at Berkeley and in the gardens of the Huntington Library, we reached difficult editorial decisions, critiqued each other's work, and brought the idea of an anthology on western regional diversity to fruition. Ironically, perhaps, it was a shared interest in the historian Frederick Jackson Turner that sparked our acquaintance and a common appreciation of the New Western History that proved the catalyst for this joint project.

Last, and most important, we wish to thank Richard Etulain and Martin Ridge whose scholarship has inspired us to think carefully about the emergence of regional identities in the West. Many years ago Martin Ridge suggested that the two of us put a panel together on western regionalism. We took his advice to heart and went a little further, putting together this book. He has been a source of inspiration to us both, ever willing to lend a sympathetic ear when we agonized over editorial decisions and always able to offer sage advice. Richard Etulain has also been a vital force looming in the background of *Many Wests,* especially during the project's early stages. He suggested contributors and provided insights that helped us save time and avoid pitfalls. For their unfailing support, advice, and wisdom we dedicate *Many Wests* to Richard Etulain and Martin Ridge.

Michael C. Steiner   David M. Wrobel
Fullerton, California   *Chester, Pennsylvania*

Many Wests

Many Wests

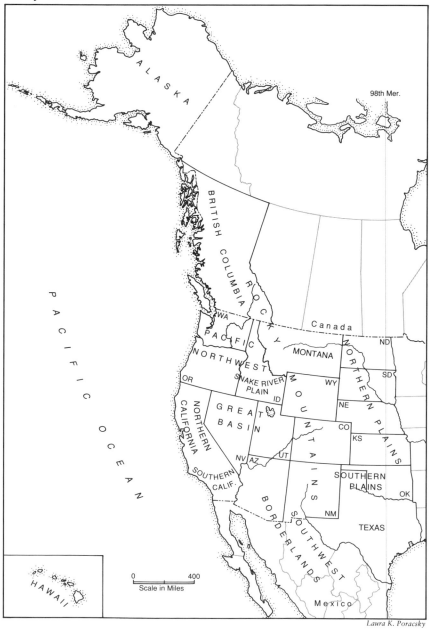

Laura K. Poracsky

Many Wests: Discovering a Dynamic Western Regionalism

Michael C. Steiner and David M. Wrobel

THE DEATH AND LIFE OF AMERICAN REGIONALISM

In 1957, western writer Wright Morris surveyed the American landscape and sounded the latest in a long series of death knells for the West and other American regions: "The *region*—the region in the sense that once fed the imagination—is now for sale on the shelf with the sugar maple Kewpies; the hand-loom ties and hand-sewn moccasins are now available, along with food and fuel, at regular intervals on our turnpikes. . . . The only regions left are those the artist must imagine. They lie beyond the usual forms of salvage. No matter where we go, in America today, we shall find what we left behind."[1] Morris's lament for a lost West reverberates throughout American culture. His eulogy to a once distinctive place now homogenized by mass culture and swallowed by the leviathan state is part of a familiar refrain and recurring narrative in American history. Like every other region, the once rugged West is dead. Crushed between corporate glaciers from the coasts—from Wall Street and from Silicon Valley, from Houston and from Hollywood—the true West as a wide-open place of promise is gone. All that remains are commercialized travesties of the real thing—manufactured moccasins and kachina dolls, franchised Santa Fe cuisine, packaged dude ranches, and other regional kitsch for bored urbanites craving tokens of authenticity.

A death-of-the-region scenario seems embedded in the modern consciousness, and the American West is often seen as the cemetery for dreams of spatial diversity. The story line is simple, straightforward, and

"Thanks—it was so fabulously regional. I mean, I can't close my eyes without seeing fajitas and Georgia O'Keeffe."

Drawing by Wm. Hamilton, copyright 1988, New Yorker Magazine.

inexorable—with regionalism cast as a lost cause doomed by the forces of modernity. Ever since the machine entered the garden and the North won the Civil War, the story goes, American regions have been battered by successive waves of nationalism, metropolitanism, capitalism, commercialism, and cyberspace. After a century and a half of incessant pounding, New England, the Midwest, the South, and finally the West have been leveled into a smooth expanse covered with interchangeable cities where Americans will always find what they left behind. Morris's turnpikes lined with regional trinket shops in the 1950s have been replaced by generic freeways connecting cloned shopping malls, housing tracts, theme parks, Kmarts, Wal-Marts, and Holiday Inns in the 1990s. Folk singer Melvina Reynolds's rows of "little boxes made of ticky tacky" are now an endless nowhere of silicon valleys and edge cities—a World Wide Web of circuit-board landscapes exemplifying theologian Herbert Richardson's belief that "the vision of a wholly artificial environment, man and society restructured by the power of the machine, is the American dream."[2] The driving of the golden spike at Promontory Point in 1869 was simply the most dramatic in a chain of technological events

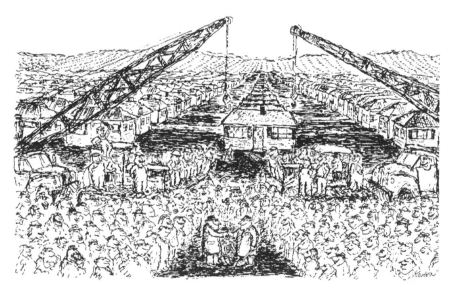

"At last! One nation, indivisible."

Drawing by Koren, copyright 1970, New Yorker Magazine.

that sealed the doom of the distinctive West, with transcontinental railroads paving the way for interstates and the placeless cosmopolitanism promised by the Internet.[3]

An inexorable leveling seems to imbue the American experience, and Westerners themselves are implicated in this process. "Something in the heart of the westerner," Richard Rodriguez writes, "must glory in the clamor of hammering, the squealing of saws, the rattle of marbles in aerosol cans. Something in the heart of the westerner must yearn for lost wilderness, once wilderness has been routed."[4] Breaking prairies, mining mountains, leveling forests, damming rivers, flooding deserts, building casinos, strips, and housing tracts—westward-yearning Americans ravage the very thing they most cherish, cropping nature as though it were a hateful presence and then mourning their victim once it's safely laid to rest.[5] Examples are legion. Almost the moment westward movement ended on the Great Plains, William F. Cody mounted his first tribute there to the departed West: "The Old Glory Blow Out" in North Platte, Nebraska, on July 4, 1882, was a nostalgic pageant complete with costumed riders and a mock stampede of ragged, remnant buffalo, the very species a younger Cody had hunted nearly to extinction. Owen Wister's farewell in 1902 to the "vanished world" of "the horseman, the cowpuncher, the last romantic figure upon our soil" and James Earl Fraser's colossal statue *End of the Trail,* depicting an Indian on horseback in slumped defeat which awed multitudes at the Panama-Pacific Exposition in San Francisco in 1915, are two more examples of how Euro-Americans have mourned their regional victim.[6]

A chorus of politicians, writers, and intellectuals has contributed to the dying-region script. "As the country grows it will inevitably grow more homogeneous," Woodrow Wilson eagerly predicted in 1897. "There has never yet been a time in our history when we were without an 'East' and a 'West,'" he admitted, "but the novel day when we shall be without them is now in sight. . . . The conditions which prevail in the ever-widening 'East' will sooner or later cover the continent, and we shall at last be one people." "I rejoice to believe that there are no longer any permanent sectional lines," the future president would soon declare in 1901. Confirming the birth of this seamless nation, the most popular play of the Progressive era, Israel Zangwill's *The Melting Pot* (1908), ends with the triumphant merging of regional and ethnic differences. "Yes, East and West, North and South, the palm and the pine, the pole and the equator, the crescent and the cross—how the great Alchemist melts and fuses them with his purging flame!" Zangwill's Americanized hero exalts from his tenement rooftop.[7]

Seventy years after Wilson and Zangwill announced the creation of one nation, indivisible, historian Daniel Boorstin imparted elegant clarity to their Progressive narrative. Noting that "the first charm and virgin promise of America were that it was so different a place," Boorstin stressed that "the fulfillment of modern America would be its power to level times and places, to erase differences between here and there, between now and then. And finally the uniqueness of America would prove to be its ability to erase uniqueness."[8] Even those who lament this process recognize its power. Bioregionalist Paul Shepard points out that although North America originally bristled with diversity, "almost everything we have done to it in the last two centuries has worked toward the destruction of these differences," and poet Wendell Berry caustically describes Euro-Americans as urban nomads "moving about on the face of this continent with a mindless destructiveness . . . that makes Sherman's march to the sea look like a prank."[9]

It seems inevitable that regions crumble as Americans bulldoze nature, that regionalism perishes as, in Joni Mitchell's words, we "pave paradise and put up a parking lot."[10] It seems irrefutable that geographical and cultural differences dwindle as we follow high-tech prophets who declare, for example, that "the 800 telephone number and the piece of plastic have made time and space obsolete," who trumpet that "the central event of the twentieth century is the overthrow of matter," or who assert that electronic media will allow us to "overcome the tyranny of geography."[11] In the face of such technocratic enthusiasm, places that resist leveling have been dismissed by other critics as quaint curiosities and embattled folk enclaves—mere "pockets of the past" and "shadowy corners of American life, which stand in contrast to the general American culture of urbanization, industrialization, and other-direction."[12] People foolish enough to promote regional cultures have been ridiculed by V. F. Calverton as "modern Don Quixotes stabbing at steel windmills" or scorned by Louis Wirth as cranky reactionaries mounting "desperate and futile protests against the tides of progress" and crackpots who would "squeeze life into a rigid mold . . . and retard the integration of life on a wider and more inclusive scale."[13]

Given the force and frequency of such reasoning, it is hardly surprising that we have been saying farewell to the West for more than a century. The western landscape is riddled with memories of last stands and last best places, and it is hardly shocking to hear poet Kenneth Hanson join fellow Westerner Wright Morris in flatly announcing the death of regionalism. "Regionalism is as dead as the carrier pigeon," the north-western writer bluntly declared in 1975. "It ended as a possibility at latest with World War II, since which time Americans have been on the move. . . . Given the facts, regionalism is an anachronism, and its reflection in literature is sentimentalism, an exercise in wishful thinking or nostalgia."[14]

Yet the truth is far more complex than the accepted scenario. At the same time that regions seem to be fading, they also appear to be flourishing. Far from being as dead as the passenger pigeon, regionalism—especially western regionalism—may be as irrepressible as the phoenix. It is a central paradox of American history that we level the land at the same time that we yearn for uneven places of belonging. During the very decades that Wilson and Zangwill, Calverton and Wirth, and Boorstin and Hanson announced the extinction of regions, many Americans proclaimed their rebirth. Early in the century, Josiah Royce saw the rise of "wise provincialism" as an antidote to the homelessness of mass society, and Frederick Jackson Turner perceived the growth of constructive sectionalism as the inevitable sequel to the fading frontier.[15] In the 1930s, Lewis Mumford, Howard W. Odum, and Walter Prescott Webb wrote monumental studies about the enduring folk-regional framework of civilization, and Franklin Roosevelt announced his devotion to regional planning as "the way of the future."[16] Since the 1970s, public intellectuals as varied as Jane Jacobs, William Appleman Williams, and Gary Snyder have championed forms of regional renewal to reach economic, political, and environmental justice, and scores of historians and artists have taken their stands as "new western" regionalists.[17]

Rather than being in a simple and steady state of decline, American regionalism has had an intricate and episodic history. As a largely unconscious source of identity, regionalism has been a compelling force throughout American history, but at certain points it becomes a *self-conscious* concern—a cause and rallying cry. It is normal for people, especially for Americans, to accept unconsciously the familiar milieu and immediate background of their daily lives—to take their region for granted like the circumambient air they breathe. Unreflective immersion in landscape or movement through space are more common than deliberate sense of place, and a degree of environmental blindness is inevitable and even necessary to function smoothly in the world.[18] "We soon cease to see what we are accustomed to seeing," novelist William Gass has shrewdly argued. "The sightless, who bump along on Braille, don't care to count what their fingers read. That would be twice blind."[19]

Yet occasionally the affective bond between people and place—their topophilia—is lifted to a more conscious level. At certain points in their personal and collective histories, Americans have been roused to a more vivid appreciation of place, creating historical rhythms in regional consciousness. From the flowering of New England in the 1840s and 1850s to the emergence of prairie architecture and populism in the 1880s and 1890s, from the southern literary renaissance and nationwide rediscovery of "native grounds" in the 1920s and 1930s to the thirst for local knowledge and rise of "new western" art, architecture, and history in the 1980s and 1990s, a gamut of regional affections has motivated large numbers of ordinary people as well as intellectual elites.[20]

Although Euro-Americans may seem the least likely of regionalists—gripped as they are by mobility, mass culture, Manifest Destiny, and the conquest of nature—a desire for regional identity looms in their lives. The uprooting, leveling nature of American experience evokes a counterdesire for stability and more intimate places of identity. We consolidate and disperse, unify and diversify at the same time. The sheer immensity of the United States engenders the need for subnational places of belonging, and regional loyalty often emerges as a conscious response to the emptiness of mass culture and the nation-state. Focusing on the growth of far western identity in the late nineteenth century, historian Earl Pomeroy concluded that "the idea of difference between West and East . . . developed almost as a consequence of the region's assimilation to standardized, nationalized ways." From a more panoramic viewpoint, philosopher John Dewey perceived regionalism as an inevitable reaction to nationalism. Praising the rich welter of local cultures flourishing beneath the dull national façade, Dewey asserted that "the locality is the only universal" and that "the wider the formal, the legal unity, the more intense becomes the local life." [21]

Pomeroy and Dewey described regionalism as an inherent response to the modern state; at the postmodern twilight of the twentieth century, their observations seem even more prescient as regionalism flourishes throughout the nation and the world. Describing how end-of-the-century

globalism engenders a countertide of pluralism and ethnoregional passions, political scientist Harold Isaacs observes that "we are fragmenting
and globalizing at the same time. We spin out as from a centrifuge, flying
apart socially and politically, at the same time that enormous centripetal
forces press us all into more and more of a single mass than ever before."
"Caught between Babel and Disneyland," Benjamin Barber argues in *Jihad
vs. McWorld,* "the planet is falling precipitously apart and coming reluctantly together at the very same moment."[22] Chechneya, Chiapas, and
Bosnia coexist with McDonalds, Microsoft, and MTV. At the same time
that the global village and the World Wide Web promise exhilarating
cosmopolitanism, they also stir up longing for more intimate loyalties. On
the threshold of a soothing small world fashioned by Michael Eisner and
Bill Gates, people resist this potentially dreary monoculture in favor of
more particular forms of identity.

What Isaacs and Barber say about the planet as a whole also applies—
though less divisively, one hopes—to the United States and to the West.
"The more Americans participate in, and indeed lead the world in, globalism," geographer Yi-Fu Tuan argues, "the more they yearn for locality,
tradition, roots—for the hearths and ethnos that they can directly experience and understand, for the small milieu that yields emotional satisfaction."[23] As we move into the twenty-first century, it is clear that regionalism is an irrepressible social force for reaction as well as renewal.
We have already listened to regionalism's critics; recent advocates are
equally persuasive. For folklorist Archie Green, "regionalism is a forever
agenda" that taps fundamental human needs of pluralism and place, while
for historian Richard Maxwell Brown, it is possible that in the near future "regionalism will not only rival but surpass nationalism as a source
for good in human life." For jurist Felix Frankfurter, "regionalism is a
recognition of the intractable diversities among men, diversities partly
shaped by nature but no less derived from the different reactions of men
to nature. . . . [R]egionalism is not a fixed concept. No region, whether
natural or cultural is stable." "At bottom, the problems of American regionalism," Frankfurter concluded, "are the problems of American civilization: the continuous process of bringing to fruition the best of which
American men and women are capable."[24]

Many Wests echoes these sentiments. Reflecting and sustaining the
wondrous diversities of nature and culture, regionalism is truly a "source
for good in human life." And it is in the West, with its sprawling varie-

gated landscapes and swirling varieties of people, that American regionalism may find its fullest expression. For the West, as Carey McWilliams
and Wallace Stegner observed, is really many Wests. The broad and bris-
tling land between the ninty-eighth meridian and the Pacific Ocean is a
constellation of many ever-changing, ever-shifting regions "all so different in their history and ethnic compositions, that . . . trying to make a
unanimous culture out of them would be a hopeless job. It would be like
wrapping five watermelons."[25] Building on the pathbreaking work of historians who regard the West as "a cohesive whole, fixed in space . . . as a
distinct place inhabited by distinct people" and who bring "down-to-earth
clarity" to this region by thinking of it as a specific place rather than an
amorphous process,[26] the thirteen contributors to this book achieve an
even sharper, earthier clarity by focusing on the many Wests within this
sprawling land.

As early as 1897, Frederick Jackson Turner urged historians to ana-
lyze the West in terms of "the regions that compose it" and "divide the
West into its proper regions and describe the spirit of each."[27] Since
Turner's early analysis of the "spirit" of four Wests—the Prairie states,
the Rocky Mountain states, the Pacific Slope, and the Southwest—there
have been innumerable efforts to outline the many Wests beyond the
Mississippi. From John Wesley Powell, Otis T. Mason, and William Morris
Davis in the 1890s to Walter Prescott Webb, Howard Odum, and A. J.
Mezerik in the 1930s and 1940s to Daniel Elazar, Raymond Gastil, Joel
Garreau, Wilbur Zelinsky, Donald Meinig, and Terry Jordan since the
1970s, scores of intellectuals and social scientists have tried, in Meinig's
words, to visualize "the West as a set of dynamic regions" and have worked
to uncover, in Howard Lamar's words, "the complex matrix of western
regions."[28] It is hoped that *Many Wests* will contribute to this worthy,
never-ending quest.

MANY WESTS AND WESTERN REGIONALISM

Recent developments in the field of western history testify to the renewed
vitality of the theme of western regional distinctiveness. The past decade
or so has witnessed an explosion of scholarly and public interest in the
American West. Sparked largely by the writings of New Western Historians, the story of the western past has taken on a new relevance in the
complex, contentious, multicultural present.[29] This revisionist approach,

historian Elliott West notes, has produced a "longer, grimmer, but more interesting story."[30] Longer, because the frontier framework that brought western history to a close with the end of the nineteenth century has been largely abandoned in favor of one that addresses developments in the twentieth-century West and emphasizes continuity between the western past and present. Grimmer, because the dark underside of the western past—featuring environmental despoliation and oppression of peoples of color, women, and the laboring classes—has been placed more squarely under the scholarly microscope than was the case when frontier triumphalism constituted the thematic framework for western history.[31] And more interesting because, as leading revisionist Patricia Nelson Limerick has pointed out, the intention of the New Western History is "to make clear that in western American history, heroism and villainy, virtue and vice, and nobility and shoddiness appear in roughly the same proportions as they appear in any other subject of human history."[32] Historical interpretation is intrinsically more interesting and more credible when stories of tragedy and triumph—and the myriad shades of gray that lie between— occupy the same stage.[33] Furthermore, the fuller inclusion of the West's formerly underrepresented peoples of color makes the new western past more interesting and relevant to more people. Heightened emphasis on topics such as urban growth, race relations, and gender and environmental issues also augments the relevance of western history.

Perhaps the most important, and probably the most enduring, of the contributions of the past decade of historical writing on the West is the emphasis on western diversity. While popular perception of the West among many Americans may still center on fictional cowboys such as John Wayne and the Marlboro Man, the public is becoming more aware of the diversity of the West's population. Yet for all the recent emphasis on western demographic diversity, it does seem that the New Western History, in its efforts to replace the frontier framework with a geographically bounded, regional West has given less attention to another important area of western diversity: regional diversity. Deemphasizing the frontier process and focusing on the West as a definable place marked by certain characteristics—such as aridity, conquest, Native Americans, racial and ethnic diversity, and boom–bust economic cycles—has amounted to a double-edged sword for western historians. On one level, it has bolstered the West's regional identity by applying to it characteristics that move beyond frontier-centered notions of the area as the final stage in a heroic

process of Euro-American settlement. But on another level, by emphasizing defining regional characteristics for the whole of the West, the new
revisionism has to some extent overlooked significant differences within
this vast region.[34]

This effort to define the West as a place (we could call it the "region-
alizing" of the West) has sparked some fascinating debates. Critics of the
New Western History have questioned whether diversity, conquest, or
aridity (or better, semiaridity) really defines the whole of the West and
distinguishes it from other regions. Semiaridity, for example, characterizes much of the West, but not all, certainly not the Pacific Northwest
(or at least that portion of it lying west of the Cascades).[35] And racial
diversity, while certainly a defining issue for much of the west coast, for
the Southwest, and for Texas, is less characteristic of Montana, Idaho,
Oregon, Washington, and the Plains states.

Such debates are important because they concern the application of
generalizations about the broader regional West to its many regions or
subregions. The West probably does have certain defining characteristics, but they are not readily and evenly applicable to all parts of the
West. Furthermore, one of the most enduring of those characteristics may
be the West's hallowed place in the American, or at least the Euro-
American, imagination. And that mythic West of the imagination is not
constructed through any conception of western regional diversity; instead,
it is derived from the application of near-intangible generalities to "the
West"—notions of striking, colorful vistas; romantic, yet challenging landscapes; breathtaking frontier dramas. The West in this context becomes
a "state of mind"—something rather difficult to map.

To fully appreciate the many Wests within the larger West, we must
move beyond both the mythic West of the frontier paradigm and the geographically bounded West of recent revisionism. We have to venture beyond the sweeping generalities to see the various subregional realities that
make up the broader West. The theoretical debates that have driven the
field—most obviously, the issue of whether "frontier" or "region" provides
the more appropriate operational paradigm for western history—have
helped western historians become very effective at defining the metaphori-
cal forest, but a little reluctant to recognize its constituent trees. Comparative studies of various issues or developments in different western
subregions could prove particularly useful in helping western historians
see beyond the forest.

In addition to the many subregional wests within the larger West, there are many locations for the broader West itself. This book focuses on the area beginning with the second tier of states west of the Mississippi. The area includes, of course, North Dakota, South Dakota, Nebraska, Kansas, Oklahoma, Texas, New Mexico, Colorado, Wyoming, Montana, Idaho, Utah, Arizona, Nevada, Oregon, Washington, and California, but also the noncontiguous Hawai'i and Alaska, and the borderlands lying beyond geopolitical boundaries, such as British Columbia and Mexico.[36] Indeed, if we are to consider British Columbia in relation to the American West, we might also consider the relationship to the West of the other western Canadian provinces. While British Columbia borders Washington and tiny portions of Idaho and Montana, Alberta borders roughly half of Montana's northern boundary, Saskatchewan borders the rest of Montana and part of North Dakota, and Manitoba also borders a portion of North Dakota. Native Americans have criss-crossed the geopolitical boundaries, and farmers and businessmen on each side have responded to economic opportunities on the other side of the border.[37]

Arguments could be made for the inclusion of the first tier of states west of the Mississippi: Minnesota (a good portion of which is west of the river yardstick), Iowa, Missouri, Arkansas, and Louisiana. Similarly, some might want to include the whole trans-Appalachian West in the larger western picture. One historian has recently called for the inclusion of the Upper Peninsula of Michigan, northern Wisconsin, and all of Minnesota and Iowa in "the West." Or, if one were to take the Census Bureau's model of four regions and nine divisions within the United States, the second tier of states west of the Mississippi—North Dakota, South Dakota, Nebraska, Kansas, Oklahoma, and Texas—would be excluded and the West would begin with the third trans-Mississippi tier—Montana, Wyoming, Colorado, and New Mexico—and would include Alaska and Hawai'i.[38]

The West we present is larger than the Census Bureau's definition, but smaller than that of some western historians. It contains, if the noncontiguous Wests are included, nineteen U.S. states and, perhaps, areas beyond both the northern and southern regional-national borders. The contiguous West, as we envision it, covers two full time zones—Pacific and Rocky Mountain—and a portion of the Central. The noncontiguous West contains two more time zones: Alaskan and Hawai'i–Aleutian.[39] Within this vast geographic area, there are diverse landscapes and climates, wildly varying degrees of racial and ethnic diversity, many economies, and multiple regional histories.

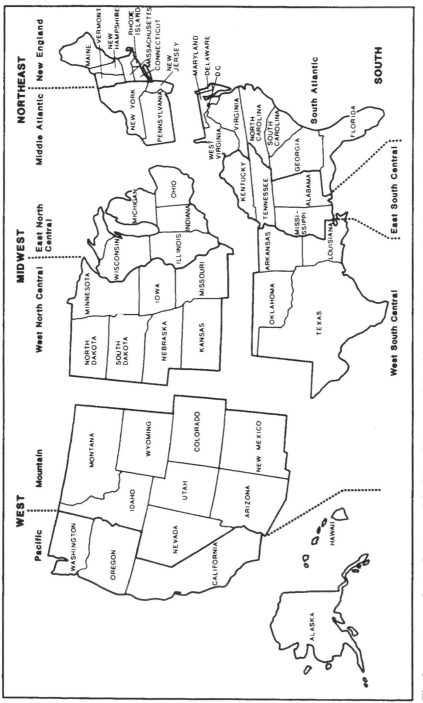

The four regions and nine divisions of the United States as defined by the U.S. Bureau of the Census. From Michael Bradshaw, Regions and Regionalism in the United States (Jackson: University Press of Mississippi, 1988). Reproduced by permission of Macmillan.

Our purpose is to build on the revisionist impulse of the past decade and present the West in all its regional diversity by focusing on many of the Wests that constitute the larger whole. Doing this much is perilous in itself. Not all readers will agree that our Wests are representative of that larger whole. For example, one might ask: Why include chapters on certain states—California, Texas, and Montana—and not others—for instance, Wyoming, Colorado, and Arizona? Why include chapters on the southern Plains and the northern Plains, and none on the central Plains?[40] How can regions as small as the Snake River Region and as large as the Rocky Mountain West, the Pacific Northwest, or the Southwest be compared? Why have two essays on California and none devoted to Nebraska?

The list of questions could go on almost indefinitely, but the purpose of this volume is to raise such questions, not to conclusively answer them all. We are not presenting a finished model of the West and its constituent subregions. Such models have been constructed by other scholars. Cultural geographers Wilbur Zelinsky and Donald Meinig, for example, have developed sophisticated models of the West as a mosaic of from six to nine cultural regions, each with a historic core and ever-shifting domain and sphere of influence.[41] At a more popular level, Raymond Gastil and Joel Garreau have presented broadscale schemes treating the West as a constellation of cultural regions. Nine of Gastil's thirteen American regions—including the Upper Midwest, the Central Midwest, the Rocky Mountain Region, the Mormon Region, the Interior Southwest, the Pacific Southwest, the Pacific Northwest, Alaska, and the Hawaiian Islands—overlap with our many Wests, while four of Garreau's "Nine Nations"—including Ecotopia, Mexamerica, the Empty Quarter, and the Breadbasket—fall squarely or partially within the larger West as we have defined it.[42] We have not presented grand designs such as Gastil's and Garreau's because such models suggest a level of finality—a confident resolution of complex regional conundrums—that we have simply not reached and that perhaps can never be reached.

Questions concerning this book's contents prompt important connected questions about regionalism: Is state identification more important than regional identification in the West or in some parts of the West? For example, do Coloradans identify with the Rocky Mountain region, with their state, or with their respective slopes—eastern or western? Do Southwesterners identify with that amorphous regional entity, or do they consider themselves Westerners first? Or does locality overshadow state,

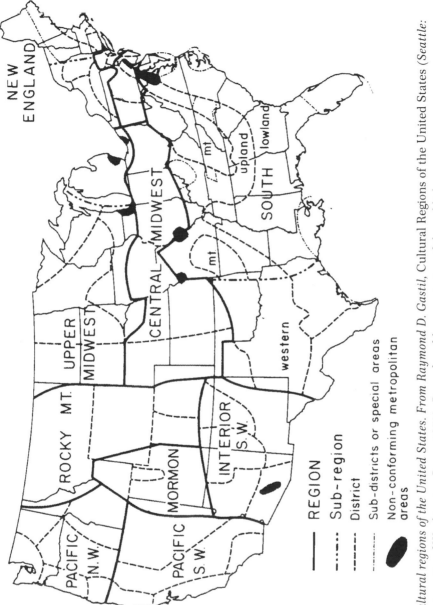

Cultural regions of the United States. From Raymond D. Gastil, Cultural Regions of the United States (Seattle: University of Washington Press, 1975). Reproduced by permission of the publisher.

subregion, and broader region as a foundation of regional consciousness? Does urban identification constitute as legitimate a "sense of place" as identification with the land? Do Portlanders or Denverites somehow have less regional consciousness than farmers in Oregon or Colorado? Have scholars slighted the regional consciousness of western urban dwellers— the bulk of the West's present population—by emphasizing the relationship between sense of place and attachment to the land?

When we add to the already complex set of equations the dynamic factor of change over time, the western regional and subregional picture becomes even more complex. Perhaps regional identification was more crucial to Pacific Northwesterners in an earlier period, but is currently overshadowed by state identification. Certainly, levels of regional consciousness are influenced by the length of residence in a particular place. But how long does it take a regional sensibility to emerge in a particular place, and how does that sensibility change from generation to generation? Those generations that settled or conquered particular places may identify differently with them than succeeding generations that were born in them. Shared memory of the pioneering process, for example, has been a significant contributor to the regional identity of many Euro-American Westerners and has been a key to the endurance of a "frontier" outlook in parts of the West. The descendants of western pioneers have often been drawn to the legacy of their predecessors and worked to keep alive the spirit of the pioneer era through "frontier days" celebrations.[43]

This "frontier heritage" has helped mold the regional consciousness of many Euro-Americans in the West and demonstrates the interconnectedness, for some Westerners at least, of the themes of frontier and region. Frontiers evolved into regions, and regional consciousness was formed, in part, through recollection of the process of moving to, adjusting to, and (to varying degrees) transforming new places. But for the West's many other groups—including Native Americans, Asians and Asian-Americans, Hispanics and Hispanic-Americans, and African-Americans— European recollections of benign and noble frontier settlement of the West may seem absurd, even obscene. While the shared memory of "frontiering" might be crucial to the regional sensibility of many Euro-American Westerners, quite different shared memories have shaped the sense of place of other ethnic groups. Different groups' memories of the past can collide, and then we are reminded that even within one unique western subregion, regional identities can be diverse and divergent.[44]

While it is a rather dissonant force, or set of forces, western regional-ism is also a dynamic force. And western regions, even while they retain a strong identity, are ever-changing entities. For example, the Pacific Northwest, the Rocky Mountain West, and the Southwest are currently the destinations of out-migrants from California. California's racial and cultural composition has been constantly altered by in-migrations of Asians, Hispanics, African-Americans, and Europeans. The cultural com-position of regions changes over time, and subregional landscapes do not remain static either: they are transformed by both natural and human forces. Even within the most racially homogenous western regions, suc-cessive generations have had to react to changing political and economic realities inside and outside the region. Thus not only do many Wests lie within the larger West, but the sense of place, or regional identity—which we might expect to be a constant among the diverse residents of those regions—is in a constant state of flux.

Among the more difficult region-related questions are two connected ones: How are regions or subregions formed? How is regional conscious-ness formed? Regions might be defined through reference to culture, landscape, or economics. Similarly, the same factors seem to have played key roles (though in varying degrees from region to region) in forming a sense of place in various parts of the West. Regions are defined by out-siders as well as by residents. Regional writers, artists, and storytellers have played a role in shaping the perceptions of regions held by outsiders and residents. Local chambers of commerce, immigration bureaus, and other resident boosters of the West worked closely with outside groups—such as railroads and land companies—to form images of regions for potential settlers, tourists, and investors. We might label the sense of place of people within a region "interior regionalism," and use the phrase "exterior regionalism" for the efforts by those outside a particular region to characterize it. We might also consider the interplay between these two forces—the sense of place of those within a region, and the efforts by outsiders to create a sense of the place—in our determinations of how regional consciousness is formed.[45]

These are complex matters. Scholars have had enough difficulty de-termining the borders of the West (partly because of the powerful mythic baggage that accompanies our sense of westernness) to guarantee that defining the West's subregions and determining how a sense of place developed and changed in each of them will be no easy task.[46] Still, if our emphasis on many Wests plays a role in shifting scholarly attention to the topic of western regional diversity, it will have served its purpose. A close reading of the chapters will not answer all the many questions raised here, but it may help us to address them with more care. Instead of asking whether the West is more racially and culturally diverse than other parts of the country, we might ask which parts of the West are most diverse, which are least diverse, what has accounted for those different settlement patterns, and how has regional consciousness developed differently in these many demographically divergent Wests. When these kinds of questions are first posed and pondered, we are better equipped to address the larger issue of the broader West's regional coherence. Is the American West as regionally significant and classifiable as the American South?[47] To address such a question, we have to know a good deal about the West's constituent regional parts.

These kinds of questions are already being asked by scholars of western regionalism. This volume makes no claims to originality by merely addressing the issues. Indeed, the growth and change in the field of western history have coincided with a heightened interest in the West's subregions. However, it seems that these two areas have been largely studied as separate entities. Recent essay collections on the Pacific Northwest, the Great Plains, the Southwest, and other western subregions demonstrate the strength of regional studies.[48] So the integration of these two burgeoning fields—regional or subregional studies and the study of the whole West as a regional entity (the "New Western Regionalism")—seems timely. Such a merger will further illuminate western diversity and highlight contrasts, connections, and contradictions among the West's many regions.

The chapters in this book are often very different from one another. All address the question of how regional consciousness or identity was formed among inhabitants of a particular western region. All draw connections between regional identity in that particular place—be it southern California, the Great Basin, or the Snake River Valley—and identification with the broader West. Furthermore, all the chapters address the larger issue of "the centrality of place—or more specifically, various western places—in determining social and cultural forms, and individual and collective identities."[49]

Beyond those similarities in intention, the authors have addressed the theme of regional consciousness from markedly different angles of vision.

Some of the essays—those by William Deverell on southern California, Glenna Matthews on northern California, and Arnoldo De León on Texas—focus largely on race and culture as the primary influences on regional consciousness. Others—by James Shortridge on the northern Plains, Anne F. Hyde on the Rocky Mountain region, Elizabeth Raymond on the Great Basin, and John Findlay on the Pacific Northwest—emphasize environmental and economic factors, and the interplay between the two, as the most significant forgers of sense of place. A few essays treat areas beyond the contiguous forty-eight states, and even beyond United States borders, examining their regional relationships to the broader West. Richard Maxwell Brown explores similarities and differences between the Pacific Northwest and the Canadian province of British Columbia, John Whitehead examines the different relationships of Alaska and Hawai'i to the broader West, and Paula Gunn Allen extends the West beyond its southern geopolitical border in her exploration of the Southwest. Finally, some of the essays focus largely on the influence of literature and other aesthetic forms in developing regional consciousness. A few essays are structured in a more literary vein. Brett Wallach tells stories about the southern Plains and reflects on how architecture mirrors regional sensibility. Peter Boag and Mary Murphy focus largely on the influence of writers shaping and reflecting the regional sensibilities of the Snake River Valley and Montana, respectively. These contributions differ in structure and design from the other chapters, which take a more strictly historical approach.

Thus the book is divided into four sections: "Environment and Economy," "Aesthetic Wests," "Race and Ethnicity," and "Extended Wests." All such arrangements are imperfect and perhaps a little artificial. Arguments could even be made for placing some of the chapters in other sections. Allen's literary approach might grace the "Aesthetic Wests" section as easily as the "Extended Wests" section. Boag's exploration of regional consciousness in the Snake River Valley focuses largely on writers, but writers who are reacting largely to the environment. And Murphy's case study of three Montana women does not focus exclusively on writers (there are two writers and one horseback rider). Furthermore, she addresses women's reactions to the environment and to racial intolerance. Her chapter could conceivably have been placed in three of the sections. Still, while there is a trace of arbitrariness in the categorization scheme, the reader will sense a good deal of order, too.

We could have organized the chapters in some discernible geographic pattern, but an east to west design would have perpetuated the Eurocentric frontier paradigm; and ordering western regions according to the time of first settlement or first effective settlement would have proved maddeningly confusing. Perhaps the chapters might just as well have been divided into sections approximating western physiographic realities[50]—we might have had sections on mountains, rivers, deserts, and plains. But a physiographic arrangement would have imposed an environmentally deterministic model on the volume when we would prefer to spark discussion about whether environmental, economic, cultural, or political factors play the most significant role in shaping regional consciousness. It is probably the case, as the various chapters suggest, that certain factors were more influential in shaping regional identity in some parts of the West than others. When it comes to the development of western regional consciousness, there do seem to be many different processes at work in the West's many places. Hopefully, the many Wests in these chapters highlight the cultural, environmental, climatic, racial, ethnic, historical, and economic diversity of the larger West and its peoples.

These essays also reflect the level of thematic complexity and variety in the field of western history. The intense media coverage of debates in the field presented a clear and rather blunt dichotomy: frontier versus region.[51] Read the newspaper and magazine reports of the scholarly "Showdown at the Politically O.K. Corral," and you might expect to find an older generation of privileged, white, male, frontier triumphalists and a more diverse group of baby-boomer, regionalist tragedians facing off against each other.[52] But these dichotomies—frontier versus region, process versus place—do not reflect the complexity and variety of current work in western history.

Perhaps the most significant long-term consequence of the New Western History will prove not to be the supplanting of one overarching thematic framework (frontier) with another (region) but the renewal of enthusiasm for a field of study, which in turn brings with it a multiplicity of perspectives. The West (almost regardless of one's specific geographic definition) is a vast place, and it is home to many and often very different people, economies, histories, and regions. It is fortunate for western history that current scholarship is equally diverse and pluralistic. That multitude of perspectives about western peoples and places promises a bright future for the field.

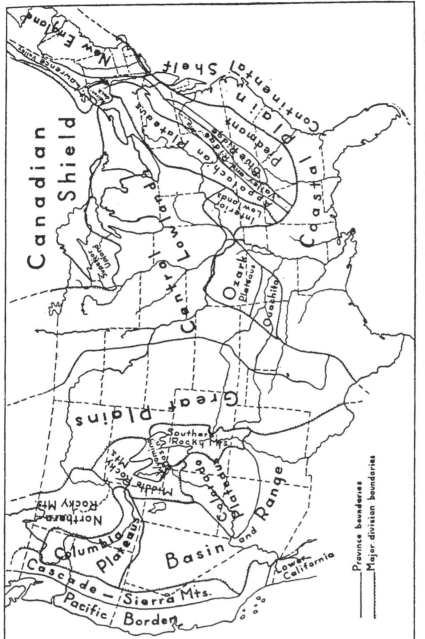

Physical provinces of the United States. As prepared by N. M. Fenneman for the U.S. Geological Survey. Reprinted from Frederic B. Loomis, Physiography of the United States (Garden City, N.Y.: Doubleday, Doran and Company, 1937).

NOTES

1. Wright Morris, *The Territory Ahead* (New York: Harcourt, Brace, 1957), 22.

2. Herbert Richardson, *Toward an American Theology* (New York: Harper & Row, 1967), 28.

3. Recent discussions of the high-tech obliteration of place include James Howard Kuntsler, *The Geography of Nowhere: The Rise and Decline of America's Man-Made Landscape* (New York: Simon and Schuster, 1993); Alexander Wilson, *The Culture of Nature: North American Landscape from Disney to the "Exxon Valdez"* (Cambridge, Mass.: Blackwell, 1992); Joshua Meyrowitz, *No Sense of Place: The Impact of Electronic Media on Social Behavior* (Berkeley: University of California Press, 1985).

4. Richard Rodriguez, "True West: Relocating the Horizon of the American Frontier," *Harper's,* September 1996, 41. Penetrating critiques of the compulsion to fabricate nature in the American West include William Cronon, ed., *Uncommon Ground: Toward Re-inventing Nature* (New York: Norton, 1995); Richard Lillard, *Eden in Jeopardy: Man's Prodigious Meddling with His Environment: The Southern California Experience* (New York: Knopf, 1966); Donald Worster, *Rivers of Empire: Water, Aridity, and the Growth of the American West* (New York: Oxford University Press, 1985); and John M. Findlay, *Magic Lands: Western Cityscapes and American Culture* (Berkeley: University of California Press, 1992).

5. Regarding our capacity to retrospectively revere the victims of our conquest, Renato Rosaldo writes: "A person kills somebody and then mourns the victim. . . . People destroy their environment, and then they worship nature" ("Imperialist Nostalgia," in his *Culture and Truth: The Remaking of Social Analysis* [Boston: Beacon Press, 1989], 70).

6. Owen Wister, *The Virginian: A Horseman on the Plains* (New York: Macmillan, 1902), viii, ix. Concerning Fraser's *End of the Trail,* see Karal Ann Marling, *The Colossus of Roads: Myth and Symbol Along the American Highway* (Minneapolis: University of Minnesota Press, 1984), 28–30. For a thorough discussion of frontier nostalgia and anxiety, see David M. Wrobel, *The End of American Exceptionalism: Frontier Anxiety from the Old West to the New Deal* (Lawrence: University Press of Kansas, 1993).

7. Woodrow Wilson, "The Making of the Nation," *Atlantic Monthly,* July 1897, 4; Wilson, "Address Before Virginia State Bar Association, August 4, 1897," in *The Politics of Woodrow Wilson: Selections from His Speeches and Writings,* ed. August Heckscher (New York: Harper and Brothers, 1956), 44. Israel Zangwill, *The Melting-Pot: A Drama in Four Acts* (New York: Macmillan, 1909), 199.

8. Daniel J. Boorstin, *The Americans: The Democratic Experience* (New York: Random House, 1973), 307.

9. Paul Shepard, "Place in American Culture," *North American Review* 262 (1977): 32; Wendell Berry, "The Regional Motive," in his *A Continuous*

Harmony: Essays Cultural and Agricultural (New York: Harcourt Brace Jovanovich, 1970), 68.

10. Joni Mitchell, "Big Yellow Taxi" (1969).

11. Walter Wriston, quoted in Michael Sorkin, *Variations on a Theme Park: The New American City and the End of Public Space* (New York: Noonday Press, 1992), xi; George Gilder, *Microcosm: The Quantum Revolution in Economics and Technology* (New York: Simon and Schuster, 1989), 17; and Allen K. Phillbrick, "Perceptions and Technologies as Determinants of Predictions About Earth, 2050," in *Human Geography in a Shrinking World*, ed. Ronald Abler, Donald Janelle, Allen K. Phillbrick, and John Sommer (North Scituate, Mass.: Duxbury Press, 1975), 33.

12. Lillian Hellman, review of *The Provincials* by Eli N. Evans, *New York Review of Books*, 11 November 1973, 5; Richard Dorson, *American Folklore and the Historian* (Chicago: University of Chicago Press, 1971), 44.

13. V. L. Calverton, *American Literature at the Crossroads*, Chapbook No. 48 (Seattle: University of Washington Press, 1931), 39; Louis Wirth, "Limitations of Regionalism," in *Regionalism in America*, ed. Merrill Jensen (Madison: University Press of Wisconsin, 1951), 392–93. Other influential critiques of regionalism as an archaic antimodern impulse include Walter M. Kollmoregen, "Crucial Deficiencies of Regionalism," *American Economic Review* 35 (1945): 377–89; and Melvin M. Webber, "Culture, Territoriality, and the Elastic Mile," *Regional Science Association Papers* 13 (1964): 283–304.

14. Kenneth O. Hanson, in John R. Milton, ed., "The Writer's Sense of Place: A Symposium and Commentaries," *South Dakota Review* 13 (1975): 21. Apparently, Hanson meant to refer to the *passenger* pigeon; it is a basic premise of *Many Wests* that, like the *carrier* pigeon, regionalism is still very much alive.

15. Josiah Royce, *Race Questions, Provincialism, and Other American Problems* (1908; reprint, New York: Books for Libraries, 1967); Frederick Jackson Turner, *The Significance of Sections in American History* (New York: Holt, 1932), 45, and throughout; Michael C. Steiner, "Frederick Jackson Turner and Western Regionalism," in *Writing Western History: Essays on Major Western Historians*, ed. Richard W. Etulain (Albuquerque: University of New Mexico Press, 1991), 103–35.

16. Lewis Mumford, *The Culture of Cities* (New York: Harcourt, Brace, 1938); Howard W. Odum and Harry Estill Moore, *American Regionalism: A Cultural-Historical Approach to National Integration* (New York: Holt, 1938); Walter Prescott Webb, *The Great Plains*, (Boston: Ginn, 1931); Franklin D. Roosevelt, "Growing Up by Plan," *Survey*, 1 February 1932, 483. Regarding regionalism in the 1930s, see Michael C. Steiner, "Regionalism in the Great Depression," *Geographical Review* 73 (1983): 430–46; and Robert Dorman, *Revolt of the Provinces: The Regionalist*

Movement in America, 1920–1945 (Chapel Hill: University of North Carolina Press, 1993).

17. Jane Jacobs, *Cities and the Wealth of Nations: Principles of Economic Life* (New York: Random House, 1984); William Appleman Williams, "Radicals and Regionalism," *Democracy* 1 (1981): 87–98; Gary Snyder, "The Bioregional Ethic," in his *The Real Work: Interviews and Talks*, ed. William Scott McLean (New York: New Directions, 1980), 138–58, and throughout.

18. Yi-Fu Tuan, "Rootedness Versus Sense of Place," *Landscape* 24 (1980): 3–8; Tuan, "In Place, Out of Place," *Geoscience and Man* 24 (1984): 3–10; Tuan, "Place and Culture: A Theoretical Perspective," in *Mapping American Culture,* ed. Wayne Franklin and Michael Steiner (Iowa City: University of Iowa Press, 1992), 27–49.

19. William H. Gass, "The Face of the City," *Harper's,* March 1986, 37.

20. The concept of "topophilia" is eloquently analyzed in Yi-Fu Tuan, *Topophilia: A Study of Environmental Perception, Attitudes, and Values* (Englewood Cliffs, N.J.: Prentice-Hall, 1974). Useful histories of American regionalism culminating in the "new western" variety include Richard Maxwell Brown, "The New Regionalism in America, 1979–1981," in *Regionalism in the Pacific Northwest,* ed. William G. Robbins, Robert J. Frank, and William E. Ross (Corvallis: Oregon State University Press, 1983), 37–96; David R. Goldfield, "The New Regionalism," *Journal of Urban History* 10 (1984): 171–86; Richard W. Etulain, "Frontier, Region, and Border: Cultural Currents in the Recent Southwest," *Montana: The Magazine of Western History* 44 (1994): 64–70; Charles S. Peterson, "Speaking for the Past," in *The Oxford History of the American West,* ed. Clyde A. Milner II, Carol A. O'Connor, and Martha R. Sandweiss (New York: Oxford University Press, 1994), 743–69; and Michael Steiner and Clarence Mondale, *Region and Regionalism in the United States: A Source Book for the Humanities and Social Sciences* (New York: Garland Press, 1988).

21. Earl Pomeroy, *The Pacific Slope: A History* (New York: Knopf, 1965), 388; John Dewey, "Americanism and Localism," *Dial* 68 (1920): 687, 686.

22. Harold R. Isaacs, *Idols of the Tribe: Group Identity and Political Change* (New York: Harper & Row, 1975), 215; Benjamin R. Barber, *Jihad vs. McWorld: How Globalism and Tribalism Are Reshaping the World* (New York: Ballantine, 1995), 4.

23. Yi-Fu Tuan, *Cosmos & Hearth: A Cosmopololite's Viewpoint* (Minneapolis: University of Minnesota Press, 1996), 104.

24. Archie Green, "Regionalism Is a Forever Agenda," *Appalachian Journal* 9 (1982): 180; Brown, "New Regionalism in America," 64; Felix Frankfurter, "Foreword," in *Regionalism in America,* ed. Jensen, xvi.

25. Wallace Stegner, "On Western History and Historians," in Wallace Stegner and Richard W. Etulain, *Stegner: Conversations on History and Literature,* rev. ed. (Reno: University of Nevada Press, 1996).

26. Donald Worster, "New West, True West: Interpreting the Region's History," *Western Historical Quarterly* 18 (1987): 145; Patricia Nelson

Limerick, *The Legacy of Conquest: The Unbroken Past of the American West* (New York: Norton, 1987), 26.

27. Frederick Jackson Turner, "The West as a Field for Historical Study," *Annual Report of the American Historical Association for 1896* (Washington, D.C.: Government Printing Office, 1897), 282; Frederick Jackson Turner to Walter Hines Page, 30 August 1896, quoted in Fulmer Mood, "The Origin, Evolution, and Application of the Sectional Concept, 1750–1900," in *Regionalism in America,* ed. Jensen, 95.

28. D. W. Meinig, "American Wests: Preface to a Geographical Interpretation," in *Regions of the United States,* ed. John Fraser Hart (New York: Harper & Row, 1972), 160; Howard R. Lamar, "Westering in the Twenty-first Century: Speculations on the Future of the Western Past," in *Under an Open Sky: Rethinking America's Western Past,* ed. William Cronon, George Miles, and Jay Gitlin (New York: Norton, 1992), 274.

29. Among the most important revisionist works of the last decade or so are Worster, *Rivers of Empire;* Limerick, *Legacy of Conquest;* William Cronon, *Nature's Metropolis: Chicago and the Great West* (New York: Norton, 1991); Richard White, *"It's Your Misfortune and None of My Own": A New History of the American West* (Norman: University of Oklahoma Press, 1991); and William G. Robbins, *Colony and Empire: The Capitalist Transformation of the American West* (Lawrence: University Press of Kansas, 1994). For a good introduction to the new western revisionism, see Patricia Nelson Limerick, Clyde A. Milner II, and Charles Rankin, eds., *Trails: Toward a New Western History* (Lawrence: University Press of Kansas, 1991).

30. Elliott West, "A Longer, Grimmer, but More Interesting Story," in *Trails,* ed. Limerick, Milner, and Rankin, 103–11.

31. While the past decade or so has certainly seen a transition of sorts from a frontier-influenced narrative to a regionally driven narrative, it is important to remember that western historians have been employing both of these organizing themes for more than a century. Indeed, before Turner delivered his famous 1893 address, "The Significance of the Frontier in American History"—the source of so much scholarly discussion and contention—Hubert Howe Bancroft had produced more than fifty volumes of western regional history and Josiah Royce had written an important regional history on California. While the New Western History has sparked a resurgence in the field of western history, it would be inappropriate to collectively categorize works that preceded the recent revisionism under the label "Old Western History." Such divisions between "new" and "old" gloss over differences and grossly oversimplify the nuances and complexities that have always been present in the field.

32. Patricia Nelson Limerick, "What on Earth Is the New Western History," in *Trails,* ed. Limerick, Milner, and Rankin, 81–88, 86.

33. Of course, some critics of the New Western History would not agree with Limerick's definition of the revisionists' purpose. Larry McMurtry, for example, has emphasized the negativism of the recent western revisionism,

labeling it "failure studies" ("Westward Ho Hum: What the New Historians Have Done to the Old West," *New Republic,* 9 October 1990, 32–38).

34.   West points to the importance of subregional diversity within the broader West and the relations between subregions in "a Longer, Grimmer, but More Interesting Story," 104. It is important to note that Limerick has responded quite effectively to this criticism of the New Western History's lack of attention to regional differences. She argues that the existence of many different subregions within the West does not exclude the West from "the club of American regions . . . on the basis of insufficient internal homogeneity and coherence." She notes that differences among the various constituent parts of the South are as great as those among the West's subregions, yet we do not disqualify the South as a coherent region because of its internal heterogeneity. See Limerick, "The Trail to Santa Fe: The Unleashing of the Western Public Intellectual," in *Trails,* ed. Limerick, Milner, and Rankin, 59–88, 70. We do not argue with Limerick's logic on this point; the West may indeed be a coherent regional entity composed of rather different constituent subregional parts. However, we do emphasize that it may be more constructive to begin with analysis of the subregional parts and move from there to a discussion of the coherence and regional integrity of the broader West. For more on the West and regional parts, see Donald Worster, *An Unsettled Country: Changing Landscapes of the American West* (Albuquerque: University of New Mexico Press, 1994), ix–xii, 1–30. For another interesting discussion of the efforts of the "New Regionalism" to redefine western parameters, see Kerwin Lee Klein, "Reclaiming the 'F' Word; Or, Being and Becoming Postwestern," *Pacific Historical Review,* 65 (1996): 179–215.

35.   See, for example, Stephen Aron, "Lessons in Conquest: Towards a Greater Western History," *Pacific Historical Review* 63 (1994): 125–47, who focuses particularly on whether the theme of conquest is more relevant to the trans-Mississippi West than to other parts of the country. Among the most significant efforts to define the West through reference to aridity and semiaridity are, in chronological order, John Wesley Powell, *Report on the Lands of the Arid Region* (Washington, D.C.: Government Printing Office, 1878); William E. Smythe, *The Conquest of Arid America* (New York: Harper, 1899; New York: Macmillan, 1905; Seattle: University of Washington Press, 1969); Walter Prescott Webb's controversial landmark article "The American West: Perpetual Mirage," *Harper's,* May 1957, 25–31, Worster, *Rivers of Empire;* and Marc Reisner, *Cadillac Desert: The American West and Its Disappearing Water* (New York: Penguin, 1986).

36.   Our definition of the West approximates that presented in Michael P. Malone and Richard W. Etulain, *The American West: A Twentieth Century History* (Lincoln: University of Nebraska Press, 1989), 9. Malone and Etulain emphasize that the second tier of states west of the Mississippi "embrace the ninety-eighth meridian . . . the dividing line between the humid plains to the

east and the increasingly arid plains to the West." We agree that the "aridity factor" is an important one, though not the only factor meriting consideration when discussing western boundaries. The ninety-eighth meridian, marking the limit of twenty inches of annual rainfall, serves as a useful eastern boundary, but northern, southern, and western edges raise further challenges. Malone and Etulain, for example, apply the phrase "noncontiguous 'western' states" to Alaska and Hawai'i, but do not group them with the broader West. We, however, in keeping with our stated purpose of sparking discussion about western regionalism, include Alaska and Hawai'i as well as borderlands with Mexico and Canada among the "many Wests" presented for consideration. Malone and Etulain's West is similar to Robert Athearn's West, as presented in *The Mythic West in Twentieth-century America* (Lawrence: University Press of Kansas, 1986), xii, though Athearn's eastern border zigzags through the second tier of trans-Mississippi western states. For more on the topic of defining western boundaries, see Walter Nugent, "Where Is the American West? A Survey Report," *Montana: The Magazine of Western History* 42 (1992): 2–23; and David M. Emmons, "Constructed Province: History and the Making of the Last American West," *Western Historical Quarterly* 25 (1994): 437–59, including the "Roundtable of Responses" to the essay, 461–86. White also provides a very useful and succinct statement about the West and its boundaries in *"It's Your Misfortune and None of My Own,"* 3–4. He notes, in the book's opening sentence, "The boundaries of the American West are a series of doors pretending to be walls."

37. For more on the relationship of western Canada to the western United States, see Robbins, "The American and Canadian Wests: Two Nations, Two Cultures," in *Colony and Empire,* 40–58; and Seymour Martin Lipset, *Continental Divide: The Values and Institutions of the United States and Canada* (New York: Routledge, 1990), 208–11.

38. In *Legacy of Conquest,* Limerick includes, albeit tentatively, the first tier of states west of the Mississippi aside from Minnesota, which she does not mention, but does not include coverage of Alaska and Hawai'i. Regarding the trans-Appalachian West, see Aron, "Lessons in Conquest"; and Stephon Aron, "The West as America: A Review of the Latest Ken Burns Documentary," in *Perspectives* [American Historical Association Newsletter], September 1996, 1, 7–11. Emmons examines the upper Midwest as part of the West in "Constructed Province." A map of the Census Bureau's four regions and nine divisions is in Michael Bradshaw, *Regions and Regionalism in the United States* (Jackson: University Press of Mississippi, 1988), 4. The Census Bureau places both Oklahoma and Texas in the West South Central Division of the South; we place them in the West.

39. For an interesting comment on time zones and western boundaries, see Maxine Benson, quoted in Nugent, "Where Is the American West?" 13.

40. For more on the central Plains, see Elliott West, *The Way to the West: Essays on the Central Plains* (Albuquerque: University of New Mexico Press, 1995).

41. Wilbur Zelinsky, *The Cultural Geography of the United States* (Englewood Cliffs, N.J.: Prentice-Hall, 1973), 109–40; Zelinsky, "General Cultural and Popular Regions," in *This Remarkable Continent: An Atlas of the United States and Canadian Societies and Cultures,* ed. John F. Rooney, Wilbur Zelinsky, and Dean R. Louder (College Station: Texas A&M Press, 1983), 3–24; Meinig, "American Wests"; Donald W. Meinig, "The Continuous Shaping of America: A Prospectus for Geographers and Historians," *American Historical Review* 83 (1978): 1185–1217. Meinig's ongoing series of volumes, *The Shaping of America: A Geographical Perspective on 500 Years of History* (New Haven, Conn.: Yale University Press, 1986–), is a magisterial realization of this dynamic vision of American regionalism.

42. Raymond D. Gastil, *Cultural Regions of the United States* (Seattle: University of Washington Press, 1975); Joel Garreau, *The Nine Nations of North America* (Boston: Houghton Mifflin, 1981).

43. For an excellent discussion of the role of shared memory in shaping regional identity, see Clyde Milner II, "The View from Wisdom: Four Layers of History and Regional Identity," in *Under an Open Sky,* ed. Cronon, Miles, and Gitlin, 203–22. Barbara Allen discusses the Fork Rock Valley (of south-central Oregon) Homesteader's Reunion in "Landscape, Memory, and the Western Past," *Montana: The Magazine of Western History* 39 (1989): 71–75. See also Allen, *Homesteading the High Desert* (Salt Lake City: University of Utah Press, 1987).

44. A powerful recent example of this phenomenon of shared memories and regional consciousnesses colliding is in the movie *Lone Star* (1996), which is set in a Texas border town where the present interests of the town's racial groups—Mexicans, Mexican-Americans, African-Americans, and whites—are reflected in debates over the social studies curriculum.

45. For more on the theme of interior and exterior regionalism, see David M. Wrobel, "Beyond the Frontier–Region Dichotomy," *Pacific Historical Review* 65 (1996): 401–29.

46. In "Becoming West: Toward a New Meaning for Western History," Cronon, Miles, and Gitlin present a sophisticated model to explain the transition from frontier to region, or from "relative newness to relative oldness," or from "flux to fixity" (*Under an Open Sky,* 3–27). This is a challenging model that cannot be summarized effectively in a limited space. The model includes the processes of "species shifting," "market making," "land taking," "boundary setting," "state forming," and "self-shaping." The model captures many of the intricate forces involved in developing regional consciousness in new environments. However, despite the authors' emphasis on the lack of finality in this process, the notion of a movement from relative flux to relative fixity does suggest a lack of regional dynamism in the postfrontier, or regional, West. We, though, are suggesting a continuing process, one in which regional identities remain in flux, despite the emergence of certain regional characteristics. Indeed, there is even a tendency to coin new regional

entities—such as the "Sunbelt"—to explain changing political and economic realities. For more on the emergence of the Sunbelt, see Raymond A. Mohl, ed., *Searching for the Sunbelt: Historical Perspectives on a Region* (Knoxville: University of Tennessee Press, 1990). The problem with the concept of the Sunbelt, a number of the contributors explain, is that the label is largely imposed on a diverse set of regional entities from the outside and does not reflect any latent or emergent regional consciousness among the residents of the Sunbelt, who do not think of themselves as "Sunbelters." Incidentally, scholars have had as much difficulty defining the geographical parameters of the Sunbelt as they have the boundaries of the West.

47. Robbins provides some useful comparative analysis of the West and the South in *Colony and Empire*, 145–61. Also worth mentioning in this context is the much earlier work of Walter Prescott Webb, *Divided We Stand: The Crisis of a Frontierless Democracy* (New York: Farrar and Rinehart, 1937). Webb argued that the two regions acquired their regional identity in part through their dependence on and exploitation by the North.

48. See, for example, Robbins, ed., *Regionalism in the Pacific Northwest;* Karen J. Blair, ed., *Women in Pacific Northwest History: An Anthology* (Seattle: University of Washington Press, 1988). For the Great Plains, see Brian C. Blouet and Frederick C. Luebke, eds., *The Great Plains: Environment and Culture* (Lincoln: University of Nebraska Press, 1979); and Frederick C. Luebke, ed., *Ethnicity on the Great Plains* (Lincoln: University of Nebraska Press, 1980). Another excellent work on a portion of the Great Plains is West, *Way to the West.* For the Southwest, see Vera Norwood and Janice Monk, eds., *The Desert Is No Lady: Southwestern Landscapes in Women's Writing and Art* (New Haven, Conn.: Yale University Press, 1987). For the Midwest, a region we have not included among our many Wests, see James R. Shortridge, *The Middle West: Its Meaning in American Culture* (Lawrence: University Press of Kansas, 1989).

49. We are indebted to David Emmons for this summary of the volume's purpose.

50. For more on western physiographic regions, see John Wesley Powell, *The Physiography of the United States* (Chicago: National Geographic Society, 1896), 66–106. Also interesting in this context is the map "Physiographic Provinces of the United States" on the inside cover of Ray Allen Billington, *Westward Expansion: A History of the American Frontier* (New York: Macmillan, 1949).

51. Among the most notable examples of the media coverage of debates in the field of western history are T. R. Reid, "Shootout in Academia over History of U.S. West," *Washington Post,* 10 October 1989, p. A3; Richard Bernstein, "Ideas and Trends: Among Historians the Old Frontier Is Turning Nastier with Each Revision," *New York Times,* 17 December 1989, E4–6; Miriam Horn, "How the West Was Really Won," *U.S. News & World Report,* 21 May 1990, 56–65; McMurtry, "Westward Ho Hum"; "Rewriting the West,"

USA Today, 7 December 1990, D1–2; Dick Kreck, "Showdown in the New West," *Denver Post Magazine,* 21 March 1993, 6–8.

52. The quotation is from Janny Scott's, "New Battleground of the Old West: Academia," *Los Angeles Times,* 18 May 1993, A5. Scott's summary, it should be noted, is quite insightful and complex. Limerick used the "showdown" motif to characterize perceptions of the debates in "Trail to Santa Fe," 59–77. William G. Robbins also provides thorough and insightful coverage of the debate in "Laying Siege to Western History: The Emergence of New Paradigms," in *Trails,* ed. Limerick, Milner, and Rankin, 182–214.

Part One:

ENVIRONMENT AND ECONOMY

The four chapters in this section share two themes: they all deal, either directly or indirectly, with the relationship between environmental and economic forces and with the role those forces play in forging regional identity; and they address the impact of outside, or "exterior," forces on the formation of regional identity.

Anglo-American folklore has assumed a special relationship between the spectacular western wilderness environments and a unique western character. The West's larger-than-life scenery and the human trials and tribulations that accompany those physiographic realities—towering mountains, bleak deserts, and vast plains—have, according to popular mythology, nurtured an exceptional and enviable western character. It is reckoned to be particularly rugged and resourceful, open and honest, though prone to violent and vengeful acts when situations warrant. In short, western mythology has constructed a western character to match the West's dramatic scenery.

More recently, revisionist western historians have deemphasized these romantic abstractions and presented the West as an environment that has been conquered, devastated, and despoiled by human and economic forces. On one level, the revisionist approach parallels the mythic approach; both assume a causal relationship between environment and culture, though for the revisionists the relationship is less romantic. They have emphasized the impact of human action on the western landscape and the impact of that environment on humans. The key themes that have emerged from these foci are western environmental limitations and fragility and the decidedly unromantic and often negative consequences of human action.

The chapters in this section examine the subtle and complex relationships between western environment and regional identity, and between economic forces and regional identity. Taken together, they perhaps suggest that neither the traditionalist nor the revisionist approach fully accounts for the varied relationships between environment and economy in different western places. Furthermore, the authors' emphasis on the impact of outside forces on Westerners' sense of place moves us beyond the common assumption that "true" regional identity is always firmly rooted in the land. Sense of place, it is generally assumed, emerges from the soil (or, sand, in the case of the Great Basin) and the scenery.

Native Americans are deemed to have a special connection to place, and Native creation stories emphasize the emergence of people from out of the land itself. Some Euro-Americans, too, have developed a strong regional rootedness in western places. Who could deny the deep sense of place, for example, of the Oklahoma and Arkansas tenant farmers in John Steinbeck's *The Grapes of Wrath* (1939) when they remark that "it's our land. We measured it and broke it up. We were born on it, and we got killed on it, died on it. Even if it's no good, it's still ours"? The displacement of the fictional Joads, and the tens of thousands of "real" families like them in the 1930s, is so heartrending because they were uprooted from the land. The stories of displacement of Native peoples from their lands by white settlers and the federal government is harrowing, too, in part because deep attachments to place were broken.

Yet as the chapters in this section point out, regional identity
does not emerge only from deep attachment to natural surroundings. Outside forces sometimes have transformed western places
and have helped form or construct regional consciousness. Or,
perhaps, the chapters suggest that regional identity has not fully
blossomed in the Pacific Northwest, the Great Basin, the Rocky
Mountains, and the northern Plains because outside influences
have proven detrimental and residents have responded to them too
readily.

James R. Shortridge's examination of the northern Plains
emphasizes the powerful and not always beneficent influence of
"the expectations of others" on that region. Anne F. Hyde's study
of Rocky Mountain regionalism focuses on the outside economic
forces that have hindered the emergence of strong community
bonds. The "social glue" necessary for community formation, Hyde
contends, has been a scarce commodity in the exploitative, extractive economy of the Rocky Mountain region. In a similar vein,
Elizabeth Raymond discusses outsiders' hopes, in the nineteenth
century, that the Great Basin desert would blossom like a rose, and
the commonly held outsiders' image of the place in the twentieth
century as a wasteland. John M. Findlay contends that Pacific
Northwestern regional identity is a fishy proposition, in part
because of the acute impact of outside forces on residents' sense of
place. "The notion of a Pacific Northwest," he notes, "has been
cultivated best by outsiders who have wanted to shape the idea of
a region for their own purposes, and by inhabitants whose sense
of place has depended extensively on their ideas and feelings about
locales elsewhere."

In "A Fishy Proposition," Findlay begins by asking why Pacific
Northwesterners have chosen salmon as their regional symbol.
Ironically, he notes, salmon was an economic commodity that
came to be a significant regional symbol only when it became an
endangered resource. Salmon has emerged as a Pacific Northwestern regional identifier since the 1960s, in tandem with a rising
environmental consciousness. In the late nineteenth and early
twentieth centuries, railroad advertising presented the spectacular
scenery of the region to outsiders in an effort to promote tourism
and settlement. In the 1930s, the New Deal government established

the Bonneville Power Administration and helped forge a sense of
regional identity in the Pacific Northwest by building a regionwide
network of dams to produce electrical power. Again and again, it
seems, the sense of place in the Pacific Northwest has been in large
part the product of forces outside the region. And when residents
of the region offer expressions of their regional sensibility, it is
often a response to "outsiders"—first Native, African-, and Asian-
Americans, and today, Californians—who are viewed as a threat to
regional purity.

In "When the Desert Won't Bloom," Raymond discusses the
emergence of a sense of place in the Great Basin, grounded in
environmental hardship. Hopes of making that desert bloom
proved forlorn. And when the environment failed to nurture the
economic and cultural development inherent in American visions
of agricultural utopia, Nevada drew on environmental reality—its
geographical remoteness—to secure economic gain. Easy divorce,
prizefighting, legalized gambling, and brothel prostitution could
thrive irrespective of infertile soil or limited rainfall. But, Raymond
concludes, even the neon glitz and glamour of Las Vegas cannot
eradicate the notion of the Great Basin as wasteland and nuclear
dumping ground.

In "Round Pegs in Square Holes," Hyde examines the exterior
environmental forces that, in tandem with interior environmental
realities, have made sense of place such an elusive commodity in
the Rocky Mountains. Spectacular mountain imagery aside, Hyde
argues, the environment is hardly pristine. Extractive industry—
from mining to skiing—has been tremendously costly for this
fragile place. And, furthermore, the extractive industries have
always been dependent on poorly paid, low-skilled wage labor. The
interplay of these economic and environmental realities, not the
spectacular mountain scenery of late-nineteenth-century landscape
artists and late-twentieth-century advertising agencies, Hyde suggests, holds the key to understanding Rocky Mountain Westerners.
She demystifies the Rocky Mountains, presenting them as com-
modities that were farmed for furs and now are mined for ores
and manicured for skiers.

In "The Expectations of Others," Shortridge describes the northern Plains as a place where grim environmental realities have

continually fostered a climate of economic uncertainty. The depressed 1890s were followed by the limited prosperity of the early twentieth century, which, in turn, was followed by harrowing agricultural depression during the 1920s and 1930s, limited prosperity in the 1940s and 1950s, and depression again in the early 1980s. Given these grim realities, Shortridge concludes that plains people have always expended "too much energy fulfilling and reacting to the expectations of others."

Unlike Hyde, however, Shortridge is hopeful that a true regional identity will emerge among plains people. He views local initiatives in areas such as business, health care, education, and religion as positive evidence that residents of the northern Plains are moving away from their traditional tendency to blame outsiders for problems that have often been internal. Such developments bode well for the formation of a strong sense of place on the northern Plains. Whether there is similar potential for the emergence of strong Pacific Northwestern and Great Basin identities is less certain. What is certain is that these essays move us beyond easy assumptions about sense of place and demonstrate that regional identity is a complex commodity influenced by environmental and economic forces and the expectations of outsiders.

A Fishy Proposition: Regional Identity
in the Pacific Northwest

John M. Findlay

"The Pacific Northwest is simply this: wherever the salmon can get to." So declares Timothy Egan, *New York Times* correspondent for the region. Many in Oregon, Idaho, and Washington have joined Egan in invoking the fish as *the* regional marker; indeed, their attachment only increases as runs of wild salmon diminish in size with each passing year. Will Stelle, head of the Northwest office of the National Marine Fisheries Service, elaborates on the sentiment when explaining why saving the species is so crucial: "Salmon are part of the heart and soul of the Pacific Northwest. They have defined its history, and its culture and hopefully its future."[1]

This identification between salmon and the Northwest is striking for bringing what may be an unprecedented sense of certainty and consensus to regional thinking. In the 1990s, people in Idaho, Oregon, and

Washington are convinced that there *is* a clearly and autonomously defined Pacific Northwest and that it is distinguished by its salmon. Moreover, like most peoples in most places and times, they tend to read their own convictions back into the past. Thus they claim that there has always been a distinct and self-defined Pacific Northwest and that salmon have always been "the heart and soul" of its identity. The equation depends on both essentialism, as though the region truly were "simply this," and timelessness, as though Northwest history and culture were always defined by "simply this."

As strongly as Northwesterners today identify the region with salmon, it has not always been so. At least until recently, the peoples who have lived in Oregon, Idaho, and Washington have generally neither defined themselves readily as belonging to the same region nor, naturally, agreed on the meaning of that region. Indeed, historical consideration of how Northwesterners managed to forge a common identity leads one to suspect that regional consciousness in the Pacific Northwest has been a fishy proposition. That is, regional identity over the years has tended to be somewhat dubious, artificial, and ever-shifting.[2]

The fishy aspects of regional consciousness, of course, contradict the essentialist and timeless formulations that Northwesterners have preferred. Wild salmon make an ideal symbol for the region because, being native and natural, they seemingly defy the contingent and constructed character of regional consciousness. Salmon are not the first instance of inhabitants of Washington, Oregon, and Idaho looking to nature as a source of regional identity. They have also seized on the Columbia River and rainy weather as ways of "naturalizing" a regional identity, of equating the Northwest with something truly homegrown and enduring, maybe even unique.[3]

The operative assumption seems to have been that something indigenous to or inherent in a place gives it some stable or fixed meaning. Historical perspective on the Pacific Northwest, however, suggests that its inhabitants have more frequently tended to import a series of meanings for the region—even "natural" ones—from outside its boundaries. Regional identity has in many respects been imposed on or adopted within Washington, Oregon, and Idaho because of these states' relationships to other places. To a significant degree, the idea of a Pacific Northwest has been the creation of outsiders to the region as well as the product of ideas about places outside the region. To understand the current regional sentiment that Salmon Are Us, we need to appreciate how regional identity came to be constructed from materials provided by terms and interests located beyond regional borders.[4]

"WHEREVER THE SALMON CAN GET TO" makes for a problematic definition of region, if taken literally. The species of Pacific salmon (genus *Oncorhynchus*) known as sockeye, pink, chum, chinook, and coho indeed begin their lives, spawn, and die in the rivers and lakes of Idaho, Washington, and Oregon. But they also spawn in North American watersheds ranging from the Sacramento and San Joaquin Rivers in California to streams in British Columbia and Alaska, as well as in Asian watersheds ranging from the Russian far east to North Korea and Japan. More than one observer has thus called salmon "the totem of the North Pacific Rim." Yet the "Pacific" salmon also run in Canadian, American, and Russian rivers emptying into the Arctic Ocean. On top of that, they have been transplanted to the Great Lakes, New Zealand, Australia, and Chile.[5] If we take at face value Egan's words "wherever the salmon can get to," the Pacific Northwest includes Coppermine in Canada's Northwest Territories and Vladivostok in Siberia; Chongjun, North Korea, and Hobart, Australia; Sacramento and Cleveland and Detroit.

At the same time, there are areas of Washington, Oregon, and Idaho where salmon cannot get to, unless they are trucked in. Parts of Oregon and Idaho drain into the Great Basin rather than the Pacific and cannot support anadromous fish. Some rivers within the Columbia River watershed, such as the Clark Fork, have proven out of the reach of spawning salmon; in one prehistoric era, even the main stem of the river was blocked. Other streams that at one time supported the fish no longer do. Dams on the Columbia and its tributaries have contributed most to the diminution of runs; those watersheds upstream from Grand Coulee, in a strict application of Egan's definition, were excommunicated from the Pacific Northwest when the dam was built during the 1930s. Additional salmon habitat has been destroyed by means other than dams.[6]

As a literal definition of the Pacific Northwest, "wherever the salmon can get to" takes us both too far and not far enough. Aiming to identify the core ingredient that all parts of the region have in common, it settles on a species of fish that is not found in every corner of the Northwest but is found in many places outside. The appropriate question appears not to be whether salmon really are the essence of the Northwest. We need to ask rather, in the late twentieth century, why so many Northwesterners have chosen salmon as the regional symbol, and, more broadly, how it is that they have come in the first place to have a common identity that requires a regional symbol.

To appreciate why salmon loom so large today in Pacific Northwest identity, we should take them figuratively rather than literally. The fish, Richard White explains, need to be viewed not so much as biological organisms but as "repositories of meaning" or "tokens of a way of life."[7] As icons, the fish convey a variety of messages. They stand, for instance, for the relative abundance of natural resources long associated with the Pacific Northwest, and they represent a concern about the environment that unites diverse peoples who have long fought over regional resources. As fish that migrate across the Cascade Range, which divides the Northwest in half, they are a symbol shared by eastern and western subregions—two parts of the Pacific Northwest that have often not agreed. Additionally, sanctification of salmon serves to mask old grievances between Indians and non-Indians, with the latter now posing as "Indian-like" in their newfound appreciation of "the land" and its resources. When Egan summarizes the disappearance of salmon as the "loss of a regional right," he is claiming for late-twentieth-century Northwesterners the same thing that Indians have claimed for decades—that salmon have been essential to their way of life and identity as members of a regional "tribe."[8] (A key difference was that some Indians' right, unlike Egan's "regional right," was actually recognized in law.)

But meanings valid or widely held today had little resonance with earlier generations. The significance of salmon as cultural "repositories" has changed dramatically over the decades. Before the arrival of Europeans, many Indians in the area regarded salmon as integral to their cultures, but they did not associate them with anything like a region, of course, because there was no notion of a Pacific Northwest until non-Indians arrived and began to incorporate the territory into Euro-American geographies. The initial newcomers—explorers and fur traders—hardly regarded salmon as a distinguishing feature of the country. If anything, many of them disliked it and complained of Indians smelling like fish. Fur traders resisted making salmon a dietary staple. They preferred the pemmican (preserved meat, often bison) they had known east of the Rocky Mountains, and when that proved unavailable in the Northwest their next preference was horseflesh, another red meat. Some who came to depend on preserved portions of the fish regularly disdained the dish as "horrid dried Salmon." Disregard for salmon continued into the 1850s when U.S. officials signed treaties recognizing some Indians' right "to fish in common" with non-Indians at "all the usual and accustomed places."[9] Surely if whites had valued salmon as a resource, they would not have allowed Indians such liberal access to it.

During the later nineteenth and early twentieth centuries, non-Indians changed their minds about salmon's value. They discovered its economic potential and began extracting it, processing it, and marketing it around the world, while increasingly denying Indians access to the fishery. Salmon became something of a symbol of the American Northwest not so much in its "natural" form, but as a canned good that permitted consumers across the globe to sample a taste of the region. Northwesterners' attachment to the fish was not strong enough, however, to afford protection to its wild runs. Partly by overfishing, partly through the exploitation of such other resources as timber, minerals, and farmland, and partly because of industrialization and urbanization, inhabitants of the region steadily diminished both the runs of salmon and their spawning habitat.[10] Their embrace of dams on northwestern rivers, culminating in the decades between 1930 and 1970, exemplified a willingness to sacrifice wild salmon for what was regarded as a greater good. New technologies such as hatcheries and salmon-farming offered some hope that the region could have its fish and consume it, too. Only when those technologies did not live up to expectations did much concern about protecting the fishery emerge, and only then were salmon widely regarded as symbols of the entire region. The idea that salmon in their "natural" state were the essence of the Pacific Northwest is a recent invention.

If salmon have served as repositories of meaning, their contents have changed continually over time. Ideas about the fish's importance have been unstable and contested, different for each group and province of the region and each period in its history. By the same token, consciousness of a Pacific Northwest—in sharp contrast to the universalist language used to express it—has also been an ever-changing, contested, contingent mentality, different for each demographic, spatial, and temporal division of the region and its history. Northwesterners today claim that salmon have always been the essence of the region. But sixty years ago, the non-Indian population was more persuaded that a combination of dams, irrigation canals, and hydroelectric power was the regional signature. These engineering projects suggested that the region deserved to be called Our Promised Land.[11] And a century before that, some non-Indian occupants focused especially on furs as the dominant feature of the region they called the Hudson's Bay Company's Columbia Department.[12] Clearly, those aiming to track regional consciousness in the Pacific Northwest must be prepared to chase a moving target through time, and to pay attention to its changing name.

They must also be prepared to follow that target from group to group and place to place. Regional consciousness has proved elusive in part because the social composition of the Pacific Northwest has been so varied and changing. Diverse groups of inhabitants have brought widely different perspectives to the idea of region, making it difficult to develop a shared sense of place. Consider the phrase "Pacific Northwest." Although reified over the years, those words began as a *relative* term. "Northwest" made sense only if understood in relation to the framework of American history, for it identified a region at the northern and western edge of today's forty-eight contiguous states. "Pacific" (or often "new") was used in large part to distinguish today's Northwest from the "old" Northwest of the late eighteenth and early nineteenth centuries—what we now might call the upper Midwest. In other words, "Pacific Northwest" has made sense only for those who imagined the territory within the context of U.S. continental expansion. The term had little meaning for, say, Indians, to Canadians and Russians eyeing the same territory for possible annexation, or to Asians migrating there in the later nineteenth century. That is, it made little sense unless and until the American context from which the phrase derived its meaning was accepted. Regional consciousness of a "Pacific Northwest" began with *American* colonization of the territory and depended primarily on the perspective of *American* citizens, most of whom regarded the eastern states as the core of their nation and the Pacific Northwest as part of the periphery.

After its incorporation into the imagined community of the United States in 1846, the Pacific Northwest seldom constituted its inhabitants' primary sense of identity.[13] The term "Northwest" hinged on the region's relationship to nation, and region did not replace nation as people's primary attachment. Newcomers from the United States regarded themselves first as Americans, not Northwesterners. Soon many of them also emphasized local attachments, saying that they belonged to Portland or the Walla Walla Valley. For most of the nineteenth and twentieth centuries, region has generally fallen behind (as well as in between) the more primary attachments of nation and locality. Regional consciousness has been not just an elusive, shifting identity, a social construction always under construction, but one—and not the strongest—of the ways that people in Idaho, Oregon, and Washington linked themselves to place.

Moreover, within the region there are many subregional divisions that, while contested and contingent and constructed, too, have over the years also generally staked strong claims on people's loyalty. Geographers identify two major physiographic provinces in the Northwest: a wetter, greener place to the west of the Cascade Range and a drier, browner place to the east. Anthropologists point out that these provinces coincide with two distinct "culture areas," the Northwest Coast and the Columbia Plateau, each of which accommodated a set of Indian peoples with certain characteristics not shared on the other side of the Cascades. From the mid-nineteenth century, non-Indians have perpetuated many east–west differences in their thinking and behavior. The more urbanized settlement, timber and fishing economies, and cultural amenities on the ocean side of the mountains, for example, have had no equivalent to the east. Economic development, furthermore, generated over time still another set of divisions between metropolis and hinterland. These differences also tend to set apart west from east, metropolis from hinterland, though lines of economic power run in other directions as well.[14] Finally, a powerful latitudinal division runs perpendicular to the longitudinal Cascade Range—the border between Washington and Oregon.[15] Interstate differences in the region have also been imagined, contingent, and contested, but over the decades the accumulating effects of law and politics have reified and strengthened the power of state boundaries in enduring ways. Between modern Oregon and Washington, differing political cultures, links to the United States government, and land-use-planning systems exemplify the Northwest's multiple personalities.

In the face of so many supraregional and subregional alternatives, regional consciousness in the Pacific Northwest—in the form of some kind of identification with the three-state area—may be said to have been generally rather weak and at times inconsequential. Inhabitants have found it difficult to agree on a single indigenous characteristic of the Pacific Northwest—apart from wild salmon in recent years—as a source of common identity, so regional consciousness has seldom papered over effectively the many fissures dividing cultures and societies in Washington, Oregon, and Idaho.

What, then, has been the basis for the limited regional consciousness that did emerge? I contend that, rather than looking mainly within the Pacific Northwest to find some sort of indigenous roots of regional consciousness, we should look more outside the three states. The notion of a Pacific Northwest has been cultivated best by outsiders who have wanted to shape the idea of region for their own purposes, and by inhabitants whose sense of place has depended extensively on their ideas and feelings about locales elsewhere. Regional consciousness in the Northwest has been largely constructed by reference to terms, interests, and images located beyond the boundaries of Washington, Oregon, and Idaho—in particular, in the vaguely defined regions of the "East" and in California.[16]

This speculation diverges from conventional explanations of regional consciousness. A more accepted model suggests that as a region matures and settles down, it acquires more resources for and interest in "indigenous cultural development." In particular, writers and artists emerge who, after interacting over time with the physical and cultural surroundings, create works that qualify as prima facie evidence of a regional mentality. Thus authors such as Ken Kesey, Ivan Doig, and William Kittredge and painters such as Mark Tobey, Morris Graves, and Guy Anderson are classified as exponents of a "Northwest" style or school.[17]

This conventional wisdom satisfyingly accounts for only some aspects of regional identity. For one thing, it holds out as exemplars of regional consciousness individuals whose work might better be associated with only part of the Northwest—for instance, the west side of the Cascades. For another, in this view regional consciousness is mediated largely through those mostly white, mostly male members of cultural elites who are supposedly best able to distill northwestern traits into some sort of creative essence. The suggestion is that less well known people and their more "mundane" lives have had little to do with shaping regional identity. Finally, the conventional wisdom assumes that regional consciousness comes only after long-term and thoughtful contact with the region, and it implies that newcomers and outsiders have not had equally significant attitudes toward the Northwest. This assumption in particular bears scrutiny. One could argue that many newcomers and outsiders have had a greater stake than "settled" residents in establishing regional identity. Because they have been less caught up in the various subregional divisions afflicting the region, newcomers and outsiders may have been capable of identifying more with an entire three-state area than with one of its subsections.

The relationship between the Northwest and its inhabitants differs from that of other American regions. John Shelton Reed, for example, identifies the South as the place that has produced Southerners.[18] And, indeed, most Americans recognize Southerners when they meet them, and know whence they came. By contrast, few Americans outside Oregon, Idaho, and Washington regard those who have left the region as Northwesterners. The Pacific Northwest has generally not been a place people come from; it has been neither a major source for internal migration within the United States nor a significant cultural hearth.[19] Rather, it has been a destination to which other Americans have gone. This fact looms large for explaining regional identity.

Instead of highlighting those who have settled down and soaked up the Northwest, we need to pay more attention to the relative mobility and newness of the non-Indian population. Voluntary migrants to the Northwest have by definition been involved in a process of regional comparison and contrast. First, they have chosen to leave one place after measuring it against prospective destinations. Then, having decided to move, they have had to choose a new place to live from among the alternatives. Once transplanted, furthermore, they have continued to compare and contrast between regions and, if not satisfied with the initial decision, sometimes opted to relocate or return. Explicit in all such comparison and contrast has been the matter of which place is best suited for migrants, and vice versa.[20]

The term "voluntary migrants" helps convey the idea that, to some extent, people *chose* the region and that their choices are important starting points for comprehending regional identity. However, I do not mean to suggest that decisions to move to and stay in the Northwest were fully democratic, always "voluntary," or equally available to all prospective migrants. There is ample evidence, for instance, that among families on the overland trail, women's and children's ability to affect the decision to move across country was quite limited.[21] Some people have always been freer to choose the Pacific Northwest than others. Moreover, even before the Euro-American population became the majority in the Pacific Northwest, it undertook concerted efforts both to marginalize people of color within its society and to inhibit or prevent people of color from migrating to the Pacific Northwest. Over the years since 1840, whites in the Pacific Northwest have discouraged African-Americans from coming; coerced Indians onto reservations and away from economic opportunities; lobbied the federal government to restrict or halt Asian-American immigration; pressured Chinese immigrants to leave, sometimes violently; prevented Japanese immigrants from owning land; and supported both the internment of people of Japanese descent during World War II and their continued exile from the region after the war.[22]

Since the Pacific Northwest became a holding of the United States, then, white Americans have dominated the region legally and, after a brief time, numerically. Their power to exclude nonwhites from outside the region and to marginalize them inside the region, combined with the area's remoteness from the sources of African-American and Hispanic migration within and to the United States, has made the regional population considerably less diversified racially than the nation's. In 1940, none of the three states had a population of less than 97.8 percent white, in a country of not quite 90 percent white. World War II began a period of substantial change in the composition of the region's population, yet in 1990 the number of white Northwesterners (especially in Oregon and Idaho, with 92.8 and 94.4 percent, respectively) once more far exceeded the national figure of 80.3 percent white. (It should come as no surprise, then, that American white supremacist groups in the late twentieth century have been attracted to the region as one place where their goal of an exclusively white population seems relatively attainable.[23]) Euro-American meanings for the Northwest have thus been defined with regard to other peoples, especially nonwhites, as well as to other places. Both by circumstance and by design, the American Northwest has been heavily white, and the prevailing constructions of regional consciousness there—the primary focus of this chapter—have been the product of American whites and, for the most part, males.

White or nonwhite, more or less voluntary in their coming, most inhabitants of the region have been either transplants to the Northwest or the children of transplants, and the process of relocating has shaped their regional identity profoundly. Comparisons and contrasts have been intrinsic to the decision making necessary for so much northwestward migration. In the 1840s, overland emigrants to the Oregon Country, as they termed the region, generally compared and contrasted conditions in the favored destination, the Willamette Valley, with those left behind, usually in the Midwest. Simultaneously, they compared and contrasted the Oregon Country with the other leading, far western destination—California. As a Mexican and therefore officially Catholic holding until 1846, and as an area with little well-watered farmland, California ranked behind the Oregon Country until the discovery of gold made it the more attractive destination by far. Prior to 1849, Oregon had attracted 11,512 overland migrants; California 2,735. Between 1849 and 1860, California attracted more than 200,000 migrants, while more than 50,000 avoided the Golden State's temptations and headed to Oregon.[24] And so began the longest running bit of humor in regional history, first reported in the 1850s: "At Pacific Springs, one of the crossroads of the western trail, a pile of gold-bearing quartz marked the road to California; the other road had a sign bearing the words 'to Oregon.' Those who could read took the trail to Oregon."[25]

The joke, of course, glossed over certain facts. Once in Oregon, the virtuous did not always remain there. Gold lured so many Oregonians to California in 1849 and 1850 that observers guessed that two-thirds of the farms in the Willamette Valley had been abandoned.[26] By the same token, some who did not succeed in California moved northward to try their luck in Oregon, Washington, and Idaho. The highly porous boundaries of virtually all American regions have made it tricky to generalize about the composition of their populations. Nonetheless, the joke about the Overland Trail contained a kernel of truth. Mid-nineteenth-century California and the Oregon Country possessed different resources and reputations; they attracted different kinds of emigrants (to summarize crudely, Oregon got more families and farmers; California, more males and miners); and the decisions made by the migrants—for many, before they ever saw the Far West—proved influential in establishing regional identity and perpetuating regional differences.[27]

Oregonians and Washingtonians of the 1850s probably had little shared identity as Northwesterners. However, if they could not much agree on who they *were*, they could surely go on at length about who they were *not*: they were no longer part of the East or Midwest they had left behind, and they were not part of the Californian destination they had decided against.

The Golden State has figured prominently over the years in Northwestern ideas about region. It was often one of the few things about which white Northwesterners could agree, even as diverse groups of them developed along distinctly different lines. Oregon gained statehood in 1859, for example, and Portland emerged as a significant metropolis; the two were integrated relatively quickly into national political and economic systems. Washington, by contrast, remained a territory and economic hinterland for thirty more years, and Seattle did not catch up to Portland until the early twentieth century. But although developing at different paces, the two shared a subservience to, and therefore a suspicion of, California.

As the center of capital, transport, and manufacturing, San Francisco dominated the Northwest economy for decades beginning in 1849. On Puget Sound, where California lumber barons prevailed until investors from Minneapolis–St. Paul arrived in 1900, the colonial nature of such outside control was well understood. "Are the people of the Territory, generally, advised as to the MANNER in which our lumbering interest is controlled?" asked the Olympia *Pioneer* in December 1853. "Are they aware that, to a very undue extent, it is controlled by irresponsible SHARP-ERS and SPECULATORS, resident in Sacramento, San Francisco, and elsewhere along the coast?" Portland newspapers railed similarly against the economic "tyranny" of California.[28]

From the perspective of the metropolis, of course, things looked rosier. Writing on the eve of the arrival of the transcontinental railroad, Henry George scarcely exaggerated when he wrote, "Not a settler in all the Pacific States and Territories but must pay San Francisco tribute; not an ounce of gold is dug, a pound of ore smelted, a field gleaned, or a tree felled in all their thousands of square miles, but must, in a greater or less degree, add to her wealth."[29] The advent of transcontinental lines only heightened San Francisco's control. By 1880, the city, with 20 percent of the inhabitants of the Pacific coast, controlled 99 percent of its imports, 83 percent of its exports, and 60 percent of its manufacturing. It "had more factories, employees, capitalization, value of materials, and value of product than the other 24 western cities combined."[30] When railroads arrived in the Northwest to stimulate growth there, San Franciscans, rather than worry about the competition, expected a new round of profits. "We *need* rich neighbor states," wrote John S. Hittell in 1890:

> The advance of Oregon, Washington, and Idaho . . . will be beneficial to California. . . . It will make a greater demand for those things we sell, and a greater supply of those we buy. It will multiply the number and the means of those people who will come to our State for pleasure and for

health. So long as men wish to escape from gloomy skies, dripping clouds, and dreary winters, and so long as they will seek a bright sunshine and a cheerful heaven . . . , so long the rich people of Oregon and Washington, Idaho and British Columbia, will enjoy much of their surplus wealth in the genial climate of the Golden State.[31]

No wonder Oregon and Washington chafed at California. Yet as much as Northwesterners resented their common economic domination from afar, they also recognized California's success—at least tacitly—in their own boosterism. James Swan imagined in 1857 that only a lack of publicity prevented Washington from surpassing its competitor: "The Territory only needs men and capital to insure its being one of the most thrifty of our possessions, and when its value is more generally appreciated, we may expect to see as rapid an increase in the population as ever California had in its palmiest days."[32] Even today, a sign on the outskirts of Yakima forlornly bills the town as the "Palm Springs" of Washington.

In the first decades of American control over the Pacific Northwest, the inhabitants of Oregon, Idaho, and Washington did not have a strong, mutual, positive identity as a single region. But they were well along in fashioning a kind of "negative" identity based on the conviction that their adopted home was *not* like other places, particularly the Midwest and imperious California. In most instances, this negative identity served to make the Pacific Northwest stand above and apart from the alternatives. But in the minds of some, it took on less favorable connotations.

Northwestern urbanites cultivated their own peculiar version of regional consciousness in worrying that their cities were not similar enough to eastern counterparts. In a metropolitan context, success seemingly depended on demographic and economic growth, which in turn depended on towns becoming familiar, congenial, and refined places, similar enough to established cities that they could attract investors and immigrants from the East.[33]

Northwestern cities tried several methods of imitating the Atlantic coast metropolis. One was in nomenclature. Before settlers on Elliott Bay accepted Seattle as their new city's name, they proposed calling it New York Alki, *alki* being a Chinook jargon term meaning "eventually" or "by-and-by." Towns in the lower Willamette Valley also went some distance to honor the East's example. A coin flip in 1845 between a Maine and a Massachusetts native resulted in a city named Portland rather than Boston; Salem took its name from another New England town. Over time, the residents of the Portland area cultivated—indeed, exaggerated—the similarities between themselves and New England urbanites because such imagery lent an economically and psychologically desirable sense of stability and refinement to urban life. A Portland that appeared as something other than a "frontier" community was a safer place for investors and immigrants because it seemed, in a word, more "eastern." Portland confirmed its place in the pantheon of mature American cities by hosting a world's fair in 1905. Not to be outdone, Seattle followed suit four years later.[34]

Early ideas about the Pacific Northwest as a region depended on its white inhabitants' perceptions of conditions in such other places as the Midwest, California, and the urban East, and these perceptions in turn emerged in large part when Americans moved to the region and attempted to develop it, all the while comparing and contrasting the Northwest with the other places. These beginnings of regional consciousness soon were supplemented by ideas that were largely imposed on the region by external powers, especially in the form of railroad companies. As before, new recipes for thinking about region would owe little to "indigenous" ingredients.

Transportation lines have loomed large in shaping notions of the Pacific Northwest because they have helped to knit together its different subregions. Commerce, cargo, and passengers moved up and down the Columbia River from a very early date, tying eastern Washington, eastern Oregon, and Idaho to the Willamette Valley and Pacific Ocean. Portland thus took its tribute before San Francisco grabbed the larger share. But the Columbia River system was never warmly or widely embraced as a source of regional mutuality. Monopoly control by Portland's Oregon Steam Navigation Company alienated many, especially in Washington. Moreover, the Columbia River system touched few residents along Puget Sound or in communities on the ocean. Residents of Coos Bay on Oregon's Pacific coast, for instance, went shopping in San Francisco, not Portland.[35]

Virtually all inhabitants of the Northwest, however, needed railroads, or at least believed they did. And using bands of steel, the transcontinental lines that arrived during the 1880s and 1890s bound the region together in entirely new and more thorough ways. Railroad companies headquartered back east suddenly exerted an enormous and unprecedented influence on Northwestern affairs. Part of their influence came from linking the region more tightly to the global capitalist system; by itself, such integration likely served to diminish some regional differences.

But the railroad companies' efforts to create a distinct regional identity may have counted for more. To be profitable in the Northwest, they needed to attract immigrants and investors who would buy their lands, ride their trains, and ship produce over their roads; they also wanted tourists to fill their passenger cars. To accomplish such goals, the companies launched continual publicity campaigns to sell Oregon, Idaho, and Washington as a single region called "the Great Northwest" or "the Great Pacific Northwest."[36]

A railroad agent once reportedly quipped, "The West is purely a railroad enterprise. We started it in our publicity department."[37] The same could be said for the Northwest. Railroad companies often paid little attention to local- or state-oriented loyalties. Owning substantial holdings in all three states, it perhaps made sense for them to advertise regionally if it meant doing it once rather than three times. But their concern for the idea of region went beyond mere efficiency. Taking a proprietary interest in the notion of a Pacific Northwest, they sought to make it a household name. In 1923, publicists associated with James J. Hill's railways criticized earlier promotions as too limited to single states, counties, or towns, and aimed now "to introduce the word 'Pacific Northwest' into the popular vocabulary—to make it convey a definite, clean-cut meaning. To make it stand for an idea."[38]

There is no precise way to gauge the power of railroads in strengthening a sense of place for the Pacific Northwest. But their influence appears to have been formidable. One measure was the frequency with which inhabitants of the region, apparently following the railroad companies' example, began to use the term "Northwest" to refer to themselves. They had made limited use of the word before the railroads' arrival. Suffragist Abigail Scott Duniway started a reformist newspaper in 1871 called the *New Northwest*,[39] for instance; Olympia's *North-Western Farmer* was published briefly in 1875; and in the same year, Portland's *West Shore*, "a family paper devoted to literature, science, art and the resources of the Pacific Northwest," began a sixteen-year run. The frequency of use of the word "Northwest" increased substantially, however, after 1883 when the first transcontinental line arrived and the railroad companies began promoting the region in earnest. In 1883, there appeared a magazine successively called, until its 1903 demise, *Northwest, Northwest Illustrated Monthly Magazine, Illustrated Monthly Northwest Magazine,* and *Northwest Magazine*. Publicist Eugene V. Smalley published the magazine in New York and St. Paul, and the Northern Pacific Railroad subsidized and distributed it around the world in order to advertise that region of the country made newly accessible by the completion of a rail line between Minnesota and Puget Sound. The magazine, along with a massive amount of other railroad publicity, appears to have increased the willingness of people in Washington, Idaho, and Oregon to view their three states as a single unit. In the 1880s and 1890s, the number of books and magazines using the term "Northwest" in their titles grew substantially. Many were produced in conjunction with the arrival of the transcontinental lines or in the course of promotions sponsored or encouraged by railroads.[40]

It likely was not accidental that around the same time another kind of enterprise also began taking the idea of region more seriously. Edmond S. Meany at the University of Washington launched the first college course devoted to Pacific Northwest history in the late 1890s. He got his start as a historian by writing about "pioneers" in his days as journalist for the *Seattle Post-Intelligencer*. He then became a state legislator and booster, helping to advertise Washington at the World's Columbian Exposition, held in Chicago in 1893. Selling Washington led directly to teaching and writing about it; it is not clear that Meany saw much difference between the two activities. Thus he became one of the leading exponents of Seattle's 1909 world's fair and helped to ensure that the exposition took place on his campus. At the University of Oregon, Joseph Schafer started teaching regional history upon his arrival in 1900 and wrote the first scholarly text on Pacific Northwest history in 1905.[41]

As railroads helped to validate the idea of a Pacific Northwest inside the region, they promoted it as well among people outside the area. The Northwest's increase in population between 1880 and 1910—from 283,000 to 2,227,000—served as ample testimony to both the greater access that trains provided the region and the power of the companies' advertising in selling it. Many newcomers admitted that the railroads' promotional materials had turned their attention to the Northwest and thus given them a conception of the place even before they arrived. Because the publicity stressed an abundance of natural resources and a relatively good life in the region, many who accepted such images at face value were disappointed upon arrival.[42] Yet regardless of the advertisements' accuracy, the terms in which the region was understood had been changed forever by railroad advertising.

Geographers have liked to discuss the Doctrine of First Effective Settlement, by which the dominant culture in an area is lastingly "imprinted" by the first colonizing "group able to effect a viable, self-perpetuating society" there.[43] But what if, because of advertising and other forms of publicity, the minds of large numbers of immigrants to an area have themselves been "imprinted" with (or colonized by) images and ideas concerning what that region is like? What if people have been conditioned to think a certain way about a place *before* they arrive? Maybe we need a Doctrine of First Effective Mass Advertising to account for the influence of modern public relations on ideas about region.[44]

Such a doctrine could help explain lasting patterns of regional thought in Washington, Oregon, and Idaho. If Northwesterners are upset about the loss of salmon as a "regional right" in the 1990s, it is due in part to earlier boosters forging links between the idea of a Northwest and its natural bounty. Railroads framed a "natural" Northwest, a place not only of resources to be extracted, but also of scenery to be appreciated and visited. In the first decade of the twentieth century, the Great Northern and Northern Pacific lines, for example, commissioned Tacoma artist Abby Williams Hill to paint mountain scenes. They sent her to work in selected areas, incorporated the resulting paintings into their publicity materials, and displayed her artwork at world's fairs.[45] Such efforts increasingly equated the region with its scenery.

Even cities became part of nature's Northwest. Appreciating that paintings like Hill's made good advertising, urbanites were encouraged by such artwork to see their towns in a new light. Prior to the advent of the railroad, their main concern had been to demonstrate that their cities met eastern standards of stability and refinement. Nature in this context was to be conquered or ignored. Tacoma's founding fathers, after all, had instructed engineers "to lose all sight of the fact that [the town] was as yet a wilderness; to forget the forest that bearded the hillsides; to forget that they were on the frontier, and to anticipate the coming of a city of hundreds of thousands." If they donned blinders, Tacomans were convinced that newcomers would do the same: "Those who come here . . . expecting to encounter and suffer the crude associations of the wild frontier towns, will be very pleasantly disappointed."[46] After 1890 or so, however, as railroad ads helped condition Northwesterners to see their region anew, the beauty of a city's surroundings became more appealing and indeed was increasingly regarded as one of the features elevating it *above* eastern counterparts. Abby Williams Hill herself summarized the emergent regional mentality while aboard a steamship leaving New York City for Europe in 1895: "Tacoma is more imposing from the water. The mountain [Mount Rainier] takes the place of the Statue of Liberty. We shall never need such a gift though our city become a metropolis."[47]

So prominent had the natural become in regional thinking that it was casually blended with the urban into a mixture taken not just to rival but to surpass the eastern city. Once devoted to imitating eastern examples, northwestern urbanites now believed that their towns would attract migrants and capital because they differed from cities back east.[48] Identity still hinged on comparison and contrast with the eastern part of the United States, but northwestern urbanites were no longer such slavish imitators.

Of course, improving on the East was one thing, competing against California was quite another. Whatever Oregon, Idaho, and Washington could manage, California always seemed able to manage better. As much as Northwesterners worried about their standing in relation to the East, they were at least equally concerned about their standing compared with that of the Golden State, whose natural resources and scenery appeared to be more alluring than the Northwest's—or at least more successfully marketed.

Promoters went to extreme lengths to overcome California's edge. In 1924, the Seattle Chamber of Commerce published a racialist booklet by Erwin L. Weber, *In the Zone of Filtered Sunshine: Why the Pacific Northwest Is Destined to Dominate the Commercial World,* that made explicit the pseduoscientific premises behind the idea of a region predominantly for whites. Weber explained that "intense and prolonged sunshine, as exists in the greater portion of the United States, is detrimental to the highest human progress. . . . The most energetic human types and the highest and most enduring civilizations have evolved in the cloudiest region of the world, Nordic Europe." He then asserted that the Pacific Northwest (by which he meant that area west of the Cascades), with its more modest sunshine, was one of earth's "few favored regions, which possess all the basic requirements necessary and desirable for the development of the most virile types of humanity, and the highest attainments of civilization." It should be home to superior Nordic peoples, Weber averred, while "the darker types" were better suited for such places as California, where the "Mediterranean races and their descendants will undoubtedly ultimately dominate." Weber predicted the "fall" and "decay" of California civilization, comparing its fate with that of other "empires" built "under the temporary stimulus of intense sunshine." The Nordic Northwest, by contrast, could expect to thrive and endure, for its productive inhabitants would be so well adapted to its weather.[49]

Selling the region required not only drawing attention to the relative homogeneity of the population, but also making virtues out of rain and overcast skies. And make no mistake: Northwesterners remained concerned above all with selling their region to immigrants and investors. Their growing interest in their physical environs did not yet make them into environmentalists. Rather, the main purpose for advertising nature remained to attract people who would help develop the country by exploiting its resources. Northwesterners continued to see their region as both underdeveloped compared with such places as California and the industrial Northeast, and in competition with those places for opportunities to grow. They lamented that the region, far from controlling its own economic destiny, was yet ruled by distant capital. Once more, they tended to define the region more by what it lacked than by what it contained.

In the 1920s and 1930s, Northwesterners planned to reduce the region's enduring subservience as some other place's hinterland. Proposals for the systematic damming of the Columbia River and its tributaries promised regionwide benefits ranging from increased inland navigation and irrigated agriculture to production of inexpensive hydroelectric power for electrifying rural households and attracting factories. Dams would move the entire region forward and ensure attainment of the "good life"— defined in terms remarkably similar to what railroad ads had pictured.[50] They would also require Oregon, Idaho, and Washington to cooperate extensively, to plan and build together as a region. The key to the success of this improbable crusade was that so much of the vision and so many of the resources required for the enormous effort and the new level of regional consciousness came once again from beyond the Northwest's borders.

The demand for dams and their attendant improvements—like that for railroads—had begun locally. But once again, the Pacific Northwest itself lacked the resources to acquire the transforming technology. Moreover, subregions and competing economic interests within the Northwest failed to agree on any one proposal because each insisted on maximizing its own advantages at the expense of the others.[51] Dams became another source of regional commonality primarily because they were somewhat imposed on the Northwest in the 1930s by the federal government, which not only possessed the resources for and interest in building them, but also provided a level of commitment to regional planning and development that Oregon, Washington, and Idaho by themselves could not attain. Like the railroad companies, the federal government had less intrinsic attachment to specific states and subregions of the Northwest; it saw the region instead as a single system to be managed. And in creating and operating that system—building the dams and power lines that further integrated the disparate fragments of Oregon, Washington, and Idaho—the federal government heightened regional consciousness. "In a sense," writes Richard White, "the Columbia River dams made the Pacific Northwest a region."[52]

Planning, building, and managing the dams required thinking on a regional scale, which came more readily to the federal government as "outsider" than to local inhabitants. Such thinking came especially readily to those federal and regional planners of the 1930s who regarded regions as more logical frameworks than states or nations for the reengineering of communities, culture, and nature.[53] And it became enshrined thereafter in the federal bureaucracy. The government has had several agencies—such as the National Park Service, National Forest Service, and National Archives and Records Administration—that, over the course of the twentieth century, have regarded the Pacific Northwest as a single administrative unit. To operate the Columbia River dams, it created in 1937 another bureaucracy tailored specifically to the region. The Bonneville Power Administration is the little-understood agency responsible for collecting hydroelectric power from federal dams on the Columbia River system and distributing it throughout the region. Its operations offered another definition of the Northwest—wherever the kilowatts can get to. "The lines of the BPA marked the region's boundaries," explains White. "Where interties with other transmission systems occurred, there the Pacific Northwest encountered other regions." Over time, the BPA's ability to shape the region expanded. Law committed it "to supplying power at the lowest possible cost, planning its distribution, and stimulating the market. Above all, the agency worked to secure its own growth," primarily by planning for and promoting regional growth.[54] Like the railroads, the BPA had its own proprietary stake in encouraging the idea of region.

The BPA promotions succeeded, in large part because the dams and their kilowatts were harnessed to national mobilization during World War

II and the Cold War. The resulting boom did not spread evenly across the region, but its inhabitants no longer regarded the Northwest as so underdeveloped.[55] They beheld themselves as more on a par with eastern centers of population, commerce, and industry, and less dominated by California. Some west coast rivalry remained, of course. Northwesterners have not minded sending kilowatts to California in the summer because they have received kilowatts back during the winter. They have resented, however, regular appeals to divert Columbia River water southward to the various California canals and pipelines, helping to integrate and create a "Pacific Southwest." At first, the issue remained one of continuing to compete with the Golden State for immigrants and investments. Thus in the later 1940s, during one of California's periodic dry spells, Portland and Seattle newspapers responded to one proposal to divert Columbia waters southward by inviting Californians northward: "Why should not the people come to the water, instead of the water being transported . . . to the people? There are no barriers of which we are aware to the migration of drouth refugees to the irrigable lands of Oregon and Washington, which are within easy reach of the great Columbia."[56]

Twenty-five years later, many Northwesterners had begun to think that erecting barriers between themselves and California was a pretty good idea. Still viewing the Golden State as a rival, they took regional identity to new heights by emphasizing not just economic distinctions, but also differences in the quality of life. Both because of and in response to sustained regional growth since 1940, environmentalism took serious hold of the Pacific Northwest during the 1960s. The region's identification with its natural resources—nurtured for so long by railroad companies and other boosters—came to have new implications; calls for preservation rather than exploitation of those resources became stronger. Continued growth—especially "unmanaged" growth—came into question; overcrowding and pollution threatened the good life that the Northwest had advertised for so long as its trademark.

In this context, overgrown and overdeveloped California became the leading negative example; Oregon and Washington vowed not to repeat its mistakes.[57] Indeed, citizens in each state, especially west of the Cascades, increasingly focused on Californians migrating northward to live in the Northwest as the single greatest threat to their environment and way of life. Northwesterners still seldom agreed on who they were or what their region signified, but they reached near consensus on what they were *not.* They were *not* Californians, and they were not shy about saying so. Oregonians made the most of this antipathy during the 1970s when they tried to make newcomers, especially Californians, unwelcome. Much of the hostility came wrapped in humor, such as Governor Tom McCall's proposal to build a "Plywood Curtain" between the two states or another wag's plan to eliminate all Oregon off-ramps from Interstate 5, which runs from California to the Canadian border. But such bumper-sticker messages as "Don't Californicate Oregon" also expressed (and continue to express) deeply felt antagonism.[58]

Washington was slower to rise to the bait, in large part because—with more people, more cities, more factories, more money, more nuclear reactors, and more of a stake in the American military–industrial complex—it resembled California too much. (Indeed, when Oregonians jokingly proposed rerouting Interstate 5 so that it went around rather than through their state, or closing down all its off-ramps, they were clearly hinting that Washingtonians were not all that welcome, either.[59]) But by the late 1980s, many in Washington, especially around Puget Sound, considered recent growth as too rapid and uncontrolled, and felt overwhelmed by such problems as urban congestion, crime, and a lack of affordable housing. They might have blamed themselves (and booming companies like Boeing and Microsoft) for these problems—after all, most of the recent population increase was "natural," and many newcomers were friends and relatives of existing residents. But Washingtonians preferred to single out migrants from California as the major source of their problem. Once again, newcomers from the Golden State were made to feel unwelcome, as one transplant noted hyperbolically: "The hostility toward Californians is worse than race relations in the South. It's just open season for contempt of Californians."[60]

By this point, California—much like the wild salmon today—clearly had to be taken figuratively rather than literally. It was hardly the main source of Washington's recent growth; in fact, between 1980 and 1987 Oregon accounted for more than one-fifth of net migration into Washington, while California accounted for less than one-eighth. Yet few were interested in blaming Oregon for the problems of growth in Washington (and nobody thought to ask whether Oregon's anti-California sentiments were infecting Washington). Instead, while Washingtonians and Oregonians preserved a sense of difference between them, they had also grown quite accustomed to deriving a Northwestern identity through comparison and contrast with the Golden State. They were not yet sure about what the Northwest *meant*—Salmon Are Us was still aspawning. But they were dead certain that the Northwest did *not* mean anything resembling California, whatever that was.

At the height of Oregon's anxiety about Californians, a Portland journalist, David Sarasohn, cast a wary eye on developments. Regionalism, he warned, was being replaced by sectionalism, and to explain the shift he referred to the American South: "regionalism is Robert Penn Warren; sectionalism is John C. Calhoun."[61] Invoking Calhoun, architect of the theory of nullifaction and extreme advocate of states' rights, may not have been an altogether untoward forecast of the direction in which one variant of regional consciousness was headed. Some in the Pacific Northwest found inspiration in the novel *Ecotopia* by Ernest Callenbach (a Californian, of course). In this story, set in 1999, Washington, Oregon, and northern California had actually seceded from the United States in 1980 after threatening to blow up eastern cities with nuclear weapons. With that act of environmental terrorism as its founding moment, the new nation of Ecotopia—significantly led more by women than men—proceeded to mold its society and economy into an ecological utopia. It outlawed the internal-combustion engine, reduced the work week to twenty hours, and required those who wanted lumber for building a house to work for several months in the forests.[62]

Ecotopia's literary qualities were debatable; twenty-five publishers rejected it before a Berkeley collective brought it out. But the novel sold surprisingly well and was bought by a paperback publisher. In 1979, it was still selling at a rate of 1,000 copies a month; Callenbach estimated that at least half of those copies were purchased in Washington and Oregon. Some Northwesterners seemed to feel that *Ecotopia* captured the essence of their region. So did reporter Joel Garreau, whose popular *Nine Nations of North America* not only dubbed the coastal strip from Monterey to Alaska "Ecotopia," but also, by calling it a "nation," weighed in on the side of sectionalism as opposed to regionalism.[63]

The idea of Ecotopia emerged from a counterculture that has perhaps passed. The concept, though, lives on today in the more mainstream garb of "Cascadia," a term used to describe the urbanized coast stretching from Vancouver, British Columbia, through the Puget Sound area to Portland and Eugene, Oregon. Cascadia means different things to different people: some see an economic unit; others, a "bioregion." But to many, it implies a relatively well-preserved and well-appreciated natural setting inhabited by people "with a love of the outdoors and reverence for the environment passed to us from the native people." Explicitly and implicitly, Cascadia suggests a population more disposed than those elsewhere to protect nature through such efforts as developing "sustainable cities."[64] With Ecotopia and Cascadia, regionalism had moved beyond sectionalism toward exceptionalism.

There could be something to the Northwest's confidence that it can avoid the mistakes made in other places and do things differently, perhaps even better. Maybe because American settlement there has been relatively recent and because it remains somewhat remote, its cities will prove more manageable, its problems more tractable, its social divisions more amenable.[65] But regional exceptionalism can certainly appear to be little more than an ill-founded conceit. If Northwesterners fancy themselves Ecotopians, how do they explain the fact that their wild salmon and spotted owls are disappearing, that their Cascade and Olympic and Blue Mountains contain enormous clear-cuts, that their highways are overburdened, or that their sprawling cities consume so much land? Inhabitants of the region have liked to point to California as the antithesis of the Pacific Northwest, but they have never had to look so far afield to see genuine environmental crises. They have also often regarded Californians as scapegoats, but the truth is that Northwesterners must bear primary responsibility for their own crises.

The region's recent fixation on salmon as markers of regional identity summarizes nicely the paradox of extinction in Ecotopia. In the same way that spotted owls serve as an indicator species for old-growth forests in the Pacific Northwest, wild salmon have evolved as a kind of indicator species for northwestern exceptionalism.[66] Decades of regional consciousness, based on the idea of an abundance of natural resources and given shape by such outsiders as railroad companies, have helped elevate salmon to their current symbolic importance. They represent the Pacific Northwest as a place of plenty where the people feel at one with their natural environs. At the same time, the wild salmon's threatened status, which in itself belies the premise of Ecotopia, has only strengthened regional attachment to the fish. As species of salmon become endangered, it seems that the region to which Northwesterners have become attached —or rather that region's chance to remain exceptional—also becomes endangered.

The salmon scenario parallels one that unfolded a century ago, albeit at the national rather than the regional level. In the 1890s, the United States faced new challenges in the form of industrialization, immigration, labor radicalism, and urbanization, to name only some. Seeing uncomfortable and often unwanted changes on the horizon, some Americans worried about losing the distinguishing traits that had supposedly made the nation special. Whereas Northwesterners in the 1990s have made salmon the measure of regional exceptionalism, in the 1890s anxieties about the nation's future came to revolve around the West. Frederick Jackson Turner, among others, declared that the frontier was what had made the country unique and good. Warning that the extinction of the frontier around 1890 or so had brought to a close "the first period of American history," Turner implied that the United States needed to reestablish its identity by pioneering new challenges.[67]

While Turner's formulation was powerful, influential, and not altogether wrong, today it seems more persuasive as evidence of national consciousness during the 1890s than as an explanation and periodization of American history.[68] One might speculate that Salmon Are Us will have the same significance for the Pacific Northwest. The region's survival as a distinct entity may seem to hinge on the fish, but in fact it does not. Even if the wild salmon themselves survive, they will likely lose their status as the premier regional talisman sooner or later. Historical perspective suggests that the Northwest has been characterized not by any one single meaning, but by a series of meanings or identities emerging over the years—each one suited to the cultures and concerns of its time; each one paradoxically expressed in essentialist language; each one contested by a variety of other ideas and a host of subregional divisions; each one also capable of building in part on, or even absorbing, its predecessors. Regional identity is always being reinvented—not always out of whole cloth entirely, but sometimes out of well-worn pieces of fabric. And, truth be told, a great deal of that reinventing has taken place outside the region.

Regional consciousness in the Pacific Northwest may seem fishy because it has been somewhat artificial and imposed, not altogether homegrown and natural. Even if it has been an ever-shifting, contested, and contingent social construction, however, regional identity has been forceful. It may seem inauthentic because it does not meet certain standards of indigenousness or durability, but the effects of regional identity on people are authentic enough, as many recently arrived Californians can attest. Just as, at the national level, there is nothing dubious about the pervasive influence of the frontier on American identity, so in the Pacific Northwest there is nothing fishy about the power of icons such as salmon.[69]

NOTES

1. Timothy Egan, *The Good Rain: Across Time and Terrain in the Pacific Northwest* (New York: Knopf, 1990), 22; Will Stelle, quoted in Scott Sonner, "U.S. Role Pondered on Rescue of Salmon," *Seattle Times,* 5 February 1995, B3. Egan's book surveys its topic by following "the historical fish arteries from the continental crest to the ocean"; one use of "wherever the salmon can get to" is establishing regional boundaries based on watersheds.

2. In taking up regional consciousness as a state of mind and sense of identity, my Pacific Northwest is subjective. Other studies have relied on more "objective" criteria, such as levels of education and kinds of religious affiliation, to define the Northwest as a "cultural region." See Raymond D. Gastil, "The Pacific Northwest as a Cultural Region," *Pacific Northwest Quarterly* 64 (1973): 147–56.

3. I am indebted to Richard White for the idea of a naturalized regional identity, and for many other helpful comments on earlier drafts of this essay.

4. Let me concede at the start that defining the Pacific Northwest as the three states of Washington, Oregon, and Idaho represents an arbitrary, if commonplace, reliance on political boundaries. One could argue that British Columbia, western Montana, far northern California, and Alaska, or parts thereof, deserve to be considered part of the same region. One could also argue that much of Oregon and Idaho should be considered parts of the Great Basin and the Mountain West, respectively, and not the Pacific Northwest. I have decided not to engage those arguments here; my concern is more about the "unnatural" nature of regional identity than it is about determining any essential Pacific Northwest. Indeed, I doubt there is any such thing as an essential Pacific Northwest. Were there such a thing, however, the weight of the evidence in this chapter would suggest that it consisted of Oregon and Washington but not Idaho, whose deep cultural and physiographic divisions illustrate the dangers of relying on political boundaries for a definition of region. On Idaho's problematic nature, see Gastil, "Pacific Northwest as a Cultural Region"; and Carlos A. Schwantes, *In Mountain Shadows: A History of Idaho* (Lincoln: University of Nebraska Press, 1991), 1–4.

5. Robert L. Burgner, "Life History of Sockeye Salmon (*Oncorhynchus nerka*)," in *Pacific Salmon Life Histories,* ed. C. Groot and L. Margolis (Vancouver: University of British Columbia Press, 1991), 4, 9; William R. Heard, "Life History of Pink Salmon (*Oncorhynchus gorbuscha*)," in ibid., 122, 127; E. O. Salo, "Life History of Chum Salmon (*Oncorhynchus keta*)," in

ibid., 233; M. C. Healy, "Life History of Chinook Salmon (*Oncorhynchus tshawytscha*)," in ibid., 315–16, 317; F. K. Sandercock, "Life History of Coho Salmon (*Oncorhynchus kisutch*)," in ibid., 398, 401; Tom Jay, "Initiation," in Natalie Fobes, *Reaching Home: Pacific Salmon, Pacific People* (Anchorage: Alaska Northwest Books, 1994), 17.

6. In *Good Rain*, Egan considers "dams a false boundary marker" (22), meaning that his Northwest extends along some of the rivers where salmon no longer swim. However, there are additional, undammed river systems where the fish have disappeared for reasons other than dams. The fate of the Columbia River salmon has been told succinctly in Richard White, *The Organic Machine: The Remaking of the Columbia River* (New York: Hill and Wang, 1995); and Charles F. Wilkinson, *Crossing the Next Meridian: Land, Water, and the Future of the West* (Washington, D.C.: Island Press, 1992), chap. 5.

7. White, *Organic Machine*, 90, 91.

8. Egan, *Good Rain*, 22.

9. Donald W. Meinig, *The Great Columbia Plain: A Historical Geography, 1805–1910* (Seattle: University of Washington Press, 1968), 59–60; Frederick Merk, *Fur Trade and Empire: George Simpson's Journal . . . 1824–1825* (Cambridge, Mass.: Harvard University Press, 1931), 40, 47–48. Quotations about the miseries of a dried-salmon diet can be found in James R. Gibson, *Farming the Frontier: The Agricultural Opening of the Oregon Country, 1786–1846* (Seattle: University of Washington Press, 1985), 24, 25. An introduction to treaty fishing rights is Fay G. Cohen, *Treaties on Trial: The Continuing Controversy over Northwest Indian Fishing Rights* (Seattle: University of Washington Press, 1986), 35–51.

10. Jay Taylor has taught me most of what I know about salmon. The destruction of salmon habitat is discussed in Joseph E. Taylor, III, "Making Salmon: Economy, Culture, and Science in the Oregon Fisheries, Precontact to 1960" (Ph.D. diss., University of Washington, 1996), chap. 2.

Quoting the annual report of the Portland Board of Trade, the *Morning Oregonian* exemplifies the emergent notion of salmon as a defining commodity: "What renders this valuable export of more importance to Oregon than anything else which she produces is the fact that while all other countries compete with us raising wheat, wool and other products no other state or country in the world has competed or can possibly compete with us in producing canned salmon in large quantities, so that practically, with careful protection and development of our salmon interests, we can as a state have a monopoly over the world in controlling the prices of an article of diet which is everywhere in daily consumption and which ought and can yield to Oregon ten or twenty years hence an immense revenue, enriching our citizens and increasing the state's wealth and prosperity" ("Board of Trade," *Morning Oregonian*, 16 August 1877, 3). Similarly, Howard H. Martin called salmon "one of the symbols of the Pacific Northwest," just as "codfish is associated with New England" ("Fisheries of the North Pacific," in *The Pacific Northwest: An Overall Appreciation,* ed. Otis W. Freeman and Howard H. Martin [New York: Wiley, 1954], 179). This recognition of salmon as symbol comes within the context of a discussion of fisheries as part of the regional extractive economy.

11. The term comes from Richard L. Neuberger, *Our Promised Land* (New York: Macmillan, 1938). The optimistic 1930s thinking about the region is summarized in Wesley Arden Dick, "When Dams Weren't Damned: The Public Power Crusade and Visions of the Good Life in the Pacific Northwest in the 1930s," *Environmental Review* 13 (1989): 113–53.

12. The Hudson's Bay Company's Columbia Department is treated in Meinig, *Great Columbia Plain;* and Gibson, *Farming the Frontier.* Both the Hudson's Bay Company and the Roman Catholic Church can be described as global entities that often paid little heed to national borders. The church in 1846 established the Archdiocese of Oregon City, which included parts of Canada as well as the United States and was roughly coterminous with the Columbia Department. But Catholic conceptions of the region did not have a lasting impact on the largely non-Catholic American arrivals. Colonization by the Roman Catholic Church is covered in Wilfred P. Schoenberg, S.J., *A History of the Catholic Church in the Pacific Northwest 1743–1983* (Washington, D.C.: Pastoral Press, 1987), chap. 4.

13. Here and throughout the chapter, I am indebted (often indirectly) to Benedict Anderson, *Imagined Communities: Reflections on the Origin and Spread of Nationalism,* 2nd ed. (London: Verso, 1991).

14. Richard E. Ross and David Brauner, "The Northwest as a Prehistoric Region," in *Regionalism and the Pacific Northwest,* ed. William G. Robbins, Robert J. Frank, and Richard E. Ross (Corvallis: Oregon State University Press, 1983), 99–108; Judith Austin, "Desert, Sagebrush, and the Pacific Northwest," in *Regionalism and the Pacific Northwest,* ed. Robbins, Frank, and Ross, 129–47. Richard Maxwell Brown skillfully portrays the coastal Northwest in "The Great Raincoast of North America: Toward a Regional History of the Pacific Northwest," in *The Changing Pacific Northwest: Interpreting Its Past,* ed. David H. Stratton and George A. Frykman (Pullman: Washington State University Press, 1988), 39–53.

15. The importance of the Oregon–Washington border, which is the same as the Columbia River for many miles, is well expressed in Richard L. Neuberger, "The Columbia," in *They Never Go Back to Pocatello: The Selected Essays of Richard Neuberger,* ed. Steve Neal (Portland: Oregon Historical Society Press, 1988), 33–34. Idaho's border with Washington and Oregon, too, has distinguished political and legal subregions.

16. David M. Emmons, "Constructed Province: History and the Making of the Last American West," *Western Historical Quarterly* 25 (1994): 437–59, argues that the entire trans-Mississippi West was a "construction" of northeastern economic, political, and ideological forces beginning in the

1840s. In his reading, the construction of region proceeded more or less according to a blueprint fashioned by ascendant external elites. I appreciate his attention to defining (or limiting) factors based outside the West. My own focus, though, is on the regional consciousness or identity of those *inside* the region, which Emmons does not really explore.

17. This model is summarized in William G. Robbins, "Introduction," in *Regionalism and the Pacific Northwest,* ed. Robbins, Frank, and Ross, 6–7; and Edwin R. Bingham, "Pacific Northwest Writing: Reaching for Regional Identity," in *Regionalism and the Pacific Northwest,* ed. Robbins, Frank, and Ross, 151–74, and it is utilized in part by Brown, "Great Raincoast of North America," 46; and Austin, "Desert, Sagebrush, and the Pacific Northwest," 136.

18. John Shelton Reed, *One South: An Ethnic Approach to Regional Culture* (Baton Rouge: Louisiana State University Press, 1982), 6, 39.

19. Some would contend that in the past decade or two Seattle has become a center for exporting clothes, coffee, and certain kinds of music and high-technology products to other parts of North America, but it is unclear whether these exports add up to a Pacific Northwest cultural hearth.

20. Students of the Pacific Northwest are fortunate that one of the most thoughtful considerations of decisions made by the westering migrant concerned the region: Dorothy O. Johansen, "A Working Hypothesis for the Study of Migrations," *Pacific Historical Review* 36 (1967): 1–12. Also of value is George W. Pierson, *The Moving American* (New York: Knopf, 1973). The idea of "voluntary regions" is explained in Wilbur Zelinsky, *The Cultural Geography of the United States* (Englewood Cliffs, N.J.: Prentice-Hall, 1973), 134–39. Zelinksy emphasizes that this type of region emerged most fully in the twentieth century.

21. Men's dominance in making the decision to migrate overland, and women's frequent opposition to moving, are treated in John Mack Faragher, *Women and Men on the Overland Trail* (New Haven, Conn.: Yale University Press, 1979); Lillian Schlissel, *Women's Diaries of the Westward Journey* (New York: Schocken Books, 1982); and Abigail Scott Duniway, *Path-Breaking: An Autobiographical History of the Equal Suffrage Movement in Pacific Coast States* (Portland, Ore.: Binford and Mort, 1914), 8.

22. Although this is not the place for it, a companion essay about how the Pacific Northwest has been defined (against the Other) as a place for whites needs to be written. Starting points for such an essay might include the following. On exclusion and discouragement of African-Americans, see Thomas C. McClintock, "James Saules, Peter Burnett, and the Oregon Black Exclusion Law of June 1844," *Pacific Northwest Quarterly* 86 (1995): 121–30; and "The Negro Exodus," *Seattle Daily Intelligencer,* 28 May 1879, 2. On the attempted marginalization of Indians, turn to, among many other works, Alexandra Harmon, "A Different Kind of Indians: Negotiating the Meanings of 'Indian' and 'Tribe' in the Puget Sound Region, 1820s–1970s"

(Ph.D. diss., University of Washington, 1995). Regarding efforts to exclude or expel Asian-Americans, consult Roger Daniels, *Asian America: Chinese and Japanese in the United States Since 1850* (Seattle: University of Washington Press, 1988); Roger Daniels, "The Exile and Return of Seattle's Japanese" (Paper presented at the symposium "World War II: What It Took to End the War," Museum of Flight, Seattle, 25 August 1995); Jules Alexander Karlin, "The Anti-Chinese Outbreak in Tacoma, 1885," *Pacific Historical Review* 23 (1954): 271–83; and Jules Alexander Karlin, "The Anti-Chinese Outbreaks in Seattle, 1885–1886," *Pacific Northwest Quarterly* 39 (1948): 103–30.

23. Kenneth S. Stern, *A Force upon the Plain: The American Militia Movement and the Politics of Hate* (New York: Simon and Schuster, 1996), 19–20.

24. John D. Unruh, *The Plains Across: The Overland Emigrants and the Trans-Mississippi West, 1840–1860* (Urbana: University of Illinois Press, 1982), 84–85. The reasoning of overland migrants to Oregon during the 1840s, which contrasted Oregon as destination to prospects in the Midwest, is examined in William A. Bowen, *The Willamette Valley: Migration and Settlement on the Oregon Frontier* (Seattle: University of Washington Press, 1978).

25. Quoted in Johansen, "Working Hypothesis," 8.

26. Hudson's Bay Company chief factor James Douglas, cited in James R. Gibson, "Furs and Food: Russian America and the Hudson's Bay Company," in *Russian America: The Forgotten Frontier*, ed. Barbara Sweetland Smith and Redmond J. Barnett (Tacoma: Washington State Historical Society, 1990), 48–49.

27. Johansen develops the ideas further in "Working Hypothesis."

28. Quoted in Robert E. Ficken, *The Forested Land: A History of Lumbering in Western Washington* (Durham, N.C.: Forest History Society, and Seattle: University of Washington Press, 1987), 33. "Tyranny" is borrowed from Rodman Paul, *The Far West and the Great Plains in Transition, 1859–1900* (New York: Harper & Row, 1988), 117. For more on the power of San Francisco, see Ficken, *Forested Land*, 26, 102–3; Paul, *Far West and Great Plains in Transition*, 115–18; E. Kimbark MacColl, *Merchants, Money, and Power: The Portland Establishment, 1843–1913* (Portland, Ore.: Georgian Press, 1988), 5; and William G. Robbins, *Hard Times in Paradise: Coos Bay, Oregon, 1850–1986* (Seattle: University of Washington Press, 1988), 12, 13, 22.

29. Henry George, "What the Railroad Will Bring Us," *Overland Monthly*, October 1868, 300.

30. William Issel and Robert W. Cherny, *San Francisco, 1865–1932: Politics, Power, and Urban Development* (Berkeley: University of California Press, 1986), 22.

31. John S. Hittell, "The Boom in Western Washington," *Overland Monthly*, 2nd ser., September 1890, 231.

32. James G. Swan, *The Northwest Coast; or, Three Years' Residence in Washington Territory* (New York: Harper and Brothers, 1857), 407.

33. These ideas about western cities are broached in John M. Findlay, "Far Western Cityscapes and American Culture Since 1940," *Western Historical Quarterly* 22 (1991): 41–43; and Findlay, "Place as a State of Mind: The Case of the Western American Cities" (Paper presented at the symposium "American Urbanism," Oregon Historical Society, Portland, November 11, 1995).

34. On "New York Alki," see Murray Morgan, *Skid Road: An Informal Portrait of Seattle*, rev. ed. (Seattle: University of Washington Press, 1982), 19, 24. On Portland's name and its New England heritage, see Carl Abbott, *Portland: Gateway to the Northwest* (Northridge, Calif.: Windsor, 1985), 19, 28, 31; and MacColl, *Merchants, Money, and Power*, 108. On worlds' fairs, see Carl Abbott, *The Great Extravaganza: Portland and the Lewis and Clark Exposition* (Portland: Oregon Historical Society Press, 1981); and John M. Findlay, "Urban Contexts for American International Expositions: World's Fairs in Washington State, 1909–1974" (Paper presented at the meeting of the Organization of American Historians, Chicago, April 1992).

35. Robbins, *Hard Times in Paradise*, 39.

36. This and the following paragraphs draw heavily on Carlos A. Schwantes, *Railroad Signatures Across the Pacific Northwest* (Seattle: University of Washington Press, 1993).

37. Quoted in ibid., 323.

38. Cited in ibid., 188.

39. Duniway no doubt used the broader term "Northwest" instead of "Oregon" because she hoped to spread the influence of her good works beyond the boundaries of one state. By referring to a *new* Northwest, she, like a host of contemporary reformers, radicals, and utopians, imagined the region as more receptive to social and political change, perhaps because it was less settled than the East and therefore less set in the "old" ways.

40. On the magazine subsidized by the Northern Pacific, see Schwantes, *Railroad Signatures*, 86–87. For the information about the dramatic increase of books and magazines using "Northwest" in their titles, I have relied on the computerized database of the University of Washington Libraries. Their holdings do not include all materials using the term "Northwest" in the title (and with some titles "Northwest" refers to Canada's Northwest Territories or America's "old" Northwest), but the library catalogue provides a reliable and convenient index of the changing frequency with which the term was used in the titles of books, journals, and magazines to refer to the three-state area. In computerized searches, I checked database for titles issued between 1870 and 1899, and found most published after 1883; then I checked the period 1900 to 1929 and found still more publications using the word. The late nineteenth century—after the arrival of railroads in 1883—appears to be when the terms "Northwest" and "Pacific Northwest" became used quite widely in print.

41. John M. Findlay, "Closing the Frontier in Washington: Edmond S. Meany and Frederick Jackson Turner," *Pacific Northwest Quarterly* 82 (1991): 59–69; Joseph Schafer, *A History of the Pacific Northwest* (New York: Macmillan, 1905). A phone conversation with the ever-helpful Richard Maxwell Brown, 13 March 1996, provided details about Schafer.

42. Schwantes, *Railroad Signatures,* 91–92; Carlos A. Schwantes, "The Concept of the Wageworkers' Frontier: A Framework for Future Research," *Western Historical Quarterly* 18 (1987): 51–53.

43. Zelinsky, *Cultural Geography of the United States,* 13–14. This doctrine offers the basis for the continued currency of the punchline "Those who could read went to Oregon." Northwesterners assume that they continue to differ from Californians because of the decisions and character of the earliest American settlers.

44. Migrants to Sun City, Arizona, for example, admitted to having their views of the retirement town shaped firmly through advertising and other means before arrival. See John M. Findlay, *Magic Lands: Western Cityscapes and American Culture Since 1940* (Berkeley: University of California Press, 1992), chap. 4.

45. Ronald Fields, *Abby Williams Hill and the Lure of the West* (Tacoma: Washington State Historical Society, 1989), chaps. 2–5.

46. Quoted in David Hamer, *New Towns in the New World: Images and Perceptions of the Nineteenth-Century Urban Frontier* (New York: Columbia University Press, 1990), 89.

47. Quoted in Fields, *Abby Williams Hill,* 20.

48. Findlay, "Far Western Cityscapes and American Culture," 41–43; Findlay, "Place as a State of Mind."

49. Erwin L. Weber, *In the Zone of Filtered Sunshine: Why the Pacific Northwest Is Destined to Dominate the Commercial World* (Seattle: Seattle Chamber of Commerce, 1924).

50. Dick, "When Dams Weren't Damned."

51. Richard Lowitt surveys how federal planning shaped regional projects in *The New Deal and the West* (Bloomington: Indiana University Press, 1984), esp. chaps. 9–10. Robert E. Ficken, *Rufus Woods, the Columbia River, and the Building of Modern Washington* (Pullman: Washington State University Press, 1995), and Paul C. Pitzer, *Grand Coulee: Harnessing a Dream* (Pullman: Washington State University Press, 1994), illuminate disagreements within the region over the dams and explain why the federal government's intervention and supervision was so influential.

52. White, *Organic Machine,* 64.

53. White develops this point with regard to the regionalist influence of Lewis Mumford in ibid., 64–65.

54. Ibid., 64, 71, 75.

55. Carlos A. Schwantes, "The Pacific Northwest in World War II," in *The Pacific Northwest in World War II,* ed. Carlos A. Schwantes (Manhattan,

Kans: Sunflower University Press, 1986), 4–19; Gerald D. Nash, *The American West Transformed: The Impact of the Second World War* (Bloomington: Indiana University Press, 1985).

56. Portland *Oregonian,* quoted in Carey McWilliams, *California: The Great Exception* (New York: Wyn, 1949), 348; "If They Want Our Water, We Have Room for Them," *Seattle Times,* 3 October 1948, 6. Among other helpful remarks on an earlier draft of this essay, William L. Lang has pointed out to me that by sending kilowatts to California, people in the Northwest *have been* sharing their water with the Golden State, in one sense.

57. The irony, of course, was that for all its environmental problems California had also pioneered many of the nation's planning and environmental initiatives designed to protect quality of life. See Samuel P. Hays, *Beauty, Health, and Permanence: Environmental Politics in the United States, 1955–1985* (Cambridge: Cambridge University Press, 1987), 44.

58. A California sociologist reports that anti-California attitudes continue to prevail in Oregon. Glenn T. Tsunokai took surveys commonly used to detect prejudice toward African-Americans, gays, and other "vulnerable groups"; substituted "Californians" for "blacks" and "homosexuals" on the forms; and sent them out to a sample of Oregonians. The respondents demonstrated fairly significant prejudice against their neighbors to the south. See Foster Church, "Oregonians Just Say No to California," Portland *Oregonian,* 12 November 1996, A1, A6.

59. On this suspicion of Washington, see David Sarasohn, "Regionalism, Tending toward Sectionalism," in *Regionalism and the Pacific Northwest,* ed. Robbins, Frank, and Ross, 224.

60. Glenn Pascall's remark on Seattle bigotry toward Californians is quoted in Mary Bruno, "Seattle Under Siege," *Lear's,* July 1991, 53. (Of course, in making this quite exaggerated comment, Pascall was also "constructing" or reinforcing certain regional stereotypes of the South—but that is the subject of another essay.) The data on the sources of Washington's growth in the early and mid-1980s, in this paragraph and the next, come from Richard Morrill and David C. Hodge, "Myths and Facts About Growth Management" (Report, 1991, in author's possession), 8–11. Jonathan Raban, *Hunting Mister Heartbreak: A Discovery of America* (New York: HarperCollins, 1991), 299–303, found in the late 1980s that Seattle was relatively welcoming to virtually all immigrants except those from California. Eloquent testimony to the survival of "California-bashing" comes from a sixteen–year-old Idaho woman who describes the hostility directed at her and other transplants from the Golden State. She regarded the "unfair treatment and blatant prejudice" against Californians as one reason that California youths had dropped out of her high school. See "Even Teachers Show Dislike for Cal Teens," Spokane *Spokesman-Review,* 25 September 1996, G1.

61. Sarasohn, "Regionalism, Tending Toward Sectionalism," 223.

62. Ernest Callenbach, *Ecotopia: The Notebooks and Reports of William Weston* (Berkeley: Banyan Tree Books, 1975).

63. Joel Garreau, *The Nine Nations of North America* (Boston: Houghton Mifflin, 1981), 251–52.

64. The literature on Cascadia is large and diverse. I have relied in part on Alan Artibise, Anne Vernez Moudon, and Ethan Seltzer, "Cascadia: A Case Study Prepared for the Conference on Cities in North America" (1995); Alan Artibise, "Cascadian Adventures: Shared Visions, Strategic Alliances, and Institutional Barriers in a Transborder Region" (Paper delivered at the symposium "'On Brotherly Terms': Canadian-American Relations West of the Rockies," Seattle, 13 September 1996); and Gary Pivo, *Toward Sustainable Urbanization on Mainstreet Cascadia* (Vancouver: International Centre for Sustainable Cities, 1995). The quotation comes from Paul Schell, "Cascadia: The North Pacific West" (Paper presented at the meeting of the North American Institute, Seattle, October 1992), 4. Like Ecotopia, Cascadia is mainly an artifact of west of the Cascade Mountains.

65. This sentiment, which runs through the Cascadia literature, has also been expressed by people ranging from Oregon's environmentalist governor Tom McCall (as cited in "The People's Choice," Pasco *Tri-City Herald*, 3 July 1969, 4) to a host of business publications ranking Northwestern cities as among America's "most liveable." Carl Abbott, *The Metropolitan Frontier: Cities in the Modern American West* (Tucson: University of Arizona Press, 1993), 177–78, holds out hope for Portland and Seattle as two of the relatively few manageable American cities where the future of urban life need not seem such a bleak prospect. After scouting other parts of the United States, the British writer Jonathan Raban relocated to the Northwest: "if I were seeking a fresh start in America," he wrote before moving, "I'd go to Seattle" (*Hunting Mister Heartbreak*, 255). And so he did.

66. A fine primer on the old-growth-forest and spotted-owl issues and on the idea of an indicator species is William Dietrich, *The Final Forest: The Battle for the Last Great Trees of the Pacific Northwest* (New York: Simon and Schuster, 1992).

67. Frederick Jackson Turner, "The Significance of the Frontier in American History," *Annual Report of the American Historical Association for the Year 1893* (Washington, D.C.: American Historical Association, 1894), 227; Findlay, "Closing the Frontier in Washington," 59–61.

68. David M. Wrobel, *The End of American Exceptionalism: Frontier Anxiety from the Old West to the New Deal* (Lawrence: University Press of Kansas, 1993).

69. One of the many works assessing the impact of ideas about the frontier on national identity is *The Frontier in American Culture: Essays by Richard White and Patricia Nelson Limerick,* ed. James R. Grossman (Chicago: Newberry Library, and Berkeley: University of California Press, 1994).

When the Desert Won't Bloom:

Environmental Limitation

and the Great Basin

Elizabeth Raymond

James Cowden spoke for many Americans in 1853 when he so casually dismissed vast acres of the interior West as good for nothing except connecting more significant parts of the country.

> From Fort Larramie [*sic*] to the Nevada Mountains, a distance of twelve or fourteen hundred miles, wild sage constitutes three fourths of the vegetation to be seen. I would give more for one county in Iowa than for all of it, except perhaps the Salt Lake Valley. Can't see any use for so much desert country, for certainly it is good for nothing only to hold the rest of Creation together.[1]

The region only then becoming known as the Great Basin was quintessential western desert—sagebrush, alkali flats, naked mountains, and no visible water. Crossing it was onerous and unrewarding. Very few people were tempted to remain. As another Iowan wrote a decade later, from the mining town of Austin, Nevada, "It is not a nice Country to live in at all. There is no fruit raised here nor crops of any kind to amount to much. . . . This is a very lonsome [sic] place, and no amusement or society."[2]

Identified by John C. Frémont in 1844 as a region of wholly interior drainage, the Great Basin was otherwise largely unknown, a "sort of neutral ground between widely separated portions of this vast country," in the words of topographical engineer Howard Stansbury. Stansbury began his 1852 account of exploring Utah's Great Salt Lake Valley with the fond wish that the area's "character should be more fully known, its hidden sources of wealth developed, and rendered available to the enterprise of our ever advancing population." The task that Stansbury set himself was not an easy one, and the Great Basin continued to confound. When novelist Walter van Tilburg Clark described his home state a century later, for readers of *Holiday* magazine in 1957, the kindest thing he could find to say about Nevada was that it was "still a white space in the mental maps of most Americans." Even today, as Reed H. Blake and Spencer H. Blake have observed, residents of the Great Basin—in contrast to denizens of other western areas—lack a strong regional identity.[3]

The Great Basin was a geographic anomaly without the dramatic and compelling physical features of a place like Yellowstone. Early accounts repeatedly attempted to convey its barren strangeness. When government geologist Israel Cook Russell set out in 1885 to provide a scientific catalogue of its characteristics, he began by explaining that the Great Basin

> stands in marked contrast in nearly all its scenic features with the remaining portions of the United States. The traveler in this region is no longer surrounded by the open, grassy parks and heavily-timbered mountains of the Pacific slope, or by the rounded and flowing outlines of the forest-crowned Appalachians, and the scenery suggests naught of the boundless plains east of the Rocky Mountains or of the rich savannas of the Gulf States. He must compare it rather to the parched and desert areas of Arabia and the shores of the Dead Sea and the Caspian.[4]

In place of such familiar American landscapes, the traveler confronted a confusing agglomeration of mountains and valleys, where all rivers drained inward and dissipated in swampy "sinks" rather than flowing to the sea. Russell estimated its extent as nearly equal in area to France, stretching from Death Valley into central Oregon, and from the Wasatch Mountains in Utah to the Sierra Nevada in California. Defying normal expectations, in this expanse, "the valleys or plains separating the mountain ranges, far from being fruitful, shady vales, with life-giving streams, are often absolute deserts, totally destitute of water, and treeless for many day's journey, the gray-green sagebrush alone giving character to the landscape."[5]

Even guidebook writers, with an incentive to make their descriptions enticing, could find little of a positive nature to report about the Great Basin. Albert D. Richardson's weak attempt in 1866 to render the region sensational is typical: "The great tract between the eastern foot of the Sierras and the western rim of the Utah basin is the most desolate upon our continent—a vast expanse of ashen desert and sandy, rocky hills, destitute of wood and grass." Yet it was difficult to get the right vantage point to see this desolation. The Carson and Humboldt Sinks, where two major basin rivers dissipated their waters into the sand, were hard to see, sometimes full of water and other times dry. It was difficult to instruct travelers what to look at. Richardson finally gave up and moved on, though not before predicting that the new state of Nevada "never will be self-sustaining for a large population, but must draw its chief supplies from Utah and California."[6]

From the beginning, then, the Great Basin posed a challenge to the prevailing American environmental ethos, grounded—during much of the nineteenth century, at least—in pride in the potential and actual resources of a bounteous terrain. Self-aggrandizement through landscape has deep roots in American culture. New England colonists, for instance, construed themselves as a chosen people in part because God had led them to such a fertile wilderness. In his now infamous 1893 frontier thesis, historian Frederick Jackson Turner argued that the exigencies of the American wilderness actually *produced* the country's vaunted democratic form of government. In 1905, irrigation promoter William E. Smythe summed up this creed when he concluded that American greatness was due to the "luminous fact" of its "continental expanse of marvelous resources awaiting the labor and genius of man." Thus landscape has long been an important element in the discourse of national identity.[7]

The twin attributes of this symbolic American landscape are great size and remarkable abundance. Grade-school classes and service clubs sing contentedly of a country "beautiful for spacious skies *and* amber waves of grain." But while the spaciousness of the United States has been construed as natural (by way of a series of conquests justified as Manifest Destiny), its abundance is more commonly viewed as a cultural artifact. Thus the continent was not just inherently productive, but was painstakingly transformed by human occupation. Indeed, European settlers justified their seizure of the land from its Native inhabitants on the grounds that the Native Americans did not put it to "proper" agricultural use. The space that Americans collectively commemorate, then, is a product—a landscape understood to have been self-consciously created, as generations of "pioneers" pitted human strength and ingenuity against the nature that otherwise constituted wasted wilderness.[8] In a few notable instances, however, the buoyant nineteenth-century American environmental faith was betrayed by the force of an intractable nature. The agricultural settlement of the western Plains in the 1890s, and subsequent depopulation of western Dakota, was one such incident. The nearly complete destruction of the western range-cattle industry in the 1880s and 1890s, and its resulting reorganization, was another. Indeed, as Euro-Americans encountered the forbidding and unfamiliar conditions of the arid West, their environmental optimism increasingly failed them. Far from yielding to their technology and their determination, the interior West proved particularly resistant to change.[9]

Nowhere was this more true than in the intermountain portion of the western United States known as the Great Basin. There, in the area that extends west from Utah's Wasatch Front to California's Sierra Nevada, nature had the reputation of being especially obdurate. Traversed by generations of east–west travelers, the region had been excoriated by many. Disgusted observers found it "extremely Barren [*sic*]," as did explorer Jedediah Smith in 1827, or of a "dreary and savage character," like John C. Frémont in 1843. An early-twentieth-century commentator was even harsher: "The mean ash-dump landscape stretches on from nowhere to nowhere, a spot of mange. No portion of the earth is more lacquered with paltry, unimportant ugliness."[10]

There is, in fact, a striking similarity among hundreds of accounts produced by those who scurried across the barren spaces of this high-desert region. Over decades, and despite considerable improvements in the technology of travel, observers of the Great Basin uniformly found the region empty, boring, and potentially threatening. In the words of contemporary essayist Rob Schultheis, it was, and remains, a kind of "geographic purgatory." Enduring its dry mountains and valleys, its saline lakes and springs, was the price people paid in order to reach places more alluring on either side. The land within its boundaries—crossed most commonly from east to west along the route of the Humboldt River and the transcontinental railroad—seemed utterly worthless.[11]

Reasons for the region's negative image are manifest. Land in the Great Basin defied the prevailing American environmental ideal of improvement and use. It provided neither opportunities for agriculture, as did California and the eastern states, nor spectacular scenery, like other areas of the mountain West. Mining produced temporary outposts of prosperity, but they were evanescent. It was not even, in Thomas Hensley's plaintive lament, "a nice Country to live in."[12]

During the nineteenth century, the main wagon route to California followed the Humboldt River west through Nevada. Diaries and letters of overland travelers customarily describe this stretch of the Great Basin as an extended physical and psychological trial from which they were fortunate to escape alive. They heightened the drama of their situation by detailing the numbers of dead and dying livestock and the increasingly frequent human graves along the trail. By their accounts, the inland desert was a place without redeeming features of any kind. Even the greater creature comforts of railroad travel did not eradicate the pain of crossing the region. Although swifter and more comfortable, the train trip was still a trial to a 1932 traveler, who complained: "One gets up in the morning and looks out of one's window at the landscape. Six hours later one is, seemingly, in exactly the same place, and it has changed little at bedtime or next morning."[13]

This refrain remained a constant. Automobile traveler Simone de Beauvoir enjoyed greater autonomy and mobility when she drove through Nevada in the late 1940s; but she still confronted an environment that she found to be blank and disorienting in its lack of human import: "At each bend of the road the country changed, yet it was always the same. We were crossing a single desert, and it could be seen in its entirety in each vision. We were even more lost than on the coast where the sea at least put limits to the land. Here, all around, the landscape disappeared into the infinite, the horizon was so vast it made one giddy. There was no sign of man." Less articulate, but no less dismayed, a cross-country driver commented of her trip through western Utah in 1916: "Much of this part of my trip was rather tiresome. The country all around looked as though it has been painted with a giant whitewash brush. One alkali bed after another—and not a living thing to break the monotony."[14]

Author T. H. White recorded a similar impression of the Great Basin as lifeless and alienating, even when viewed from the air, in 1965: "Why go to the moon? For half an hour, at our great airplane speed, it was an endless dried ocean bed . . . not flat, but seared and gulleyed like a sea-side beach whose trickles had dried." Speed ate up greater distances and height provided a commanding perspective, but neither made the landscape any more palatable. White revealed his own environmental biases when he remarked plaintively on the presence "here and there [of] a lonely farm-field won from the chaos."[15]

Initially, few Euro-Americans settled permanently in this landscape. The prevailing American environmental ethic of the nineteenth century had been shaped by eastern standards of humid agriculture. Land was prized to the extent that it produced crops. By this measure, the Great Basin environment seemed hopeless.[16] It is exceptionally dry, with average precipitation of less than seven inches annually. The soil is thin and often alkali; the terrain is mountainous; and even the indigenous peoples had no agriculture, living in small bands of nomadic hunter-gatherers. The area is a desert, even though occasional mining booms such as the discovery of Nevada's Comstock Lode in 1859 brought in hordes of eager fortune seekers like the young Samuel Clemens. Mining towns, however, usually died as suddenly and dramatically as they had been born, leaving behind no permanent or significant vestiges of human presence. In John Muir's estimation they were "sins against science." Their ruins resembled "the bones of cattle that have died of thirst."[17]

Mining booms, and the temporary towns that accompanied them, were the exception that proved the rule. Nature in the Great Basin was judged to be hostile, entirely unsuited to conventional settlement. Those who tried, like the Mormons in the eastern reaches of the Great Basin, succeeded only in limited areas, and then by dint of extraordinary effort. Mormon settlements were sustained against overwhelming odds by a spiritual imperative to establish an agricultural society in their 1847 State of Deseret. Accordingly, they officially eschewed mining and established rudimentary irrigation projects through church initiative and communal labor. At great cost, they reproduced and maintained midwestern-style farms in the valleys of Utah and eastern Nevada.[18]

Since then, observers have noted with amazement the contrast between the green areas of Mormon settlement and the rest of the Great Basin. As early as 1858, one traveler remarked with surprise that the Mormons were practicing field agriculture in the middle of the wilderness, though he also observed that "certain years despite the most intensive precautions everything withers and dies." A history of Utah published in 1916 conceded that although "tillage, aided by irrigation, has done much to redeem the waste and render it fruitful," the desert was not yet vanquished: "Desert it was, uncultivated, uninhabited; and desert it is, in many places, despite the wondrous changes that time and toil have wrought."[19]

The risks of a short growing season at the high altitudes of the Great Basin, and the tremendous costs of constructing and maintaining irrigation works without government subsidy, were sufficient to deter agriculture in most of the region. Ranches in Nevada were scattered thinly along the western margins and watercourses. In the interior, they clustered in those few places where mountain drainages supplied water year round. Indeed, the nature of the soil itself mitigated against agriculture, as Captain J. H. Simpson observed during his 1859 survey. Even dedicated Mormon farmers were helpless to contend with alkali:

> This saline efflorescence is a sure poison to vegetation, and hopelessly worthless is any soil where it is seen. It is the fact, too (and it is one of great importance in this Territory), that soils which have been originally quite productive under cultivation have, by that very process, gradually become more and more alkaline, until at length, on account of their unproductiveness from this cause, they have of necessity been abandoned. This has been the history of many a field in Great Salt Lake and Utah Valleys, and I am inclined to the belief that it will be the history of the greater portion of the cultivable land of the Territory.[20]

Yet the cultural imperative that equated a healthy society with an agricultural economy remained strong, and late-nineteenth-century confidence in the efficacy of science and technology was virtually unlimited. In Nevada, between 1890 and 1920, irrigated farming was one of the principal tenets of this faith. Simpson's cautions were long forgotten. Observing the stubborn persistence, if not the prosperity, of the Mormon farms and the potential for profit from large-scale irrigation projects in the Central Valley of California, enthusiasts like William E. Smythe championed federally sponsored irrigation efforts in his book *The Conquest of Arid America*. Preaching a gospel of scientific farming through the systematic application of moisture to crops only when it was needed, Smythe prepared to do battle with the intransigent desert environment of the Great Basin. He addressed himself in 1900 to a generation of "homeseekers, who, under the leadership of the paternal Nation, are to grapple with the desert, translate its gray barrenness into green fields and gardens, banish its silence with the laughter of children."[21]

He was not alone in his faith. Commentators throughout the nation eagerly accepted the Progressive dogma of irrigation science. The history of American landscape change encouraged them to expect great things in the future. In 1914, one eastern horticulturist chronicled the changes he had witnessed since moving from New York to Illinois in 1845. Citing his own history as his guide, B. F. Ferris confidently forecast similar triumphs in the west:

> In 1845 Illinois was almost a wilderness of prairie, Iowa entirely so. Since I can remember, Chicago has changed from what it was to what it is, and Iowa has surprised the world. What does it portend for the "farther West?" . . . The millions of acres from northern Montana to southern Arizona, on both sides of the Rocky mountains [sic] will be cropped and the settlers will grow their own fruits and flowers. . . . The days of miracles have passed, but the days of progress have not . . . the same energy that has made Chicago what she is, and Iowa what she is, will fruit and flower the farther West.[22]

Invoking that energy, Smythe lent his publicity efforts to the ongoing irrigation campaign stimulated in the 1880s by John Wesley Powell and promoted, among others, by Nevada senators William Stewart and Francis Newlands. Newlands was largely responsible, in 1902, for passage of the National Reclamation Act, commonly known as the Newlands Act, which involved the federal government in financing irrigated farming. The Newlands Act established a revolving fund for the construction of large-scale irrigation projects. Using proceeds from the sale of public lands, the government would construct the dams, reservoirs, and canals that would bring water to arid land. Purchasers of irrigated farmsteads would repay the cost of the construction over a ten-year period, thus replenishing the fund for future use. Among the first such projects was one in Nevada, along the Truckee and Carson Rivers at the western edge of the Great Basin.[23]

The irrepressible Smythe eagerly predicted a state socially and politically transformed by the introduction of irrigated agriculture. In the late nineteenth century, there had been public discussion of whether a state like Nevada, with only 47,000 people inhabiting 110,000 square miles in 1890, even deserved to retain its statehood. Mining was moribund by then, and it was charged (with some justification) that Nevada was simply a huge rotten borough controlled by the railroad. Similar controversy plagued Utah, still a territory in 1890 despite denser settlement and greater agricultural development than its western neighbor, because of the practice of polygyny sanctioned by the Church of Jesus Christ of Latter-Day Saints. Throughout the Great Basin in the nineteenth century, not only the landscape, but also the resulting society and economy seemed blighted.[24]

But Smythe was sanguine, evoking in defense of his vision an unfamiliar positive image of a Great Basin environment redeemed through the beneficial influence of agriculture: "A big, splendid, American State, blest with the climate in which English-speaking man has won nearly all his triumphs, except that its skies are cleared by aridity and its sunshine brightened by altitude, a land of prosperous little farms, tilled by their owners . . . and a people so economically freed and politically untrammelled that they may make their institutions what they will—this is the Nevada of the future."[25] And Smythe was not alone. Some Nevadans, too, believed that farms could help sanctify a morally and socially suspect state.

Economically, agriculture represented potential prosperity amid the severe economic decline of the 1890s. This was a practical appeal that Newlands was making as early as 1890, and William Stewart before him. But agriculture also entailed the tantalizing possibility of an alternative culture, a reform vision articulated in a speech delivered at the University of Nevada in 1893 by Reno newspaper editor Robert L. Fulton. In his address, Fulton drew a clear distinction between Nevada's traditional economy and the kind of state that would emerge as a result of irrigation: "But we must go to work right to make a State. We cannot do it with a lottery, with prize fighting nor stock gambling. Up to this time Nevada has been too much like a man who when hungry takes a drink of whisky instead of a beefsteak to sustain his strength. . . . When times were dull, instead of going into some new place and developing wealth, we would ask where we can make a boom and how can we get in." Fulton disdained the hectic artificiality of the mining world and the kind of people it attracted: "Men who come in to engage in the exciting pursuits of mining and stock raising in the barren wastes of a desert country are not going to reclaim it and cultivate it." He preferred instead the sober industry of the farmer, who realizes that "it is steady, quiet endeavor pursued through patient years that makes a State."[26]

For a generation, hopes for that new state ran high. From the first national irrigation congresses in the 1890s until passage of the National Reclamation Act and the opening of the Truckee–Carson Irrigation Project in 1905, Nevadans like Fulton eagerly anticipated the dawn of the predicted new day. In June 1905, when water from the Truckee River was first turned into the headgates of the main canal to flow toward newly created fields, journal editor Mrs. M. M. Garwood proposed to celebrate "Irrigation Day" as "the most significant of all holidays." Future celebrants would realize "the immensity of the Government Reclamation Service," she predicted, "when the lands through which we are now passing, white hot and bare, should be green with whispering trees and the broad waving fields, healthy happy homes for future generations." The engineer in charge of the project, L. H. Taylor, confidently predicted that it would ultimately irrigate between 350,000 and 400,000 acres.[27]

Smythe's optimistic faith in the promise of irrigation resonated for a group of Nevada boosters with backgrounds in education and Progressive reform. These men and women saw in the early-twentieth-century marriage of technology and federal funds the opportunity to remake their state from a political and economic pariah into a respectable agricultural commonwealth. They supported improbable ventures like the Pacific Reclamation Company's attempt at Metropolis, in northeastern Nevada, to build a dry-farming colony in the high desert. They believed devoutly in the state's newly developed system of soil classification based on the height of the sagebrush, which confidently predicted that any land that could grow sagebrush at least two feet high could grow rye or wheat without irrigation. Nevada patriots, they agreed with the state's commissioner of agriculture, C. A. Norcross, that any failure of irrigation would inevitably be regarded by the outside world as a result of deficient soil and climate. Tirelessly, they promoted Nevada agriculture and initiated newcomers into the intricacies of a desert climate. They built demonstration farms, invested in dairies and other food-processing plants, and confidently anticipated the achievement of a permanent economic foundation for their much maligned state.[28]

Unfortunately, and much to their sorrow, irrigated agriculture had only a very limited future in Nevada. Natural watercourses are few; the climate is unpredictable; and the soil proved far less fertile than that of California, regardless of the height of the sagebrush. Over time, Nevada farmers experimented with sugar beets, melons, potatoes, and turkeys, but had difficulty establishing any dependably profitable crops. Poorly designed drainage systems wasted precious water, and irrigation eventually leached naturally occurring toxic minerals like arsenic to the surface of the soil, thereby poisoning nearby wetland areas in which the runoff collected. By 1929, only 87,500 acres of the predicted 350,000 in the Truckee–Carson Irrigation Project were actually irrigable, and cropped acreage came to just 51,000 acres. Eventually, much of that cropland was devoted to alfalfa, used by local ranchers who needed hay as a winter feed to supplement the natural vegetation on which their cattle grazed during the rest of the year.[29]

Smythe's prosperous little farms, for the most part, gave way to ranch operations that simply supplemented an existing system of grazing on the public range. In the end, only small corners of the Great Basin were permanently transformed by irrigation. The occasional green fields glimpsed by T. H. White during his airplane flight were artifacts of an oasis civilization, minor technological marvels, achieved at tremendous cost in terms of capital investment, technology, and human effort. In the fervent words of a guidebook to Utah: "If houses could not stand as monuments to a culture, trees, gardens, and sheer greenness could." Despite Smythe's high hopes for the "religious rite" of irrigation, most of the Great Basin did *not* blossom like the proverbial rose.[30]

In the intermountain desert, nature was a more formidable opponent than Smythe or Fulton could conceive, and dominion was less easily or convincingly achieved. Few stayed when they could manage to leave. Environmental limitation was the ultimate lesson of the harsh, empty, desert country, and the ethos of those people who endured was extractive rather than nurturing. They mined nature, literally or figuratively, for resources in the form of ore, timber, or range grasses. In the eastern half of the basin, only the strong religious influence of Mormonism convinced otherwise reluctant residents to remain in the harshest areas. The Great Basin portions of Utah were devoted primarily to mining and, in the twentieth century, to military bases.

In the heavily male western half of the region, transience was the rule for those not held by bonds of family or church. Few expected to remain once they found happiness in the form of a "stake" large enough to take them elsewhere. When the mines played out or drought killed the cattle, they admitted defeat, took their losses, and moved on. There were not many other options. The few cities like Reno and Elko were small and isolated, heavily dependent for their continued existence on the transcontinental railroad and their status as distribution centers. A spectacular mining boom in southern Nevada in the first decade of the twentieth century briefly revived the state's fortunes and population, but both declined again by the 1920s and the state slipped back into economic torpor. Nevada's declining population remained heavily male even in the 1930 census.[31]

Despite the best efforts of irrigation prophets, mining promoters, and railroad interests, the Great Basin remained in fact as in image an unredeemed desert, an environmental obstacle for travelers, and an environmental gamble for those who sought to make a living there. It was unyielding. People who persisted did not conquer it, but merely survived. In their accounts, they prided themselves on having managed to persist in a place that so many found so distasteful.

Even those who found beauty in this landscape remained mindful of its inhospitability. Frances Fuller Victor described the effect in an 1869 poem entitled "Nevada," written during the Comstock silver boom:

> Nevada—desert, waste,
> Mighty, and inhospitable, and stern;
> Hiding a meaning over which we yearn
>   In eager, panting haste—
>   Grasping and losing
> Still being deluded ever by our choosing
> Answer us, Sphinx: What is thy meaning double
>   But endless toil and trouble?
>
> Inscrutable, men strive
> To rend thy secret from thy rocky breast;
> Breaking their hearts, and periling heaven's rest
>   For hopes that can not thrive;
>   Whilst unrelenting,
> Upon thy mountain throne, and unrepenting,
> Thou sittest, basking in a fervid sun,
>   Seeing or hearing none.

Seventy-five years later, the Works Progress Administration guide to Utah repeated the theme in its description of the state:

In Utahns there is universally a consciousness of the earth, in part because of the recency of its pioneering, but principally because Utah is an uncertainly subdued land, instinct with hardship. . . . Life does not come easy. Perhaps some of the especial flavor of Utah comes from this quality of things coming hard. Its beauty is not wholehearted; always there is something withheld. Utah's loveliness is a desert loveliness, unyielding and frequently sterile; its one sea, Great Salt Lake, is lethal and worthless. This kind of country does not appeal to everyone.[32]

Residents of the Great Basin thus developed in self-defense a regional identity that grew from their pride in the basic accomplishment of simply having endured in such an unlikely place. Whether they loved the desert landscape or hated it, residents uniformly catalogued its challenges. Far from transforming the landscape, they constantly risked annihilation by it. Their accounts did not differ significantly from those of the disaffected sojourners. Their sense of place was founded in the same environmental hardship.[33]

With such a venerable tradition of negative imagery and environmental constraint, this region might have seemed the most unlikely of tourist attractions. Yet in the mid-twentieth century, in a creative response to its environmental limitations, Nevada transformed itself from purgatory to playground. Taking cynical advantage of the very isolation and lack of development that had condemned it in the eyes of so many generations of sojourners, Nevada promoted itself, beginning in the 1920s, as the last bastion of the individualistic morality of the Old West.

From 1897 on, a series of legislative decisions legalized or liberalized social practices such as prizefighting, horse-racing, divorce, and gambling, which were elsewhere regarded as vices. Famous prizefights like the Corbett–Fitzsimmons fight in 1897; the Gans–Nelson bout in 1906, in the southern boom town of Goldfield; and the pairing of Johnson and Jeffries in Reno in 1910 popularized the state as a place to see and bet on boxing. So many attended the latter two fights that special trains had to be scheduled to accommodate the crowds. Increasingly liberal divorce provisions, aided by compliant judges, produced a substantial divorce business in Reno in the 1920s and 1930s that was effectively promoted by extensive newspaper coverage of various celebrity divorces and by plays and movies like Clare Booth Luce's *The Women*. Divorce required a six-month period of residence during which the plaintiff could not leave the state. Predictably, a host of hotels, nightclubs, dude ranches, and other tourist services grew up to distract and entertain the involuntary visitors.[34]

This new direction was lamented by Progressive reformers like Anne Martin, who still yearned to realize Fulton's 1893 dream of an agricultural society. By 1922, however, any such wish was vain, as she admitted in an article entitled "Nevada: Beautiful Desert of Buried Hopes." Lax enforcement of existing prohibition and antigambling legislation had given Reno, in particular, a well-deserved reputation as a wide-open town. Bootleggers and hotel owners alike profited from the tourist traffic, and they spent money to promote events that would attract even more visitors, including rodeos, highway expositions, and more prizefights. Hotel owners lobbied the federal government for highway funds to improve automobile access to the emerging Nevada metropolis of Reno, which in 1926 proudly proclaimed itself, in a burst of bravado, "The Biggest Little City in the World."[35]

Almost overnight, the tiny town of Reno went from a desert outpost of 15,000 souls, to a sophisticated urban playground. In this context, full legalization of casino gambling in 1931—an event that prompted the characterization of Nevada as a "prostitute state" and prompted a flurry of disapproving national publicity—was almost anticlimactic. It was a logical step in a continuing process of self-promotion for economic gain, which resumed with the reestablishment of brothel prostitution in rural areas of Nevada after World War II.[36]

This new identity transformed Nevada from traveler's hindrance to tourist's mecca. The same environmental barrenness that had intimidated so many observers still remained, and travelers still remarked on it. The Great Basin itself was not physically transformed. Its image, however, was marvellously altered. Formerly dismissed as wasteland, the natural environment was now used to justify the development of an economy in its western reaches that was based on sin and self-indulgence. Indeed, as many national commentators suggested in the 1930s, any rational observer was forced to admit that Nevada had few substantial resources and no significant prospect for self-support other than its legislated vices. In the words of historian Donald Worster, "Even the sterile deserts of the Great Basin have been made to produce countless flocks of bleating sheep, on the range and in the casinos."[37]

In the new casino culture that resulted, an artificial Old West atmosphere was invoked specifically in order to reassure visitors that their departure from moralistic standards of behavior was acceptable, indeed traditional. Agriculture, and the conservative morality represented by farm families, was superseded by an individualistic rhetoric of male independence associated with the open range. Thus the railroad town of Las Vegas, a creation of the twentieth century that was virtually moribund until the construction of Boulder Dam in the 1930s, instituted in the 1940s a Frontier Days festival to celebrate an ersatz cowboy heritage it had never actually shared.[38]

The blatant artificiality of this Old West imagery disturbed few. Longtime residents who knew better were scarce in Nevada. Many, agreeing that the state had few natural advantages to draw on, welcomed the new economic opportunities inaugurated by resort gambling. Newcomers attracted by the boom cheerfully manipulated familiar cultural images in order to attract tourists and legitimate their nascent industry. Linking casinos to popular American icons like cowboys and rodeos was good for business, confirming their status as harmless entertainment in a society still vaguely titillated by the spectacle of public gambling. As sociologists Louis Turner and John Ash described the phenomenon, twentieth-century gambling could substitute for the nineteenth-century drive to dominate and control the natural world: "These less adventurous souls will seek their novelty in twenty-first-century fantasy—in pleasure cities like Las Vegas and Disney World, where all our frustrations can be soothed away. Gambling provides the *ersatz* experience of being Man against Nature; unlike the mountaineer or ocean yachtsman, the only thing one can lose is one's money."[39]

The newest environmental image of the western Great Basin is thus not sagebrush and isolation, but nighttime neon. As observer John McPhee has commented, the flashy casino culture that developed after World War II somehow seems entirely appropriate in those surroundings: "Neon looks good in Nevada. The tawdriness is refined out of it in so much wide black space." More so than Reno, Las Vegas capitalized on this recognition, taking garish display to a happy extreme in the gargantuan resort hotels that developed in the 1950s along the area known as "the Strip." Their 1990s incarnations—in the form of the Luxor, the Stratosphere, and New York, New York—are frequently and favorably compared with Disneyland, as they promote a more wholesome family image.[40]

In this new tourist-dominated culture, Nevada's traditional extractive practices continue in a new vein. Residents, growing more numerous daily as the state explodes in its newly found prosperity, no longer rely on undependable nature, but on interchangeable tourists, who have proved more consistently profitable. In a variation on traditional western tourism, Nevada draws visitors neither for its natural beauty nor for its historical associations, but for the opportunity it offers for socially sanctioned self-indulgence, for recreational fantasy. Yet although tourism has at last provided a reasonably secure economic base for the state, its costs have been substantial. As humorist Bill Bryson splenetically observed: "Here's a riddle for you. What is the difference between Nevada and a toilet? Answer: You can flush a toilet." Bryson further notes, "Nevada has the highest crime rate of any state, the highest rape rate. . . . It has a long history of corruption and strong links with organized crime. And its most popular entertainer is Wayne Newton. So you may understand why I crossed the border from Utah with a certain sense of disquiet." At first Bryson is pleasantly surprised at Las Vegas, where instead of hookers and high rollers, "there were just ordinary folks like you and me, people who wear a lot of nylon and Velcro"; but after experiencing the buffet at Caesar's Palace, his disillusion returns. Seeking refuge from the unpleasant experience, he finds everywhere he goes "the same noise, the same stupid people losing all their money, the same hideous carpets. It all just gave me a headache."[41]

Even today, despite all the glitter and profit associated in particular with Las Vegas, negative environmental images of the Great Basin persist. Many concur with historian W. Eugene Hollon, for example, that the consignment of large sections of Nevada to a military bombing range is appropriate, because then "at least it serves some useful purpose." Although Utah, too, has recently developed a significant tourist economy, it is generally centered in areas of the state outside the Great Basin. As former Salt Lake City major Ted Wilson observes, Utahans treat their West Desert as a dumping ground: "When we want to dump something we go west with it. Our idea of a dumping hole is out there. Now it's the whole country's notion." Americans from outside the region are only too willing to envision filling up Walter van Tilburg Clark's white space with the nuclear waste they do not want in their own backyards. The Great Basin desert may no longer be physically threatening, but all the pleasure palaces of Las Vegas are not sufficient to redeem this landscape from its enduring symbolic role as America's resolutely unblooming wasteland.[42]

NOTES

1. "Diary Kept by James S. Cowden on His Trip 'Overland' from Iowa to California in 1853, with Ox Teams and Wagons" (typescript manuscript, Iowa State Historical Society, Iowa City), 21–22.

2. Thomas Jefferson Hensley to Mary J[ennette] Boles, 27 September 1863, Manuscript Collection, Iowa State Historical Society, Iowa City.

3. Howard Stansbury, *Exploration of the Valley of the Great Salt Lake* (1852; reprint, Washington, D.C.: Smithsonian Institution Press, 1988), 6; Walter van Tilburg Clark, "Nevada's Fateful Desert," *Holiday,* November 1957, 76; Reed H. Blake and Spencer H. Blake, "Regional Identity in the Interior Mountains: A Latent Emergent" (Paper presented at the meeting of the Western Social Science Association, Reno, 17–20 April 1996). This uncertain regional identification is exacerbated by the recent influx of California refugees into the Great Basin. See Paul F. Starrs and John B. Wright, "California, Out—Great Basin Growth and the Withering of the Pacific Idyll," *Geographical Review* 85 (1994): 224–44.

4. Israel Cook Russell, *Geological History of Lake Lahontan: A Quarternary Lake of Northwestern Nevada* (Washington, D.C.: Government Printing Office, 1885), 7.

5. Ibid., 9. Although regional boundaries are notoriously vague, the Great Basin is generally defined hydrologically and is considered to include most of Nevada, western Utah, parts of southern Oregon and Idaho, and parts of eastern California. One scholar estimates its extent to be in excess of 220,000 square miles. See Samuel G. Houghton, *A Trace of Desert Waters: The Great Basin Story* (1976; reprint, Reno: University of Nevada Press, 1994).

6. Albert D. Richardson, *Our New States and Territories . . .* (New York: Beadle, 1866), 41, 45.

7. The history of American attitudes toward nature is traced in Roderick Nash, *Wilderness and the American Mind,* 3rd ed. (New Haven, Conn.: Yale University Press, 1982). For New England, see Edward Johnson, *God's Wonder Working Providence in New England,* ed. J. Franklin Jameson (New York: Scribner, 1910). Amid considerable debate about the environmental and historiographic consequences of Turner's infamous frontier thesis, the political thrust of his original argument has largely been overlooked. For a comprehensive review, see Wilbur R. Jacobs, ed., *On Turner's Trail: 100 Years of Writing Western History* (Lawrence: University Press of Kansas, 1994). Smythe's remark is from *The Conquest of Arid America* (New York: Macmillan, 1900, 1905), 11. Discussions of landscape as a factor in national culture include Anne Farrar Hyde, *An American Vision: Far Western Landscape and National Culture, 1820–1920* (New York: New York University Press, 1990); John F. Sears, *Sacred Places: American Tourist Attractions in*

the Nineteenth Century (New York: Oxford University Press, 1989); and Peter Schmitt, *Back to Nature: The Arcadian Myth in Urban America* (New York: Oxford University Press, 1969).

8. For the clash over environmental practices and attitudes between New England settlers and the Native peoples, see William Cronon, *Changes on the Land* (New York: Hill & Wang, 1983). John Stilgoe chronicles the tremendous physical transformations made by American settlers in *Common Landscape of America, 1580–1845* (New Haven, Conn.: Yale University Press, 1982). The same theme is treated in Michael Conzen, ed., *The Making of the American Landscape* (Boston: Unwin Hyman, 1992). Classic studies of the varying consequences of these attitudes include Patricia Nelson Limerick, *Legacy of Conquest: The Unbroken Past of the American West* (New York: Norton, 1987); and Donald Worster, *Dust Bowl: The Southern Plains in the 1930s* (New York: Oxford University Press, 1979).

9. Henry Nash Smith gives a thorough summary of the disappointed expectations of Plains "boomers" in *Virgin Land* (Cambridge, Mass.: Harvard University Press, 1950) See also David Emmons, *Garden in the Grasslands: Boomer Literature of the Central Great Plains* (Lincoln: University of Nebraska Press, 1971); and Brian W. Blouet and Merlin P. Lawson, eds., *Images of the Plains: The Role of Human Nature in Settlement* (Lincoln: University of Nebraska Press, 1975). James A. Young and B. Abbot Sparks chronicle the development of the cattle industry in the Great Basin in *Cattle in the Cold Desert* (Logan: Utah State University Press, 1985). Susan Rhoades Neel points out the culturally specific nature of such beliefs in "A Place of Extremes: Nature, History, and the American West," in *A New Significance: Re-envisioning the History of the American West,* ed. Clyde A. Milner II, (New York: Oxford University Press, 1996), 105–24. She observes that the West is arid only in the eyes of Easterners accustomed to greater rainfall.

10. Jedediah S. Smith, *The Southwest Expedition of Jedediah S. Smith: His Personal Account of the Journey to California, 1826–1827* (Glendale, Calif.: Clark, 1977), 178; John C. Frémont, *A Report of the Exploring Expedition to Oregon and North California in the Years 1843–44,* in *The Expedition of John Charles Frémont,* ed. Donald Jackson and Mary Lee Spence (Urbana: University of Illinois Press, 1970), 1:599; Smythe, *Conquest of Arid America,* 214.

11. Rob Schultheis, *The Hidden West: Journeys in the American Outback* (New York: Random House, 1982), 138. For the historical difficulties of incorporating the Great Basin into national culture, see Hyde, *American Vision,* 128–29, 138–39, 192. Hyde has argued elsewhere that changes in transportation technology significantly altered landscape perception. See Anne Hyde, "Cultural Filters: The Significance of Perception in the History of the American West," *Western Historical Quarterly* 24 (1993): 351–74. This is not the case in the Great Basin, where reports of travelers bear a striking similarity over the course of 150 years.

12. For the power and pervasiveness of such environmental ideals, see Virginia S. Jenkins, "A Green Velvety Carpet: The Front Lawn in America," *Journal of American Culture* 17 (1994): 43–47.

13. For the California travelers, see Stephen Fender, *Plotting the Golden West: American Literature and the Rhetoric of the California Trail* (Cambridge: Cambridge University Press, 1981); A. Edward Newton, "Westward," *Atlantic Monthly,* May 1932, 534. An account of the range of positive and negative reactions to Great Basin landscape can be found in Elizabeth Raymond, "Desert/Paradise: Images of Great Basin Landscape," *Nevada Public Affairs Review,* 1988, 12–18. See also Patricia Nelson Limerick, *Desert Passages: Encounters with the American Desert* (Albuquerque: University of New Mexico Press, 1985).

14. Simone de Beauvoir, *America Day by Day* (London: Duckworth, 1948), 121; [Amanda Preuss], *A Girl—A Record and an Oldsmobile by the Girl Herself* (Lansing, Mich.: Olds Motor Works, 1916), 10–11.

15. T. H. White, *America at Last* (New York: Putnam, 1965), 134.

16. In her book *American Vision,* Hyde portrays the steps by which Americans came to understand and appreciate an initially alien western landscape. Her argument about the mechanics and implications of acceptance, while convincing for the Rocky Mountain West and the desert Southwest, does not include the Great Basin. I have suggested elsewhere that Americans, in fact, never came fully to accept or appreciate the Great Basin landscape. See Elizabeth Raymond, "Sense of Place in the Great Basin," in *East of Eden, West of Zion: Essays on Nevada,* ed. Wilbur S. Shepperson (Reno: University of Nevada Press, 1989), 17–29. This view is supported by Limerick, who concludes in *Desert Passages* that desert landscapes finally became appealing to Americans because they remained intractable, thus offering refuges from the complications of mass urban society.

17. For the Native peoples of the Great Basin, see Warren d'Azevedo, ed., *Handbook of North American Indians,* vol. 11, *Great Basin* (Washington, D.C.: Smithsonian Institution Press, 1986); Steven J. Crum, *The Road on Which We Came: A History of the Western Shoshone* (Salt Lake City: University of Utah Press, 1994); and Martha C. Knack and Omer C. Stewart, *As Long as the River Shall Run: An Ethnohistory of Pyramid Lake Indian Reservation* (Berkeley: University of California Press, 1984). Historical descriptions of eastern basin peoples are included in Stansbury, *Exploration of the Valley of the Great Salt Lake,* and in Captain J. H. Simpson, *Report of the Explorations Across the Great Basin of the Territory of Utah in 1859* (Reno: University of Nevada Press, 1983). It is worth emphasizing the obvious point that none of the indigenous tribes experienced the Great Basin as deficient in the same ways that Euro-Americans did. The Indian groups' itinerancy allowed them to take full advantage of the seasonal nature of resources in the region. John Muir's comment on mining towns is found in *Steep Trails* (Boston: Houghton

Mifflin, 1918), 203. The environmental legacies of mining in the Great Basin are only recently beginning to be recognized and recorded.

18. For Mormon settlement, see Leonard B. Arrington, *Great Basin Kingdom: An Economic History of the Latter-Day Saints, 1830–1900* (Cambridge, Mass.: Harvard University Press, 1958); Dan L. Flores, "Zion in Eden: Phases of the Environmental History of Utah," *Environmental Review* 7 (1983): 325–44; and Richard H. Jackson, "Mormon Perception and Settlement," *Annals of the Association of American Geographers* 68 (1978): 317–34.

19. Auguste Nicaise, *A Year in the Desert,* ed. and trans. Edward J. Kowrach (Fairfield, Wash.: Ye Galleon Press, 1980), 57; Orson F. Whitney, *Popular History of Utah* (Salt Lake City: Desert News, 1916), 5. Wallace Stegner comments on the myriad Lombardy poplars, "Mormon trees," planted to demarcate fields in the eastern Great Basin, in *Mormon Country* (1942; reprint, Lincoln: University of Nebraska Press, 1970), 21–22. For more on perceptions of areas of Mormon settlement, see Raymond, "Sense of Place."

20. Simpson, *Report of the Explorations,* 31.

21. Smythe, *Conquest of Arid America,* xii–xiii. For Smythe, see Limerick, *Desert Passages,* 77–90.

22. B. F. Ferris, "West and Farther West," *Report of the Iowa State Historical Society for the Year 1914* (Des Moines: Robert Henderson, State Printer, 1915), 86. For irrigation fever in Nevada, see Wilbur S. Shepperson, with the assistance of Ann Harvey, *Mirage-Land: Images of Nevada* (Reno: University of Nevada Press, 1992). For the Midwestern experience of landscape alteration, see Elizabeth Raymond, "Alternative Narratives of Nature: Middle Western Sense of Place," *Canon* 2 (1994): 26–43.

23. For the checkered history of the Bureau of Reclamation, from initial high hopes shaped by a "Christian ideal" of greening the desert to more recent debacles, see Marc Reisner, *Cadillac Desert: The American West and Its Disappearing Water* (New York: Penguin, 1986). For the Newlands Act, see Donald Worster, *Rivers of Empire: Water, Aridity, and the Growth of the American West* (New York: Pantheon, 1985), 160–69. Worster has explored the negative environmental and social consequences of large-scale irrigation culture in the American West, though largely outside the Great Basin, where its failures may have been of a different sort.

24. For the rotten-borough argument and resultant challenges to statehood, see Richard G. Lillard, *Desert Challenge: An Interpretation of Nevada* (Lincoln: University of Nebraska Press, 1942), 41–43; and Gilman M. Ostrander, *Nevada: The Great Rotten Borough, 1859–1964* (New York: Knopf, 1966). This chapter devotes its attention primarily to the social and economic consequences of environmental constraint in the western part of the Great Basin. While it is clear that Utah environment and culture were subjected to similar national condemnation, the religious foundation of that state, as well as the fact that only a portion of its area was within the Great Basin, dictated differing responses.

25. Smythe, *Conquest of Arid America,* 220.

26. "An Address to the People of Nevada on Water Storage and Irrigation by Francis G. Newlands" (Reno, 1890); R. L. Fulton, "The Future of Nevada," 14 April 1893, both Nevada Historical Society, Reno.

27. Mrs. M. M. Garwood, "Irrigation Day," *Progressive West,* July 1905, 35–37; L. H. Taylor, "The Truckee–Carson Project," *Progressive West,* August 1905, 59–61. The connection between irrigation and progressive reform in Nevada is an observation of Shepperson in *Mirage-Land.*

28. For Great Basin homesteading, see Marshall E. Bowen, *Utah People in the Nevada Desert: Homestead and Community on a Twentieth-Century Farmers' Frontier* (Logan: Utah State University Press, 1994). The system of soil classification, which mimics the standard methods of gauging soil fertility according to the kinds of trees that grow in a particular area, is discussed in C. A. Norcross, *Agricultural Nevada* (San Francisco: Sunset Magazine Homeseekers Bureau [1912]), 4. His fear of failure is discussed in C. A. Norcross to Tasker L. Oddie, 19 November 1913, Tasker L. Oddie Papers, Huntington Library, San Marino, Calif. An example of Nevada patriotism is George Wharton James, "What's the Matter with Nevada?" *Out West,* April 1914, 173–82.

29. For the 1929 statistics, see James G. Scrugham, *Nevada: A Narrative of the Conquest of a Frontier Land* (Chicago: American Historical Society, 1925), 1:539. For the failure of the Truckee–Carson Irrigation Project to live up to its early promise, see Lillard, *Desert Challenge,* 64–73.

30. Federal Writer's Project of the Works Projects Administration, *Utah: A Guide to the State* (New York: Hastings House, 1945), 4; Smythe, *Conquest of Arid America,* 330.

31. As late as 1930, there were still 1.3 men for every woman in Nevada. For a discussion of the transience see Lillard, *Desert Challenge,* 75–80.

32. Frances Fuller Victor, "Nevada," *Overland Monthly,* December 1869, 423–24; WPA, *Utah,* 8.

33. This argument is developed at greater length in Raymond, "Sense of Place." David Wrobel makes the important distinction between internal and exterior regionalism in "Beyond the Frontier–Region Dichotomy," *Pacific Historical Review* 65 (1996): 401–29. In the Great Basin, however, the two generally did not diverge significantly. As successive generations of observers recognized, it was the "irrigation vision," whether sustained by the Mormons in Utah or the Progressives in Nevada, that was anomalous. For 150 years, Euro-American reactions to the Great Basin have varied remarkably little, whether recorded by temporary sojourners or life-long residents.

34. One of the major figures involved in this transformation was George Wingfield (1876–1959). As a politician, banker, and hotel owner, Wingfield was a powerful central figure in the legislative shifts that created the twentieth-century tourist culture in Nevada. See Elizabeth Raymond, *George Wingfield: Owner and Operator of Nevada* (Reno: University of Nevada Press,

1992). For the impact of boxing, see Shepperson, *Mirage-Land*. The creation
of a divorce business is treated in Anita Watson, "Tarnished Silver: Popular
Image and Business Reality of Divorce in Nevada, 1900–1939" (M.A. thesis,
University of Nevada, Reno, 1989).

35. Anne Martin, "Nevada: Beautiful Desert of Buried Hopes," *Nation,* 26
July 1922, 89–92; Paul Hutchinson, "Nevada—a Prostitute State," *Christian
Century,* 25 November 1931, 1488–90. See also Earl Pomeroy, *In Search of
the Golden West: The Tourist in Western America* (New York: Knopf, 1957),
184–92.

36. Nevada's divorce legislation attracted considerably more media
attention than legalized gambling in 1931. Most accounts sensationalized the
state's new legislated industries, but a few acknowledged that legalized vice
was at least paying the bills. See "Passion in the Desert," *Fortune,* April 1934,
100–107, 124–32; and Anthony M. Turano, "Nevada's Trial of Licensed
Gambling," *American Mercury,* February 1933.

37. Donald Worster, *The Wealth of Nature: Environmental History and the
Ecological Imagination* (New York: Oxford University Press, 1993), 103.

38. For a history of the development of gambling in Las Vegas, see John M.
Findlay, *People of Chance: Gambling in American Society from Jamestown to
Las Vegas* (New York: Oxford University Press, 1986); Eugene P. Moehring,
Resort City in the Sunbelt: Las Vegas, 1930–1970 (Reno: University of Nevada
Press, 1989); and Eric N. Moody, "Regulation of Nevada Casino Gambling,
1931–1945" (Ph.D. diss., University of Nevada, Reno, 1997).

39. Louis Turner and John Ash, *The Golden Hordes: International Tourism
and the Pleasure Periphery* (New York: St. Martin's Press, 1976), 185–86. On
taming nature through popular culture images, see William W. Savage, Jr.,
"What You'd Like the World to Be: The West and the American Mind,"
Journal of American Culture 3 (1980): 302–10; and Robert G. Athearn, *The
Mythic West in Twentieth-Century America* (Lawrence: University Press of
Kansas, 1986).

40. John McPhee, *Basin and Range* (New York: Farrar, Strauss & Giroux,
1981), 54. Among others, Findlay makes the Disneyland comparison in *People
of Chance.*

41. Bill Bryson, *The Lost Continent: Travels in Small-Town America* (New
York: Harper & Row, 1989), 244, 245, 248. For a similarly iconoclastic vision
of modern Las Vegas, see Mike Davis, "House of Cards," *Sierra,*
November–December 1995, 37–41, 76.

42. W. Eugene Hollon, *The Great American Desert: Then and Now* (New
York: Oxford University Press, 1966), 203; Ted Wilson, quoted in "Land's
Puzzle: The Great Basin's Uncharismatic Wilderness," *Great Basin News,*
Winter 1996, 9.

Round Pegs in Square Holes: The Rocky Mountains and Extractive Industry

Anne F. Hyde

When people think about the American West, whether they define it as a place, a process, or a mythic landscape, the Rocky Mountains stand tall in these definitions. No one denies that the landscape crumbling and thrusting from the Continental Divide is West. The stark beauty and physical challenges these mountains represent are central to our definition of national history and culture. Although these monoliths are important in our understanding of what we have been and might be, they are anything but monolithic in the ways that they affect human life. The presence of these mountains determines much about the economy, society, and culture of the people who live in them.

The Rocky Mountains encompass a miraculously varied region. Its extremes of climate, topography, and human use make describing it as a coherent region difficult. Geography and human use link high mountains, plains, and deserts in complex ways. Definition gets even messier when political lines impose themselves on top of topographical ones, so that the Rocky Mountain states are simply "the square ones." Indeed, Colorado and Wyoming are the only states in the United States whose borders are made up of four straight lines. This could be indicative of the impossibility of making rational political and geographical delineations in such a challenging landscape or of the absence of social glue that connects the people who live in and around these mountains. Trying to characterize a region that includes 14,000-foot peaks, desert, high valley, and rolling plains might be folly. Think about what the following situations might have in common:

> All the sublimest glories of the Swiss and Italian Alps, all the picturesque savagery of the Tyrol, and all the softer beauty of Killarny and Como and Naples dwindle to insignificance by comparison with the stupendous scenes that meet the gaze at every turn in Colorado.[1]

> A Wyoming joke has it that one of the two most beautiful sights in the world is the Grand Tetons, and the other is Rock Springs in a rear-view mirror. . . . Rock Springs is an appalling sprawl of shacks, trailers, mobile homes, rutted dirt streets, dust, trash, and beer parlors, a polluted non-community of 26,000 people who are as transient as the papers that blow through the streets.[2]

> It dawned what this treeless, flowing pastureland meant to us just then. There was not one upright particle on all these miles of range for a sheep to rub up against, and an attack of ticks was beginning to make the ewes itch beneath their heavy fleeces. Now the sheep were rolling themselves on the ground to scratch—a roll which easily carried them too far onto their deep-wooled backs to be able to get up again, and within minutes in the summer heat, their struggling would bloat them to death. We had the prospect of endless bloated corpses around us.[3]

> When I looked into this close and dirty hole, I could hear the miner's pick striking the coal, but at this distance, I failed to see the miner. . . . The air was almost stagnant and densely charged with coal dust, and in a few minutes I could feel the effects of carbonic acid gas, better known to the miners as black damp. . . . In its pure state, it is a most deadly poison, and will support neither life nor combustion.[4]

> What had looked so beautiful in the winter—white slopes, snow-covered trees, lifts carrying brightly colored skiers quietly through the air—looked

different in August. Stumps of clear-cut trees, pipes carrying water up the mountain to service snow-making equipment, ponds of stagnant water to fill those pipes, trash heaps smelling ripe outside of the lodge all revealed the sacrifice necessary to create my ski fantasy. The land and people had given a lot for me to ski effortlessly down the mountain.[5]

What seems oddly combined in these scenes—stunning beauty, hideous destruction, and human pain—characterizes much of the culture and landscape that has developed in the Rocky Mountain region. I define this region to include Montana, Wyoming, Colorado, and parts of Utah and Idaho—in other words, all the states or parts of states that have a significant chunk of both the Continental Divide and sweeps of high plains running through them. Water, politics, human use, and geology make these geographic features inseparable and grant them the power to create water, fur, precious metals, coal, and vacation resorts. The presence of tremendous mountains in combination with high plains has made life in the area distinctive, especially the culture and society that developed in the nineteenth and twentieth centuries.[6]

Two major features make it distinctive: the inhospitable but spectacular nature of mountains and high plains, and the overwhelming presence of extractive industries, which has created a variety of peculiar adjustments in society and culture.[7] Certainly the beauty of the landscape is significant in the way people have come to define the region, but this chapter focuses on extractive industries because they are crucial in understanding the "place" that has developed here. The reality of this place stands in stark opposition to the "Rocky Mountain High" imagined by wannabe Westerners and Westerners themselves, largely because of the shaping power of extractive industries. I define "extractive" broadly—as an industry that relies primarily on raw materials produced directly by the environment—so that it includes furs, mining, ranching, water sales, and skiing. Other regions of the West certainly have extractive industries, but because the Rocky Mountain states traditionally have had little else, the region highlights the peculiar cultural and environmental roles that these industries have played there.

Extractive industries leave a particular imprint on land and society, and it is this imprint that I want to explore. Throughout the Rocky Mountain region, extractive industries have created a relationship with the federal government different from that in parts of the West that have more varied economies. Because the region developed during a crucial and intensive phase of industrialization in the United States, corporate capitalism, class tensions, technological prowess—all sustained by the federal government—decided its shape and culture.[8] The result of this, as many historians have argued, is a destructive colonial relationship with the rest of the United States, making the region a "plundered province."[9]

These industries exacerbated a rapid and dislocating process of urbanization and industrialization in a region that was isolated and raw. With almost no farming and with railroad and mining towns accounting for well over 90 percent of the population in the Rocky Mountain states and territories, in the nineteenth century this region was the most urban part of the United States. The presence of this kind of economy created a distinctively unrooted culture that combined hyper-individualism with industrial processes and boom-and-bust economies that severely limited personal control. In addition, the entire region has experienced tension between traditional extractive industries that bored mountains out and tore them down and the tourism that worshiped the mountains. These facets of regional identity that developed in the nineteenth century continue to characterize the region at the end of the twentieth.[10]

We can trace important similarities among the fur trade, mining, ranching, and skiing, largely because all of them are intricately connected to high mountains and plains. These industries emerged in extremely isolated areas, developed rapidly, were characterized by intense urbanization and industrialization, and relied on non-Anglo labor for most of the work. Perhaps most significantly, they all came about both because of and in spite of the Rocky Mountains.

The rapidity of industrial development in the Rocky Mountains is an issue that would make Frederick Jackson Turner blanch. Nothing happened in the grand and orderly fashion ordained by Turner. In 1820, when Stephen Long made his depressing assessment of the easternmost part of the Rockies, the fur trade barely existed in the region. The scarcity of navigable river systems, the unfriendliness of the Spanish, and the imposing nature of the mountains themselves made it impossible to transport the pelts to the markets. With the sudden opening of the Santa Fe trade; the death of Manuel Lisa, who had served as overlord of the remnants of the St. Louis–Missouri River fur trade; and the implacability of the Blackfeet Indians along the upper Missouri, the fur trade underwent a huge change in direction and operation. It moved south and west, and by the early 1830s thriving communities had developed along the South Platte and Arkansas Rivers.[11]

Bent's Fort, founded in 1833 along the Arkansas in what is now southeastern Colorado, provides a good example of how "urban" these settlements were. The fort was a complex mixture of trading post, factory, and boarding house for men. A newspaper correspondent for the New Orleans *Picayune* called it "an air castle dropped to earth and covered with mud." The structure was 137 feet square, with 18-foot walls that encircled a complex housing a library, a wine cellar, and a factory for processing furs. It also included a huge corral with 6-foot walls, making the biggest problem in the fort the removal of manure, which started fires if left too long. In its heyday, Bent's Fort employed more than 100 men: traders, hunters, herders, teamsters, and laborers. Most of the laborers were Mexicans who were paid about $6 a month, usually in goods.[12]

The mining industry, as is well documented, developed equally quickly in the Rocky Mountains. In the 1840s when an aristocratic young traveler named Rufus Sage made a tour of the Rocky Mountains, he wished to acquaint himself "with the geography of these comparatively unexplored regions."[13] Discovering gold was the farthest thing from his mind. Similarly, the "rude and stern scenes of the prairie and the mountains" appealed to historian Francis Parkman because of their utter isolation from the civilization he wanted to escape.[14] By the summer of 1858, however, 50,000 people had poured into what would become Colorado Territory to find gold. By 1859, Denver was home to more than 2,000 people, and Central City, Nevada City, Blackhawk, French Gulch, California Gulch, and Gold Hill were thriving communities. In Montana, excitement over gold in Bannack in 1862 and Virginia City in 1864 created suddenly wealthy communities that would change the landscape forever.[15] This process occurred over and over again, with "mining excitement" and the resulting urban development spreading throughout the region between 1858 and the 1910s.

Ranching appeared with equal speed. Cheyenne, Wyoming, and Miles City, Montana, reigned as early centers of the cattle industry in the 1870s in areas where few people would have considered investing their money only a few years earlier. Enormous and well-organized capital made the cattle industry boom, largely because of eager British investment. In 1873, W. J. Menzies organized the Scottish-American Investment Company, and by 1883 Moreton Frewen of London directed the Powder River Cattle Company in Wyoming, which ran 50,000 head of cattle.[16]

A twentieth-century example, the ski industry, appeared out of no-where after World War II. Tiny mountain communities, struggling to maintain their populations after the mining booms ended, suddenly became vacation resorts. Sun Valley, Idaho, chosen by W. Averell Harriman, head of the Union Pacific Railroad, as the site of a ski resort, had been a dwindling mining community. In 1936, a Hollywood cast gathered in the new 250–room lodge to introduce Sun Valley to the world. Union Pacific trains brought eager skiers, and a new industry was born. Aspen, Colorado, is another prime example. The town boasted a population of nearly 30,000 in the 1890s boom years, but by the 1930s the population had dwindled to only a few hundred. In 1947, a combination of local veterans of the Tenth Mountain Division who had trained as ski troops in the Colorado Rockies and a wealthy Chicago industrialist, Walter Paepcke, pooled ideas and resources and put the first chairlifts on Ajax Mountain. Suddenly, Aspen became a resort, complete with a housing boom and floods of visitors in summer and winter.[17]

These "instant cities" built by the power of extractive industries had another unique feature: extreme isolation. The cigars, wines, and books that made Bent's Fort a haven in the 1840s came from the nearest city, St. Louis, which could be reached only by a strenuous wagon trip that took several weeks. When Helena, Montana, metamorphosed from a gathering of ragged tents in the summer of 1864 to a city with a population of over 4,000 a year later, it achieved this growth without the help of a railroad or even a reliable wagon road into the community. The materials to build houses, to print newspapers, to clothe and feed miners, and to process ore had to be carried over a mountainous track grandly called the Bozeman Road, a path deeply resented by powerful Indian tribes, or along the upper Missouri River, made hazardous by sandbars and snags.[18] After silver was discovered in the late 1870s, Leadville, Colorado, quickly became a city of nearly 30,000 people, all of whom got there along a terrifying mountain road well described by Mary Hallock Foote in 1879: "On the last and steepest grade, a sharp turn with a precipice on one side narrowed the road suddenly. The view was cut off ahead, and here we met the stage coming down, all six horses at full speed. . . . We had to go up the side of the bank if only on two wheels. . . . [A]nd we did get by with only a few inches to spare."[19] Similarly, when miners rushed into Aspen in the early 1880s, supplies, ore, and people had to be transported via Leadville over 12,000-foot Independence Pass. The word "road" referred to a partially cleared track with tree stumps a foot high that was impassable in the winter and for much of the spring.[20] The ranching communities of Montana, beautifully described by Ivan Doig in his memoir, *This House of Sky,* remained so isolated in the years after World War II that in order to attend school, Doig, like most ranch children, had to board away from his family, when "winter was sealing the Sixteen country into long frozen months of aloneness."[21]

The combination of isolation and urbanization that characterized settlements based on extractive industries in the Rocky Mountains also created a crucial shortage of labor. The fur trade, mining, ranching, and skiing required large numbers of low-skilled and expendable workers to extract value from the landscape. The fur industry relied heavily on the labor of Indian men to trap or shoot animals and on the work of Indian women to process dead animals into usable pelts and hides. Plains Indians, under pressure from Euro-American migration and settlement, vastly increased the number of animals they were killing. In the 1850s, long after the heyday of the fur and hide trade, an agent on the upper Arkansas River estimated that the 11,000 Indians in his charge were killing 112,000 bison, 40,000 deer, 7,000 bear, and 3,000 elk every year as participants in the hide trade.[22] We can only imagine what the total numbers must have been.

In the forts where these hides were traded and sold, Indians and Mexicans provided essential labor. Indian women had value both as workers and as wives. White traders who married them often gained trading advantages. William Bent married a succession of chiefs' daughters, which helped his company develop important trading relationships with the Cheyennes. Mexican men were hired because of their valuable skills in farming and in making adobe brick. They also worked at trading, herding horses, and packing mules. In the 1830s and 1840s, hundreds of Mexicans were employed at posts on the Arkansas and Platte Rivers.[23]

The mining industry, of course, is notorious for its inhumane use of labor. Because of the extreme isolation of mining communities in the Rocky Mountain West, the situation seems especially stark. In most mining communities, the industry evolved from placer mining, in which a single miner could hope to find a fortune, to capital-intensive hard-rock mining in less than a season. Miners and prospectors who had expected to work independently rapidly found themselves digging in dark holes for someone else. Working underground involved dangerous and backbreaking work, and in many places, white miners preferred to move on to other diggings than to work underground. Because law and local practice in many districts forbade "foreign" miners from staking claims of their own, Chinese and Mexican laborers were left with the most undesirable work.

The Chinese provide an especially distressing case of exploited and persecuted workers in the Rocky Mountain West. Because mining boomed in those regions as the transcontinental railroads were completed, Chinese workers who had been hired by the railroads found themselves at loose ends. They settled in the new mining communities, opening restaurants and laundries and working at day-labor jobs in the mines. In 1870, the Chinese made up 27 percent of Idaho's population and 9.4 percent of Montana's, with Colorado and Wyoming having much smaller numbers, though the Chinese were heavily concentrated in some communities.[24] Even though the Chinese did "women's work" like cooking, cleaning, and washing, and rarely competed directly with Euro-Americans, workers resented even their presence. A newsletter published by the Butte Chamber of Commerce complained, "A great many buildings that contain furnished rooms for rent are attended and cleaned by Chinese. Why cannot we get white persons to do this work?"[25]

Given such racial attitudes and the economic instability of mining communities, violence seemed inevitable. Anti-Chinese riots rocked Butte, Helena, and Denver in the early 1880s, resulting in the expulsion of the Chinese from some communities, the destruction of property, and the injury and death of scores of Chinese people. One of the most horrifying incidents occurred in Rock Springs, Wyoming, where the Union Pacific Railroad hired Chinese workers to serve as strikebreakers in their coal-mining operations. In the fall of 1885, after the strike had been broken and white and Chinese workers were mining together, a dispute broke out over which group could work a certain "room." That evening a mob gathered, and the Anglo miners burned 79 houses, killed 28 Chinese, and drove 550 Chinese out of town.[26]

Although riots have not broken out in ski towns, the same labor practices and racial tensions exist in many of these communities that led to violence in late-nineteenth-century mining towns. In the 1960s and 1970s, towns like Aspen, Crested Butte, and Park City made the transition from dying mining town to booming ski town. As resort operators harvested another natural resource, snow, they needed cheap labor to manage the snow and the tourists who came to ski on it. At first, locals filled the need, but as skiing became a national pastime, labor had to be imported. As large corporations like Vail Associates and Marriot bought up interests in ski resorts, service workers came increasingly from outside the region. In Colorado and Utah, young Hispanic workers fill low-paying jobs in the restaurants and hotels surrounding ski mountains. Most of the work is seasonal, with employees coming in for the winter season and leaving for the summer—not at all dissimilar to the patterns in the fur and hide trade and in the coal-mining industry.[27]

The intensity of the boom created another problem. As wealthy tourists bought up land and houses for vacation property, real-estate values skyrocketed, making it nearly impossible for local people to remain in their own communities. Ski towns became commuter towns, with service workers commuting long distances in dangerous winter weather to get to their jobs. In some cases, to combat this problem, resort operators have built on-site dormitories for some of their workers, again reminiscent of nineteenth- and early-twentieth-century practices.[28]

Clearly, extractive industries have played a significant role in the development of the Rocky Mountain region in the nineteenth and twentieth centuries. The distinctive features of these industries in combination with the stark and often harsh landscape affected the society and culture of the area in important ways. Since few people intended to stay in a place after they had extracted its wealth, poorly planned, rootless communities emerged without thought for the future. The landscape—scraped, uprooted, excavated, deforested, and eaten—became a testament to the junk-heap mentality encouraged by extractive industries. The rapidity of development and the calamity of decline, characterized by the boom–bust cycle of these industries, affected families, communities, and landscapes, creating, in journalist Ed Marston's words, a world "without social glue."[29]

The lack of social glue has serious implications. Without it, communities and cultures cannot hope to weather the storms of instability and social change, and few places show much success at this in the Rocky Mountain region. Community in general in the West does not have a high profile. Our most famous western characters, many of whom emerge out of the Rocky Mountains, celebrate their disconnectedness to place and to community. Whether or not we take seriously the utterly dysfunctional sorts like Jeremiah Johnson or any of Clint Eastwood's characters, this personality type represents reality. However, whether this disconnectedness is chosen or imposed is an important question. I would argue that it is imposed by the dynamics of extractive industry.

This dynamic affected nearly every imaginable aspect of life in the region. Look at the example of the buffalo and the southern Plains Indians. For years, we have assumed that the sudden and nearly fatal decline of the buffalo in the late nineteenth century was solely the fault of Euro-American intruders on the Plains. These Anglos hunted the buffalo to near extinction to facilitate the building of railroads and to deprive the Plains Indians of their staff of life. But the story is more complicated. The buffalo were disappearing long before Euro-Americans wandered onto the Plains—as early as the 1830s. Plains Indians traded buffalo hides for commodity goods as soon as trade opened up on the Santa Fe Trail. This trade began just as more tribes began to compete for the same buffalo herds because of pressures on Indian land far to the east of the Plains. The process accelerated as white emigrants and their wagons, cattle, and horses destroyed the winter forage areas so crucial to the buffalo and to the Indians. Now Indians had to use the buffalo to meet far too many of their traditional needs as well as needs created by new goods.[30]

Along the Arkansas and Platte Rivers, buffalo hunting had become an extractive industry, complete with boom–bust cycles and corporate organization. The effect on Indian families, especially those in the westernmost part of the Plains, was devastating. As the boom began to bust, the Indians began to starve, leaving them victims of disease and social destruction. Seasons like the "Winter When the Big Cramps Take Place" and reports from overlanders of trees filled with burial platforms holding dead Indian children demonstrate the horror of what was happening. Records indicate that alcohol exacerbated the problem and that Indians demonstrated their despair with the lack of care given to their children, a precipitously dropping birth rate, and rashes of violent murders. The overhunting of the buffalo dissolved the social glue that bound Indian families.[31]

The same kinds of dynamics operated in mining towns. Prospectors and miners never intended these places to be permanent settlements, so family life was slow to develop and when it did, wives and children were a tiny portion of the population. For example, in Summit County, Colorado, in 1870 there were five times as many men as women and nearly nine times as many men as children.[32] This demographic pattern was reflected in civic arrangements. Schools, libraries, and housing were low priorities for people who daily expected to make their "pile" and go home.

Children received their education in other ways: peering through knotholes at the action inside the cribs of prostitutes, accepting bets of gold dust and silver ore on their sled races, learning to make the rounds of saloons, enduring beatings from their underemployed and desperate parents, and working in the mines themselves.[33] Given the dangers inherent in mining, many children grew up without parents at all. Between 1910 and 1913 alone, 162 men died in the mines of Butte, Montana. Another 5,233 suffered debilitating accidents. Thousands more died of respiratory illness, as at least 30 percent of all hard-rock miners eventually contracted silicosis. Such human disasters made a continuing impact as widows and orphans struggled to survive without family ties in communities lacking any social services.[34]

There were, of course, exceptions to these dismal conditions. Pride in civic culture among businessmen and community leaders appeared in the form of opera houses and libraries in towns like Aspen, Helena, and Leadville, but these points of architectural pride did not affect the material conditions of many of the towns' inhabitants. Tightly knit ethnic communities did provide a significant social network for workers in towns like Butte, Virginia City, and Pueblo, which often countered the force of social disorganization.

Certain kinds of social crises, however, characterize nearly all booms in extractive industries. In the 1970s, the entire Colorado Plateau—including western Colorado, eastern Utah, Wyoming, and northern New Mexico—underwent a terrific energy boom. Coal, shale oil, and uranium lured people into these unpopulated rural areas, which were completely unprepared for the thousands of eager workers who descended on them. Much like Leadville, Helena, or even Denver in the nineteenth century, these places lacked housing, water and sewer systems, courts, schools, and jails to handle the new population. The strains created showed up immediately. In Silt, Colorado, old wooden sewer lines burst. In Rock Springs, Wyoming, housing rentals exploded by 3,000 percent in a single year. Social costs expanded even more dramatically. In Craig, Colorado, for example, when the population suddenly doubled, family disturbances rose by 352 percent between 1973 and 1976, child abuse jumped by 130 percent, substance abuse increased by 632 percent, and crimes against persons soared by 900 percent.[35]

In addition to social disarray, extractive industries and their boom–bust cycles have had a tremendous impact on the environment. The Rocky

Mountain West provides depressing evidence of the long-term environmental costs of these industries. Because people rushed in with no intention of staying, they never considered the wastes and leavings of their endeavors. When industry boomed, people were too busy making money to worry about industrial waste, and when it busted, no one had the money or the desire to clean up, leaving the region as combination charnel house and toxic junkyard.

Mining both scarred the land and poisoned the air. An English visitor to Central City, Colorado, noted the laissez-faire attitude and its results: "Men dig a shallow shaft or deep, and leave it gaping for anyone to tumble into. Trees are cut down and stumps all left. . . . The hills surrounding us have been flayed of their grass, and scalped of their timber; and they are scarred and gashed and ulcerated all over from past mining operations; so ferociously does little man scratch at the breasts of his great calm mother."[36] A few years later, Butte, Montana, may have been the most polluted city on earth. By 1890, six smelters spewed smoke into the air, creating a gray, sulfur-and arsenic-poisoned world in which no flowers, grass, or trees would grow. Mining corporations insisted that such pollution was a cost of doing business and that people should expect such conditions in a mining town.[37]

Conditions like those in Butte may have been extreme, but environmental devastation characterized other industries as well. As a result of the fur and hide trades, buffalo nearly disappeared, and populations of nearly every fur-bearing animal in the region declined precipitously. The cattle boom of the 1880s brought more than 2 million head of cattle onto Rocky Mountain rangeland. Because the land was overstocked and overgrazed, a few seasons of drought and blizzard completely destroyed the open-range industry.[38]

The twentieth century still reels from nineteenth-century damage, while creating its own. Old mining towns—with their tailings piles, mine-drainage tunnels, and chemical smelters—have become Superfund sites that many officials doubt can ever be cleaned up. Strip mining, cyanide-leaching processes, and dredge mining create environmental havoc that never could have been imagined in the nineteenth century.[39] Farming on the westernmost lands of the Great Plains, in Colorado, Wyoming, and Montana, surely qualifies as an extractive industry. In a series of wet boom years and dry bust years, water and nutrients were extracted, leaving a landscape that the Council on Environmental Quality classifies as "severely desertified." Population has declined, the land is unsaleable, aquifers have been sucked dry, and Dust Bowl conditions characterize many counties.[40]

Less obvious, but perhaps as dangerous as environmental devastation, is the stunning concentration of power that extractive industries allow and even encourage. Because these industries required so much capital, technical expertise, and machinery, and because they developed in regions with little political or social undergirding, those who controlled the industry often controlled the state. In politics, then as now, money talked. With the economy and well-being of a state dependent on extractive industries, political leaders were unlikely to challenge the will of these industrial giants.

In Montana, copper ran much of the state. The legendary and often exaggerated War of the Copper Kings still illustrates the astounding control that a few men had over an entire industry and the state that supported it. William Clark, a Butte mine and smelter owner, and Marcus Daly, owner of Amalgamated Copper (which eventually became Anaconda Copper), battled over the location of the state capital, a Senate seat, and, finally, which one would dominate the copper industry. Daly died after this initial skirmish, and Clark won the Senate seat. The war continued, however, when an upstart outsider, Frederick Augustus Heinze, decided to take on Daly's legacy, Anaconda Copper, which now controlled all mines and smelters, including those once owned by Clark and Daly, as well as coal mines, lumber mills, and all but one newspaper in the state. To stop Heinze, Anaconda simply shut down all its operations, throwing 20,000 people out of work. In the company-owned newspapers, unemployed Montanans read that Heinze had caused all their troubles by forcing the shutdown. Under tremendous pressure, Heinze sold his mining properties to Anaconda, leaving it the uncontested economic, political, and journalistic power in the state. For nearly fifty years, western Montana operated as a gigantic company town.[41]

A different concentration of power, based on land and cattle, emerged in Wyoming. In the 1870s, as nearly free cattle from Texas poured onto the entirely free grazing lands of the northern Plains, cattlemen faced the problem of trying to figure out whose cattle were whose on the open range. They formed associations to register brands and to deal with the problem of rustlers. In 1879, these local associations merged to form the Wyoming Stock Growers Association, which evolved to control the entire state. The Stock Growers dictated freight rates, judicial appointments, and even elections. When the Cheyenne Club, social haven for the stock growers, was built with one of the nation's earliest electric-light systems, its gaudy and well-lighted interior served as a meeting place for the territorial legislature as well.

The ultimate indicator of the stockmen's power came with the Johnson County War in 1891/1892, when the cattlemen, frustrated by cattle theft, decided to take on small homesteaders who they blamed for all the stealing. Instead of using the legal system, they hired Texas gunmen to "invade" Johnson County and to round up, threaten, and murder a long list of supposed rustlers. Local homesteaders, well aware of the plan, cornered the vigilantes and kept them from finding any of the "rustlers." However, with the help of the powerful Wyoming Stock Growers Association, federal troops rescued the Texans, who were eventually released without trial.[42] This moment represented both the apogee of the cattlemen's power and the end of their reign, mostly because the cattle industry had busted due to its abuse of both environment and economy.

Other parts of the Rocky Mountains did not have the same dramatic examples of political and economic control, but the concentration of power was impressive just the same. In southern Colorado, for example, Colorado Fuel and Iron, the coal-mining and steel-producing giant controlled by the Rockefeller family, influenced all aspects of people's lives. In scores of small towns, CF&I controlled housing, stores, schools, saloons, sheriffs, judges, mine inspectors, state militias, and newspapers, making the corporation immune to demands for health and safety reforms in an industry that had the highest fatality rate in the nation. Nonunionized and non-English-speaking workers had little chance of challenging the overwhelming power of CF&I. Only after the horrible event of the Ludlow Massacre in 1914, when hired gunmen and state militia fired on the encampments of striking workers, burning eleven women and children to death, did this utter control come into question.[43] And only after national magazines began to draw attention to "the barony of the Colorado Fuel and Iron Company whose officials owned the mayors, the ministers, the merchants, and the lawyers" and stated that "working conditions are perhaps the worst in the country," did the corporation make any effort to change its behavior.[44]

This concentration of power, usually in the hands of eastern capitalists and investors, led to a long-standing characterization of the region as a "plundered province."[45] Although Bernard DeVoto coined the phrase in the 1930s, it reflected sentiments long held and obviously true, especially in the Rocky Mountain West. In the late nineteenth century, all big capital did come from the East. Industrialization had already taken hold there, building fortunes that could be reinvested in the West. In the Rocky Mountains, where nature had left vast riches in natural resources that could be developed only with enormous investment, regional boosters eagerly sought the necessary capital. A mine or a smelter or a railroad or a ski resort or an irrigation project required huge sums of money that small and new communities could never muster.

Aspen provides a good example. When a party of four prospectors led by Charles E. Bennett discovered indications of silver in the Roaring Fork Valley in the summer of 1879, they recognized the potential value of the strike. Quickly, a town developed with roads, banks, and brick buildings, and a population of miners, storekeepers, bankers, laundresses, saloon keepers, and boardinghouse owners filled its streets. Very little mining occurred, however. The entire town had been built on potential, but that potential could not be reached without a huge infusion of capital to sink deep shafts and to build smelters and railroads. Finally, in 1883, a New Yorker named Jerome B. Wheeler came to town, bringing the R. H. Macy fortune, which he had married and increased. As Malcolm Rohrbough writes, "Even those few in the camp who were skeptical of religious figures came to regard Wheeler as virtually God."[46] Wheeler "made" Aspen by building a smelter and a railroad and, most important, by giving other investors the confidence to spend their money there. Similarly, in the 1940s, when Aspen's silver fortunes had faded completely, local boosters recognized its potential as a national ski resort, but did not have the capital to build it. Walter Paepcke, a Chicagoan and head of the Container Corporation of America, provided the necessary millions to build ski lifts, lodges, and hotels.[47]

These kinds of investments, of course, came with strings attached. These strings inevitably created a complicated love–hate relationship with eastern capital. People who invested large sums of money expected not only profits, but a large measure of control over the communities they had built. Marcus Daly in Butte, Jerome Wheeler in Aspen, and William Palmer, the Denver and Rio Grande magnate, in Colorado Springs demanded political and social power as well as economic domination. The situation was even worse in communities where an absentee landlord controlled the economy. When Rockefeller interests, for example, held Anaconda Copper and Colorado Fuel and Iron, or when the Union Pacific or Northern Pacific Railroads had a significant stake, communities had little control over their own affairs and no place to seek redress. A faceless "eastern corporation" made financial decisions with little thought to local needs and concerns. This was as true for the St. Louis–based directors of fur-trading forts as it is for the officials of Ralston-Purina who own many of the big ski resorts in Summit County, Colorado, or, indeed, for the United States government, which serves as faceless landlord for most of the land in the Rocky Mountain West. The desire for eastern capital has coexisted with the fear of losing local control since the late nineteenth century.

Especially in volatile western industries, where bust followed boom with both suddenness and inevitability, eastern capital was a mixed blessing. When the bottom fell out of the silver market in 1893, many big investors had made their piles, leaving local people, those who owned small businesses and real estate, holding the bag. In Colorado, Utah, and Idaho, nearly every silver mine shut down with little warning, and as a local newspaper put it: "the dreaded emergency is now upon us. . . . At least 200,000 in Colorado alone are made destitute."[48] Men like Jerome Wheeler simply retired from the mining business to take up other interests. Other people lost their jobs as mines closed, their savings as banks failed, and their homes when they could no longer pay rent.[49]

Even in less drastic situations, the inequity in power between local citizen and corporate investor glared. A corporation like the Union Pacific or the Swan Land and Cattle Company or Anaconda Copper could simply absorb the losses of a bad year, a strike, or a drought. Most other people could not. When Exxon suddenly pulled out of its projected $500 billion Colony Shale Oil Project on the western slope of Colorado in May 1982, local people were left with big debts and even bigger resentment at "eastern capital" and the predicament in which it had placed them.[50]

This resentment, developed over a 100-year experience with big investors, has repeatedly boiled over into political action, each time using the same mix of mythology and fact about the region as a "plundered province." The Populist message carried by William Jennings Bryan of being sacrificed on a cross of gold resonated in a region that saw itself as having been destroyed by eastern bankers monomaniacally protecting an outmoded gold standard. In the depths of the Depression, DeVoto's claim that "an unending stream of gold and silver and copper and oil . . . has not made the West wealthy. It has, to be brief, made the East wealthy," seemed entirely appropriate. His bitter conclusion that Westerners had been "looted, betrayed, and sold out" by Easterners demonstrates a powerful truth and a powerful mythology.[51] Westerners were at the mercy of eastern capital or the federal government or, today, California capital; but they had, of course, invited it in, had ticker-tape parades for it, and showered it with praise in boom cycles—a part of their history many people in the Rocky Mountains forget.

Such historical "partial amnesia" is evident in the outpouring of anger labeled the "Sagebrush Rebellion" in the early 1980s. This time, Westerners directed their anger at both corporate capital and the federal government, but the unifying word was always "eastern." The story went that the West had been a quiet place, where little men built an economy and loved the land, only to have Easterners destroy it or lock it up. Governor Richard Lamm of Colorado evoked this mythic past when he wrote about the early twentieth century: "There were so few people in the mountains then. It was like having your own magnificent kingdom. We would seldom meet other people. . . . The mountains were a refuge from the noise and stench of the city. No airplanes, no litter, no sound. Only occasional civilization." Then, in Lamm's narrative, the post–World War II period brought apocalypse: "Energy combines, unleashed by the government, invade the West. Seeking profit, unconcerned with local fears, they ignore social, political, and economic considerations in the process of building. Huge profits accrue to them and flow out. Little is left to the people and their communities. . . . Ways of life crumble forever. Values, attitudes, customs—the core of western life—shatter."[52] This is a tragedy of epic proportions.

Lamm, of course, is partly right, but the scenario he describes is flawed in several ways. First, the pristine mountains never existed. Leadville in 1879, Telluride in 1890, Coeur d'Alene in 1891, and Butte in 1900 were anything but quiet places. Even the world of fur trappers in the 1830s seemed overly crowded to them. A rendezvous in those years made veritable cities in the wilderness, complete with smog, garbage heaps, and noise pollution. Second, energy combines, much like British capital in the cattle industry or eastern capital in mining, did not invade. Local, state, and regional boosters desperately sought out and courted them and rewarded them when they came.

Finally, and perhaps most important, Lamm's myth alludes to a set of western core values that reflects life in the Rocky Mountains. What might these be? Lamm, and many others of various flavors of Sagebrush Rebel, imagine a world of hardy individuals who both appreciated and single-handedly tamed a landscape. Such deeply conflicting values created individuals, and their descendants, who were tenacious, stubborn, and deeply devoted to the land, but also intent on extracting wealth. Certainly, Westerners exist who fit this definition. Many of the people who reacted with such horror to Frank and Deborah Popper's analysis of the depopulation of the northern Plains, for example, reflect exactly that tenacious drive and dedication to land.[53]

The historical record suggests a set of values that often is quite different. Most people went to the Rocky Mountains to make a quick killing and leave. They had no regard for land whatsoever and, indeed, considered it a barrier to their instant wealth. Land captured resources—whether precious metals, coal, furs, beef, mutton, water, or ski trails—and the task of the individual was to pry them from the land. Most people found themselves unequal to the task, and only by becoming employees of large corporations or subsidees of the federal government could they succeed. And even then, success was at best temporary, as resources ran out or became too expensive to harvest. Most people, reflecting self-preservation rather than tenacity, moved on to the next boom area.

Quick profit as a motive created distinctive communities. Transient, tough, and highly insular, the communities of the Rocky Mountains have always modeled themselves after mobile-home parks rather than New England towns. Plunked down amid heaps of animal carcasses, tailings piles, smelter refuse, or snowmaking equipment created by corporate entities, communities had little chance of developing the social glue that might have allowed them to make the best of a bad situation. Extractive industries have molded the environmental, social, and cultural patterns of the region in ways that many residents would rather not recognize. The region has been plundered by "outsiders," but not because the people who lived here were entirely powerless. While the beauty of the landscape is continually celebrated, its plundering has been encouraged, even upheld as a cultural value in the region. To have an impact on the future, the people of the Rocky Mountain region have to see the shape of their history more clearly and to recognize the conflict at its core. It explains much of how we use, imagine, and fear the Rocky Mountains themselves.

NOTES

1. Denver and Rio Grande Railroad, *The Heart of the Continent* (Chicago, 1892), 28–29.

2. Wallace Stegner and Page Stegner, "Rocky Mountain Country," *Atlantic Monthly*, April 1978, 59.

3. Ivan Doig, *This House of Sky: Landscapes of a Western Mind* (New York: Harcourt Brace Jovanovich, 1978), 206.

4. *First Annual Report of the State Inspector of Coal Mines, 1884* (Denver, 1884), 4–5.

5. Ian Davidson, "The Costs of a Day of Skiing" (Manuscript, 1995).

6. There is a complex history of the use that Indians have made of the Rocky Mountain region that I have not included here largely because the Indians recognized the climatic and topographical limitations of living in the mountains. Few tribes made their homes in the mountains, though they used them for hunting, gathering wood and medicinal plants, and summer retreats. For interesting material on this subject, see Karl Butzer, "The Indian Legacy in the American Landscape," in *The Making of the American Landscape,* ed. Michael P. Conzen (Cambridge, Mass.: MIT Press, 1990), 27–59; and Ronald L. Ives, "Early Human Occupation of the Caribou Lake Site, Colorado Front Range," *Plains Anthropology* 19 (1974): 1–14.

7. Historical geographers have made observations along these lines. See especially William Wyckoff and Lary M. Dilsaver, "Defining the Mountainous West," in *The Mountainous West: Explorations in Historical Geography,* ed. William Wyckoff and Lary M. Dilsaver (Lincoln: University of Nebraska Press, 1995), 3–8.

8. David M. Emmons, "Constructed Province: History and the Making of the Last American West," *Western Historical Quarterly* 25 (1994): 437–59.

9. For an overview of the history of this idea, see William G. Robbins, "The 'Plundered Province' Thesis and the Recent Historiography of the American West," *Pacific Historical Review* 55 (1986): 577–94.

10. In different ways, David Emmons and William Robbins have explored the process of urbanization and industrialization for the entire West. See Emmons, "Constructed Province"; William G. Robbins, "Creating a 'New West': Big Money Returns to the Hinterland," *Montana: The Magazine of Western History* 46 (1996): 66–72; and Robbins, *Colony and Empire: The Capitalist Transformation of the American West* (Lawrence: University Press of Kansas, 1994).

11. David J. Wishart, *The Fur Trade of the American West, 1807–1840* (Lincoln: University of Nebraska Press, 1979); David Lavender, *Bent's Fort* (Garden City, N.Y.: Doubleday, 1954), 28–135.

12. Janet Lecompte, *Pueblo, Hardscrabble, and Greenhorn: Society on the High Plains, 1832–1856* (Norman: University of Oklahoma Press, 1978), 12–18.

13. Rufus Sage, *Rocky Mountain Life* (Cincinnati: Rulison, 1857), 29.

14. Francis Parkman, Jr., *The Oregon Trail* (1849; reprint, New York: Penguin, 1982), 47.

15. Robert G. Athearn, *High Country Empire: The High Plains and Rockies* (New York: McGraw-Hill, 1960), 73–75, 84–86; Duane A. Smith, *Rocky Mountain West: Colorado, Wyoming, and Montana, 1859–1915* (Albuquerque: University of New Mexico Press, 1992), 6–7, 31–32.

16. Athearn, *High Country Empire*, 138–41.

17. John B. Allen, *From Skisport to Skiing: One Hundred Years of an American Sport* (Amherst: University of Massachusetts Press, 1993); "East Goes West to Idaho's Sun Valley, Society's Newest Winter Playground," *Life*, 8 March 1937, 20–27.

18. Athearn, *High Country Empire*, 88; Paula Petrik, *No Step Backward: Women and Family on the Rocky Mountain Mining Frontier, Helena, Montana, 1865–1900* (Helena: Montana Historical Society Press, 1987), 3–4.

19. Mary Hallock Foote to Helena Gilder, 12 May 1879, in *A Victorian Gentlewoman in the Far West: Reminiscences of Mary Hallock Foote*, ed. Rodman W. Paul (San Marino, Calif.: Huntington Library, 1972), 171.

20. Malcolm J. Rohrbough, *Aspen: The History of a Silver Mining Town, 1879–1893* (New York: Oxford University Press, 1986), 24–27.

21. Doig, *This House of Sky*, 95.

22. Elliott West, *The Way to the West: Essays on the Central Plains* (Albuquerque: University of New Mexico Press, 1995), 66.

23. LeCompte, *Pueblo, Hardscrabble, and Greenhorn*, 63–64, 12.

24. Roger Daniels, *Asian America: Chinese and Japanese in the United States Since 1850* (Seattle: University of Washington Press, 1988), 60.

25. Butte Chamber of Commerce, "Chinese Question," *Resources of Butte*, July 1890, 14.

26. Sucheng Chan, *Asian Americans: An Interpretive History* (Boston: Twayne, 1990), 49–50. See also Paul Crane and Alfred Larson, "The Chinese Massacre," *Annals of Wyoming* 12 (1940): 155–56.

27. Peggy Clifford and John Macauley Smith, "The Distressing Rebirth," *Empire Magazine*, 16 August 1970, 9–12; see also Vail Associates Collection, Clippings Files, Denver Public Library.

28. *Denver Post*, Ski Industry Clippings Files, Denver Public Library.

29. Ed Marston, "The West Lacks Social Glue," in *Reopening the Western Frontier*, ed. Ed Marston (Washington, D.C.: Island Press, 1989), 69.

30. West, *Way to the West*, 59–73; Dan Flores, "Bison Ecology and Bison Diplomacy," *Journal of American History* 78 (1991): 470–77.

31. West, *Way to the West*, 87–91

32. Elliott West, *Growing Up with the Country: Childhood on the Far Western Frontier* (Albuquerque: University of New Mexico Press, 1989), 18.

33. Ibid., 150–55.

34. David Emmons, *The Butte Irish: Class and Ethnicity in an American Mining Town, 1875–1925* (Urbana: University of Illinois Press, 1990), 148–53. See also Alan Derickson, *Workers' Health, Workers' Democracy: The Western Miners' Struggle, 1891–1925* (Ithaca, N.Y.: Cornell University Press, 1988), 50–51.

35. Andrew Gulliford, *Boomtown Blues: Colorado Oil Shale, 1885–1985* (Niwot: University of Colorado Press, 1989), 90–93, 99–102.

36. James Thomson, 16 June 1867, in *Poems and Some Letters of James Thomson,* ed. Anne Ridler (London: Centaur Books, 1963), 246.

37. Smith, *Rocky Mountain West,* 202.

38. Ibid., 125–27; Donald Worster, *Under Western Skies: Nature and History in the American West* (New York: Oxford University Press, 1992), 34–52; Karl J. Hess, Jr., *Visions Upon the Land: Man and Nature on the Western Range* (Washington, D.C.: Cato Institute, 1992),

39. Duane A. Smith, *Mining America: The Industry and the Environment, 1800–1980* (Lawrence: University Press of Kansas, 1987), 13–18; Stephen M. Voynick, *The Making of a Hardrock Miner* (Berkeley, Calif.: Howell-North Books, 1978), 65–68.

40. K. Ross Toole, *The Rape of the Great Plains: Northwest America, Cattle, and Coal* (Boston: Little, Brown, 1976), 136–40; Deborah Epstein Popper and Frank J. Popper, Jr., "The Fate of the Plains," in *Reopening the Western Frontier,* ed. Marston, 106–7.

41. Smith, *Rocky Mountain West,* 166–71.

42. T. A. Larson, *History of Wyoming,* 2nd ed. (Lincoln: University of Nebraska Press, 1978), 270–83; Athearn, *High Country Empire,* 134–46.

43. Howard M. Gitelman, *Legacy of the Ludlow Massacre: A Chapter in American Industrial Relations* (Philadelphia: Temple University Press, 1988), 7–11; Anne F. Hyde, "Presenting and Protecting Power: Public Relations and the Remaking of John D Rockefeller, Jr." (Manuscript, 1994).

44. Helen Ring Robinson, "The War in Colorado," *Independent,* 11 May 1914, 245; "The Colorado Slaughter," *Literary Digest,* 7 February 1914, 247.

45. Bernard DeVoto, "The West: A Plundered Province," *Harper's,* August 1934, 355–64.

46. Rohrbough, *Aspen,* 67.

47. Bill Sonn, "The Life and Times of Aspen," *Colorful Colorado Magazine,* Summer 1977, 71–74.

48. *Rocky Mountain Sun,* 1 July 1893, quoted in Rohrbaugh, *Aspen,* 219.

49. Rohrbough, *Aspen,* 225–33.

50. Gulliford, *Boomtown Blues,* 152–71.

51. DeVoto, "West," 358, 364.

52. Richard D. Lamm and Michael McCarthy, *The Angry West: A Vulnerable Land and Its Future* (Boston: Houghton Mifflin, 1982), 3, 5.

53. For an interesting analysis of the reaction the Poppers got, see Anne Matthews, *Where the Buffalo Roam* (New York: Grove Weidenfeld, 1992).

The Expectations of Others:

Struggles Toward a Sense of Place

in the Northern Plains

James R. Shortridge

Skeptics might question how anyone could devote an entire chapter to so simple a topic as regional identity in the northern Plains. The image of the place is straightforward, they would say. It is flat and semiarid, a land filled with farms and small towns. Its people reflect this rurality: honest, but rather naive and homogeneous. Such observers have a point. Their assertions can find support in demographic and topographic statistics. More important, they are repeated daily in the national media. As I write these words, for example, a new poll has been released that asked 13,500 "veteran vacationers" to rate their favorite destinations. Kansas scored dead last among the states, and was joined in the bottom grouping by its Plains neighbors North Dakota, Nebraska, and Oklahoma.

(Presumably, only the presence of the Black Hills kept South Dakota off the list.) When interviewed about these results, an official with the Kansas Department of Commerce noted that state tourism is hindered by a small budget for promotion.[1] This is true, but nearly irrelevant. No one in or out of the state seriously believes that even major promotional pushes would change the image perceptibly. Most Americans today regard Kansas and the rest of the northern Plains as isolated, nearly forgotten, places. To use another popular epithet, they are the essence of "flyover country."

The simplicity of this interpretation is appealing. But before accepting it as complete, one should note its source. The flyover image is almost entirely the creation of outsiders. Whether or not local residents agree is a question rarely asked. Plains people certainly are aware of the popular view, and some of them agree with it. Other scenarios can be easily imagined, though. It even is possible that the self-image of some residents has been constructed completely in opposition to this outsider judgment. People could emphasize that their region today is far more urban than rural, and Dakotans, at least, could stress that they have more ethnic diversity than most states. Isolation could be claimed to produce contemplation rather than ignorance. These are not idle issues, and their importance grows if one looks at past representations. Plains people, with their small populations, have never had much control over how others have seen them. The possibilities for distortion, misunderstanding, and general mythmaking are enormous.

My goal here is to sketch the complicated emergence of regional consciousness in the northern Plains. I will pay attention to the views of insider and outsider alike, for the latter clearly have influenced how local people see themselves. The approach is chronological for the most part, but chorography comes into play toward the end, where I compare the Plains identity with that of the West as a whole and note some major anomalies and variations that exist within the region.

THE PLACE

Regardless of their views on cultural characteristics, observers have always agreed on the location and extent of the northern Plains. This consensus reflects physical geography in some places, settlement history in others. A generally abrupt transition between mountain and flatland in western Montana, eastern Wyoming, and central Colorado makes for a logical border on the west. Similarly obvious is the political line between the United States and Canada, where differing national purposes over the decades have created distinct cultures. To the east is a major transition zone. People usually talk about a climatic change there between arid and humid, but topography and time of settlement also are involved. No one can agree on an exact line, but everyone acknowledges that the changes begin about one state west of the Mississippi River and are complete in the vicinity of the hundredth meridian. The most common practice has been to adopt the eastern borders of Kansas, Nebraska, and the Dakotas as the operational limit, and I do so here as well.

Dividing the Plains north and south is more subtle, but still quite a clear process for residents. Southern Plains always means Oklahoma and Texas. The term implies a distinctive mix of Euro-, African-, and Native American peoples who immigrated there in the nineteenth century from the south midland and lower southern states. North of Oklahoma, Illinoisans, Hoosiers, Ohioans, and Pennsylvanians dominated the influx of new settlers. Yankees, Germans, Scandinavians, and Ontarians were important, too, along with the native Sioux. The cultural influence of these peoples remains: the southern Plains is Baptist country; the northern, a quilt of Methodist, Lutheran, and Catholic. Detailed research by Michael Roark has shown that the meeting point between these two flows actually occurred in central Oklahoma, near the Canadian River. During the land-rush days, this stream lay midway between a contingent of settlers who moved southward from Kansas and another who trekked northward from Texas.[2] Subsequent history (some of it growing out of the outlaw, "Sooner" mentality of the land rush itself) has largely relocated this perceptual divide, however, and it now runs along the Kansas–Oklahoma border.

EARLY ASSESSMENTS

Most modern accounts of how the American public saw the Plains before and during the early years of Euro-American settlement have cast the imagery as dichotomous. An overly negative desert interpretation, established in the 1820s, yielded some forty years later to that of a garden. This garden concept, so the story continues, attracted large numbers of settlers in the 1870s, 1880s, and beyond, people filled with humid-land ideas about how to farm and live. Major droughts during the 1890s and 1930s supposedly then ended the era of mythmaking.

This conventional wisdom is far too simple. Now, thanks largely to research by Martyn Bowden and four of his doctoral students at Clark University, we know that past Americans held views that were far more complex.[3] Although fur traders had provided some early (and largely pessimistic) accounts, the Plains first became newsworthy in 1803 following their purchase from France by Thomas Jefferson. Buoyed by nationalistic feelings, journalistic reports soon were full of unbridled praise. A garden became the operative image, and a nationwide sampling of newspapers and periodicals shows that most people believed it.

As excitement about the new land subsided and more explorations of it took place, the unanimity of opinion unraveled. A report by Edwin James on the 1820 expedition made by Major Stephen Long across the central Plains was critical. Not only was it extremely negative, but excerpts from it were reprinted in a number of major urban newspapers in the Northeast. A typical account described a "barren desert" stretching for 400 miles eastward from the Rockies whose "elevated surface is . . . covered with sand, gravel, pebbles, etc."[4] This vivid word picture of a Great American Desert quickly moved from the newspapers into several textbooks. Still, it was far from universally accepted. Bowden's meticulous research has shown it to be dominant only in major eastern cities. In contrast, desert descriptions were rare in papers from the urban South, rarer still in small-town papers from both North and South, and virtually nonexistent in all accounts published west of the Appalachian Mountains. This striking discrepancy along regional and social lines corresponds nicely with the split between people who favored rapid westward expansion and those who opposed it.

The instigation of mass overland migrations to California and Oregon in the 1840s reinforced the concept of the Plains as a desert in the minds of the urban Northeasterners. After all, why would Missourians, Illinoisans, and others travel 2,000 miles if good land were available closer at hand? The answer, again from Bowden's research, was not that the Plains lacked good potential for agriculture, but that the combination of mining, farming, and business opportunities on the west coast was even better. Textbooks (most of which were published in the Northeast) continued to promote the desert concept until the time of the Civil War, but it was countered by the beginnings of firsthand experience with the region and by a series of idyllic images created in the initial wave of regional guidebooks. People could believe whichever source supported their own prejudices, and the sectional distribution of this opinion continued as before. Southerners, Westerners, and rural Northerners sided with the writers of the guidebooks; the urban elite in the Northeast, with the textbooks.

Following the war years, the Janus-like imagery of the Plains coalesced briefly on a new theme. Livestock raising, the first major economic venture in the area by Euro-Americans, proved so successful between 1865 and 1875 that the national press rechristened the desert–garden as "the Great Western Pastoral Region."[5] A grazing theme struck many observers of the time as well suited to the place. Cattle and sheep would utilize the same natural grasses as had the buffalo. Grazing also would provide a convenient compromise for the old competing images, a position midway along the continuum between garden and desert. Although events would soon erode the pervasiveness of pastoralism, the ecological match between image and place has helped it to endure as a Plains theme. For most observers, of course, its viability owes even more to Frederic Remington, Owen Wister, Zane Grey, Hollywood movie producers, and others who began to romanticize the American cowboy after the 1880s.

The day of the cattleman on the northern Plains is usually said to have ended with the killing blizzards of 1886/1887. This is factually true, but by this date eastern Americans were already far advanced on a plan to reconceptualize the region once again. This time, the rationale was profit. Cattle created money, to be sure, but for only a few. The free-labor ideology of the ascendant Republican Party helped farmers in the Old Northwest Territory, railroad investors, and urban entrepreneurs to see the Plains (and the rest of the West) as a place to implement their dreams. The Homestead Act of 1862 was a part of this plan, the land grants to railroads were another, but image manipulation lay at its core. The desert concept was quickly discredited by an avalanche of propaganda created by railroad companies and others. Rain would follow the advance of settlement, they said. Plowing the prairie sod and planting new trees would increase transpiration and thereby the supply of moisture. Next, the promoters attacked the grazing ideal. Horace Greeley was one of many who became skilled at designing exactly the right cultural attack on this front: "I fear this cattle-ranching, with long intervals between the ranches, is destined to half-barbarize many thousands of the next generation, whom schools can scarcely reach, and to whom the sound of the church-going bell will be a stranger."[6]

The direct and massive involvement of national corporations and the federal government in the settlement of the Plains gave what historian David Emmons has called "a distinctly imperial character" to the region in the 1870s and 1880s.[7] It was market capitalism at its best: a conquest marked by unprecedented speed and ferocity. This interpretation is consistent with that of other modern scholars, but at first it seems far removed from the idyllic, agrarian imagery so commonly expressed in the promotional literature of the time. Such depictions were everywhere. Bowden's surveys show that by 1880 even the newspapers in Boston, New York, and Philadelphia—the centers of reluctance in the past—offered editorial opinion that ran 3 to 1 in favor of the garden.[8]

Emmons has explained the paradox between the simultaneously held concepts of a ruthless, profit-minded conquest and of an egalitarian paradise. The latter, he argues, was a "myth of concern" contrived by corporate America. Garden symbolism played to the dreams of young, postwar Americans who sought places to build new homes. Conveniently, it also shielded avarice. In Emmons's words: "it gave to the dominant element of that society—mostly eastern—a powerful argument against those who challenged their dominance." With the myth in place, the complaints of those who might fail could be ignored. After all, a paradise would easily support anyone who made an honest effort.[9]

LIFE IN THE GARDEN

Surviving accounts of life on the Plains in the 1870s and 1880s suggest that garden symbolism was embraced by the majority of settlers. It is uncertain how many of these people realized that promoters were a source of these ideas, but the source really was unimportant. Everyone wanted to believe. The modern technology of railroads and barbed wire gave the settlers confidence, and weather conditions also cooperated for the most part. Other than a bad grasshopper year in 1874 and droughts from 1878 to 1880, crops generally fared well. The frontier pushed north and west steadily, and people convinced themselves that they could duplicate Iowa's prosperous rural landscape. As for social democracy, the Plains might do even better. An air of progress was omnipresent.

The heady frontier optimism ended abruptly. Drought came in 1888 and stayed continually until 1901. It gave lie to earlier claims that rains would follow the plow, and caused human suffering unmatched in more recent decades. The experience of Johnson City, Kansas, the seat of newly formed Stanton County on the Colorado border, symbolized the troubles. After an early peak of several hundred people, the town was completely deserted by 1897; it had recovered to only sixty-two people by 1913, and remained too small to require any local elections until 1923.[10]

Ranchers, who had been forced out by high land prices in the late 1880s, staged a comeback as the drought held on. Their reappearance signaled that the overall conceptualization of the region was about to change again. William Allen White, among others, editorialized in 1895 that Kansas (and presumably the entire Great Plains) should no longer be thought of as homogeneous. Like Gaul, it was better conceived as tripartite: "Eastern Kansas has proven herself good for agriculture; central Kansas is proving herself worthy; [but] western Kansas is a dead failure in everything except the herd."[11]

Had the dryness of the 1890s persisted for a few more years, it is likely that White's vision would have become accepted. Instead, one moist year followed another between 1901 and 1911, farmers began to move westward again, and the garden image returned. This time, however, the symbolism was modified somewhat. The Plains still were said to offer marvelous potential, but now they were seen to yield their bounty only with effort. Weak-willed settlers would fail, and even the strong would have to dedicate themselves completely to the task at hand. This story of commitment and sacrifice as the price of success made sense. Not only did it accommodate the now obvious climatic extremes, but it also flattered the residents who had endured and promised them hope during the difficult times. The conception quickly found widespread acceptance in the region, and it persists today as the core of local self-identity. Many characters from Plains fiction stand as icons in this regard, including two of its most memorable: Cather's Alexandra Bergson and Rolvaag's Per Hansa.

The reconstitution of regional character actually had begun even as the drought of the 1890s persisted. Contemporary social commentators reported that hardships brought people together and winnowed out those who did not belong. The experience also tempered blatant boosterism and, by causing investments to fail, acted to sever many of the existing ties between East and West. Eastern speculators tended to blame their losses on local spendthrifts, while Plains men came to regard the Easterners as selfish, unfeeling exploiters. The process turned transplanted Easterners into real Nebraskans or Dakotans. A New York journalist visiting in Kansas caught the mood well in 1898:

> It was interesting to watch the effect of this [return to] prosperity upon the farmers. So far as I could observe and learn there was little elation. . . . The joy that came to the thousands upon thousands of homes . . . is the kind that expresses itself oftenest in tears. With the money that they made last year the farmers purchased the necessities they had gone without, and the luxuries that their wives and daughters craved, and then they went home ready to face the problems of this and the coming years with renewed courage, longing for more years of plenty, but prepared, with their surplus earnings and their experience in economy and improved methods of farming, to meet fearlessly another drought of one or even more years.[12]

The self-conception of Plains people as an especially hardy breed of yeoman farmers went largely unchallenged over the next two decades. Good prices were accompanied by adequate moisture throughout the period. This combination enabled older county seats to acquire more educational and cultural facilities, and encouraged a new wave of Euro-American frontiersmen to push the Sioux aside and to plant crops all the way to the Rocky Mountain front. These settlers did not fear even another drought, for they had been sold on a new, "scientific" method of farming. Promoters argued that the fallowing of fields in alternate years would allow the "banking" of rainfall in the subsoil. Wheat thus could grow easily in places that received only ten inches of precipitation annually.[13]

The only specter in the agrarian dream was control of the commercial market by nonresident forces. Railroads often charged more than local people thought they should to transport grain, and elevators did likewise for storage. Some of the dissatisfaction was voiced toward businessmen in Minneapolis–St. Paul, Chicago, Omaha, and Kansas City, but the favorite targets were more remote: financiers in Boston and New York, and politicians in Washington, D.C. This manipulation sensed by residents was correct. Railroads and grain elevators were simply the two most visible local manifestations of the imperialism that had underlain the entire settlement structure of the West ever since the Civil War. The only change was the growing local awareness of this fact. To acknowledge the situation fully, of course, Plains people would have had to admit that their society was part of the world-market economy instead of a separate, self-contained, and self-controlled garden. For the moment, they instead chose to believe that yeomanry remained and that the intrusiveness could be rectified through local political action.

Grassroots protest movements began in the 1880s as a series of farmers' alliances. They grew rapidly, coalesced as the Populist Party in 1892, and found acceptance throughout the northern Plains. Fusion with the Democrats sapped some of their energy after 1896, but seventeen years later the spirit emerged strong again in North Dakota as the Nonpartisan League. There, with strong support from Norwegian settlers who were used to socialistic enterprises in Europe, reform achieved its zenith. League candidates assumed control of the state government in 1918. The next year, they passed bills to increase taxes on existing banks, railroads, and utilities; bills to exempt many farm improvements from taxation; and, most significantly, bills to establish a state-owned system of banks and grain elevators.[14] Their feat was one of agrarianism's finest hours, and state banks and elevators remain as fixtures on the modern North Dakota scene.

A LOSS OF CONFIDENCE

The reforms passed by the Nonpartisan League in 1919 represent the pinnacle of local optimism and self-confidence on the northern Plains. The league itself declined rapidly after that point, a victim of its own success and of linkages made between its brand of socialism and that being practiced in the new Soviet Union of Vladimir Lenin. More generally, a combination of bad agricultural years and of changing national values made it increasingly difficult to sustain any sense of idealism. Willa Cather, one of the most sensitive observers of that period, wrote that "the world broke in two in 1922 or thereabouts."[15] Her words have general meaning, but she was thinking specifically about the northern Plains, which she knew best. She made the contrast between the two periods a central issue in two novels, and expressed herself clearly through the thoughts of Niel Herbert in *A Lost Lady:*

> The Old West had been settled by dreamers, great-hearted adventurers
> who were unpractical to the point of magnificence; a courteous
> brotherhood, strong in attack but weak in defense, who could conquer but

could not hold. Now all the vast territory they had won was to be at the mercy of men like Ivy Peters, who had never dared anything. They would drink up the mirage, dispell the morning freshness, root out the great brooding spirit of freedom. . . . All the way from the Missouri to the mountains this generation of shrewd young men, trained to petty economies by hard times, would do exactly what Ivy Peters had done when he drained the Forrester marsh.[16]

Cather's views were prescient. With the death of the generation of pioneers, belief in the yeoman myth that had sustained them also was faltering. The process was gradual and came later to the newly settled areas of eastern Montana than to Cather's older south-central Nebraska. Still, in retrospect, it was easy for her and others to identify the early 1920s as the divide. The defining event was a sustained agricultural depression, one that proved to many American farmers that world markets had much more control over their personal destinies than they had realized. Reaction to the farmers' plight also was revealing. People in the Plains showed major concern, of course, but those on the eastern and western seaboards expressed only a modest one. Anyone who pondered the situation could see that coastal Americans had declared agrarianism to be passé. They embraced a new sustaining myth: technological–industrial progress.

As the agricultural depression of the rural heartland in the 1920s turned into the Great Depression of the 1930s, and then into the crisis of World War II, all segments of American society were affected. People temporarily played down their regional differences and the competing myths of identity. These differences could not be ignored after 1945, though, because the events of depression and war had widened the gap between sectional perceptions even farther. Conditions during the Depression had painted rural life on the Plains in vividly negative terms. After all, the dust bowl was located there, and its human tragedy was documented for everyone to see through the photographs of Dorothea Lange and Arthur Rothstein and the words of John Steinbeck. In this testimony, the Plains were the antithesis of a garden, and the farmers anything but hardy yeomen. This extreme negativity was countered somewhat in the 1940s by images of grain production for the war effort. Such conceptions still had a rural base, however, and by this time anything rural had to compete in people's minds with the gleaming factories of America's wartime cities. Outside observers easily judged the urban scene as far superior to rural life. For such people, the Plains had become a societal backwater.

Two lines of reaction emerged among Plains residents. One, more common in the earlier years, was resistance. This could be considered a cultural addendum to the economic agenda of the earlier Populists. With the same goals of propping up the besieged yeoman myth and of perfecting rural society, proponents lobbied for prohibition, church attendance, and isolationist politics; they railed against aliens, cigarettes, and jazz. The second, and often simultaneous, response was to embrace the same industrial–technological dream that had materialized elsewhere in the nation. If Ohio could be home to factories and farms alike, this argument went, so could Nebraska and North Dakota. The use of oil and natural gas to attract industry to southeastern Kansas early in the century might be a model for the rest of the northern Plains; the infusion of government funds to transform California into a manufacturing center during World War II, another.

The appeal of industrialization was strong on the Plains in the years immediately following World War II. It seemed to offer a means of sidestepping the obvious and apparently insoluble problems of dependence on a narrow agricultural base. It also provided a means for replacing a fading American myth—agrarianism—with a newer, now brighter one. Some industrialization had already come to the region by this time, of course, but it was concentrated in eastern border cities, in Wichita, and along the well-watered Platte valley. This success meant that officials in Kansas and Nebraska could afford to take a relatively laissez-faire attitude toward recruitment. Promoters for the more isolated Dakotas knew they would have to work harder.

The promise, politics, and ultimate failure of industrialization in Montana and the Dakotas is nicely encapsulated by the quest for a Missouri Valley Authority. This idea began in the early 1940s when a federal plan for irrigation in the upper basin of the Missouri was merged with another to control floods downstream. Nearly simultaneously, a study commissioned by the North Dakota legislature suggested that low-cost electrical power might offer a way for the region to attract manufacturers. State officials immediately began to lobby for an expansion of the river project, now known as the Pick–Sloan plan. They took as their model the Tennessee Valley Authority, a multipurpose federal project from the 1930s that had been widely credited with revitalizing the economy of the Upper South.[17]

The tone of the arguments in the debate is more important than the outcome. Those opposing the plan stressed an old Populist position: resist federal intervention at any cost. Those in favor adopted a variation on the same theme: the Plains as victim. Influenced by unsympathetic outsiders, this scenario went, federal officials were going to destroy valuable farms with their big dams on the main stem of the Missouri but offer nothing in return; Dakotans were morally entitled to major irrigation projects and cheap electrical power. As things actually happened, schemes for power generation and irrigation were incorporated into the existing Pick–Sloan plan. The irrigation never materialized (though North Dakotans still lobby for it), but the new electricity came on line beginning in 1956. This reduced rates by some 30 percent, but the amount proved inadequate as an incentive to overcome the more pervasive problem of market isolation.[18]

If electricity failed to attract industry to the northern Plains, its coming at least made life better in the rural areas. This, plus a period of prosperous agriculture in the 1940s and 1950s, not only kept hard times at bay, but actually fostered an interval during which people seemed to be reasonably happy with their circumstances. Having discovered the victim argument, Plains people now began to employ it successfully with federal officials for new school buildings, highways, sewage plants, and other construction projects that enhanced their quality of life. Population numbers, though declining slightly in most rural counties, were not yet low enough to affect the prosperity of small-town merchants. The average county seat actually grew during this period, drawing in residents from the surrounding countryside. It was a time soon to be remembered as a golden age.

PARANOIA

It can be argued that the prosperity of the 1950s represented the closest that many Plains communities have ever come to fulfilling the dreams of their founders. This contentment, though, rested on a fragile foundation. Most industries had already decided that the region was too isolated for their needs, and agricultural prices would inevitably fall. Trends for local businesses and populations were even more frightening. Merchants in the county-seat towns, who had smiled as their superior size and facilities had lured customers away from country stores, now began to wince as their own trade was pulled away to even larger emporia. Others noticed that fewer young people than before were remaining in town beyond their high-school years. The logical first step for dealing effectively with such problems would have been a clear-headed assessment of the causes. Here it was an enlarging scale of human activity produced by modern transportation. Isolation, which ironically had guaranteed a captive audience for local merchants at the same time that it had discouraged outside manufacturers, was waning. The local economy was connected ever more tightly with that of the outside world. Businesses, schools, and whole towns would have to change if they were to survive.

A wave of school consolidations in the 1960s is proof that town and county officials took some positive actions to alleviate their crisis, but in cities of from 1,000 to 5,000 people the predominant stance was another retreat from reality. Again, the residents championed the ideas of self-sufficiency and victimization. The whole world may be changing, but they need not. They had been prosperous before, and could be again. The problem was meddling outsiders.

Kathleen Norris, a poet and resident of Lemmon, South Dakota, has labeled this retreat from reality as "the small-town death wish." She points out that whereas farmers, ranchers, and villagers have no more illusions about their role in the modern economy, people in slightly larger towns persist in seeing themselves as important cogs. They alienate the farmers they need as allies by wrongly holding them responsible for business decline. They refuse to offer incentives that might attract new business. They distrust suggestions from teachers, doctors, lawyers, ministers, and other professional people in town, arguing that they, too, are outsiders, and therefore "don't understand."[19]

Norris's portrait may not ring true for people who visit only briefly in towns like Lemmon; residents there display a long-practiced surface veneer of smiles and cooperation. Her indictment matches my experience, though. Such behavior also should not be surprising from citizens who truly have been exploited to some degree, and who now begin to sense that they may be nearly powerless. Denial can be a group as well as an individual experience. The problems to be faced actually go beyond those of recent shifts in population. North Dakota historian Elwyn Robinson, for example, identified the "too much mistake" more than a generation ago. This is a legacy of belief in the garden imagery, whereby too many counties were established, too many churches built, and too many miles of roads constructed for the region to support on a long-term basis.[20] The Plains are infrastructure heavy, but to admit this and to change is to cast doubt on the identity-sustaining premise that the past was golden. On the issue of counties, North Dakotans have chosen a typical halfway response. They passed legislation that would allow consolidation to occur, but so far have refrained from actual mergers.

Still another burden for Plains people is the nearly universal dismissal of their region by outsiders. Since the dust bowl days, writers have varied little from the themes of remoteness, desolation, and dullness. Journalist Eric Sevareid called his home state of North Dakota "a large rectangular blank spot in the nation's mind" in 1946, and his words still apply.[21] Rand-McNally forgot to include the state in one of its atlases in 1989. Surveys show that residents are thought of as simple country bumpkins when they are thought of at all. Anecdotal information backs this up. Erskine Caldwell once described Dakotans and ground squirrels in similar words ("chubby-faced, friendly-mannered"), and officials at the University of Nebraska considering dumping Herbie the Husker, their longtime and similarly endowed mascot, in a move to improve the university's outside image.[22] Plains people also realize that nearly all the celebrities native to their states moved away either to achieve their fame or to enjoy it. Dwight Eisenhower retired to Pennsylvania; Willa Cather wrote in New York; Lawrence Welk toured the country.

What can residents do to cope? While many cleave to an imagined golden age of the 1950s, others succumb to the outsider view and make plans to move. In student surveys of favorite places to live, only Plains residents gave their states less than top ratings. Dakotans preferred Minnesota to home, Kansans said Colorado. For young people, at least, state pride in the Plains does not approach that in, say, New York or Alabama, and their exodus makes the states gray even faster.[23]

Between the courses of capitulation to outside negativity and belief in outdated myths of self-sufficiency lies a path of moral outrage. This, too, has become common, especially during the most recent episode of farm depression in the early 1980s. Some people, after working hard all their lives and yet still losing their farms and small businesses, demanded and found a scapegoat. Leaders of groups called the Aryan Nations, Christian Identity, and Posse Comitatus told them that a conspiracy was afoot. Eastern (largely Jewish) banking interests—in league with the Internal Revenue Service, the Federal Reserve Board, and other agencies—coveted their land; the goal was one-world government and the enslavement of all white Christians. To most people this scenario was ludicrous, but it

echoed old regional fears, and zealots argued that the theory could explain much of the moral and economic decay of the times. Believers found
a martyr in 1983 in the person of Gordon Kahl, a North Dakota farmer
and fugitive tax evader.[24]

A proposal that envisions a huge national parkland on the Plains has
generated the most recent voicing of moral outrage. This plan, known as
the Buffalo Commons, was conceived rather innocently by two scholars
from Rutgers University. Frank and Deborah Popper noted the statistics
on severe population decline in many Plains counties, argued that planning for the ongoing abandonment process would make sense, and, in
1987, proposed the commons as a worthy goal. They published in a
standard academic journal, but their ideas immediately hit raw nerves
throughout the Plains. Newspapers, radio waves, and political speeches
have been laced with rebuttals ever since. "Never underestimate our grit"
is one standard response, followed by "we feed the world" and "fix your
own eastern slums before meddling in our lives." The issue has galva-
nized regional pride, but, significantly, no one challenges the basic facts
of a declining and aging population.[25]

THE SEARCH FOR A GENUINE IDENTITY

History demonstrates that nothing unites a people so easily as a common
enemy. From this perspective, the Plains have been blessed because, for
over a century now, railroad owners, Jewish bankers, Frank and Deborah
Popper, and other residents of the evil cities of the American East have
taken turns portraying their villain. Such constant attribution of local
troubles to an outside party is a dangerous game, though. Along with unity
comes repression of the true nature of a place and of the self-knowledge
essential to the correct conceptualization and effective resolution of regional problems.

Plains people still expend too much energy fulfilling and reacting to
the expectations of others. The groundswell of emotion unleashed by the
Buffalo Commons proposal, for example, is demonstration that paranoia
remains strong. All this notwithstanding, I am beginning to see signs of
change. For one thing, the negativity with which outsiders have labeled
the region has lessened markedly. Urban culture has proved itself far from
perfect in the United States; costs of living are high, neighborhoods un-
safe, and streets dirty. A man confuses heaven with Iowa in the movie

Field of Dreams, and some of this sentiment has begun to spread into the Plains. Many small towns report recent population gains from a combination of retirees coming home after urban careers and of others seeking safety, traditional values, and/or less expensive housing. Similarly, regional athletic teams are finding some of the same features help to lure prospects away from urban campuses to towns such as Manhattan, Kansas, and Laramie, Wyoming.

Evidence that Plains people are finally overcoming some of the negative legacies of the garden myth is strong as well. If one looks again at the striking figures on population decline prepared by the Poppers, for example, it is clear that the worst is now over in the heart of the Plains. Counties have stabilized, and usually now contain a single town and school district apiece; they are forming effective cooperative ventures with their neighbors for health care, special education, and similar issues. When I travel across northern Kansas, I see more signs of economic vitality in the far west (St. Francis, Atwood, and Oberlin) than I do in Plains-border communities where consolidation is still ongoing (Mankato, Belleville, Washington). Larger, true Plains cities such as Colby and Hays are similarly prosperous. This pattern is fast becoming the rule in the northern Plains.

My optimism that people in the Plains may be approaching a regional identity of their own has been bolstered by a series of locally initiated innovations. The cooperative arrangements successfully pioneered by education and health organizations, for example, have spread to churches. In 1992, when the pulpits of eight small Lutheran and Presbyterian congregations became vacant in Griggs County, North Dakota, the congregants came up with a plan to create a combined ministry. The four pastors who were hired like the arrangement because the teamwork reduces their individual isolation. The local churches survive, parishioners get to see a variety of ministerial styles, and everyone profits financially. Officials with the Evangelical Lutheran Church in America see this experiment as a "wonderful model" for the future.[26]

Another recent North Dakota cooperative arrangement involves industry. Tired of seeing profits from the processing of their durum wheat go to out-of-state companies, 1,000 farmers have raised a total of $12 million to build their own pasta plant in Carrington. The state-owned Bank of North Dakota, itself created during the older Nonpartisan League drive for increased local control of resources, is a second major investor in the plant.[27]

Beyond the cooperative ventures, the dream of attracting traditional industry that could take advantage of the low regional costs for land and labor and the low taxes also has been revived in North Dakota recently. Lawyers in Mott and Hettinger created the Dakota Management Corporation in 1993. Their idea was to search the nation's bankruptcy courts for small manufacturing companies that could perhaps be made profitable in a Plains setting. Local townspeople would supply the needed capital. In return, the companies would provide steady jobs. So far, the results have been mixed. A pilot plan to bring a manufacturer of safes to Edmund, South Dakota, was successful, but efforts to establish a vitamin manufacturer in Mott and a futon maker in Hettinger stalled because of inadequate local funding. Outside experts continue to term the concept "very creative," though, and the corporation is pressing ahead.[28]

The noted anthropologist John Bennett has argued that Plains culture is shaped by the realities of an economy based on resource extraction under marginal climatic and marketing conditions. Once Plains people accept this truth, and stop imagining their region to be more Edenic than it is or their troubles to be caused more by outside people than they are, they can begin to recognize and to celebrate their essence. Bennett suggests that individualistic attitudes are basic to the evolving system, with "an emphasis on physical strength, competence, and active performance, rather than on the use of words, sedentary skills, and manipulative capabilities."[29]

How can we measure whether or not Bennett has his finger on the regional pulse? The cooperative projects suggest that people have tempered the concept of individualism somewhat, but recent evidence from folklore and other studies supports Bennett's thesis overall. Folklore provides especially convincing testimony, for this set of materials and ideas is passed along only informally. Without a solid consensus of opinion, it cannot exist. Tom Isern, Roger Welsch, and other fieldworkers report that such consensus is strong in the northern Plains. The stories take many forms, but focus on the tall tale, that basic means of mitigating the hardships of life. During a recent drought, for example, farmers told about being mystified by the disappearance of their chore buckets until they discovered that raccoons had borrowed them to carry water to the sweet corn. Likewise, the farm crisis of the 1980s produced predictable gallows humor such as the following riddle: Did you hear about the new John Deere tractor with no seat and no steering wheel? (It's for the farmer who has lost his ass and doesn't know where to turn.)[30]

Tornado stories and what Isern calls folk monuments are among the most enduring grassroots statements of modern Plains culture. The former, frequently told and always rich in bizarre imagery, convey pride on the part of their tellers. Without histrionics, they say that we are a people able to cope and survive in a potentially dangerous environment. The latter genre is best represented by old grain separators placed on the crests of hills and by old boots stuck atop fence posts, sometimes forty in a row. Isern interprets these as "lectures to frivolous folk speeding by," true monuments to hard work.[31]

Finally, I am convinced that Plains people have begun to acknowledge and appreciate the aesthetics of their environment. Little research exists on this subject, but in quiet moments residents will sometimes talk about their love for the prairie and its big sky. If strangers are present, they may apologize a little about this because they realize that the Plains world lacks mountain ridges, seashores, and the other common cues for beauty. Their emotion is real, though, a response to the absence of things. Without "things," there is nothing for us to control, and egos begin to melt away. Some call the experience prairie zen.[32]

THE PLAINS IN PERSPECTIVE

Anyone who attempts a regional description encounters the somewhat opposed geographical principles that every place is unique and that everything depends on scale. Inevitably, much of what I write about the Plains will apply as well to the American West and even to larger regions. Just as inevitably, my words will not match the experience of all peoples and sections of the northern Plains. Proper exploration of either end of this equation is impossible here, but some consideration of context seems appropriate by way of conclusion.

The most obvious ties between the northern Plains and the greater West lie in the general time and conditions of settlement. Both were quite literally conquered in the latter half of the nineteenth century by a Euro-American society confident of its imperial power and moral right. Existing peoples were largely exterminated and the new landscapes manipulated and defaced to conform to the expectations of the invaders. Nature was essentially denied a voice.

Both the Plains and the larger West were projected as sources of wealth and then were endowed with myths to sustain these projections. The particulars were different, of course: traditional farming in the Plains versus the products of forest, mine, and irrigation ditch in the West; the yeoman-garden concept versus the idea of an eternally youthful land of general opportunity. The two places have shared a difficulty in escaping from their respective myths, however, a difficulty that has many ramifications. Clearly, it has impeded the development of rational policies toward the use of natural resources and has retarded the development of authentic senses of place.

If we change the focus to an intra-Plains comparison, the accuracy of my words is highest for rural, isolated, and Euro-American places. People in the string of urban areas from Topeka and Kansas City northward to Fargo and Grand Forks obviously operate in a different, more mainstream American, cultural system. Indeed, they spend part of their time actively dissociating themselves from images of Plains backwardness. The tourist-oriented Black Hills of South Dakota are also a world apart, but the various ranching islands set amid the Plains wheat field are not so distinctive culturally as their landscape would suggest.

If life in the cities differs from the Plains norm in being more like that in the rest of the country, life on the reservations of the Oglala Sioux and other Indians of the region differs from that norm in being vastly more isolated, dependent, and victimized. The nadir is Shannon County, South Dakota, site of the Pine Ridge Reservation, where 16,000 people faced an unemployment rate of 75 percent in 1995; Shannon is the poorest county in the United States. Problems became bad in the 1920s and 1930s when the local cattle-raising economy failed to recover from agricultural depression. Since then, because this and other major reservation sites were selected deliberately by federal officials for their isolation and limited natural resources, industrialization has been almost impossible. Attitudes of Euro-American neighbors, ranging between outright resentment toward the Indians and cautious avoidance of them, add to the difficulties, as does a quasi-socialistic tradition of local governance that hinders tribal efforts to adopt free-enterprise techniques.[33]

The sense of identity among the Sioux and other tribes of the region obviously is different from that found in the Plains as a whole, but it is still an issue of considerable uncertainty. Since most of these peoples have resided in the Plains environment for longer than their white neighbors and have never bought into the myth of the garden, they enjoy a comfortable relationship with their physical surroundings. Even more than the

Anglos, though, they must deal with the expectations of others. Caught between traditional values and the allure of the modern economy, yet somewhat removed from both worlds, Pine Ridge is in many ways the dilemma of the Plains intensified.

NOTES

1. "Kansas Ranks Last in Rating of Vacation Spots," *Lawrence* [Kansas] *Journal-World,* 16 October 1995, 3B.

2. Michael O. Roark, "Oklahoma Territory: Frontier Development, Migration, and Culture Areas" (Ph.D. diss., Syracuse University, 1979).

3. This work is cited in and summarized in John L. Allen, "The Garden–Desert Continuum: Competing Views of the Great Plains in the Nineteenth Century," *Great Plains Quarterly* 5 (1985): 207–20. Martyn Bowden's two major studies are "The Perception of the Western Interior of the United States, 1800–1870," *Proceedings of the Association of American Geographers* 1 (1969): 16–21, and "The Great American Desert and the American Frontier, 1800–1882," in *Anonymous Americans,* ed. Tamara K. Hareven (Englewood Cliffs, N.J.: Prentice-Hall, 1971), 48–79.

4. *National Intelligencer* (Alexandria, Va.), 11 October 1825, quoted in Allen, "Garden–Desert Continuum," 211.

5. Allen, "Garden–Desert Continuum," 214.

6. Horace Greeley, *An Overland Journey from New York to San Francisco in the Summer of 1859,* ed. C. T. Duncan (New York: Knopf, 1964), 253. See also Walter M. Kollmorgen, "The Woodsman's Assaults on the Domain of the Cattleman," *Annals of the Association of American Geographers* 59 (1969): 215–39.

7. David M. Emmons, "Constructed Province: History and the Making of the Last American West," *Western Historical Quarterly* 25 (1994): 437–59, quotation on 445.

8. Allen, "Garden–Desert Continuum," 215.

9. Emmons, "Constructed Province," 451.

10. Book Committee, *Stanton County, Kansas: 1887–1987* (n.p., 1987), 73–77.

11. William Allen White, *Forty Years on Main Street,* comp. Russell H. Fitzgibbon (New York: Farrar and Rinehart, 1937), 74.

12. Franklin Matthews, "Bright Skies in the West," *Harper's Weekly,* 12 February 1898, 163. See also James R. Shortridge, *The Middle West: Its Meaning in American Culture* (Lawrence: University Press of Kansas, 1989), 16–20.

13. Mary W. M. Hargreaves, *Dry Farming in the Northern Great Plains, 1900–1925* (Cambridge, Mass.: Harvard University Press, 1957).

14. Robert Morlan, *Political Prairie Fire: The Nonpartisan League,*

1915–1922 (Minneapolis: University of Minnesota Press, 1955); Kathleen Moum, "The Social Origins of the Nonpartisan League," *North Dakota History* 53 (Spring 1986): 18–22; William C. Pratt, "Socialism on the Northern Plains, 1900–1924," *South Dakota History* 18 (1988): 1–35.

15. Willa Cather, *Not Under Forty* (New York: Knopf, 1936), v.

16. Willa Cather, *A Lost Lady* (New York: Knopf, 1923), 106–7.

17. Mark W. T. Harvey, "North Dakota, the Northern Plains, and the Missouri Valley Authority," *North Dakota History* 59 (Summer 1992): 28–39.

18. Ibid., 38; Priya A. Kurian and Robert V. Bartlett, "The Garrison Diversion Dream and the Politics of Landscape Engineering," *North Dakota History* 59 (Summer 1992): 40–51; John Farrell, "Developing the Missouri: South Dakota and the Pick–Sloan Plan," *South Dakota History* 19 (1989): 306–41.

19. Kathleen Norris, "Gatsby on the Plains: The Small-Town Death Wish," *North Dakota Quarterly* 53 (Fall 1985): 44–54; G. Keith Gunderson, "Letter: A Reply to 'Gatsby on the Plains,'" *North Dakota Quarterly* 53 (Fall 1985): 55–61. Norris has expanded her thoughts in *Dakota: A Spiritual Geography* (Boston: Houghton Mifflin, 1994).

20. Elwyn B. Robinson, "The Themes of North Dakota History," *North Dakota History* 26 (Winter 1959): 5–24. A personal case history of McDonald, in extreme northwestern Kansas, is James R. Dickenson, *Home on the Range: A Century on the High Plains* (New York: Scribner, 1995).

21. Eric Sevareid, *Not So Wild a Dream* (New York: Knopf, 1946), 5.

22. Erskine Caldwell, *Afternoons in Mid-America* (New York: Dodd, Mead, 1976), 143. Good surveys of regional imagery include Wynona H. Wilkins, "The Idea of North Dakota," *North Dakota Quarterly* 39 (1971): 5–28; Robert S. Bader, *Hayseeds, Moralizers, and Methodists: The Twentieth-Century Image of Kansas* (Lawrence: University Press of Kansas, 1988); and Ann Rathke, "The Image of North Dakota in Recent American Travel Literature," *North Dakota Quarterly* 56 (1988): 86–98.

23. Peter Gould and Rodney White, *Mental Maps* (Baltimore: Penguin, 1974), 93–118.

24. James Corcoran, *Bitter Harvest: Gordon Kahl and the Posse Comitatus: Murder in the Heartland* (New York: Viking, 1990).

25. Anne Matthews provides the best overview of reaction to the Buffalo Commons idea in *Where the Buffalo Roam: The Storm over the Revolutionary Plan to Restore America's Great Plains* (New York: Grove Weidenfeld, 1992). The original paper by Frank and Deborah Popper is "The Great Plains: From Dust to Dust, a Daring Proposal for Dealing with an Inevitable Disaster," *Planning* 53 (1987): 12–18. For more recent reflections, see their "The Great Plains: Checkered Past, Hopeful Future," *Forum for Applied Research and Public Policy* 9 (Winter 1994): 89–100.

26. Gustav Niebuhr, "In Isolated U.S. Churches, Innovative Plans Fill Pulpits," *New York Times*, 12 March 1995, sec. 1, 1, 15.

27. Bob Moen, "Pasta Plant Just Another Calculated Risk for Farmers," *Lawrence* [Kansas] *Journal-World,* 16 August 1992, 8D.

28. Barnaby J. Feder, "Building Up from Ground Zero," *New York Times,* 15 January 1995, sec. 3, 1, 6.

29. John W. Bennett, "Range Culture and Society in the North American West," in *Folklife Annual, 1985,* ed. Alan Jabbour and James Hardin (Washington, D.C.: American Folklife Center, 1985), 89.

30. Thomas D. Isern, "The Folklore of Farming in the North American Plains," *North Dakota History* 56 (1989): 31–36; Isern, "How to Kill a Chinch Bug: The Folk Technology of Farming on the North American Plains," *Journal of the West* 31 October (1992): 45–50; Roger Welsch, "Reflections on Plains Folklore," *North Dakota History* 56 Fall (1989): 59; Welsch, *It's Not the End of the Earth, but You Can See It from Here: Tales of the Great Plains* (New York: Villard Books, 1990). The raccoon story is in Welsch, "Reflections," 6; the John Deere one in Isern, "Folklore of Farming," 34.

31. Larry Danielson, "Tornado Stories in the Breadbasket: Weather and Regional Identity," in *Sense of Place: American Regional Cultures,* ed. Barbara Allen and Thomas J. Schlereth (Lexington: University Press of Kentucky, 1990), 28–39; Isern, "Folklore of Farming," 36.

32. Neil Evernden, "Beauty and Nothingness: Prairie as Failed Resource," *Landscape* 27, no. 3 (1983): 1–8; Cary de Wit, "Sense of Place on the Kansas High Plains" (M.A. thesis, University of Kansas, 1992).

33. Richmond L. Clow, "Tribal Populations in Transition: Sioux Reservations and Federal Policy, 1934–1965," *South Dakota History* 19 (1989): 362–91; *New York Times,* 20 September 1992, Peter T. Kilborn, "Sad Distribution for the Sioux: Homeland is No. 1 in Poverty," sec. 1, 1, 14; *New York Times,* 15 October 1995, James Brooke, "In the Budget Talk from Washington, Indians See the Cruelest Cuts of All," sec. 1, 10.

Part Two:

AESTHETIC WESTS

The three chapters in this part examine the role of creative expression in forging regional identity. The three authors emphasize the aesthetic over the concrete and materialistic and, on occasion—as in Bret Wallach's precise treatment of southern Plains architecture—render the concrete and materialistic aesthetic.

In "The Telltale Southern Plains," Wallach begins with an account of how the understated architecture of the southern Plains reflects regional sensibilities. There is a certain honesty about the place and its utilitarian architectural forms that Wallach finds straightforward, decidedly "unfaddish," and acutely unpretentious. Contemporary houses, he tells us, are glitzier, infinitely less practical, and more expensive, and seem remarkably out of place in a simple, honest environment. With the vernacular architecture of the region outlined in detail and elevated to a level of respectability, even enviability, Wallach proceeds to tell the stories of some of those who lived in these houses, such as Lucile Searcy and Jean Sugden, who built one and occupied it for four decades together—

Lucile remained there into a fifth decade. Their unpretentious lives in that unpretentious house constitute for Wallach an object lesson in "life . . . lived as it must be, not as people would like to live it." Such simple, yet fascinating stories capture the quintessential essence of southern Plains regional identity.

By way of contrast with Wallach, Mary Murphy and Peter Boag focus on the stories of individuals who gained greater notoriety. In "Searching for an Angle of Repose," Murphy moves away from, or beyond, the "last best place" theme, which has characterized much of the writing on and imagery relating to Montana. She focuses instead on the lives of three women: rodeo rider Fanny Sperry Steele, novelist Mourning Dove, and poet Gwendolen Haste, all of whom searched for an "angle of repose"—a balanced sense of place—in Montana. Although only Sperry was a native of the place, all three were profoundly affected by Montana's "diverse landscapes."

The achievements of Fanny Sperry, who in 1912 became "Ladies' Bucking Horse Champion of the World," should do much to qualify the quintessentially male imagery—centering on the Anglo cowboy beneath the big sky—that supposedly speaks volumes about Montana regional identity. And the Montana myth is further qualified by the story of the mixed-blood writer Mourning Dove, who addressed her divided consciousness—between Indian and white cultures—in her work. Mourning Dove tried to find her angle of repose by straddling those two cultures, but early-twentieth-century Montana was not receptive to such efforts; she died in 1936, the victim of spousal abuse. Gwendolen Haste, too, tried to reconcile various cultures—the rural and urban, and the male and female. She helped her father edit the *Scientific Farmer,* but provided a fuller testimony to her uneasy sense of place in her poems about women's lives in Montana. All three women, in their efforts to secure an angle of repose, spoke volumes about the complexities and the inequities that are a part of the story of Montana identity. By emphasizing their search and their stories, Murphy helps us see through the traditional "master narrative of Montana."

In "Mountain, Plain, Desert, River," Boag examines the Snake River Plain, viewing it as a significant physical crossroads between three major western physiographic regions: the Pacific Northwest, the Great Basin, and the Rocky Mountains. Given this, his analysis can be considered not just in relation to Wallach's and Murphy's chapters, but also in connection with those by Findlay, Raymond, and Hyde in the section "Environment and Economy." While drawing its identity from all three of the major subregions that are its physiographic neighbors, the Snake River Plain, Boag contends, is "a distinctive physical space," even if a "distinct regional consciousness has not yet fully emerged there." Nonetheless, he points out that residents of the region do have a sense of place related to landscape, and it has been nurtured in the regional literature about that landscape. Focusing on the works of Washington Irving, Mary Hallock Foote, and Vardis Fisher, Boag demonstrates how the three are linked by "their common equivocation toward the varied Snake region landscapes."

Wallach, Murphy, and Boag write about western places that some might argue are not full-fledged regions. Murphy focuses on a state, though a particularly large one in terms of acreage. Wallach's conception of the southern Plains encompasses only Oklahoma and the Texas panhandle. Boag's Snake River Plain is similarly small—approximately 400 miles long, from east to west, and 60 miles wide. But taken together, the chapters raise the issue of state boundaries and distinct landscapes as regional identifiers. They also testify to the importance of stories as forgers and illuminators of regional consciousness. The aesthetic West of artists and writers is often reckoned to be a colorful, grandiose, romantic, and mythic place. And while those elements certainly exist in some of the stories in this part, the variety of stories told here—some heartrending, some harrowing, some uplifting, some simple, some complex, some by literary giants, others by literary nobodies—together enlarge our conception of the "Aesthetic West."

The Telltale Southern Plains

Bret Wallach

My wife and I were sitting in the dining room of an old friend. This was out on the west coast, and Margaret had just finished building a spectacular house, with huge windows that overlooked a precipitous, fir-covered slope and distant islands set in blue ocean waters. Somehow the conversation turned to the Great Plains, where Margaret had been born and had lived until her marriage some forty years earlier. And she mentioned with a laugh that the first time she came west to meet her mother-in-law, the woman told her, in a characteristically no-nonsense way, that the only reason people lived on the Plains was that they didn't know better.

It's not true, of course. There are plenty of people living on the Great Plains who "know better," but who stay put on that grassy apron of the Rockies. Still, Margaret's mother-in-law wasn't really wrong: most of the people on the Plains would indeed leave if they knew where to go and how to survive once they got there. It's common knowledge—and common utterance, except among people staring into cameras or speaking into microphones. Indeed, it's a national truism that can be traced back to and actually past the 1930s, with their archetypal photographs of migrants on Route 66. It's a judgment rooted in the grim history of the American Indians; on the southern Plains, it's a judgment based on the additional misery of homesteaders coming from mostly poor, southern roots and quickly dispossessed of their homesteads and degraded into sharecropping tenants.

Recovering from such abuse is slow, and today, sixty years after the dust bowl, supermarkets on the Plains just don't have the variety found in markets on the coasts. But there's a superabundance of religiosity, at least south of Kansas and its well-tempered Methodists. A recent addition is the Cross of the High Plains, just east of Amarillo, Texas, on Interstate 40. Two hundred feet tall in its corrugated-aluminum majesty, the surreal cross fits nicely with communities where dogs bark all night and where few people would think of asking for quiet. Sidewalks are scarce, and the older ones are pretty thoroughly broken up now by tree roots. The trees themselves are dying of old age, and town councils aren't replanting them; after all, government doesn't know how to spend money wisely. Downtowns are dying: brick blocks abandoned store by store—even the few that, in a last gasp of commercial optimism, were sided with blue aluminum in the duplicitous 1950s.

Then there's the physical environment. On the High Plains proper (a remnant of the Tertiary period that stretches from Nebraska's Pine Bluff Escarpment south to about Midland, Texas), you can rarely see as far as a mile: the land is simply too flat for vistas. Instead, there is an uncomfortable illusion that you're sitting in the center of a shallow plate that has been elevated into the sky. Blue the sky may be, but it sits right down on you and can feel psychologically uncomfortable, compressing.

Most of the Great Plains aren't so "planed," and even with local relief of 100 feet or so they offer tremendous vistas from one rolling summit to the next. Still, it's hard for normal human beings to make peace with the wind. It blows unobstructed from the north in winter and the south in summer; the northern Plains have their blizzards, while the southern Plains have their famous tornadoes—hundreds each year—combined with desiccating summer winds that need only a few seasons to reduce painted surfaces to a sea of flakes.

No wonder Margaret eventually came to agree with her mother-in-law; she has no interest in the Great Plains any longer. Still, dark clouds and booming thunder outside my Oklahoma window this warm August morning seem to say that I should speak honestly, and in that honesty I think lies the greatest virtue and the best defense of the Great Plains. (Lightning just flashed outside the window, an approving and vaguely threatening exclamation point: damned right, it seemed to say.) Perhaps honesty may not redeem the Plains, but how much I prefer our plainness, barren as it often seems, to the cock-of-the-walk, flavor-of-the-week, opulent, bragging, condescending coasts.

What exactly is this honesty? It's certainly not anything people here say or espouse, for in such matters there is as much hypocrisy here as anywhere. Rather, it's in the things people make—plain things, severe things. These things are icons: windmills, section-line roads, grain elevators, most of all the common frame houses that sit by the dozens and hundreds in towns and smaller cities, particularly in the southern Plains. Here houses are smaller, both because winters are shorter and because settlement came later and usually involved people who were closer to dirt-poor. Such houses can be found outside the southern Plains, but the natural understatedness of the Plains frames them best, distracts from them least. On the Plains, these houses speak and are heard.

The footprint of the house is an inviolate rectangle. Typically, it might measure twenty-six by thirty-nine feet. (It sounds awfully arbitrary, but those are the measurements of one house that I happened to measure; perhaps the numbers arise from some multiple of joists or rafters.) The house rises from that footprint as a simple box under an equally simple pitched roof, two planes broken only by two brick chimneys and some plumbing standpipes. The roof as built was of cedar shingles; but fifty southern Plains summers destroy even the best cedar shingles, and today the roof is almost always of asbestos shingles, though the cedar may still be there, underneath.

The walls were originally wrapped in clapboards, sometimes narrow, sometimes broad. Invariably, they were painted a puritanical white, a punishing color in bright sun. Today the paint is almost always flaking, unless it's been masked by plastic siding that was stapled on in a couple of days and is always a nurse-uniform white. The windows, usually mounted in pairs, are double hung. The upper sash is probably painted stuck, and even the lower one no longer opens very easily—the counter-weight ropes frayed years ago. Aluminum storm windows have probably been added sometime in the past twenty or thirty years; I think of them and think of nails scratched on a blackboard.

The house can sit equally well with the ridgepole either parallel to or perpendicular to the street, but the perpendicular form is probably com-moner, perhaps because the house requires less frontage that way. (Cost is always a factor: a house like this, land aside, cost about $4,000 in the mid-1930s. That was a good year's wage.) Whatever the reason, a pass-erby usually gets a temple façade minus the columns, unless you count the two posts that hold up the front porch. The porch is obligatory. It must be big enough for two large chairs, and it has to have at least a couple of steps down to the ground. It can be mounted along the long wall of the house, if that's the way the house sits; sometimes it's even cut into a corner of the house, with the front door recessed in the cutout square. In any case, there shall be a porch. Many a southern Plains child has been given strict orders never to crawl underneath it for fear of rattlesnakes and scorpions and brown-recluse spiders.

Perhaps the house has 800 or 900 square feet of living space. It's di-vided into four rooms: a living room and kitchen on one side and two bedrooms separated by a bath on the other. (The garage is a separate structure. It's the house in miniature, and it's set back at the end of a long driveway. Often as not, nobody parks in it, and it's used for storage.)

Come into the living room, and you see a hardwood floor: pine in the budget version, oak in the upscale one. The walls are lath-and-plaster, much cracked and probably covered now with many layers of paper. Per-haps there's a picture rail—a nice touch. Certainly there are ceiling-light fixtures. Still, to modern taste the room seems small and dark, an effect compounded by the dark wood of the varnished pine doors and by the window-unit air conditioner, which takes up precious window space. (There's too much humidity here for evaporative coolers to be effective, at least until you climb onto the High Plains.)

The kitchen has a hardwood floor, too, but it always has been covered with battleship linoleum. There's an unspoiled wooden countertop, how-ever, and there are solid wooden cupboards and drawers, too—no Formica anywhere in sight. There's a water heater next to the kitchen chimney, which was once connected to a coal stove, now removed. There's an elec-tric or a gas stove now and, somewhere, a refrigerator. Where? Out the kitchen door, where a back porch has been enclosed to make a utility room. There's the refrigerator, along with a washer and a drier.

The other plumbed room, of course, is the bathroom. It, too, has a hardwood floor covered with linoleum. It has what plumbers here call a stool; it also has a wall-mounted sink fitted with two separate taps. The tub has a mixing valve but no shower, and it sits under a single, small, double-hung window.

What else? Not much. There is no basement, only a crawl space entered through a tiny hole in the brick wall of the foundation. Inside is an orchard: three rows of short brick piers about two feet high. They hold up a central beam and, on either side of it, two less massive ones, all in parallel and all running the thirty-nine feet of the house's main axis. Wooden wedges have been tapped between the piers and the beams to get the beams level; joists, still fragrant after sixty years, have then been laid across the beams long wall to long wall. The floor of the crawl space is hard dirt, with a scattering of old nails. Despite the simplicity of the construction, there's a chaos of pipes—hot, cold, and drain.

Up above, the house has an attic, but it's entered with some difficulty through a trapdoor in a bedroom closet. There's nothing in it, not even floorboards, so to inspect the rafters you must walk carefully joist to joist. The rafters often protrude outside; only in the upscale version of the house have carpenters hidden the rafter ends behind soffits.

The lot isn't fenced, and very few homeowners pay any attention to the garden. Something grows: nature's that way. But landscaping generally extends to wreaking periodic vengeance on whatever comes up. Landscaping, in fact, is close to proof that the owner wasn't born here.

Now I am afraid that I am likely to be misunderstood at this point. What I want to say, simply, is that I like these houses—and I fear that readers will think that I am being sarcastic. I am not. I don't say that I like scrofulous lawns. I don't like flaked paint, and I like plastic siding even less. I don't like the detritus that accumulates inside these houses— you can see it on display at the garage and estate sales that constitute a major regional industry—and I despair at the *Reader's Digest* condensed novels from whose cumulative mass in this part of the world one could, I am sure, build pyramids, great walls, and whatever other imperial works struck one's fancy. I don't like any of this, I say, but I like the houses. I don't say they're beautiful; I don't say they're works of high craftsmanship. I say only that they're honest, that honesty is a prerequisite to beauty, and that in a cultural landscape wanton in its devotion to falseness, you take what you can get. I say that in a nation whose cultural landscape overflows with pretension, it's reassuring to find structures—lots of structures, towns full of them—that aren't trying to fool anybody.

Perhaps a comparison will help. And, unfortunately, I don't have to go to southern California or even Texas to find one. I think simply of the houses that Oklahomans began to build after World War II. The ranch house came first: a national style, of course, rectangular but always long side to the street, framed but always faced in brick, big but always half-garage. The claim, in short, was one of stately affluence—but it was only a claim, buttressed by the hypocrisy of looking bigger than you were, more substantial than you were.

Even better, I think of the houses being built today. Here's one: the "Cambridge II Model Home," offered by a developer in Norman, Oklahoma. The name "Cambridge" is wonderful; it has a clear edge over two nearby competitive models: the meaningless "Kingsbury" and the grotty "Yorkshire." It's good to know, I think, that there are peerages for sale. After all, the builder's literature carries the name Cambridge in a heavy wedding-text font: Isn't that the typeface used on the cover of Debrett's? It's disturbing at first to see on the next page a sketch of two boys fishing from a pier. You see it, too, don't you? Straw hats, torn pants cut just below the knee, bare feet, tousled hair: it's Tom Sawyer and his friend Huck. The caption reads, "the kind of neighborhood that builds childhood memories." But after a while, it grows on you. I definitely like it. Sure, the juxtaposition of democracy and aristocracy seems a bit forced, but you have to defer to the judgment of the builder, who must have learned from experience that people think they can combine Oxbridge and Hannibal "just one mile west of *Sooner Fashion Mall.*"

The Cambridge house costs about $190,000. It contains some 3,000 square feet, though several hundred lie in what is here termed a "bonus room." I do not know the provenance or the domain of bonus rooms, and on the assumption that my readers are equally benighted I shall explain that in this part of the country and in the past twenty years or so, every house of any pretension has had a "Dallas roof," which is to say a great heaped up windowless attic. Strictly, I suppose, this roof is derived from the old pyramidal roof characteristic of the South, but the Dallas roof is also broken up into as many planes as possible. I do not think this is an elegant allusion to Cubism—more likely it's an echo of Benjamin Disraeli's baronial pile. In any event, the Dallas roof might also be called the Roofer's Revenge, for homeowners must reshingle with alarming frequency. After all, wood shingles are a common subdivision covenant here, expressive of the community's refined tastes. And do you see the bonus room yet? It is the windowless space created in this attic, around whose central portion some wallboard has been thrown up.

Earnest women tell me that bonus rooms make wonderful play spaces for children, and I can see it. But I still feel cheated. The stairs up—from the dining area as it happens—have a handrail (balustrade, I mean) that, according to the literature, is "handrubbed" with walnut stain. I believe we are now in the vicinity of rich budgetwood, but I can handle that, and you probably can too. Still, I resent being led—misled, it turns out—to expect something more up those stairs than a windowless shoebox. After all, when we came in we noticed the "Beautiful Brass Carriage Light Fixtures on Each Side of Garage Door." And in the living room (living area, I mean—sorry), we loved the "Handcrafted Oak or Ash Front Door with Leaded Glass." There was the "Dazzling Display of Natural Light from Sloped 10ft. Ceilings" and the "Elegant Divided Light Window Wall." The quality features just went on and on: remember the designer kitchen, with its wine rack and its many glued-on lengths of elegant pilasters? Even the driveway demonstrated impeccably good taste, for its concrete had been molded into genuine simulated cobblestones. I don't know about you, but I think I'm ready to talk about financing.[1]

So, the southern Plains have come a long way in the past fifty years along that path blazed by the treacherous, culture-commanding coasts. But having acknowledged this triumph of deceit, I want to return to the older houses and to the inner honesty of the lives lived in them.

I'd like you to meet Martha Lucile Searcy, born in 1898 in Wartrace, a hamlet east of Shelbyville, Tennessee, but coming as a young girl with her parents to Elk City, Oklahoma Territory. Lucile was an only child, and perhaps that made it easier for her parents to help her along. Like a surprising number of poor children of that generation, she got to Southwestern State College in Weatherford, Oklahoma, which these days is a bit over an hour's drive west of Oklahoma City. She went on to graduate from the University of Oklahoma at Norman, where in 1930 she received a master's in English. I look at her thesis and marvel at the tone of the opening sentence. She writes: "Knowing fully the 'poor psychology' of beginning anything with an apology, I yet feel it not beyond the province of a thesis to offer some explanation of a title as possibly vague as 'Problems in the Text of King Lear.'" A sentence like this makes me realize that we really have very little idea about the kind of people who settled Oklahoma—and that what we do know, or think we know, is probably inaccurate.

By 1930, Lucile Searcy had almost certainly met Jean Sugden, another graduate student in the University of Oklahoma English department. Sugden came from a big family in Weatherford, where she had already earned an undergraduate degree. In 1931, she would finish her master's at Norman, with a thesis on old English ballads, as revised by one Bishop Percy.

Lucile Searcy was taken on by the English department as an instructor; in 1936, Jean Sugden was offered a similar appointment. The two women had ambitions, and in 1936 they published a book with Macmillan. *Foundation English* went through fifteen printings and did well; years later, Searcy recalled that the book "bought our first Chevrolet." By 1937, with the book out and with both women appointed to the university staff, Searcy and Sugden felt settled enough to build a house. One of them, I am not sure which, had inherited a lot with about seventy-five feet of frontage on Pickard Avenue, which runs north–south in Norman five blocks west of campus. Pickard Avenue at the time was the edge of town: to the west lay Imhoff Creek, a tributary of the Canadian River; beyond the creek were cotton farms that would stay intact until after World War II.

The house Searcy and Sugden built, of course, was just the sort I've described. Because the lot was wider than usual, however, and because the house was oriented with the gable toward the street, it sat surrounded by yard. And Searcy and Sugden were a departure from the norm when it came to gardening. They planted an elm on the south side of the front yard, to cast summer-afternoon shade over the house. They planted two sycamores north of the house and on the far side of the driveway to the garage. They planted a sweetgum out back. They planted a sour cherry on the south side of the house—sweet cherries had not yet been bred to stand the winters here. They fenced the lot with square-weave wire, and then planted a heady combination of honeysuckle and dawn roses along the fence line. Closer to the house, they planted pheasant's-eye narcissus along the south foundation wall and a large deutzia at the northwest corner. They planted lilacs square in the middle of the backyard and deep-purple iris against the garage. Against the back fence they put in a separately fenced vegetable garden, with a chicken coop under the shade of the sweetgum. As for lawn, they relied on the old local standby, Bermuda grass, which is well suited to the climate, though it goes to straw both in winter and in dry summers. The driveway remained gravel, and, of course there were no underground sprinklers.

Searcy would later write that "our house, a four-roomed frame house, was built in the spring of 1937, and we moved in in June." The two women, who were Bundesbankers on the subject of debt, nonetheless spent whatever money was needed to keep the house in perfect shape. Eventually, they decided to quit painting and cover the clapboard with a gloomy gray asbestos siding, but the paint on the clapboard under that siding was tight. The house was cold, too, because the women refused to install gas—told everybody that they had once been hauled unconscious from a gas-heated house. Instead, they had fiberglass batts stuffed between the floor and ceiling joists, the floor ones neatly kept in place by a screen of chickenwire. They continued to heat with coal—neat scoops and buckets were kept next to the two cast-iron stoves—but they also installed electric baseboard heating.

Despite their book, Searcy and Sugden remained instructors, and their teaching loads were heavy, with four courses each term. The university class schedule for the fall of 1939 shows each of them with fourteen hours of class a week: both women taught a section of "Grammar and Composition," two sections of the first semester of "Principles of English Composition," and one section of either "English Usage" or the second semester of the principles course.[2] It seems clear that they were teaching the courses that the senior faculty didn't want to teach, and it is probably true that they would have taught them forever. Perhaps it was with some bitterness, therefore, that both women resigned in 1944 to take positions as teachers at Norman High School. Sugden switched to mathematics, but Searcy stayed with English. Both women continued on at Norman High until their retirements in 1968. They never married, and they never moved.

McKinley Elementary school stood—and still stands—half a block north of their house, and a neighbor told me a couple of years ago that when he was a boy enrolled there Searcy and Sugden always had him come over after school for cookies and tutoring. The place always smelled of baking, he says. Other neighbors remember the two women—especially Searcy—as crotchety and fiercely independent. She would poison stray cats, these people recall. Once, it seems, she shot a paperboy with buck-shot. There was family trouble, too: one of Sugden's sisters later wrote that "because of a personality conflict with her 'house-mate,' Lucile Searcy, none of the Sugdens have been permitted to have a close rela-tionship with Jean for several years." The hostility must have run deep, for the two women originally drew up matching wills in which their com-bined estate was willed to a nephew of Sugden's, Lawrence Dan Schreiner. The will was changed in 1980, and Schreiner was given nothing; instead, everything was given to the McFarlin Methodist Church of Norman. The estate—which eventually amounted to about $130,000, split evenly be-tween the house and other assets—came with instructions that it was to be used for University of Oklahoma scholarships to aid nonminority stu-dents. "Bigotry," I said to myself when I first learned this; now I'm in-clined to see it as evidence of Searcy's independence.

In retirement during the 1970s, Searcy developed severe arthritis; Sugden was incapacitated with Parkinson's disease. Searcy nursed her, writing to a friend, "I spend more hours on my feet and 'on duty' than I did when I was in my twenties and teaching one hundred students a day." Eventually it became too much, and Sugden was taken to Rosewood Manor Living Center. (I wonder what a time the two women might have had in a class with that name.) Searcy stayed behind in the house, alone. In a letter to a friend, she wrote, "I did not choose growing old in this fashion." She seems to have feared senility, though people who knew her say she was fine. Perhaps she was angry at the thought of being humored. "I think people meet senility as they must," she insisted, "not as they would like to." Certainly, she remained as difficult as ever. "Truly there are al-ways two sides to a quarrel," she wrote to a neighbor who had stormed out, slamming the door and determined never to help her again, "and you did try to boss me terribly. My time is short, my strength so scant." Another neighbor—also a retired schoolteacher—recalls going to the store for Searcy on August 15, 1982. That was the day Searcy died—right there in the front bedroom, the woman told me.

Lucile Searcy was buried next to her parents, in the Roselawn Ceme-tery in Elk City. You can go out there now and see the parents' shared stone. Next to it, laid flat in the turf, is a small rose-granite slab that says only "Martha Lucile Searcy, 1898–1982." Next to it, a perfect twin, is a stone that reads "Jean Louise Sugden, 1903–1983."

The Searcy and Sugden house stood empty for two years after Searcy's death. Then, in May 1984, after the estates of both women had been probated, the house was sold; it went in a flash, with the realtor getting an offer the same day his sign went up. There was an estate sale. The newspaper ad promised "over 40 years accumulation" and listed eight rocking chairs, a pie safe, oak library tables, and cedar chests. There were hand-made quilts and plenty of hand-sewn clothes, too—none of the fabrics synthetic. The old coal stoves were there, and garden tools. The new owners, who were from the Pacific Northwest, bought as much as they could; the rest flew away. Then, over the next few years, the new owners stripped the flowered wallpaper and sanded the floors—all the floors, even the ones that had been covered with linoleum. The old water heater and refrigerator and stove stayed. Why not? They had lasted for thirty years, would last for another thirty—and had a degree of character. The garage became a studio, complete with a skylight. Nothing could be done with the asbestos-tile siding—not unless the owners wanted to replace it or go back to painting—but the house was brightened by painting the eaves and window frames a color like brick; although it was heretical at first, a few people around town picked up the hint and adopted the same color, which comes close to matching the Permian sandstone that underlies this part of Oklahoma. The new owners worked hard on the garden, leaving the trees but adding thickets of flowers and gradually replacing the Bermuda grass with lush if thirsty fescue. Perhaps it was a foolish choice, but there was now too much shade for Bermuda.

So there it is: Lucile Searcy and her house—unprepossessing, militantly plain, modest, competent, without affectation; two lessons, one in the flesh, the other in a house, and both saying that life is lived as it must be, not as people would like to live it. I compare that with a hypermarket I saw on the west coast; a neon sign over the doorway said, "Enter the Excitement," and I think that the hard part in all this is that the honesty of the southern Plains expresses a truth that we don't want to hear. We prefer the sensuous lies of goat-cheese toastlets in west coast fern bars.

And what, again, is this truth of which the lightning tells me to speak? It's just what Lucile Searcy said: recognizing what life is, rather than believing in some illusion.[3]

I go out along the abandoned stretches of old U.S. 66, see the square blocks of concrete with tar expansion joints, and recall those old black-and-white photographs of men and women leaning against old, loaded-down cars. I can show you places in the southern Plains today that have a grimness to match those photos. Sometime when you're passing through and are in no hurry (but when is that?), I'll show you Bridgeport. You'll have to know where it is, since the engineers who designed Interstate 40 didn't even give it a sign. Still, take the "Exit 99" off-ramp and head to the water tower you see a mile to the north. That's Bridgeport's only land-mark. It was erected, as the builder's plate says, by the Chicago Bridge and Iron Company in 1903. Once there was a bridge across the Cana-dian River here—hence the town and its name. But U.S. 66 bypassed Bridgeport; so did Interstate 40. Now there's nothing left except maybe fifty houses, occupied but in disrepair. Bridgeport has no commercial establishments, no post office, not even a bridge—just that water tower as a reminder of ambition defeated.

Or I run a few miles south to Anadarko. You recall the government's deciding that the best way to help Oklahoma's Indians was to assimilate them and that the best way to assimilate them was to take their reserva-tions, cut them up into homestead-size parcels, allot those parcels to tribal members, and then open the rest of the reservations to settlement by whites. Most of western Oklahoma was thus parceled out. But the Chey-enne and Arapaho near Bridgeport—like the Comanche, Kiowa, and Apache just to the south—weren't interested in farming. So they leased their allotments to whites and after a while quit even living on the land.

Many went to Anadarko, which became and remains a ghetto. Bad enough that they are desperately poor; drive through Anadarko, and you'll see that the local theater is named the Redskin, yes indeed—and its marquee has a war bonnet in 1950s-style neon. Go a mile north of town to see the regional headquarters of the Bureau of Indian Affairs. You'll have to hunt, I'm afraid, even though the building is big enough to house the Strategic Air Command. It's all one story, with massive prefabricated concrete walls, tiny slit windows like loopholes, and not a sign on the place. Sure, there is a nearby concrete wall with the lonely letters "BIA," but they sit there looking as though they hope nobody sees them. It's the most invisible federal presence I've ever seen.

You can understand, of course, why the BIA lies low. I once visited the Army War College in Carlisle, Pennsylvania. You can see there the careful plaques commemorating the time a century ago when the college was the Carlisle Indian Industrial School. Indian children didn't volun-teer to go there, of course; they were rounded up. There's a cemetery on the base; it has tombstones labeled with every Indian tribe you can think of. And there's a fine old building that makes nice barracks for officers today, but that was once the girls' dormitory. A sign on the wall tells you that much, but it doesn't quite tell the whole story; it sure doesn't say anything about the girls uprooted and confined here a century ago to learn how to use chairs and spoons and all those things that did not exist when, years later, they returned to their parents.

Down along Cache Creek, south of Lawton, there's an old man living in an original allotment house with walls covered with photographs of his ancestors dressed in buckskin and feathers. He has an old war bow, and he knows stories about places like Rainy Mountain and the great Medicine Bluff cliffs on the grounds of Fort Sill, near Lawton. You can see the cliffs yourself, if you're interested. The Fort Sill authorities are proud of their ecology program. You just can't climb them: they're "off limits."

The Plains don't let you kid yourself; they give it to you straight.

A while ago, I was talking with a successful third-generation wheat farmer who lives a few miles north of Bridgeport. Mike's about fifty, tall, husky, carrying more of a gut than he'd probably like. He drives a big diesel Suburban with a cellular phone, and no doubt he could buy me six times over. He's got a sense of humor that sneaks up on you, except when he's talking about taxes.

Mike owns about 2,000 acres of choice land, mostly upland but some North Canadian bottomland. On it he grows about 1,600 acres of wheat, which he sells, and a few hundred acres of alfalfa, which he sells or feeds to a couple of hundred head of cattle he owns. His grandfather, Jacob, came from Ohio in 1900 and settled on the same eighty acres on which Mike's house and farm buildings stand. For that land, Jacob paid $6,000— astronomical, but the land was good and the years were optimistic. Jacob survived World War I, though he came out of it with a new, non-Germanic name. He didn't fare so well in the Depression, and quit farming in the early 1930s—sold the place to his son Clarence and moved for good to McAllen, Texas.

Clarence hung on, and eventually he thrived. In 1933 he had the brains to build a 30,000–bushel grain storehouse in which he could hold a crop when prices were bad. His real opportunity to profit from this strategy came after World War II. Clarence's neighbors began to disappear, one by one, while he bought their land and expanded his holdings to about 1,000 acres. In 1948 Clarence built a new house—nothing fancy, and Mike's place today—and he got rid of Jacob's house, which was sold, cut down, put on a truck, and hauled to the nearby town of Geary. It's still occupied.

Michael bought the farm from Clarence in the late 1960s, and Clarence followed his own father, Jacob, to retirement in McAllen. Since then, Clarence has come up now and then to visit. Mike has meanwhile doubled his father's on-farm grain store. (I asked him about mice in that old wooden structure. He smiled and said that's why he had cats.) Mike's own secret for success is that he not only stores his grain, but bypasses the local grain merchants altogether and trucks his crop all the way down to the Gulf. I was flabbergasted; surely, I said, the transportation cost killed him. "Nope," he replied. Trucking his grain cost him 55 cents a bushel, 7 cents more than shipping by rail. And the advantages of timely sale more than compensated for that extra cost.

Mike was a gambler through and through, and he admitted it. When I saw him, wheat was selling for over $5 a bushel, the highest price in years. Yet he had 30,000 bushels of last year's crop still in storage. Why? Well, he said with a quiet smile, he was betting that prices would go still higher. People told him he was crazy, he added, but that's what he was going to do. No, he said in answer to the next question, he didn't hedge his crop in the futures market. He preferred out-and-out gambling.

When I saw him, he was still excited by a new toy, a Cat Challenger— a 325–horsepower diesel crawler with rubber treads. With it, he said, he could pull a 30–foot drill and plant twenty acres of wheat an hour. A good investment? Absolutely, he said. His crop this April was green, while many of his neighbors had no crop at all. Back in the fall, he explained, there had been a foot of rain in one brief period. He had gone out and planted right on top of it. Since then, there had been almost nothing, and the seed planted by his neighbors, who didn't get their seed in the ground so fast, had never germinated.

By most standards, mine included, this is a success story. But what about Mike's own father and grandfather? Why had they left Oklahoma? Why had Jacob never returned even to visit? Mike didn't know—said he'd ask his dad. Meanwhile, his own son Randall wanted to take over. There didn't seem to be any question about it, even though Mike acknowledged that the trend to larger farms shows no sign of abating. And why shouldn't farms get bigger? Mike and Randall alone do almost everything on their 2,000 acres—and Randall rents and farms another 800 acres on his own. Even at harvest, the busiest time of the year, the two men hire only two extra hands. How, then, I ask myself, can the family be sure that it will do the swallowing and not be one of the swallowed? Somebody's sure going to be swallowed as the engine of agribusiness rolls on.

The wind was blowing hard from the south as Mike talked, and the soil of one unlucky neighbor was blowing past in clouds. It was funny, Mike said, the way the wind blew around here. Just the other day, the dust had been coming from the north.

Isn't it so with us, too? Blown this way and then that, anchored for a while, and then drifting? Isn't that Lucile Searcy's story and the story of the allotment Indians? Isn't it the story of farmers and everybody else? And where, I ask, can you learn this lesson as well as you can here on the Plains, which, if you only knew better, you'd leave tomorrow?

NOTES

1. Regarding my discussion of houses on the southern Plains, I leave it to readers to gauge whether my greatest debt is to John Ruskin, James Agee, or Bob Vilas.

2. The details of the University of Oklahoma's Fall 1939 semester come from the Western History Collection, University of Oklahoma, Norman.

3. I am grateful to the McFarlin Methodist Church of Norman, Oklahoma, for sharing with me its correspondence and materials regarding Lucile Searcy and Jean Sugden.

Searching for an Angle of Repose:

Women, Work, and Creativity

in Early Montana

Mary Murphy

In Montana during the winter—the greater part of the year—conversation about the season roams comfortably among many topics. Snow is a big one—its beauty, its skiability, its promise of summer water, the way people don't remove it from sidewalks. Temperature and its effects is another—who recorded the lowest, why the coldest spell came at calving time, how much ice coated the inside of windows on any particular morning. Montanans watch the incremental lengthening of the day following the winter solstice, waiting for that first day when they can go to and come from work in daylight. Around mid-April, people get desperate for spring, and the conversation turns to lilacs. Will they be early or late this year? The blossoms profuse or skimpy? Will a heavy snow kill the buds or, even later, crack the blooming branches?

Lilacs are the only verdant, lush flower that blooms everywhere in Montana. In Butte, where poisonous fumes from copper smelters exterminated virtually every green thing in the city in the late nineteenth century, where homegrown root vegetables still provide more than the daily allowance of heavy metals, and where one group of gardeners called themselves the Plant and Pray Club, lilacs are rampant. On the Montana plains, homesteaders planted lilacs to remind themselves of past homes and greener landscapes. In a good lilac year, you can drive across Montana with your windows down, and your nose will lead you to old homesteads, cabins deserted, crumbled, and dwarfed by great shaggy stands of overgrown fragrant purple shrubs. Lilacs bear silent testimony to the men and women who built and later abandoned those homesteads, men and women who sought, but did not find, their "angle of repose" in Montana.[1]

"Angle of repose" is a geological term. Also known as a "critical slope," it refers to the angle at which a material, such as soil or loose rock, remains stable—a little steeper, and it will start to slip. Wallace Stegner made the phrase famous when he used it to title his fictional biography of Mary Hallock Foote, a New Yorker who married a mining engineer and came west to search restlessly for a home. Angle of repose implies both tension and rest, finding the balance point at which a person can place herself in the western landscape without slipping—without falling into despair at its harshness, without being so seduced by its beauty and wildness that she forsakes civil society.

MONTANA CONSCIOUSNESS

States impose political boundaries on a land, often with little regard for topographical or cultural divides. What we now call Montana was historically occupied and claimed by a variety of tribal groups and imperial powers. Between 1805 and 1864, this piece of ground was embraced by the shifting borders first of Indian Territory, and then of Louisiana, Missouri, Nebraska, Dakota, Oregon, Washington, and Idaho Territories. As a political entity, Montana is a toddler; it gained statehood in 1889. Its population, including the Natives who now occupy seven reservations, still numbers less than 1 million.

Like many other western states, Montana has always had a divided consciousness, rooted in the geographic rift between the mountainous western part of the state—home to loggers, miners, and industrial corporations—and the eastern high plains—home to farmers, ranchers, and agricultural corporations. The western part of the state, rich in minerals and timber, boomed between 1875 and 1920. Tens of thousands of hopeful agriculturalists rolled into eastern Montana between 1910 and 1918 on a wave of twentieth-century homesteading. By 1914, main-line railroads crisscrossed Montana, jammed with men and women seeking work and new homes in the copper-mining and -smelting cities of Butte, Great Falls, and Anaconda, or on the reputedly rich farmlands of the eastern plains. As early as 1918, however, Montana witnessed the beginnings of a great exodus of people and of hope.

The 1920s and 1930s were years of drought and depression in both agricultural and industrial sectors. While the economy recovered in the 1940s, thousands left to work in better paying west coast war plants and never returned. Montana enjoyed the national prosperity of the postwar period, though its economy, based on natural-resource extraction, continued to follow familiar boom–bust cycles. The oil embargoes of the 1970s sparked sharp rises in domestic energy production in Montana and other western states rich in oil, gas, and coal. But the bust was nearly as spectacular as the boom.

By the 1990s, Montana was a different state, and a poor one. According to the 1990 census, the two sectors employing the greatest number of people were retail trade and education, neither particularly well paying. Whereas in 1920, 82,000 Montanans worked in agriculture, by 1990 that number was down to 33,813, including forestry workers. From being 8 percent above the national average in 1950, in 1993 Montana's per capita income ranked fortieth in the United States.[2]

Despite these economic conditions, in the past ten years advertisers of all stripes have appropriated the phrase "The Last Best Place," taken from the title of an anthology of Montana literature, to tout the state.[3] The Last Best Place has become the catchphrase that sums up Montanans' sense of place and the image they project outside the state, one of sparse population, a pristine environment, a sense of freedom and possibility associated with the quintessential West, a place of cowboys and Indians, wild animals, big skies, and wide-open spaces: in short, a place protected from the present.

This Montana consciousness demonstrates the power of history, for its structure was created in the half-century between 1870 and 1920, when each decade seemed to hold the promise of more people, more minerals, more crops, all achieved through struggles of heroic proportion. By the early twentieth century, the story line of Montana history had taken shape, and it has persisted ever since. The stories of those years are the tales widely known and shared by Montanans today. They follow a well-established western plot, but with particular Montana actors: the conquest of the Indians, starring Crazy Horse and Custer; the battles between labor and capital, featuring the Industrial Workers of the World and the Anaconda Copper Mining Company; the struggle of homesteaders, not a bloody contest between farmers and ranchers, but a conflict among farmers, railroad barons, and a drought-riven land; and the burgeoning of a mythic cowboy West rendered in vibrant color by Charlie Russell.

This "master narrative" has been peopled by and recorded by characters who are, for the most part, male and white, as was most of early Montana. In 1900, 61.6 percent of the population was male, and 93 percent was white. In 1990, the population was 50 percent female, but still 93 percent white.[4] Yet from Montana's earliest days, there have been counternarratives of this place, tales that put women in the center of traditionally male-defined pursuits, move "the Indian question" off the battlefield, and probe the issue of how women dealt with the spaces and places of the West. They reveal alternative consciousnesses about the Last Best Place and divides of power as well as space.[5] Women, such as bohemian writer Mary MacLane, documentary photographer Evelyn Cameron, Impressionist painter Fra Dana, and Crow narrator Pretty Shield—from rural and urban spaces—created works that presented alternative visions of Montana. This chapter focuses on the lives and works of three of their contemporaries: rodeo rider Fannie Sperry Steele, novelist Mourning Dove, and poet Gwendolen Haste. Only Fannie Sperry was a native Montanan, but Montana shaped the work of all three. In many ways, each challenged the standard history of the state and of the West.[6]

Fannie Sperry, raised on a small ranch near Helena, learned how to ride from her mother. In 1912 she became the "Ladies' Bucking Horse Champion of the World," riding a horse that had thrown a cowboy to his death the week before. Mourning Dove, one of the first Native American women to write fiction, wrote about the life of a mixed-blood woman on the cattle range in western Montana. Gwendolen Haste moved to Billings in 1915 to help her father edit the *Scientific Farmer*. Her series of poems about rural women's lives shared her father's political sensibilities, but put a human face on the process of scientifically mastering the plains.

The diverse landscapes of Montana had profound effects on each of these women. Fannie Sperry and Mourning Dove, growing up in the rural West, spent their entire lives working with the land and animals. If they had problems with the West, it was with two-legged creatures, not four-legged ones or the ground they trod on. Haste had a more ambivalent attitude toward Montana. She left the state to take up satisfying work in New York, yet many of her most moving works were written in and about Montana and its women. The lives of these three women demonstrate the range and limits of opportunity available to women in early Montana; their creative works express their responses to Montana's space.

Fannie Sperry Steele

According to one scholar, Montana produces rodeo stars out of all proportion to its population. The roster includes several women, but Fannie Sperry Steele (1887–1983) was the first. Fannie Sperry was the fourth child of Rachel and Datus Sperry. She once said, "[I]f there is a horse in the zodiac then I am sure I must have been born under its sign, for the horse has shaped and determined my whole way of life." At a young age, Fannie earned her reputation as a girl who could ride horses men wouldn't or couldn't.[7]

Like many families, the Sperrys made their living from a variety of pursuits, and all five children worked at daily chores. The ranch was primarily a dairy operation, but the Sperrys also broke horses, sold surplus hay, and skidded logs. Indians used to pass by the ranch on their way to Fort Benton, and one year Datus bought a colt from a group of Natives who did not think he would survive the trip. Datus gave his oldest child the colt, who sired foals for every sibling right down the line. Fannie began her riding career at age six on an Indian pony.[8]

Fannie Sperry loved horses. She and her brother Walter used to round up wild horses, herd them into a corral, and see how hard they would buck. Fannie rode for pleasure and for work, and in the summer of 1903, at the age of sixteen, she rode for money. At a small fair in the nearby community of Mitchell, Fannie gave such a great ride on a white bucking stallion that the spectators passed a hat. She soon joined a women's relay team, billed as the "Montana Girls," that competed in races throughout the Midwest. They earned $100 a week plus expenses. At the same time, a domestic servant—the most common form of employment for women in the West—earned between $5 and $7 a week. In 1907 Fannie won a bucking-horse contest in Lewis and Clark County, and for the next five years she raced and rode broncs in fairs and shows throughout Montana. She had begun earning a reputation as a good bronc rider and one who always rode "slick." Unlike many other cowgirls, who rode "hobbled" or with their stirrups tied together beneath the horse, Fannie rode broncs in the same manner as cowboys.[9]

There were undoubtedly thousands of ranch girls like Fannie, who were raised on horseback, doing men's work, but only a few went on to become rodeo stars or Wild West show riders. The transition required a special combination of traits: exceptional equestrian skill, the willingness to breach traditional expectations of women and, often, defy their families' wishes, and the creativity to turn everyday working skills into showy public performances. For instance, the Buckley sisters of eastern Montana, known as the "Red Yearlings" for their "manes" of red-blond hair and renowned riding skills, were too shy to accept offers to ride in Wild West shows.[10]

Fannie, unlike many cowgirls, had the support of her family. She once said, "I was raised to be lady-like and refined, if rugged and wiry and independent."[11] The rodeo circuit reinforced these seemingly dichotomous values. Although the Montana Girls rode in racing silks, when Fannie performed in the rodeo she always wore ankle-length divided skirts, though they sometimes hampered her movement. Until 1913, all but the most scandalous of female riders did the same. Rodeo prizes rewarded equestrian skill and daring, but also reminded female contestants that their mastery of masculine skills was anomalous. No cowgirl rode sidesaddle in a Roman race or on a bucking horse, but female riders often received sidesaddles or lemonade sets as trophies.[12]

In 1912 Fannie was invited to participate in the first Calgary Stampede. As a result of her performance, she became one of only a dozen or so prominent cowgirls in the country. In the practice session before the stampede began, an outlaw bronc named Red Wing had thrown and stomped a cowboy to death. On the first day of the stampede, Goldie St. Clair, a popular hobble rider and seasoned Wild West performer, rode Red Wing in the bucking-horse competition. He bucked her against a wall, severely cutting her leg, but she completed the ride and competed for the rest of the week as the favorite. On the last day of the contest, Fannie drew Red Wing. After giving what some called the "most spectacular ride ever seen by a slick riding cowgirl," Fannie was awarded the title "Lady Bucking Horse Champion of the World," along with an engraved belt buckle, a saddle hand-tooled with roses, and $1,000.[13]

Now a Montana celebrity, Fannie appeared at local rodeos, fairs, and horse shows. At the 1912 county fair in Deer Lodge she met Bill Steele, a cowpuncher, rodeo rider, and rodeo clown. Fannie was twenty-five, and she had not been very interested in men. One neighbor recalled that Fannie "had more beaus than a dog has fleas, but she was more interested in horses than boy friends." Fannie agreed. "I hardly saw men," she recalled, "yet let a horse go down the road and I noted all there was to see about it!" When Fannie was eighty-nine, she could not remember anything about her meeting Bill Steele or their courtship except that he bought for $10 "a little blue-grey mare" that she had admired.[14]

Fannie and Bill married in 1913 and traveled the rodeo circuit together. The next year, they founded their own small company, called the Powder River Wild West Show. For the next few years, in between major competitions in New York, Chicago, Kansas City, and Pendleton, Oregon, they toured across Montana. Fannie gave exhibitions of bronc riding and sharpshooting, targeting china eggs that Bill held between his fingers or shooting the ash off a cigar clenched between his teeth.[15]

Fannie made her last professional appearance in Bozeman, Montana, in 1925. Her legacy to rodeo was carried on by cowgirls she had taught, like Marg Brander, and others she inspired, like Alice and Margie Greenough. Giving up rodeo did not mean giving up horses. The year they retired from rodeo, the Steeles began working as dude ranchers and outfitters. Bill died in 1940; Fannie carried on the business until 1965. She died at the age of ninety-five; she had ridden horseback until she was eighty-seven.[16]

The cowboy is the dominant figure in western popular culture. An enormous amount has been written about him and about the single feature that distinguished him from other working-class men in the West—his horse. A horse gave a cowboy mobility, power, a sense of physical mastery over the landscape and over horseless men, and intimacy with a large, warm-blooded, sentient, fairly undemanding companion.

Cowgirls shared the same privilege. Their lives revolved around horses, and in the early part of the twentieth century they had the unique opportunity of working with wild horses. It was their experience breaking wild horses that gave women like Fannie and the Greenough and Buckley sisters their love of horses and their skill in working with them. Fannie believed, as did several other cowgirls of her generation, that while rodeo riders of the late twentieth century were as good as those of her time, the horses were not. She once stated, "I am of the belief that the days of the bucking horse are numbered, for no more are there wild horse bands scattered across the country. . . . Where I was born and raised, they ran in large numbers and we spent glorious days chasing them. . . . [T]he spirit of the bronc is not what it used to be." For Fannie, the passing of the best of Montana came with the passing of the herds of wild horses. Yet she confessed to no regrets about her life, for Fannie had found her angle of repose. In her late sixties, she stated, "[I]f, with my present arthritis, I must pay the price of every bronco ride that I have ever made, then I pay for it gladly. Pain is not too great a price to pay for the freedom of the saddle and horse between the legs."[17]

Mourning Dove

Horses had revolutionized the lives of western Indians. The adoption of the horse and the ability it gave to travel widely, hunt greater numbers of bison, and acquire and transport more goods transformed the social and economic life of many tribes. Horses were transportation, tools, wealth, and the means of achieving status. They were also central to the consciousness of writer and novelist Mourning Dove.[18]

Mourning Dove (ca. 1885–1936) was a member of the Colville Confederated Tribes of Eastern Washington. One of the first generation of inland Salish-speaking people to grow up on a reservation in a period of enforced assimilation, she attended Catholic school, and then government Indian schools. It is unclear when she gained her determination to become a writer of fiction, but she actively pursued the skills she believed necessary to the task. In 1904 she agreed to be a matron at the Fort Shaw Indian School in Montana in exchange for further classwork. Later she learned typing at a secretarial school in Calgary. In 1908 she married Hector McLeod, a mixed-blood Flathead Indian, whom she had met at

Fort Shaw. McLeod was an alcoholic and abusive. The couple separated in 1912. Seven years later, Mourning Dove married Fred Galler, a Colville of Wenatchee, Washington, who later in life also abused alcohol.[19]

In the years between her first and second marriages, Mourning Dove, a mixed-blood herself, completed a draft of a western romance novel, set on the Flathead Reservation: *Cogewea, the Half-Blood: A Depiction of the Great Montana Cattle Range.* The main character, Cogewea, is a mixed-blood woman who is faced with the choice of two beaus: Jim LaGrinder, the half-blood foreman of her brother-in-law's ranch; and Albert Densmore, a white Easterner. Verbally seduced by Densmore, Cogewea ends up betrayed, robbed, and beaten by him, and finally rescued and happily paired with LaGrinder.[20]

This short summary of the novel's formula belies the fascinating presentation of divided consciousness and divided society that Mourning Dove relates. The most obvious opposition in the novel is between white and Indian cultures. Stemteema, Cogewea's Indian grandmother, is the wise seer who sees through Densmore's smarmy patter and tries to protect her granddaughter. Cogewea's two sisters represent the obvious choices of mixed bloods—to live by white ways or by Indian ones. One sister, Julia, married a good white man, the owner of the ranch that is the novel's setting; she facilitates the romance between Cogewea and Densmore. Mary, or Shy-girl, Cogewea's other sister, is her grandmother's student and ally in trying to reveal Densmore's duplicity.

But other oppositions are also present: between men and women, as in any romance; between savvy cowboy and inept tenderfoot; between East and West. The last is best illustrated by a description of city slickers who have come west to prey on innocent women. Jim rallies his cowhands to support a basket social and make a good appearance, since "there'll be city guys with hair parted in the middle, all dressed in shiny shoes, white shirts, and a wearin' stiff standin' collars and choke rags. Out here from Noo York, Chicago and Omyhaw, they're huntin' lonely schoolmarms with payin' homesteads." He urges the cowboys not only to outbid the Easterners, but to outdress them as well.[21]

Cogewea does not want to live on either side of the Indian–white divide; she seeks some way to straddle it, to live comfortably as a mixed-blood. But Montana in the first decade of the twentieth century had no easy place for "breeds." Despised by whites and Indians alike, Cogewea—like her literary creator, Mourning Dove—is hard pressed to find an angle of repose in a racist society, in which miscegenation is regarded as racial pollution. While western history records many lasting and loving relationships between white men and Indian women, the exploitation of Indian women by white men was often more characteristic of the sexual encounter between these two peoples. Cogewea's very existence is testimony to a brutal history. White men's betrayal and abandonment of Indian women is a relentless theme of Mourning Dove's novel.

The chapter that most damningly portrays Cogewea's situation also highlights the skill she possesses that gives her superiority over others. Like Fannie Sperry Steele, Cogewea is a great horsewoman, and her true love is also destined to be a horseman. We learn in the author's initial description of Jim that "as a rider he had no equal on the range and was an artist with the rope"; his sobriquet is "the best rider of the Flathead." Although Densmore gains some riding skills by the end of the novel, it is clear he could never be a real Westerner or a proper mate for Cogewea because he can't sit a horse. Jim puts it baldly when he states, "If I know my own name, no pretender that can't ride is a goin' get her."[22]

Throughout the novel, Cogewea's horse is her most faithful, trustworthy companion. Like Fannie, Cogewea rides horses that even cowboys think are dangerous. Her horse, Wan-a-wish, is her escape, her companion, her instrument of exhibiting her pride and her ability. In the chapter "The 'Ladies' and the 'Squaw' Races," two horse races illustrate "the half-blood's" plight. During the Fourth of July festivities, Cogewea, dressed in a corduroy riding habit with red, white, and blue ribbons in her hair, enters the "ladies" race. "Ladies," not surprisingly, is a euphemism for white women. Cogewea competes, subjected to the contempt of the white riders and the whip of one white woman. Then, dressed in buckskin, she enters the "squaw" race, where the Indian riders also revile her. Cogewea, of course, wins both races. But in a confrontation with Jim at her side, she throws back with disdain the prize money for the squaw race, when the judge rules that she cannot claim the prize money in the ladies' race, since a mixed-blood can be neither a lady nor white. Cogewea does not go unrewarded. During the powwow after the races, a Nez Perce chief presents her with a splendid blanket and a Pend d'Oreille chief gives her the pinto horse on which his wife had won second place—both gifts of great honor.

Cogewea is a complicated novel in many ways, but its richness lies in its portrayal of people, in this case Cogewea and Jim, who are trying to live in a place that is no longer Indian, but not completely white either. Cogewea is torn between two identities, but she does not value each equally. Part of Densmore's allure is that his courtship allows her to believe that she could be accepted in white society. Yet while she admires elements of white culture, she also condemns its decimation of Indians and their cultures. Cogewea treasures her Indian heritage, represented in the novel by her grandmother. Yet her grandmother is old, her ways are clearly "vanishing," and it is impossible for Cogewea to re-create the life that Stemteema led. Nor does she really want to. Through the character of Cogewea, Mourning Dove portrays her own difficult choice not to try to pass as white or as Indian, but to live with the scorn of both and, in her own person, reconcile two opposing cultures.

Mourning Dove's novel ends happily. Jim and Cogewea are united, and Cogewea discovers that due to a legal technicality, she will inherit a substantial sum from her white father, who had long ago abandoned his Indian family. Unlike Cogewea, Mourning Dove did not have a heroic lover or a substantial fortune. Mourning Dove drew elements of the novel from her life: her deep familiarity with the Flathead Reservation, her family history, her knowledge of Native stories and customs, her skill as a horse-woman. Alanna Brown has called *Cogewea* Mourning Dove's "spiritual autobiography," for author and protagonist knew the pain of a mixed-blood life. In a letter written to her friend L. V. McWhorter in 1916, Mourning Dove confessed that when she was with Indians on the reservation, "if they are not mixed bloods like myself I feel sadly out of place with them."[23]

Mourning Dove's life was one of unremitting hard work. She squeezed her writing into the interstices of long days of migrant farm labor, housework, caregiving, and political activism on behalf of her tribe. In the early 1930s, life became even more difficult as the effects of the Great Depression, combined with her husband's alcoholism and gambling, spiraled them deeper into debt and occasional mutual violence. In July 1936, Mourning Dove was admitted to a Washington hospital, "in extreme mental distress, with abrasion marks and bruises on her chest, shins, and buttocks." She died ten days later of what appeared to be a cerebral hemorrhage.[24]

Mourning Dove could not exercise the same control over her fate that she could over Cogewea's. A poor mixed-blood woman in a racist, patriarchal society, she expressed her hopes for women like herself in her novel, but she did not have the power or resources to shape a happy ending for her own life. Cogewea with her symbolically named horse, Wan-a-wish, found peace at the end of her struggle, but for Mourning Dove there was no angle of repose in the early-twentieth-century West.

Gwendolen Haste

The work of Gwendolen Haste (1889–1979) also sought to reconcile cultures—in her case, that of dry-land farmers and city dwellers. Haste, a graduate of the University of Chicago, moved to Montana when she was twenty-six to help her father, Richard Haste, edit the *Scientific Farmer,* a paper devoted to encouraging and disseminating information about dry-land farming. The Hastes and the *Scientific Farmer* moved to Billings in 1915 in the middle of Montana's homesteading boom, when thousands of women and men turned their hands to farming the High Plains with-out benefit of irrigation, dependent on only sparse rainfall. Except for an interval during World War I when Gwendolen worked in a New Jersey munitions plant and then in an office in New York, she remained in Bill-ings until 1924, writing poetry based on her observations of Montana's land and people. Years after she left the West, she remarked that even after her departure, many of her poems grew out of impressions she gath-ered there and the sense of life "in a new state."[25]

"As Ye Cultivate, So Shall the Harvest Be" read the masthead of the *Scientific Farmer.* Richard Haste's editorship of the paper was clinical, offering advice and remedies for the agricultural problems that plagued dry-land farmers. Detailed articles on farm management, plant breeding, soil bacteria, summer tillage, and drainage systems filled the monthly's pages. There was surprisingly little boosterism, no attempt to seduce newcomers through a romanticized portrait of farm life. Haste's farm writing was dispassionate; he reserved his fervor for politics. An ardent supporter of the Nonpartisan League, his support for it and its candidates demonstrated his empathy with farmers. Yet the *Scientific Farmer* re-veals little about the human conditions on eastern Montana's farms. It is in Gwendolen Haste's verse that the dry-landers become more than ele-ments of a social and scientific experiment.

In the early 1920s, Gwendolen composed a suite of ten poems that she called "Montana Wives." The lead poem, "The Ranch in the Coulee," won the *Nation*'s poetry prize in 1922, judged the best of 2,500 poems submitted. Both her poetry and her unpublished autobiography convey a sense of women's lives in Billings and on the homesteads of eastern Montana in the late 1910s and early 1920s, and of the differences between men's and women's reactions to the High Plains.

Gwendolen frequently traveled with her father as he visited various ranches and homesteads. Calling on a couple who had a home on a bluff above the Clarks Fork of the Yellowstone River, she talked to the woman, who had stopped her husband from building their cabin at the foot of the escarpment. Gwendolen recalled that she had told him that she'd "rather carry water up that hill four times a day" and have the view than be stuck at the bottom.[26] The theme of women's enclosure and their desire for sight reverberates through Gwendolen's work. The division of labor that took men out into fields and onto the range, while women's orbit revolved around a cabin and house garden, is a constant in her verse. One senses that men's greater mobility across the land and increasing familiarity with it made it easier for them to adapt to the West. The women in Gwendolen's poems are the women who plant lilacs, seeking to introduce into a new landscape elements of an old and mourned-for familiar one. In her poem "The Stoic," she recounts the cost of life on a homestead for one woman whose children,

> Searching through barren hill or ragged butte,
> Would heap her lap with loco blooms, and bring
> Clouds of blue larkspur and bright bitter-root,
> Then would she run away to hide her pain
> For memory of old gardens drenched with rain.[27]

In "The Ranch in the Coulee," a woman did not survive being transplanted to eastern Montana:

> He built the ranch house down a little draw,
> So that he should have wood and water near.
> The bluffs rose all around. She never saw
> The arching sky, the mountains lifting clear;
> But to the west the close hills fell away
> And she could glimpse a few feet of the road.
> The stage to Roundup went by every day,
> Sometimes a rancher town-bound with his load,
> An auto swirling dusty through the heat,
> Or children trudging home on tired feet.

At first she watched it as she did her work,
A horseman pounding by gave her a thrill,
But then within her brain began to lurk
The fear that if she lingered from the sill
Someone might pass unseen. So she began
To keep the highroad always within sight,
And when she found it empty long she ran
And beat upon the pane and cried with fright.
The winter was the worst. When snow would fall
He found it hard to quiet her at all.[28]

"The Ranch in the Coulee" provoked a wide response. A woman from Connecticut wrote that the circumstances Gwendolen evoked were not unique to the West: "You have read the soul of a lonely woman. It might have been mine." Another commiserated with her, first assuming that it was Gwendolen's experience she wrote about, but asking that if it was another's to send her the woman's address because she would "love to write to someone as lonely as that." Gwendolen's own doctor asked her what the next verse was. When she replied, "Don't you *know*?" he answered, "I certainly do. They come in here every day and there is nothing we can do. Hard work, excessive child bearing, loneliness. It gets them and we can't help them." Another reader commented, "That last line is wrong. The husband would *never* notice how she felt."[29]

In poem after poem, simply by her attention to women's experience of the High Plains, Gwendolen addressed a divided consciousness between men and women, the drudgery of women's work, and their isolation—isolation from friends and neighbors and from their husbands. In the 1920s, her own ill health, the drought, and the political repression that had curtailed the Nonpartisan League also shaped Gwendolen's poetry. In "Deliverance," she chronicled a woman's contemplation of suicide; a reader told her, "It made me think of a woman I used to know who lived not far from here. She had just hung out a big wash when the line broke and the whole thing fell down into the dust. She didn't stop to pick up the clothes. She just turned away and walked down to the river and drowned herself."[30]

Yet not all of Gwendolen's verse relegated women to perpetual drudges blind to the beauty of Montana. In "Horizons," a poem that contrasted the views of a woman who lived along the Clarks Fork with those of a woman who lived in Billings, she mocked the city woman who pitied the loneliness of the country dweller. The farm woman looked out her window onto "the Beartooth Mountains fairly screaming with light and blue and snow." Through her curtains, the city dweller saw "another white stucco house,

> And a brick house,
> And a yellow frame house,
> And six trimmed poplar trees,
> And little squares of shaved grass."[31]

Gwendolen was fascinated by "the two worlds of Montana" she knew. One was Billings and the Yellowstone Valley. In the late 1910s, Billings was "an attractive little city" of paved, tree-lined streets, flanked by neat houses. It was the transportation and commercial center of a well-irrigated valley whose cottonwood-shaded farmhouses charmed her. But away from the Yellowstone Valley, "the towns were brutal clusters of shacks, huddled around a railroad station or set down along a road running from one bleak hillside to another." There were no trees, lawns, or gardens. "While the spring rains encouraged a blooming of pasque flowers, yellow balls, violets and black-eyed susans, the terrible dry heat of the summer seared these away."[32]

Gwendolen admired the dry-landers, "with skins burned and hair bleached by the constant light." And she loved the views of the world they had, of the Beartooths, the Judiths, the Snowies, and the Big Horns, views that were "full of hope" prior to the drought of 1918. Her poems, while tuned to the hardships of women on isolated ranches and farms, were also keyed to the beauty of Montana and the satisfaction of work. Nor did she neglect the toll that the land took on men. In the poem "Cumae," she describes the nightmare of a farmer's failure and his subsequent suicide.[33]

In 1920 when Gwendolen returned to Montana from New York, she found her father deeply involved in state politics. The drought and post-war depression had politicized many farmers, who had turned for help to the Nonpartisan League. Richard Haste was running for secretary of state on the same Democratic ticket, supported by the league, that featured Burton K. Wheeler for governor. They lost that election. But two years later, with Haste managing his campaign, Wheeler won a seat in the United States Senate and took Haste with him to Washington as his secretary. With her parents gone, Gwendolen left for New York in 1924.[34]

Gwendolen had documented and dramatized Montana homesteaders' search for an angle of repose. Like many of them, hers was not to be found in eastern Montana. Yet the light and space, the pleasures and pains of those years remained with her. Gwendolen continued her life as a poet when she moved to New York. Joining the editorial staff of the *Survey,* a progressive magazine of social work, she wrote to Harriet Monroe, founder and editor of *Poetry* magazine, that "I don't accomplish as much reading as in the spacious days in Montana, but I find I get quite as many poems written." She spent the rest of her life in New York, but Montana continued to resonate through her verse.[35]

CONCLUSION

In searching for an angle of repose, women in Montana sought the same kinds of things that men did: meaningful work—work that allowed them to express some sense of creativity, whether it was shaping a family, a poem, or a performance. And they sought mobility—not social mobility, necessarily, but physical mobility, the means to move across space freely and comfortably, and the acquisition of a sense of place which that comfort can endow. Horses, and later automobiles, allowed women to free themselves from the tether of kitchen and garden, though not all women had access to horsepower of one kind or the other.

Fannie Sperry Steele, Mourning Dove, and Gwendolen Haste were unusual women. Enmeshed in family responsibilities, they determinedly carved out time to engage in publicly creative works, thus providing us with some notion of the social and physical spaces that women occupied and shaped in early-twentieth-century Montana. They did not presume to speak for all women or to advocate their personal choices for others. In order to succeed at their work, however, each woman needed to know how to read an audience. That made them canny observers of life around them, and their observations led each to activism. Haste supported a variety of Progressive causes, including woman suffrage; Mourning Dove worked for Native American rights; Steele passed on her skills to other cowgirls.

Fannie Sperry Steele found her angle of repose in Lewis and Clark County. For Mourning Dove and Gwendolen Haste, Montana provided fertile ground for their creative efforts, but not a place to call home for long. The characters that each portrayed in their work challenged the main story line of Montana history. The most painful wounds of the Indian wars were not always acquired on the battlefield; many struggles of the homestead frontier took place within the confines of family; and Montana ranches, which generated cowboys, also spawned cowgirls.

Examining the history of women's creative work in early-twentieth-century Montana reveals a divided consciousness, marked by gender and race, that when incorporated into Montana history would make a far more complex and more interesting story. But simply to say that there were divided consciousnesses in Montana is to ignore how those divides marked inequities of power. To fail to rewrite the narrative of Montana history so that it acknowledges those inequities is to perpetuate a story that has the Indian question settled in the nineteenth century, that enshrines the cowboy as the symbol of admirable western values, and that keeps women—unless they were extraordinary in some fashion—virtually invisible. Euro-American men and their exploits have dominated the master narrative of Montana not simply because they were the numerical majority by the twentieth century, but because their system of power dominated the state's institutions and ideology. Patriarchal values suffuse the Montana consciousness of both men and women. Contrary voices, no matter how eloquent, are often feeble by comparison, tucked into the corners of otherness.

Montana is everything that the phrase "the Last Best Place" implies. It is beautiful, wide open, sparsely populated. If they choose and can afford to, people here can live close to the land and animals. It is "safe" compared with many parts of America. But the Last Best Place also reflects a less benign consciousness. Montana is insular, racially homogeneous, often anti-intellectual, and increasingly xenophobic. Insider-outsider is one of the most common oppositions in Montana today. While sipping their cappucinos and lattes, Montanans complain about the influx of Californians and the changing sensibilities they import. Coffee becomes the metaphor for how complicated these issues are.

The Last Best Place, for too many, means the ultimate destination on the white-flight highway—the last best hiding place from the rest of America.[36] Montana has given room to those who would twist virtues like self-determination and self-reliance into selfish indulgence. Fortunately, many Montanans reject that particular worldview and hold other values, those rooted in collective enterprise and political action; in familial affection, tribal loyalty, and mestizo culture; in intimate and respectful relationships with land and animals. The lives and stories of Fannie Sperry Steele, Mourning Dove, and Gwendolen Haste remind us that love of lilacs and horses, poetry and political dissent, meaningful work and racial equality are also "western," the ingredients of an alternative consciousness of the Last Best Place.

NOTES

The author would like to thank Doris Loeser, Alanna Kathleen Brown, and Sue Hart for generously sharing their research material on, respectively, Fannie Sperry Steele, Mourning Dove, and Gwendolen Haste. The essay benefits greatly from the careful reading of Alanna Kathleen Brown, Joan Jensen, Linda Karell, Dale Martin, Anastatia Sims, and the supportive and patient volume editors, Michael Steiner and David Wrobel.

1. Lilacs are an Old World shrub that originated in western China. No one knows exactly when they were introduced to North America. See Susan Delano McKelvey, *The Lilac: A Monograph* (New York: Macmillan, 1928), vii, 3.

2. On the general history of Montana, see Michael P. Malone, Richard B. Roeder, and William L. Lang, *Montana: A History of Two Centuries,* rev. ed. (Seattle: University of Washington Press, 1991). On the recent past, see Michael P. Malone, *Montana: A Contemporary Profile* (Helena, Mont.: American & World Geographic, 1996); and U.S. Department of Commerce, Bureau of the Census, *1990 Census of Population and Housing, Summary Tape File 3A* [CD-ROM] (Washington, D.C.: Government Printing Office, 1992).

3. William Kittredge and Annick Smith, eds., *The Last Best Place: A Montana Anthology* (Helena: Montana Historical Society Press, 1988).

4. U.S. Department of Commerce, Bureau of the Census, *Abstract of the Twelfth Census, 1900* (Washington, D.C.: Government Printing Office, 1904), 32, 39, 40; U.S. Department of Commerce, Economics and Statistics Administration, Bureau of the Census, *1990 Census of Population, Social & Economic Characteristics, Montana* (Washington, D.C.: Government Printing Office, 1993), 7, 33.

5. Several anthologies present historic reflections on the meaning of Montana. Kittredge and Smith, eds., *The Last Best Place,* is a grand anthology of Montana literature, ranging from Native stories to modern poetry. It updates Joseph Kinsey Howard, ed., *Montana Margins: A State Anthology* (New Haven, Conn.: Yale University Press, 1946). In *Ten Tough Trips: Montana Writers and the West* (Seattle: University of Washington Press, 1990), William W. Bevis offers interpretative essays on those novelists, such as A. B. Guthrie, Ivan Doig, and James Welch, who have shaped popular representations of Montana. Rick Newby and Suzanne Hunger, eds., *Writing*

Montana: Literature Under the Big Sky (Helena: Montana Center for the Book, 1996), discusses the works of many lesser known Montana writers and genres other than fiction. William Kittredge, ed., *Montana Spaces: Essays and Photographs in Celebration of Montana* (New York: Lyons & Burford, 1988), was published to commemorate the state's centennial. William L. Lang, ed., *Stories from an Open Country: Essays on the Yellowstone River Valley* (Billings, Mont.: Western Heritage Press, 1995), focuses on one part of Montana and explores its culture from the point of view of tribal elders, historians, folklorists, and essayists.

6. For brief biographical entries on Pretty Shield, Evelyn Cameron, and Fra Dana, see Gayle C. Shirley, *More than Petticoats: Remarkable Montana Women* (Helena, Mont.: Falcon Press, 1995). On Mary MacLane, as well as Dana and Cameron, see Kimberly J. Davitt, "Female Visions and Verse: Turn-of-the-Century Women Artists and Writers in the Montana Landscape" (M.A. thesis, University of Montana, 1993). MacLane's works are out of print, but a good selection is reprinted in Elisabeth Pruitt, ed., *Tender Darkness: A Mary MacLane Anthology* (Belmont, Calif.: Abernathy & Brown, 1993). Women painters of the region are discussed in Patricia Trenton, ed., *Independent Spirits: Women Painters of the American West, 1890–1945* (Los Angeles: Autry Museum of Western Heritage, 1995)

7. MaryLou LeCompte, *Cowgirls of the Rodeo: Pioneer Professional Athletes* (Urbana: University of Illinois Press, 1993), 22; Fannie Sperry Steele, as told to Helen Clark, "A Horse Beneath Me Sometimes," *True West*, January–February 1956, 8; Liz Stiffler and Tona Blake, "Fannie Sperry Steele: Montana's Champion Bronc Rider," *Montana Magazine of Western History* 32 (1982): 44.

8. Stiffler and Blake, "Fannie Sperry Steele," 46–47; Fannie Sperry Steele, interview with Kathy White, 22 October 1976, Helena (Untranscribed, Mansfield Library, University of Montana, Missoula).

9. LeCompte, *Cowgirls of the Rodeo*, 54.

10. Ibid., 8, 61; Steele interview; Donna M. Lucey, *Photographing Montana, 1894–1928: The Life and Work of Evelyn Cameron* (New York: Knopf, 1991), 174; Evelyn Cameron, "The 'Cowgirl' in Montana," *Country Life*, 6 June 1914, 829–32.

11. Steele, "Horse Beneath Me," 10–11.

12. LeCompte, *Cowgirls of the Rodeo*, 49, 21.

13. On Fannie's experiences at Calgary, see ibid., 49–55; and Dee Marvine, "Fannie Sperry Wowed 'Em at First Calgary Stampede," *American West*, August 1987, 30–36.

14. "Fannie Sperry Steele," Clipping File, Montana Historical Society Library, Helena; Steele, "Horse Beneath Me," 11; Steele interview.

15. LeCompte, *Cowgirls of the Rodeo*, 62–64; Stiffler and Blake, "Fanny Sperry Steele," 54. The Steeles followed a well-established pattern. LeCompte

calculated that from the nineteenth century through World War II, 90 percent of all rodeo cowgirls married rodeo cowboys (3).

16. Stiffler and Blake, "Fannie Sperry Steele," 56; Doris Loeser, in her film *"I'll Ride That Horse!": Montana Women Bronc Riders* (1994), covers Fannie's career and interviews Marg Brander, Alice and Margie Greenough, and Bobby Kramer.

17. Steele, "Horse Beneath Me," 46, 12; Loeser, *"I'll Ride That Horse!"*

18. As was customary among many Indian peoples, Mourning Dove had several names: Humishuma, which translated to Mourning Dove, and her English birth name, Christine Quintasket. She also later used her two married names: Mrs. Hector McLeod and Mrs. Fred Galler. She signed her written works Mourning Dove.

19. The most accurate biographical information on Mourning Dove is in Alanna Kathleen Brown, "Mourning Dove (Humishuma)," in *Dictionary of Literary Biography: Native American Writers of the U.S.* (Columbia, S.C.: Bruccoli Clark Layman, 1997), 187–97. See also Jay Miller, ed., *Mourning Dove: A Salishan Autobiography* (Lincoln: University of Nebraska Press, 1990). My thanks to Alanna Brown for sharing her unpublished work, research photographs, and conversation about Mourning Dove.

20. Mourning Dove had completed a draft of *Cogewea* in 1912. In 1914 she met Lucullus Virgil McWhorter, a writer and reformer, with whom she subsequently formed a lifelong friendship and collaboration, and who worked with her to get *Cogewea* published. It was finally published in 1927. The topic of McWhorter's collaboration with Mourning Dove and his role in producing *Cogewea* is the main issue for literary scholars who have studied this work. See, for example, Susan K. Bernardin, "Mixed Messages: Authority and Authorship in Mourning Dove's *Cogewea, the Half-Blood: A Depiction of the Great Montana Cattle Range*," *American Literature* 67 (1995): 487–509; Alanna Kathleen Brown, "The Choice to Write: Mourning Dove's Search for Survival," in *Old West–New West: Centennial Essays*, ed. Barbara Howard Meldrum (Moscow: University of Idaho Press, 1993), 261–71; Brown, "Looking Through the Glass Darkly: The Editorialized Mourning Dove" in *New Voices in Native American Literary Criticism*, ed. Arnold Krupat (Washington, D.C.: Smithsonian Institution Press, 1993), 274–90; Brown, "Mourning Dove, Trickster Energy, and Assimilation-Period Native Texts," in *Tricksterism in Turn-of-the-Century American Literature*, ed. Elizabeth Ammons and Annette White-Parks (Hanover, N.H.: University Press of New England, 1994), 126–36; Brown, "Mourning Dove's Voice in *Cogewea*," *Wicazo Sa Review* 4 (1988): 2–15; Maureen Honey, "'So Far Away from Home': Minority Women Writers and the New Woman," *Women's Studies International Forum* 15 (1992): 473–85; and Linda K. Karell, "'This Story I Am Telling You Is True': Collaboration and Literary Authority in Mourning Dove's *Cogewea*," *American Indian Quarterly* 19 (1995): 1–15.

21. Mourning Dove, *Cogewea, the Half-Blood: A Depiction of the Great Montana Cattle Range* (Boston: Four Seas, 1927; reprint, Lincoln: University of Nebraska Press, 1981), 195–96.

22. Mourning Dove, *Cogewea,* 107. On Indians as cowboys, see Peter Iverson, *When Indians Became Cowboys: Native Peoples and Cattle Ranching in the American West* (Norman: University of Oklahoma Press, 1994).

23. Mourning Dove to Lucullus Virgil McWhorter, 4 September 1916, in Brown, "Mourning Dove's Voice in *Cogewea,*" 6. This essay traces the autobiographical elements of *Cogewea.*

24. Brown, "Mourning Dove (Humishuma)," 192–93.

25. "Gwendolen Haste," Vertical File, Montana Historical Society Library. Haste's poems were published in a variety of literary magazines throughout her life and in two volumes: *Young Land* (New York: Coward-McCann, 1930) and *The Selected Poems of Gwendolen Haste* (Boise, Idaho: Ahsahta Press, 1976).

26. Gwendolen Haste, untitled, unpublished autobiography, 54. My thanks to Sue Hart for sharing this manuscript with me.

27. Haste, "The Stoic," in *Young Land,* 40–41.

28. Haste, "The Ranch in the Coulee," in *Young Land,* 36.

29. Haste autobiography, 60–61.

30. Ibid., 79.

31. Haste, "Horizons," in *Young Land,* 41–42.

32. Haste autobiography, 75–76.

33. Ibid., 76; Haste, "Cumae," in *Selected Poems,* 28.

34. Gwendolen describes her father's political activities in her autobiography. They are also evident in his editorials in the *Scientific Farmer.* He was strongly antimilitaristic, and supported Jeannette Rankin, Burton K. Wheeler, and the Nonpartisan League.

35. Gwendolen Haste to Harriet Monroe, 19 June 1925, Poetry Magazine Papers, Series I, 1912–1935, box 10, folder 10, General Manuscripts Special Collections, University of Chicago Library.

36. I wish I could lay claim to the phrase "last best hiding place," but I credit my colleague, Bob Rydell.

Mountain, Plain, Desert, River:

The Snake River Region as a

Western Crossroads

Peter Boag

I came to southeastern Idaho in the late 1980s from Oregon's soggy, green Willamette Valley (my childhood home) in order to take a position in the history department at Idaho State University in Pocatello. Especially in the beginning, southeastern Idaho presented me with a variety of social, cultural, and environmental obstacles to feeling at home. For a while, I was literally a duck out of water, but I have slowly evolved from webfoot into desert rat (or lizard, if one considers the condition of my skin).

During the process of exchanging one home and one epidermis for others in the West, I collected a number of instructive, if not amusing, personal stories about my changing relationship with and understanding of just a few of the "many Wests" that this volume considers. For example, even before coming to Idaho State, my soon-to-be colleagues (who in retrospect understandably seemed quite sensitive about Idaho) quizzed me about my readiness to offer a course entitled "Idaho and the Northwest." At the time I felt more than confident, as I was teaching Pacific Northwest history at the University of Oregon, and I was reworking into a book my dissertation about the environmental history of the Willamette Valley.[1] But during my first few semesters of teaching this course, I found that my primarily southeastern Idaho students only patiently sat through seemingly endless lectures on Chinook Indians, rain, salmon, Seattle, the Willamette Valley, and Douglas fir forests. And they literally *waded* through pages and pages of Don Berry's *Trask* and Margaret Craven's *I Heard the Owl Call My Name*. With this syllabus, I attempted to impart to my students *my* sense of place and *my* understanding of regional consciousness in the Pacific Northwest—a Pacific Northwest that somehow included southern Idaho as though only because the university catalogue specified so.[2]

Certainly, this syllabus held little relevance to southern Idaho and my students, who knew better. Since those very naive years, I have learned a great deal about deserts, sagebrush, the Shoshone, Latter-Day Saints, and the Carey and Newlands Acts. These elements of the social, cultural, and natural environment of southern Idaho are much more relevant to my "Idaho and Northwest" students. They also offer a clearer perspective on how the whole of Idaho relates to the rest of the Oregon Country and to other subregions of the West. As I have come to terms with this part of the West through teaching about it as well as living in it, I have come to understand that southern Idaho—dominated by the readily identifiable landscape known as the Snake River Plain—is a crossroads of the West. As such, it offers instructive lessons on both what impedes and what aids the development of a regional consciousness on a local level as well as in the West generally.

As a physical crossroads, three of the West's major subregions—the Pacific Northwest, the Great Basin, and the Rocky Mountains—contribute to the Snake River region its primary and seemingly contradictory landscape features: towering mountains, desert plains, and abundant waters. On a raised-relief map of the United States, the Snake River Plain readily pops out to the eye. It appears as a broad, open, relatively flat, crescent-shaped plateau in the heart of the rugged Intermountain West.

Over 400 miles from west to east, the plain ascends from approximately 2,000 to 6,000 feet in elevation. At the most, it is perhaps 60 miles wide. It formed, geologically, over some 17 million years. As the North American continent moved southwestward, southern "Idaho" passed over a "hot spot" in the earth's mantle. The hot spot is now under Yellowstone and creates there the unique landscape of America's first national park. As the continent continues to move toward the southwest, Yellowstone will, theoretically, someday look like the Snake River Plain to its west: a relatively flat, barren landscape formed when basalt lava flows filled up a succession of collapsing calderas. Almost completely encircling the path of the hot spot (now the floor of the Snake's plain) are the mountain ranges of the northern Great Basin, the Middle Rockies (which include the Tetons), the Blue Mountains, and the Northern Rockies. These towering behemoths provide a dramatic horizon to the plain. They make this region part of the Mountain West.[3]

These mountains also provide the snowmelt that makes the Snake a significant river of the West. It is the fourth longest United States river to drain into the Pacific, it is the Columbia River's largest tributary, and it carries more than two and a half times the amount of water that the Colorado does. As far as water drainage goes, it is southern Idaho's connection to the Pacific Northwest. The Snake also attaches southern Idaho to the Northwest through fish runs. Although Pacific salmon and steelhead no longer come to southern Idaho because of the Brownlee, Oxbow, and Hells Canyon Dams (constructed on the lower Snake in the 1950s and 1960s), southern Idahoans' control of the upper Snake's waters is one of the keys to the viability of salmon runs lower down in the drainage system. In recent years, because of the obsessive emphasis on saving the salmon, Idaho has become increasingly tied to the other northwestern states both politically and environmentally. In 1990, for example, the governors of Montana, Oregon, Washington, and Idaho convened the "Salmon Summit" and together worked out short-term measures to aid the dwindling salmon runs of the region. Subsequently, the Northwest Power Planning Council, which contains two representatives from each of the northwestern states, has worked on long-range regional solutions.[4]

While the Snake is in a couple of ways southern Idaho's link to the Northwest, other physical features prevent a stronger connection. At the western margin of the plain, the Snake flows northward and cuts through the Blue Mountains the deepest gorge in North America: Hells Canyon.

Because of the depth, length, and treachery of Hells Canyon, historically it has presented a barrier to travel and communication between southern Idaho and the rest of the Northwest. It makes southern Idaho feel separate from Oregon and Washington. The historian David H. Stratton has even termed Hells Canyon the "missing link in Pacific Northwest regionalism." It detaches the Snake River Plain from the rest of the Northwest in most ways other than in water drainage.[5]

For much of its way across—or through—the plain, the Snake courses through a deep gorge whose walls are made of dark-colored basalt. Technology such as dams and pumps, however, makes the water accessible to farms and has transformed into productive cropland a landscape that is in reality a desert. The most apparent native vegetation is sagebrush, but there are also various grasses, prickly pear cactus, and, in moister places, juniper trees. Although technically an extension of the physiogeographic region known as the Columbia Plateau, in its climate, natural plants and animals, Native peoples' prehistoric culture, and general appearance, the Snake River Plain is an extension of the Great Basin, which borders it on the south.[6]

The Snake River Plain is, therefore, a singular geographic region of the larger American West. Its physical and climatic characteristics combine to make it part of three different western subregions: its abundant river waters and drainage system make it part of the Northwest; its bordering mountains place it in the Rockies; and its climate and native life attach it to the Great Basin. It is certain that, when compared with these and other major subregions of the West, the Snake River Plain is relatively small in size. But because it blends different major subregions, and its physical form visibly sets it off from its neighbors, the Snake River Plain is a distinctive space in the West and might truly be considered, at least physically speaking, a separate western subregion. Perhaps it might best be compared with other identifiably smaller western spaces, such as California's Central Valley, Utah's Wasatch Front, Oregon's Willamette Valley, and Washington's Puget Sound lowlands.

While the Snake River Plain is indeed a single, identifiable landscape, a regional consciousness has not yet fully emerged here. Residents of the Snake recognize that they are themselves divided by various social, cultural, and historical factors, a condition also apparent in the larger West. For example, in the eastern part of the region, also known as the Upper Snake River Plain, Mormons have dominated the relatively thinly populated area since the earliest historic times. Between 1878 and 1884, Mormons established numerous villages in the Snake River Plain along the route that the Utah and Northern Railroad pushed northeastward from Pocatello to Montana. These communities were, according to church directive, agriculturally based and, more important, self-sustaining. Although this situation has changed considerably from 120 years ago, the Mormons continue to look to Salt Lake City for leadership, particularly in the realm of spirituality. Because a city based outside the Snake River region plays such an important part in their lives and because the Mormons have regarded themselves as a distinctive people are only a couple of the various impediments to the development of a common regional consciousness growing up among all Snake River Plain inhabitants. Indeed, because of these factors, non-Mormons in Idaho (as elsewhere) have looked with suspicion on the Latter-Day Saints, resulting in some deep political and cultural divisions that run across both region and state.[7]

While the Mormons have oriented the Upper Snake River Plain to the influences of Salt Lake City, the western portion of the region, known as the Treasure Valley, has instead centered around Boise. Boise got its start in the early 1860s as a trading center for the military's Fort Boise and especially for the rich Boise Basin gold-strike country, located a few miles to the north and east. With the development of irrigation projects on the Boise River just shortly after the arrival of settlers, agriculture spread, and the town of Boise grew and soon came to dominate southwestern Idaho. Once Boise became the territorial capital in 1865 and then the state capital in 1890, its position of dominance was secured. Today this rapidly growing metropolis is known throughout the West as the headquarters not only for many of Idaho's largest firms—such as Simplot, Albertson's, Micron Technology, and Morrison Knudsen—but also for multinational corporations, such as Boise-Cascade, whose interests necessarily lay outside of southern Idaho. That other areas of Idaho, including those farther up the Snake River, should look on the success and dominance of Boise with jealousy and envy also prevents a feeling of common cause from developing across the region.[8]

The dominance of Mormons in the east and Boise in the west creates two essential divisions in the Snake River Plain. The western historian Leonard J. Arrington has identified a possible third segment of the region: south-central Idaho, which is known as the Magic Valley. The people there are strongly rooted in a history of independent, irrigated farms made possible by one of the West's few successful Carey Act irrigation ventures. In 1900, resident and visionary Ira B. Perrine incorporated the Twin Falls Land and Water Company and entered into a contract with the state to construct Milner Dam and deliver water from it to 270,000 acres on the south side of the Snake, and later to another 185,000 acres on the north side. The success of this unique project sustained the growth of the city of Twin Falls through the remainder of the century. Today, Twin Falls is Idaho's sixth largest city and the Snake River Plain's fifth largest community. It is precisely halfway along the 240 miles that separate Pocatello and Boise. This relative isolation contributes to the fact that Twin Falls is truly a regional center for agriculture and the small service industry that has developed around it.[9]

In addition to the three subregions that culture, economics, distance, and history have created in the Snake River Plain, ethnicity and race have divided the population and thus prevented a fully developed common consciousness from developing here. Although when compared with so many other areas of the West, the Snake River Plain is ethnically homogenous—91 percent of its more than 720,000 people are white—there are various minority groups spread across the area. The largest minority by far is the Hispanic community, which began to develop during World War II and now has a total of about 46,000 members (6.3 percent of the total population). Although African-Americans number under 3,000 (0.4 percent of the population), they have been part of the southern Idaho population since the nineteenth century. They live in twenty of the twenty-two counties of the Snake River Plain, and the largest communities are in Boise, Pocatello, and Mountain Home (where there is also a United States Air Force base). While today the population of Asians in the region is small—about 7,400, or 1 percent of the total population—historically their numbers have been larger, especially that of ethnic Chinese during the gold-rush era. The other viable minority on the Snake River Plain are Native Americans, who in 1990 totaled 8,662, for 1.2 percent of the total regional population.[10]

While both today and in the past, any number of conditions prevent a full-fledged regional consciousness from developing among the inhabitants of the Snake River Plain, some factors have indeed contributed to at least a rudimentary form of regional awareness. For example, one of the strongest adhesives binding together Snake River Plain inhabitants is their mutual dependence on the Snake River's waters for agricultural, industrial, domestic, and environmental purposes. Five of Idaho's six largest communities are located near the Snake River (or its tributaries) on the Snake River Plain. And because of geographic, political, and land-use boundaries, southern Idahoans maintain almost a complete monopoly on the Snake's water. So used or overused is the Snake in Idaho that it is known as two rivers. By the time it reaches Milner Dam, near Twin Falls (and halfway across its journey through the state), the Snake is almost completely carried away by irrigation canals. On a trip down the length of the Snake, environmental writer Tim Palmer found that directly above Milner Dam the flow of the Snake the summer he visited it was about 8,000 cubic feet per second (cfs). Directly below the dam, the riverbed was bone dry, with about 6 cfs leaking "from the cracks between the boards of the antiquated structure." But due to the porous nature of the Snake's volcanic rocks and soils, the irrigation waters quickly seep down into the immense aquifer and surge back through the river's canyon walls and into the river at Thousand Springs, about twenty miles downstream.

Of course, competing river uses—especially agricultural and environmental—have also acted as a disintegrating force among southern Idaho's people. But their essential reliance on the river in this desert land contributes to commonality across southern Idaho. Although southern Idahoans might share this characteristic with inhabitants of other desert regions of the West, this does not suggest that they wish to share "their" river with outsiders. For example, when thirsty Californians periodically propose elaborate schemes to channel the Snake to their doors and transform southern Idaho into another Owens Valley, Idahoans rally together to defend their prized possession.[11]

Another major factor that contributes to a regional consciousness in the Snake River Plain is the political boundaries that define these people as Idahoans first—but Idahoans of a particular sort. Since very early in Idaho state and territorial history, the Blue Mountains and Northern Rockies—which demarcate significant climatic and landscape differences between northern and southern Idaho—have divided the state in two. No freeway, no railway, and only one road connect southern and northern Idaho. To get from one part of the state to another, most choose instead to travel outside Idaho altogether, through Montana or Oregon.

Geographic and climatic differences have led to various social, cultural, and historical variations between these two parts of the state, too. For example, the north has historically been known for mining and logging, while the south relies on agriculture. But the differences go deeper; the two regions just have not always gotten on together. At times in early Idaho history, the northern panhandle attempted to separate itself from the rest of Idaho and attach itself to Washington, to which northern Idahoans have felt a closer tie. And Lewiston in the north has probably never forgiven Boise in the south for "stealing" the capital in 1865. Also, the Snake River Plain supports five of the state's six largest cities, and all of southern Idaho constitutes 80 percent of the state's total population. While southern Idaho residents do identify themselves as Idahoans, when using this term they do not necessarily associate themselves automatically with those in the north.[12]

There is yet another factor that helps unite the Snake River Plain's peoples—their strong sense of place as derived from their association with the region's three principal and often contradictory landscapes: towering mountains, a vast desert plain, and the deep gorge and abundant waters of a significant river. Their strong identification with their unique landscape reflects an essential condition found in the larger West. I would propose that although the West is an enormous area composed of many regions and subregions that are different and often divided from one another, what unites the people across the region and gives them a consciousness as Westerners is their close identity with the region's distinctive landscapes.

Scholars have employed different means to attempt to identify Westerners' strong sense of place as related to landscape. For example, in my earlier work on the nineteenth-century Willamette Valley, I tried to show how western landscapes were an essential component in the life and thought of the relatively unlettered as well as the inarticulate. Of course, the more traditional approach to the study of landscape and Westerners has been through the assessment of regional literature. Historic and contemporary writers of the West—such as Willa Cather, H. L. Davis, Mari Sandoz, John Steinbeck, A. B. Guthrie, Ivan Doig, Mary Austin, Craig Lesley, Don Berry, and Wallace Stegner—have utilized the region's landscape as an essential component in their work.

Although assessing literature is assessing an elite's consciousness, a task that might not necessarily uncover the broader populace's feelings, the strength of the literary tradition of regional writing throughout the West makes it an appropriate subject of consideration for several reasons. First, western literature does reflect the experience of a significant proportion of the West's populace. Second, that the writers themselves come from varied backgrounds and different parts of the West would suggest that less articulate people here also identified with landscape. Finally, in both past and recent years, western writers from minority ethnic groups—notably Native American and Hispanic—have also contributed mightily to regional literature. They too, to varying degrees, utilize landscape as an integral component in their work. Among these writers are N. Scott Momaday, Leslie Marmon Silko, James Welch, Louise Erdrich, and Rudolfo Anaya. This all goes to suggest that the significance of western landscape in sense of place also cuts across ethnic barriers.[13]

For the Snake River Plain, regional writing has largely been confined to Euro-Americans, who today make up about 91 percent of the population. Their literature shows that landscape has helped to create a common consciousness among them. Because of their numbers and because the region's varied landscapes have played a common role in their literature, their experience is certainly worthy of consideration. To show that landscape is an imperative to regional consciousness on the Snake River Plain, the remainder of this chapter offers a brief analysis of the work of three writers from three periods of the region's history. Each utilized landscape in a central role in his or her works. But each also shows how the significance of landscape evolved over time in the lives and especially thoughts of the people who frequented and lived in the Snake River region.

Although all were Euro-American, they came from contrasting backgrounds, as will become clear. The first of these is Washington Irving, who in the 1830s wrote some of the earliest literature about the Snake River Plain. Through his descriptions and stories, he offered a primitive sense about this place for a larger American audience. A few decades later came the writer and artist Mary Hallock Foote, who moved with her husband to the Boise area. Unlike Irving, Foote actually resided on the Snake River Plain for some years. The sense of place we can detect in her work is that of both outsider and insider. Our trajectory of the historic development of an indigenous sense of place appropriately concludes with the writer Vardis Fisher. Not only did he write prolifically about the region, but he was born there, raised there, and, though gone for a short time, lived much the rest of his life in the Snake country. He also died there. Because Fisher was an insider, it is especially his early-twentieth-century works that offer a climax to the evolution of sense of place in the Snake.

While Washington Irving (1783–1859) never traveled to the Far West, his name is certainly associated with some of the best early literature about the region. In 1836 he published *Astoria,* a history of John Jacob Astor's ill-fated attempt to develop an early fur trade in the Oregon Country. The next year Irving produced *Bonneville,* a narrative of Captain B.L.E. Bonneville's explorations of the West. *Astoria* was the more popular of the two. By the time of Irving's death in 1859, it had gone through two editions and a number of printings and ranked "next to the journals of Lewis and Clark as perhaps the most exciting introduction to the history of the American West." For both these volumes, Irving utilized the records of the fur trade, especially those of John Jacob Astor, as well as interviews and records of Bonneville.[14]

Astoria and *Bonneville* offer us glimpses into Irving's—and therefore his audience's—growing sense of place about the West in the 1830s and 1840s. Both are among the first works of literature that, through details about plants, animals, Native people, and contours of the land, brought to the American consciousness a more specific awareness of the Far West—particularly the Snake River and its plain. Among other things, *Astoria* tells the story of the Wilson Price Hunt expedition, which, in 1811, became the first European–Euro-American journey through a region that Lewis and Clark had bypassed six years earlier. The Hunt party's lack of precise geographical knowledge about the Snake River Plain resulted in near tragedy for them and Astor's whole plan in the West. Consequently, in *Astoria* the plain is a formidable landscape of misery. Irving's words and prose are as terse, austere, and direct as the Snake's landscape is stark. For example, a pivotal point in the story comes on the Snake River at Caldron Linn where one of the Hunt party's canoes shatters on a rock and its navigator drowns. Irving writes that the Snake River's waters present a "furious aspect, brawling and boiling along a narrow and rugged channel, between rocks that rose like walls." At this point, the party can go no farther by canoe. They abandon the river—as well as a good many of their supplies—for a different route. But the only alternative is, in Irving's words, the "vast trackless plains destitute of all means of subsistence, where they might perish of hunger and thirst. A dreary desert of sand and gravel."[15] With such brief phrases characterizing the land as "bleak and barren," Irving reveals the essence of his sense of place for the Snake at the time of *Astoria.*

Astoria is in large part a narrative of men confronting, challenging, acquiescing to, and overcoming landscape. It is not about men absorbing landscape into their minds, emotions, and spirits. This should come as no surprise, of course, since Irving had no firsthand knowledge of the Snake's landscapes. Rather, he relied primarily on the journals of men who had been preoccupied with survival. In contrast, in *Bonneville,* which appeared only a year after *Astoria,* Irving describes the Snake River Plain in much more elaborate terms. In this narrative, he devotes ample space to a description of the area's strange geologic formations such as lava plains, volcanic convulsions, alluvial bottoms, chasms whose depth might be gauged only from the reverberating sounds made by stones dropped into them, and streams that disappear into the plains and find subterranean outlets. But as singular features of the region, Irving concentrates his efforts on its three principal landscapes: mountains, desert plain, and the waters and gorge of the Snake. Relatively brief examples include Irving's description of the Snake's plain, where "nothing meets the eye but a desolate and awful waste; where no grass grows nor water runs, and where nothing is to be seen but lava." Of the encircling mountains, he adds, "Ranges of mountains skirt this plain. . . . Far to the east, the Three Tetons lift their heads sublimely, and dominate this wide sea of lava;— one of the most striking features of a wilderness where every thing seems on a scale of stern and simple grandeur." But the most impressive feature of the landscape, as it is in *Astoria,* is the Snake River. Irving here writes from the descriptive perspective of Bonneville:

> Whenever he approached [the] Snake River, he found it running through a broad chasm, with steep, perpendicular sides of basaltic rock. After several days' travel across a level plain, he came to a part of the river which filled him with astonishment and admiration. As far as the eye could reach, the river was walled in by perpendicular cliffs two hundred and fifty feet high, beetling like dark and gloomy battlements, while blocks and fragments lay in masses at their feet, in the midst of the boiling and whirling current. Just above, the whole stream pitched in one cascade, above forty feet in height, with a thundering sound, casting up a volume of spray that hung in the air like silver mist.[16]

Bonneville is not just a story of men confronting and surmounting landscape, but also an account of how the landscape influenced the minds and emotions of Bonneville and his men. At one point, Bonneville directs his men to scout the country. But they "soon returned, having proceeded no further than the edge of the plain; pretending that their horses were lame, but it was evident that they had feared to venture, with so small a force, into these exposed and dangerous regions." Another time, Irving describes the desert of the Snake as "one of the most remarkable tracts beyond the mountains . . . [an] immense landscape . . . calculated to inspire admiration," which "Captain Bonneville had the soul to appreciate." As for the other men's feelings about the landscape, Irving writes that after certain setbacks the "poor wanderers . . . were in no mood to enjoy the glories of these brilliant scenes . . . though they stamped pictures on their memory, which have been recalled with delight in more genial situations." These "stamped pictures . . . recalled with delight" intimate that the men of *Bonneville*—and by this time Irving himself—had acquired a more refined sense of place about the Snake than had the earlier Hunt party men of *Astoria*.[17]

A more complex sense of place about the Snake River Plain emerged over time in Irving's writings about the region. Not surprisingly, the greater Irving's familiarity with the Snake, the more detailed became his, his characters', and ultimately his audience's sense of place. By the time of *Bonneville,* three principal landscapes were essential to Irving's sense of place for the region: the Snake River, the Snake River Plain, and the mountains skirting the plain's periphery. Not only had Irving singled these out without actually seeing them himself—suggesting the magnitude of their importance to those who had and on whom Irving relied—but he also attached distinctive characterizations to these landscapes. These characterizations would recur in later literature about the region. The plain was a desolate waste that could provoke fear. The mountains had a sublime beauty that excited admiration. But the river had the most complex nature of all. Its form presented contradiction: it was immutable, but shifting; it was serene, but raucous. Such disparity in form could also call forth from observers conflicting responses, as the history of the evolution of a sense of place here demonstrates. Aesthetic conflict with and between contradictory landscapes and its evocation of discrepant emotions in observers is the key to understanding sense of place for the whole of the region.

In 1884, twenty-five years after Irving died, and almost the same amount of time since settlement began in the Snake River region, the western artist and writer Mary Hallock Foote (1847–1938) took up residence here for almost a dozen years. Foote hailed from eastern society and only unwillingly moved to the West with her husband, Arthur. She never came completely to accept life here, but she was able to create a very successful career out of what she found in the West.[18] Indeed, in the late nineteenth and early twentieth centuries, Foote was one of the best known writers and illustrators of the region, filling the fervent demand in the East for "local color" from the West.

From 1876 to 1895, Foote followed her husband, an engineer, to various western and Mexican locales, including New Almaden and Grass Valley, California; Leadville, Colorado; and Morelia, Mexico. Except for Grass Valley, where Foote spent the greater part of the remainder of her life, her most extensive stay in any one locale was in the Snake River region. It was also in Idaho where Foote experienced her most difficult years, filled with heartbreak, discouragement, and failure as she nursed ill family members, suffered miscarriage and sickness herself, and tolerated Arthur's growing drinking problem, which only worsened as his scheme to irrigate the Boise River washed up and financially ruined the Footes and Mary's sister's family. Mary's art was all that kept the Footes afloat during these years, and consequently, when they left the Snake for California in 1895, Foote had become "the first writer and illustrator to publish a substantial body of work set in Idaho." Her Idaho writings, done between 1884 and 1895, deal largely with romance, loneliness, tragedy, and the life of women in the West, and through these works, Foote added to a national audience's growing knowledge about the Snake River region as she illustrated and wrote about its rivers, deserts, mining, irrigation, farms, and ranches.[19]

As with Irving, Foote offered to her readers an equivocal sense of place about the Snake River region. Foote's uncertainty was at least partly due to her own feelings about a life of exile in the West and her husband's successive failures there. But her ambiguity must also be seen in the context of the pattern of response to the region's landscapes that is identifiable in her predecessor's work. On the one hand, the general Snake River region scenery struck a positive chord in Foote's life. In 1887, for example, after about three years of residence in the Snake country, Foote wrote in personal correspondence: "There is something terribly sobering about these solitudes, these waste places of the Earth. They belittle everything one is, or tries to do. The vast wonderful sunsets, the solemn moonlights, and the noise the river makes on dark nights. The wash of the water and of land and the immense dignity of it all." And of her initial arrival on the Snake River Plain in 1884, Foote wrote, "It was a place where silence closed about you. . . . miles and miles of pallid sagebrush: as moonlight unto sunlight is that desert sage to other greens. It gives a great intensity to the blue of the sky and to the deeper blue of the mountains lifting their snowcapped peaks, the highest light along the far horizon." On the other hand, in her fictional writings, the landscape generally performed a more somber function, providing a barren backdrop for her stories. In "Maverick," Foote wrote, "To say that [the country] is 'thirsty' is to mock with vain imagery the dead and mummied land on the borders of the Black Lava."[20]

Foote's feelings for the Snake River region's landscape generally also applies specifically to her interpretation of the region's rivers. As with Irving, Foote was both drawn to and repulsed by this particular landscape feature. In her reminiscences, written in the 1920s, Foote revealed her interpretation of the meaning that the Snake's rivers had for her even before moving to Idaho. She confessed that for her the Snake "had an evil name," but it was the Boise River that was of greatest concern, as it held the key to the success or failure of Arthur's irrigation scheme, and consequently the fortunes of the entire family. Mary felt "adrift, as it were, cast off on a raft with my babies, swept past these wild shores uninhabited for us. My husband steering us with a surveyor's rod or some such futile thing—and where were we going on this flood of uncertainties?"[21]

Foote's tendency to view the Snake with dread is notably suspended in her short story "The Harshaw Bride." This piece depicts a young Englishwoman, Kitty Comyn, who travels to Idaho believing that she will be married to a long-term fiancé. As it turns out, Kitty's hopes are destroyed when she discovers that her fiancé has turned his romantic attentions elsewhere and that it was his cousin, the uninteresting Cecil, who lured Kitty to the West for himself. The narrator of the story is Mrs. Daly (really Foote), who, along with her husband, Tom, offer lodging to Kitty. Tom and Cecil plan a scheme to develop electrical generation on the Snake River at Thousand Springs. When the four main characters venture to the springs for a survey, Mrs. Daly writes positively about the scene: "The wall of the river canyon is built up in stories of basalt rock . . . out of which these mysterious waters gush. . . . It looks cold until the rocks warm it with their gem-like tints, like a bride's jewels gleaming through her veil.

Back of the bluffs where it might be supposed to come from, there is nothing for a hundred miles but drought and desert plains. I don't care for any of their theories concerning its source. It is better as it is—the miracle of the smitten rock."[22]

While at Thousand Springs, the group comes upon Miss Malcolm, daughter of a famous painter, who owns an island in the river beneath Thousand Springs. The island is the only place where Tom and Cecil could locate the power plant. But Miss Malcolm resists their request for a right-of-way, as she "will not have the place all littered up with their pipes and power plants." She posits, "Has anyone the right to come here and spoil such a lovely thing as that?"[23]

It is also here that Kitty obtains two letters. From one she learns yet more about her fiancé's treachery. From the other she receives a humiliating counteroffer from his father. But rather than becoming the typical scene of tragedy, the Snake emerges in the story as a place of comedy as Mrs. Daly and Kitty heartily laugh off the contents of the letters. For Mrs. Daly, this is "a place for a honeymoon." And indeed it does become such in a sense as Kitty softens toward Cecil, and the two eventually do marry. In the meantime, Miss Malcolm also softens but to Tom's desire for a plant on her island. This saddens Mrs. Daly for the future of the springs, but at the same time gladdens her for Tom's sake. But the springs—like Kitty and Cecil—eventually seem to be saved, as Mrs. Daly writes that when Cecil takes Kitty back to England it will be the end of the scheme.

"The Harshaw Bride," when judged against Foote's other Idaho stories and her own life in Idaho, is instructive for understanding her sense of place. As in Irving's works, the Snake's landscape, especially its waters, offered two possibilities: affliction and promise. These possibilities take on deeper meaning in Foote's work, however, because of her residence in the region. Foote could envision a refined Victorian woman—Miss Malcolm—whose only purpose in the middle of the isolated Snake desert was to admire a feature of the landscape. We can see Foote not only as Mrs. Daly, who appreciated Thousand Springs' beauty, but as Miss Malcolm, who advocated its preservation. In this light, we plumb the depths of Foote's relationship with the Snake River landscapes. While she admired and desired to preserve the scenery, Foote's own husband, like Tom Daly, wished to alter the region's scenery for profit. For the sake of her husband and her own family's well-being, like Mrs. Daly, Foote found it necessary to support this effort (even when it brought the ruin of her own sister). But she felt equivocal about doing so. Mrs. Daly writes, "For the sake of consistency, and that pure devotion to the Beautiful, so rare in this sordid age, I could have wished that [Miss Malcolm] had not weakened so suddenly; but for Tom's sake I am very glad."[24] Without Foote's having to take a firmer position in "The Harshaw Bride," however, fate intervened to end the developmental scheme that threatened the land. It may be that as an artist, Foote's love for the Snake River scenery influenced how she felt about her own husband's desire to change that landscape (and how he, an engineer, could scientifically explain the phenomenon of Thousand Springs; but she rejected that explanation, contending instead that it was a miracle). Yet she also felt a desire to support him. When in the end Arthur's real-life scheme failed, Mary might have at least taken some solace in the fact that, as in Mrs. Daly's experience with Thousand Springs, beauty would be preserved (at least for the time being).

Despite the importance of landscape in Foote's Idaho writings, it usually plays the role of backdrop. The work of writer Vardis Fisher, however, elevates landscape to the role of actor. With this feat, the development of an indigenous sense of place for the Snake River Plain truly culminates. In 1895, the year Mary Hallock Foote left Idaho, Fisher was born in the small Mormon community of Annis, located at the easternmost fringes of the Snake River Plain. In 1901, with his parents and two siblings, Fisher moved to the bottom of the rugged and steep Snake River canyon. There the Fishers inhabited a two-room, dirt-floor, dirt-roof cabin that was thirty miles from town and ten miles from neighbors other than a family that lived across the furious waters of the Snake. Fisher described this place as the bottom of the world. Until he was able to leave for school in Annis in 1907, he lived an insular, lonely, gloomy, bitter, and nervous childhood. The overpoweringly bleak landscape of the vertical canyon, roaring waters of the Snake, and barren hills and towering mountains above his home became during these early years an ingrained part of Fisher's psyche. Later in life, Fisher struggled with these elements of his early universe in his novels about the upper Snake country. In his writings, as in Foote's, this landscape does provide background. But more important, it works its way into the minds, souls, and emotions of his characters in a way that no previous writer had achieved. Because of the influence the eastern ranges of the Snake River country had on Fisher, one scholar declared in 1972 that Fisher was "the only significant literary interpreter of frontier life in that region."[25] Fisher undoubtedly retains this honor.

Although Fisher's literary production was so prodigious and varied that he defies labeling as a writer, much of his early work concerns the landscape and people of his youth. Indeed, his first products were regional novels, written at roughly the same time that other American greats like Willa Cather and William Faulkner—concerning themselves with the Great Plains and the South, respectively—were developing regional writing into a genre. Among Fisher's greatest regional works are his earliest novels, *Toilers of the Hills* and *Dark Bridwell*.[26] These two works deal in great detail with the landscapes of the eastern ranges of the Snake River region. The first concerns especially the rolling hill country above the Snake River. The second, and more haunting of the two, centers on the Snake River. The dichotomous interpretation of the Snake that Irving was the first to identify and Foote later echoed becomes, in *Dark Bridwell,* fully developed.

Fisher's first book, *Toilers of the Hills,* relates the story of Dock and Opal Hunter, who at the beginning of the novel are making their way by wagon through the lonely, rolling hill country of the eastern Snake River Plain. Dock's intention is to homestead and try his hand at dry-land farming high above the Snake River, which flows through the valley below. From the outset, Opal hates the landscape of these barren hills and declares "Oh, I'm lonely in this place! . . . Can't we get a ranch somewhere in the valley? . . . I can't stand these hills and them lonely mountains!"[27]

Even though farming a new country provides Dock with any number of difficulties—grubbing sagebrush, plowing hardpan, enduring summer drought, and fighting weeds—he loves the hill country from the outset. Dock is originally from the region, while Opal is not, which accounts in part for their differing affinities for this place. Dock's kinship with the hills only mystifies Opal, and he himself finds it difficult to explain. At one point Opal declares, "You seem to think them ugly hills is your kids or something. You seem just like a big chunk of them to me. . . . I'm mistook if you don't think all them hills is alive." Dock responds that, of course, the hills are alive: "And he strove to make her feel, as he felt, the liveness of all things about him, of the hills and the clouds and even the mountains across the way. His mind groped for words that would make her understand. . . . Between all these and himself, he admitted, there existed a kinship, something for which he could find no words, a feeling of love sometimes, or of fear and wonder."[28]

Opal never does share Dock's feelings for the landscape. Indeed, the story is primarily about her and her growing weariness with life on the hills as Dock succeeds in becoming the best farmer in the region. As this happens and Opal advances in years, she slowly concedes that she will forever remain in the hills she has hated so much and that the "long gray road leading valleyward" out of the hills has to be a "road to forget, for she had closed the door to her dreams." Through these years, however, Opal has succeeded in some sort of uneasy reconciliation with landscape, developing a meaningful sense of place—a sense of place that possesses the basic duality others before her experienced in this land of contradictory landscapes: "She hated this country, but . . . the ugly things . . . had grown to be a part of her with roots deep in her being. She wanted to leave here and she wanted to stay, she hated and she loved."[29]

Whereas *Toilers of the Hills* is set above the Snake River, *Dark Bridwell* is set at the bottom of the bleak Snake canyon (precisely where Fisher himself spent his strange childhood). In this book, the river has primary influence on the principal characters and it directs the plot of the novel. As in *Toilers of the Hills*, in *Dark Bridwell* there is a tension between a husband and wife: Charley and Lela Bridwell. This tension parallels the two characters' differing responses to the Snake River and the surrounding, varied landscapes. In addition, each of their respective reactions is filled with contradiction. Charley is essentially lazy and carefree. To him, the general setting of the Upper Snake River Plain seems "full of timeless laziness and centuries of peace. It was a huge bowl of sunshine and solitude, inviting to drowsy indolence and murmurous afternoon hours." To Charley, the "mountains were . . . great hulks of philosophy and peace. Instead of rushing around and shaking the earth, they sat on their heels and let it move over them with good things." But this world is disrupted by the river, and "the river . . . was where no river should be. Its silly frenzy, the impetuous nonsense of its blustering journey, belonged to another part of the world. . . . The river annoyed him. It came violently around a curve, as if it were going somewhere and knew where it was going; as if it had work to do between its source and its graveyard of the sea. But it has nothing to do that was worth doing."[30]

Lela also has two responses to the landscape. She comes from the town of Pocatello, whose "flat smoky houses and coal-yards, had borne down on her spirit." However, "the extravagant beauty of her new home" on the upper Snake liberates her, but ultimately, she discovers, imprisons her as well. Like Charley, Lela loves the serenity of the mountains— at least initially. But unlike her husband, she also loves the power and inexorable movement of the river. To Lela, the quiet meaning of the mountains and the "eternal language of this river, were related. . . . The quiet of the former and the frantic haste of the latter, were but a larger vision of something that had lived . . . in her own soul." But this large vision she has realized in her soul only at the end of seventeen years of enforced isolation at the bottom of the Snake canyon. Lela "was as ambitious as her husband was lazy. She did not like a quiet life," but by this time Charley has "almost convinced her . . . that she did. In consequence, she became more and more unhappy, more dissatisfied with the chloroformed seasons of her life." At this point, Lela realizes she is "a prisoner, walled in by mountains, roofed by an ageless sky." The frenetic energy of the river, however, has kept something alive in her through these years. Indeed, from the time she initially came to the canyon the river "haunted her most. If it had been a deep quiet lake . . . [S]he might have killed the restless part of her. . . . But the river was . . . a great unrest, . . . speaking the eager language of life." In the end, this landscape shows her the way out of the canyon. It is, "a door to a new life, and she was slowly opening that door." Indeed, at the end of the novel, fed up with the ways of her husband, Lela, unlike Opal, her counterpart on the hills above, is able to leave this hated but loved landscape. As the landscape has entrapped her, so too does it provide her escape.[31]

Toilers of the Hills and, in particular, *Dark Bridwell* are as haunting as their author's real life in the very landscape where the stories take place. Undoubtedly, as Mary Hallock Foote drew on her own life and experiences on the western Snake River Plain to inform her plots, develop her characters, and interpret her settings, so did Vardis Fisher draw on his childhood and youth in the Upper Snake River Valley. It is clear that the region's contrasting landscapes held much power over Fisher's life and psychological development. Because of his intimate relationship with the land during his formative years, it is only to be expected that in Fisher's works landscape takes on a much greater, sustained, and pervasive role than it does in any of the writings of those who came before him. With Vardis Fisher, we have the emergence of a native of the Snake River Plain who articulated how local landscapes were significant in the minds and lives of other residents. Consequently, in Fisher's work we find the most developed sense of place of any of those writers whose work this chapter has explored.

While Vardis Fisher's work might logically and qualitatively be set apart from others because of the depth of his understanding of and experience in the Snake River region, his writings still reflect the principal themes successively reinforced in the work of Irving and Foote, each of whom experienced a different level of personal relationship with the area. In their common equivocation toward the varied Snake region landscapes, Fisher, Irving, and Foote are directly linked. For the most part, for all these writers the Snake River Plain's mountainous backdrop was a landscape of peaceful, sublime beauty, but the desert plain was a desolate waste to be avoided. In the two different primary landscapes of mountains and desert expanse, observers identified aesthetic, psychological, and emotional conflict within the same region. More fascinating, they also discovered contradiction in the third principal element of the region: the Snake River. To them and to others, it was and is a "furious aspect," a "flood of uncertainties," and it belongs "to another part of the world." But at the same time, it also fills its observers with "astonishment and admiration." For Irving, Foote, Fisher, and others, the Snake, in the heart of a barren desert, provides a place of rest and aesthetic consideration; it offers escape, freedom, and "life."

A strong sense of place as related to the land is the additional element in the Snake River Plain that helps unite its inhabitants, giving them a regional consciousness. Their sense of place, as reflected in the few works of their literary chroniclers, is derived from a mixture of positive and negative emotional and psychological responses to a unique combination of singular and vast landscapes. In addition to a distinctive relationship with the land, this chapter has outlined a variety of factors that have contributed to a regional consciousness on the Snake River Plain. These include a unique geology, a unique configuration of landscapes, and a host of distinctive problems—the persistent divisions as a result of a strong Mormon minority, the perpetual intralocal rivalries between subregional centers, and the responsibility of the people of the Snake River Plain to the viability of salmon runs downstream, even when no salmon run exists in their own home.

While the Snake can be regarded as a unique place, it might also be aptly termed the crossroads of the West. Its location at the nexus of the Pacific Northwest, the Great Basin, and the Rocky Mountains—three large subregions of the West—gives this sobriquet credence. In addition to general location, the Snake combines several of the most significant landscape forms identified with the West and with each of these various sub-regions: towering mountains, desert plains, and abundant waters. But the crossroads metaphor encompasses more than simply location and geography; it also refers to the fact that the Snake River region is in striking ways a social, cultural, and historical microcosm of the West. Although perhaps more socially homogenous than other Wests, its inhabitants represent the larger region's various ethnic groups. Ethnic and accompanying cultural differences also help to divide the people of the Snake, as they do people elsewhere in the West. And the people of the Snake, like so many in other parts of the West, also have a very special relationship with water in an otherwise arid land. But most important, the Snake River inhabitants' closeness to landscape, which helps make a specific regional consciousness, also reflects a general condition of the rest of the West: Westerners' regionalism is directly tied to the land. As such, what makes the Snake River Plain a distinctive region also makes it a part of the larger West.

NOTES

1. Peter G. Boag, *Environment and Experience: Settlement Culture in Nineteenth-Century Oregon* (Berkeley: University of California Press, 1992).

2. Don Berry, *Trask: The Coast of Oregon, 1848* (New York: Ballantine, 1960); Margaret Craven, *I Heard the Owl Call My Name* (New York: Dell, 1980).

3. Until recently, geologists believed that the Snake River Plain was geologically part of the Columbia River Plateau. Now they recognize it as originating from distinctive volcanic processes. On Snake River Plain geology, see Bill Hackett and Bill Bonnichsen, "Volcanic Crescent," in *Snake: The Plain and Its People,* ed. Todd Shallat (Boise, Idaho: Boise State University Press, 1995), 15–59; Paul Karl Link and E. Chilton Phoenix, *Rocks, Rails and Trails* (Pocatello: Idaho State University Press, 1994), 21–24; and Earl H. Swanson, Jr., "The Snake River Plain," *Idaho Yesterdays* 18 (1974): 2–11. For an impression of how recent migration ties Idaho into the Rocky Mountain West, see "Eastward, Ho! The Great Move Reverses," *New York Times,* 30 May 1993, 1, 12.

4. On Idaho and the salmon, see Keith Peterson, *River of Life, Channel of Death: Fish and Dams on the Lower Snake* (Lewiston, Idaho.: Confluence Press, 1995); Tim Palmer, *The Snake River: Window to the West* (Washington, D.C.: Island Press, 1991); and Steven Peterson, Joel R. Hamilton, and Norman K. Whittlesey, *What Role Can Idaho Water Play in Salmon Recovery Efforts?* (Corvallis: Oregon State University Extension

Service, 1994). And on the salmon crisis in the Pacific Northwest generally, see Joseph Cone, *A Common Fate: Endangered Salmon and the People of the Pacific Northwest* (New York: Holt, 1996).

   5. David H. Stratton, "Hells Canyon: The Missing Link in Pacific Northwest Regionalism," *Idaho Yesterdays* 28 (1984): 3–9. Still the best source for understanding how the Snake River Plain fits into a larger Pacific Northwest region is D. W. Meinig's exceptional study, *The Great Columbia Plain* (Seattle: University of Washington Press, 1968). For other impressions on how the interior Northwest and especially Idaho is and is not part of the Pacific Northwest, see Judith Austin, "Desert, Sagebrush, and the Pacific Northwest," in *Regionalism and the Pacific Northwest,* ed. William G. Robbins, Robert J. Frank, and Richard E. Ross (Corvallis: Oregon State University Press, 1983), 129–47; and Lancaster Pollard, "The Pacific Northwest," in *Regionalism in America,* ed. Merrill Jensen with a foreword by Felix Frankfurter (Madison: University of Wisconsin Press, 1951), 187–212. Textbooks that have included Idaho with Oregon and Washington include Dorothy O. Johansen and Charles M. Gates, *Empire of the Columbia: A History of the Pacific Northwest* 2nd ed. (New York: Harper & Row, 1967); and Carlos A. Schwantes, *The Pacific Northwest: An Interpretive History* (Lincoln: University of Nebraska, 1989). But a textbook that does not include Idaho with Oregon and Washington is Gordon B. Dodds, *The American Northwest: A History of Oregon and Washington* (Arlington Heights, Ill.: Forum Press, 1986). On Idaho's relation to an economic megaregion that includes Oregon, Washington, British Columbia, Alberta, and Alaska, see Eric Scigliano, "The Northwest Megastate," *Horizon Air Magazine,* January 1990, 12–16; and Robert R. Gilbert, "Erasing National Borders to Build a Trade Region: Movement Strives to Create a Vast Area in the Northwest that Will Be Known as Cascadia," *Christian Science Monitor,* 20 July 1992, 9. Some studies on sense of place for specific Idaho locales include Thomas Edward Cheney, *Voices from the Bottom of the Bowl: A Folk History of Teton Valley, Idaho, 1823–1952* (Salt Lake City: University of Utah Press, 1991); and Louie W. Attebery, *Idaho Folklife: Homesteaders to Headsteaders* (Salt Lake City: University of Utah Press and Idaho State Historical Society, 1985).

   6. James A. MacMahon, *The Audubon Nature Guides: Deserts* (New York: Knopf, 1987). An important point with regard to internal Snake River regional divisions concerns Native Americans. Cultural ethnographers note that although prehistoric and early historic Natives of the Snake River region belonged to the larger Great Basin, there were notable differences between them. For example, just before the arrival of Europeans, the Shoshone of eastern Idaho relied to an extent on bison while the Shoshone of the west depended more on salmon or mountain sheep, depending on their location. These made for significant cultural differences. Whereas the eastern Shoshone had taken on many outward signs of the Great Plains culture east of the Rockies, the western Shoshone had more in common with Columbia

Plateau and other Great Basin Indians. See Sven Liljeblad, *The Idaho Indians in Transition, 1805–1960,* with a preface by Earl H. Swanson, Jr. (Pocatello: Idaho State University Museum, 1972); Deward E. Walker, Jr., *Indians of Idaho* (Moscow: University of Idaho Press, 1978); and Robert H. Ruby and John A. Brown, *Indians of the Pacific Northwest: A History,* with a foreword by Alvin M. Josephy, Jr. (Norman: University of Oklahoma Press, 1981).

7. For a discussion of political divisions not only in the Snake River region (which includes a discussion of the Mormon region) but in Idaho generally, see Randy Stapilus, *Paradox Politics: People and Power in Idaho* (Boise, Idaho: Ridenbaugh Books, 1988). On the division between Mormons and non-Mormons in Idaho and on Mormons as distinctive people, see Carlos A. Schwantes, *In Mountain Shadows: A History of Idaho* (Lincoln: University of Nebraska Press, 1991), 123–27; Leonard J. Arrington, *History of Idaho* (Moscow: University of Idaho Press and Idaho State Historical Society, 1994), 1: 429–33; Arrington, *History of Idaho* (Moscow: University of Idaho Press and Idaho State Historical Society, 1994), 2:268; Dennis C. Colson, *Idaho's Constitution: The Tie that Binds* (Moscow: University of Idaho Press, 1991), 35–37, 110–11, 148–59; A. J. Simmonds, "Idaho's Last Colony: Northern Cache Valley Under the Test Oath, 1872–1896," *Idaho Yesterdays* 32 (1988): 2–14; and Merle W. Wells, *Anti-Mormonism in Idaho, 1972–92* (Provo, Utah: Brigham Young University Press, 1978). For general discussions of Mormon settlement in southeastern Idaho and the Upper Snake River Plain, see Arrington, *History of Idaho,* 1:165–80, 329–31; Lawrence G. Coates, Peter G. Boag, Ronald L. Hatzenbuehler, and Merwin R. Swanson, "The Mormon Settlement of Southeastern Idaho, 1845–1900," *Journal of Mormon History* 20 (1994): 46–62; Michael S. Durham, "This Is the Place," *American Heritage* 44 (1993): 65–82; Schwantes, *In Mountain Shadows,* 54–57, 96–97; Susan Hendricks Swetnam, *Lives of the Saints in Southeast Idaho: An Introduction to Mormon Pioneer Life Story Writing* (Moscow: University of Idaho Press, 1991); and Ronald R. Boyce, "The Mormon Invasion and Settlement of the Upper Snake River Plain in the 1880s: The Case of Lewisville, Idaho," *Pacific Northwest Quarterly* 78 (1987): 50–58.

8. Merle Wells, *Boise: An Illustrated History* (Woodland Hills, Calif..: Windsor, 1982); Schwantes, *In Mountain Shadows,* 116–17, 124–25; Arrington, *History of Idaho,* 1:196–97; Arrington, *History of Idaho,* 2:346; Arthur A. Hart, *The Boiseans: At Home* (Boise, Idaho: Historic Boise, 1984). On early Boise Valley history, see Dean L. May, *Three Frontiers: Family, Land, and Society in the American West, 1850–1900* (New York: Cambridge University Press, 1994). On Boise's remarkable business climate, see L. J. Davis, "Unlikely, but Boise Means Big Business," *New York Times Magazine,* 11 June 1989, 24–25, 70–72

9. Arrington, *History of Idaho,* 1: xv; Hugh T. Lovin, "Free Enterprise and Large Scale Reclamation on the Twin Falls–North Side Tract, 1907–1930," *Idaho Yesterdays* 29 (1985): 2–14; Lovin, "The Carey Act in Idaho,

1895–1925: An Experiment in Free Enterprise Reclamation," *Pacific Northwest Quarterly* 78 (1987): 122–33.

10. I have included in my tabulations populations from the counties that are at least partly on the Snake River Plain. This leaves out some counties in the extreme southwestern part of the state as well as a couple of others that are traditionally considered part of southern Idaho. My figures come from *Idaho Statistical Abstract*, 4th ed., vol. 1 (Moscow: University of Idaho Press, 1996), which utilizes 1990 United States census figures. A few sources on the history of minority groups in the Snake River region include Nancy Lee Prichard, "Paradise Found? Opportunity for Mexican, Irish, Italian and Chinese Born Individuals in Jerome Copper Mining District, 1890–1910" (Ph.D. diss., University of Colorado, 1993); Ronald L. James, "Why No Chinamen Are Found in Twin Falls," *Idaho Yesterdays* 36 (1993): 14–24; George M. Blackburn and Sherman L. Ricards, "Unequal Opportunity on a Mining Frontier: The Role of Gender, Race, and Birthplace," *Pacific Historical Review* 62 (1993): 19–38; Francis P. Odom, *A Century of Quiet Accomplishment* (n.p., 1991); Alan Lifton (producer), *Other Faces, Other Lives: Asian Americans in Idaho* [videocassette] (Moscow, Idaho: Rocksteady Productions, ca. 1990); J. Patrick Bieter, "Letemendi's Boarding House: A Basque Cultural Institution in Idaho," *Idaho Yesterdays* 37 (1993): 2–10; and Mary Katsilometes Scott, "The Greek Community in Pocatello, 1890–1940," *Idaho Yesterdays* 28 (1984): 29–36.

11. Palmer, *Snake River,* 51. Palmer is excellent on both the contemporary unifying and disintegrating forces that water contributes to southern Idaho. For historical and potential divisions, see also Marc Reisner, *Cadillac Desert: The American West and Its Disappearing Water* (New York: Penguin, 1986), chap. 11; Hugh Lovin, "Water, Arid Land, and Visions of Advancement on the Snake River Plain," *Idaho Yesterdays* 35 (1991): 3–18; Bookman-Edmonston Engineering, *Water Management Opportunities with the Snake River Basin, Oregon and Idaho: Report of the Snake River Basin Water Committee* (Sacramento, Calif.: Bookman-Edmonston Engineering, 1994); and U.S. Congress, House, Committee on Resources, Subcommittee on Water and Power Resources, *Water Rights: Oversight Hearings Before the Subcommittee on Water and Power Resources of the Committee on Resources* (Washington, D.C.: Government Printing Office, 1996). On irrigation history, ecology, and social conditions of the Snake River Plain between 1880 and the 1920s, see also Mark Fiege, "A World in the Making: The Social and Ecological Construction of Idaho's Irrigated Landscape" (Ph.D. diss., University of Utah, 1994). For a general study on irrigation history, see Leonard J. Arrington, "Irrigation in the Snake River Valley, an Historical Overview," *Idaho Yesterdays* 30 (1986): 3–11.

12. An example of the independence-minded north occurred at the time of statehood and is described in Colson, *Idaho's Constitution;* and Arrington, *History of Idaho*, 1:419–40. On the story about the capital's move, see D. Duff

McKee, "'The People vs. Caleb Lyon and Others': The Capital Relocation Case Revisited," *Idaho Yesterdays* 36 (1992): 2–18.

13. The fiction and nonfiction works that these authors have written on the West and its subregions could fill libraries (and do). A sampling of their best work includes Willa Cather, *Death Comes for the Archbishop* (New York: Knopf, 1927); Cather, *My Ántonia* (Boston: Houghton Mifflin, 1926); Cather, *O Pioneers!* (Boston: Houghton Mifflin, 1913); H. L. Davis, *Honey in the Horn* (New York: Harper, 1935); Mari Sandoz, *Old Jules* (Lincoln: University of Nebraska Press, 1935); John Steinbeck, *Cannery Row* (New York: Viking, 1945); Steinbeck, *The Grapes of Wrath* (New York: Viking, 1939); A. B. Guthrie, *The Big Sky* (New York: Sloane, 1947); Guthrie, *The Way West* (Boston: Houghton Mifflin, 1949); Ivan Doig, *This House of Sky: Landscapes of a Western Mind* (New York: Harcourt Brace Jovanovich, 1978); Doig, *Winter Brothers: A Season at the Edge of America* (New York: Harcourt Brace Jovanovich, 1980); Mary Austin, *This Land of Little Rain* (Boston: Houghton Mifflin, 1903); Craig Lesley, *Winter Kill* (Boston: Houghton Mifflin, 1984); Lesley, *River Song* (Boston: Houghton Mifflin, 1989); Berry, *Trask;* Don Berry, *Moontrap* (Sausalito, Calif.: Comstock, 1962); Berry, *To Build a Ship* (Sausalito, Calif.: Comstock, 1963); Wallace Stegner, *Beyond the Hundredth Meridian: John Wesley Powell and the Second Opening of the West* (Boston: Houghton Mifflin, 1954); Stegner, *The Big Rock Candy Mountain* (New York: Sagamae Press, 1957); Stegner, *Mormon Country* (New York: Duell, Sloan & Pearce, 1942); N. Scott Momaday, *House Made of Dawn* (New York: Harper & Row, 1968); Leslie Marmon Silko, *Ceremony* (New York: Viking, 1977); James Welch, *Fools Crow* (New York: Penguin, 1986); Welch, *The Death of Jim Loney* (New York: Penguin, 1979); Louise Erdrich, *The Beet Queen* (New York: Bantam, 1986); Erdrich, *Love Medicine: A Novel* (New York: Holt, Rinehart and Winston, 1984); Rudolfo A. Anaya, *Heart of Aztlán* (Berkeley, Calif.: Justa, 1976); and Rudolfo A. Anaya and Francisco A. Lomelí, *Aztlán: Essays on the Chicano Homeland* (Albuquerque: University of New Mexico Press, 1991).

14. Edwin R. Bingham, "Washington Irving's 'Astoria': An 1836 Classic Retains that Status Today," *Oregon Magazine*, October 1980, 56. Irving's relationship with the West has been the subject of various recent scholarly studies: John L. Allen, "Horizons of the Sublime: The Invention of the Romantic West," *Journal of Historical Geography* 18 (1992): 27–40; Elizabeth L. Broach, "Angels, Architecture, and Erosion: The Dakota Badlands as Cultural Symbol," *North Dakota History* 59 (1992): 2–15; Kris Lackey, "Eighteenth-Century Aesthetic Theory and the Nineteenth-Century Traveller in Trans-Allegheny America: F. Trollope, Dickens, Irving and Parkman," *American Studies* 32 (1991): 33–48; Peter Antelyes, *Tales of Adventurous Enterprise: Washington Irving and the Poetics of Western Expansion* (New York: Columbia University Press, 1990); I. S. MacLaren, "Washington Irving's Problems with History and Romance in Astoria,"

Canadian Review of American Studies, 21 (1990): 1–13; Hugh Egam, "The Second-Hand Wilderness: History and Art in Irving's Astoria," *ATQ* 2 (1988): 253–70.

15. Richard Holton Cracroft, "The American West of Washington Irving: The Quest for National Tradition" (Ph.D. diss., University of Wisconsin, 1970), 36, 52–53, 59, 190–91. The "boiling, seething" Caldron Linn has also been called "Devil's Scuttle Hole," according to Lalia Boone, *Idaho Place Names: A Geographical Dictionary* (Moscow: University of Idaho Press, 1988), 61; Washington Irving, *Astoria, Or Anecdotes of an Enterprise Beyond the Rocky Mountains* (Philadelphia: Carey, Lea, & Blanchard, 1836), 2:31, 33.

16. Irving, *Astoria,* 2:30; Washington Irving, *The Rocky Mountains: Or, Scenes, Incidents, and Adventures in the Far West; Digested from the Journal of Captain B.L.E. Bonneville, of the Army of the United States, and Illustrated from Various Other Sources,* 2 vols. (Philadelphia: Carey, Lea, & Blanchard, 1837), 2:44–45.

17. Irving, *Bonneville,* 1:131, 156.

18. It should be pointed out that before coming to the West, Foote had become a noted illustrator. However, it was in the West that her artistic career took off and she also began writing. A somewhat controversial fictitious biography of Mary Hallock Foote is Wallace Stegner, *Angle of Repose* (New York: Doubleday, 1971).

19. Barbara Cragg, Dennis Walsh, and Mary Ellen Walsh, eds., *The Idaho Stories and Far West Illustrations of Mary Hallock Foote* (Pocatello: Idaho State University Press, 1988). On Foote in the West generally, see Rodman Paul, ed., *A Victorian Gentlewomen in the Far West: The Reminiscences of Mary Hallock Foote* (San Marino, Calif.: The Huntington Library, 1972); Lee Ann Johnson, *Mary Hallock Foote* (Boston: Twayne, 1980); and Barbara Cragg, "Mary Hallock Foote's Images of the Old West," *Landscape* 24 (1980): 43–47. On Foote's difficult domestic life, see Melody Graulich, "Mary Hallock Foote, 1847–1938," *Legacy* 3 (1986): 43–52. And on Foote in Idaho, see Rodman W. Paul, "When Culture Came to Boise: Mary Hallock Foote in Idaho," *Idaho Yesterdays* 20 (1976): 2–12.

20. Mary Hallock Foote to Helena de Kay Gilder, 6–8 June 1887, quoted in Johnson, *Mary Hallock Foote,* 70; Foote, *Reminiscences,* 275; Foote, "Maverick," in *Idaho Stories,* 77.

21. Foote, *Reminiscences,* 265–66. The Footes' residence in Idaho— residence due to Arthur's desire to control the region's waters—certainly ended with financial tragedy. Not surprisingly, the region's waters also provide tragic endings for some of Foote's characters. For example, Henniker in "The Trumpeter" drowns himself in the Snake River. And Ruth Mary Tully in Foote's first Idaho story, "A Cloud on the Mountain," drowns in the rising waters of the Boise River as she attempts to bring warning of the coming flood to the mining engineer she loves. See Foote, "The Trumpeter" and "A Cloud on the Mountain," in *Idaho Stories,* 92–135, 1–23.

22. Foote, "The Harshaw Bride," in *Idaho Stories*, 252.

23. Ibid., 258.

24. Ibid., 266

25. Tim Woodward, *Tiger on the Road* (Caldwell, Idaho: Caxton Printers, 1989), 31; Wayne Chatterton, *Vardis Fisher: The Frontier and Regional Works*, Western Writers Series, No. 1 (Boise, Idaho: Boise State College, 1972), 6. Woodward's is the only full-length biography of Fisher.

26. Another early novel, *In Tragic Life* (1932), is the first in an autobiographical tetralogy. While part of *In Tragic Life* takes place outside eastern Idaho, most of it is set within. Consequently, it too is considered a regional novel. For the subsequent volumes of the series, southeastern Idaho is a secondary setting. Consequently, *In Tragic Life* is considered the only truly regional novel of the four. But showing the significance of the Snake River landscape on Fisher in these subsequent works, one literary critic pointed out that although the hero of the tetralogy moves to many places, "the determining background is always the Idaho benchland." See Chatterton, *Vardis Fisher*, 21; and John Peale Bishop, "The Strange Case of Vardis Fisher," in *The Collected Essays of John Peale Bishop*, ed. Edmund Wilson (New York: Scribner, 1948), 57, quoted in Chatterton, *Vardis Fisher*, 24.

27. Vardis Fisher, *Toilers of the Hills* (1928; Caldwell, Idaho: Caxton Printers, 1933), 14.

28. Ibid., 99, 100.

29. Ibid., 360, 359.

30. Vardis Fisher, *Dark Bridwell* (Boston: Houghton Mifflin, 1931; reprint, Boise, Idaho: Opal Laurel Holmes, n.d.), 43, 44, 45.

31. Ibid., 268, 269, 270, 271, 355.

Part Three:

RACE AND ETHNICITY

Although the western half of the United States is a vast
kaleidoscope of places and people, it is usually reduced to a much
simpler image. In its mythic role, the variegated West is distilled to
a lone horseman against a distant butte; in the popular mind, it
becomes an immense Monument Valley where the Marlboro Man,
John Wayne, or Clint Eastwood ride under a big sky through an
endless open range. An occasional Indian, Mexican, school marm,
or rancher's wife might lurk in a few box canyons on the edge of
this rugged terrain, but the imagined West remains a white man's
refuge. This white, macho, nearly empty land was marketed by
Frederic Remington, Theodore Roosevelt, and Owen Wister a century
ago, and it is merchandised by Ralph Lauren, Walt Disney, and the
Phillip Morris people today. This is the glossy landscape that sells so
many cars, computers, clothes, cigarettes, and cappuccinos to aging
urban baby boomers, and this is the mythic place that tourists
discover in Disney's Frontierlands where friendly Indian robots and
a few dance-hall girls are the only nonwhite, nonmale presence.

The urge to condense the multivarious West to one landscape ruled by white men moves beyond theme parks and consumer culture. In the previous part of this book, Mary Murphy warns that the master narrative of pioneer conquest and recent notion of Montana as the "Last Best Place" can be twisted to mean "the ultimate destination on the white-flight highway—the last best hiding place from the rest of America." There are just enough militia men and Ted Kosinski−types in pockets of the West to justify her warning and highlight the importance of counternarratives of women and Native Americans. In this section, Arnoldo De León points out how Texas schoolchildren of all cultures were taught the glories of Anglo supremacy in the Lone Star State, while William Deverell outlines how southern Californians learned the wonders of white hegemony through the subtle lessons of real estate, popular entertainment, and architecture.

Despite such coercive campaigns and escapist fantasies, the West remains an infinitely complex constellation of people and places. Far from being a big safe place for a few white folk, the land beyond the ninty-eighth meridian bristles with natural and cultural variety. Its daunting geographical diversity is surpassed by its human richness. The differences between the Olympic rain forest and the Mojave Desert, the Rocky Mountains and the Great Plains, for example, are overshadowed by contrasts between Koreans in Los Angeles and Mormons in Salt Lake City, African-Americans in San Francisco and Navajos in New Mexico, Tejanos in San Antonio and Irish in Butte.

This Whitmanesque list could easily continue, but the point is clear: the nation's 60 million Westerners are as various as their landscape, and only a small fraction of them fit the stock rural profile. With 86 percent of its people living in cities, and with Los Angeles, San Diego, Las Vegas, Phoenix, Denver, and Seattle among the fastest-growing metropolitan areas in the nation, the West remains the most urban American region in the 1990s. The Census Bureau's West, which excludes Texas and the five Plains states, contains the country's highest percentage of foreign-born residents; and with only 22 percent of the nation's people, the census West has 48 percent of its Native American population and 45 percent and 56 percent of its Hispanic and Asian residents, respectively.

Laced with cities and brimming with immigrants, the West has always been a place where cultures collide with creative as well as destructive consequences. A piebald cast of characters from every continent converged on the West from the beginning, and this frontier pluralism endures wherever cultures meet today. Although ethnic patterns and concentrations have varied throughout the West, each of the many Wests has been a testing ground, at one time or another, for versions of cultural diversity. Paula Gunn Allen's portrait of Anglo-Hispanic-Native American mixtures in the Southwest, John Whitehead's sketch of Hawai'i's Anglo-Asian milieu, Anne F. Hyde's discussions of cultural contention in the Rocky Mountains and in early Montana—these and other essays shed light on shifting multicultural arrangements within the many Wests that are the actual arenas of people's lives.

The chapters in this part of the book heighten our understanding of cultural pluralism in the Pacific Rim and Sunbelt portions of the West. Focusing on northern California, southern California, and Texas—regions with large urban centers experiencing massive immigration from Asia and Latin America—these studies trace the emergence of at least three ethnoregional systems and intercultural possibilities, ranging from flexible cosmopolitanism to syncretic blending to harsher patterns of white hegemony. Each author explores, furthermore, how the creation of these systems and attitudes toward "the other" lies at the heart of regional consciousness and identity.

In "Forging a Cosmopolitan Civic Culture," Glenna Matthews shrewdly argues that the liberal, pluralistic identity of San Francisco and its hinterlands is rooted in the polyglot gold-rush frontier of the 1840s and 1850s. The future city and burgeoning goldfields were engulfed by so many self-sustaining cultures during these formative years that no single group—not even white Protestants—could dominate the emerging region. "San Francisco was not born enlightened," she notes, "but it was born in such a way that many groups could contend in its public sphere." At the same time that Matthews carefully avoids portraying the region as a racial utopia, noting the persistence of brutal scapegoating and xenophobia, she also traces the city's evolution from the primitive cosmopolitanism of a conglomeration of competing groups in the nineteenth century to the fuller civic culture embodied by the expansiveness of a Willie Brown or a Lawrence Ferlinghetti today.

While Matthews's northern California is a model of cosmopolitan openness, Deverell's southern California is an object lesson of hegemonic control. There are remarkable similarities between the regions—both are dominated by large cities characterized by racial diversity and both began as a potpourri of cultures—yet an Anglo elite emerged south of the Tehachipis, while a more even balance of power prevailed in the north. In "Privileging the Mission over the Mexican," Deverell focuses on the period between 1880 and 1920 when a southern California identity was forged from Anglo interpretations of Mexican culture. By the 1880s, the region's ethnic equilibrium was shattered as railroads and a wondrous climate brought in a flood tide of Americans, and a subtle set of strategies emerged to "freeze" the Mexican in time and place. Nostalgic evocations of a Spanish Fantasy Past in melodrama and preserved ruins, postcards and citrus-crate labels depicting the "typical Mexican" as a happy worker and real-estate campaigns designed to keep him out of sight—such images taught, and perhaps continue to teach, southern Californians about ethnic compliance and regional identity.

In "Region and Ethnicity," De León is also concerned with the construction of regional myths and the ethnic realities they hide. Just as Deverell warns that the mission myth masks the "extraordinarily diverse society . . . being forged in southern California," De León succinctly describes how the romantic image of the rugged cowboy smothers Texas's cultural complexity. Looking beneath the Anglo-manufactured myth of "Texanism," De León masterfully traces the movement of four groups into the Lone Star State—Mexicans from the south, Anglo and African-Americans from the east, and Commanches from the north—and describes how three ethnoregional identities emerged by the end of the nineteenth century as a result of the interaction of these cultures. Tejano-textured border Texas, African-American–influenced East Texas, and Anglo-flavored West Texas constitute the real cultural matrix of the state, though Texans of all backgrounds have multiple loyalties to their specific ethno-region, the state as a whole, and the larger West. De León's concluding image of cultural syncretism and creative cross-fertilization—so remindful of John Sayles's film *Lone Star*—stands as a compelling model for western regional identity.

Forging a Cosmopolitan Civic Culture:

The Regional Identity

of San Francisco and

Northern California

Glenna Matthews

In 1995, in the wake of the Republican landslide of 1994, could the flamboyant—and liberal—former speaker of the California Assembly, Willie Brown, have been elected mayor of any other big city in the country besides San Francisco? Assuming that the answer to this question is no, the next question is: What makes politics in San Francisco unique? How does one account for the plethora of causes, cultural phenomena, and social movements that have been born in the Bay Area and in northern California, from the Sierra Club 100 or so years ago to the Beats of the 1950s, the hippies of the 1960s, and beyond—to say nothing of the powerful labor movement during the glory days of American labor? What is the relationship between the Bay Area and the rest of the region? Is there a downside to all this openness to social experimentation? These are all tough questions, in part because grappling with them compels us to confront the possibility that the northern portion of the Golden State resembles no place else on earth.

The men (for men they largely were) who flocked to the region following the discovery of gold in 1848 and precipitated the region's growth as a substantial Euro-American settlement had no notion of creating a unique environment. They came to strike it rich—or at least to seize another chance from life—and, with rare exceptions, they brought no special complement of idealism along with them. The history of the region is pockmarked with episodes of violence, especially violence directed against people of color, reflecting the racism and ethnocentrism that the Euro-American forty-niners carried with them from wherever they came. A superficial glance at the past, thus, would seem to offer little in the way of a clue to the nature of one of the most liberal portions of the United States in the 1990s. Yet if one lingers to examine the past more closely, the gaze backward in time can fill in important parts of the puzzle.

Writing in 1949, Carey McWilliams suggested that the whole state of California constituted one vast "Great Exception" to the larger national pattern.[1] He singled out a number of factors that, he thought, underlie California exceptionalism, such as the peculiar nature of the state's agriculture, the unusual character of the state's demography, and the especially feisty relationship between capital and labor. But in most instances, the precipitating cause of what he chose to emphasize can be traced back to the gold rush. In short, one of the most perceptive observers ever to write about California saw this early period as essential to understanding later developments.

By way of contrast, after having been long dominated by paradigms emphasizing the paramount importance of the pioneer period—above all, by Frederick Jackson Turner's frontier thesis—the field of western history has moved in an altogether different direction in recent years. Indeed, one of the outstanding books in the field, Richard White's *"It's Your Misfortune and None of My Own,"* contains not a single use of the word "frontier," by no means an accident.[2] Turner's frontier was one of triumphant individualism, thanks to the abundance of "free land," and his insensitivity to those who suffered at the hands of the Euro-American pioneers has discredited this focus as a means of understanding the West. Moreover, to talk about "exceptionalism," whether American or Californian, has seemed to many to be an act of implicit cultural imperialism.

Yet McWilliams shows us that it is possible to talk about exceptionalism without being triumphalist and to emphasize the pioneer era without stinting on recognition of the injustice that came with development. Where Turner spoke of "free land" and gave short shrift to those—the Native Americans—who had been dispossessed, McWilliams went out of his way to demonstrate that the land was far from free: the sheer number of those who rushed to California after 1848 led to an unusual land hunger and a particularly brutal treatment for the indigenous population that stood between the forty-niners and their dreamed-of riches. Giving the figures for the decimation of the Indian population in California, McWilliams writes that: "California 'solved' its Indian problem by liquidating the Indians."[3] The land in California was free only if you discount the cost of what verged on genocide.

Although Turner and McWilliams agree on the critical importance of the early stages of development to a region's subsequent history, McWilliams's early California does not much resemble Turner's frontier. McWilliams not only builds the harsh treatment of the indigenous people into his analysis, but also argues that the land in California began to be swallowed up by rapacious entrepreneurs at an early stage, thus limiting migrants' access to land.[4] California was settled by an explosion of Euro-American population (as well as by smaller numbers of people from other parts of the world), the Native peoples suffered extraordinary depredations as a consequence, and the capitalists moved in with remarkable dispatch. This is not Turner's frontier as incubator of democracy.

So California exceptionalism in McWilliams's formulation did not entail an exemption from guilt and sin à la that prototypical "American Adam" before the fall who stands at the forefront or lurks in the background of social portraits delineated by frontier enthusiasts. Rather, there was guilt aplenty for those who flocked to the Golden State early on, and, in his reckoning in 1949, California remained a problem for its western neighbors, because it was so much bigger and richer than they. In short, conceived in greed, California still had the mid-twentieth-century identity of the neighborhood bully, according to McWilliams.

Many current scholars of American regional identity—as opposed to western historians—also emphasize the ways in which "distinctive variations related to the time and scale of settlement" interact with "natural, demographic, economic, social, and political characteristics."[5] In other words, regional identity and regional consciousness are regarded as greatly shaped by factors that are artifacts of the process of settlement by Euro-Americans. In northern California, that settlement process was shaped most powerfully by the shiny metal that James Marshall discovered at Sutter's Mill in January 1848. Once again, we find ourselves back at the gold rush.

In this chapter, I argue that because the gold rush brought together a group of people who had never before lived in the same jurisdiction in the history of the world—from Asia, Latin America, Europe, and North America as well as a small number of African-Americans—northern California was "born cosmopolitan" to an unprecedented extent, and that this phenomenon has shaped all of its subsequent history. I want to make clear that I am using "cosmopolitan" in the sense meaning "composed of elements gathered from all or various parts of the world," not in the sense connoting "citizen of the world," because many decades would elapse before the use of the word in the latter connotation to characterize the region would be warranted.[6] People came from everywhere, creating an atmosphere so heady that over time some began to value the cosmopolitanism for its own sake and to act to lessen the cognitive dissonance between it and the ethnocentrism and racial antipathy that were also so manifest, thus creating a unique regional consciousness.[7] Moreover, the sheer amount of wealth created in the early stages of the region's history, not only by the mining but also by ancillary economic activities, underwrote cultural developments as diverse as the population, thus enhancing the cosmopolitanism. And the wealth also created an opportunity structure such that, over the long haul, the people of northern California had relatively less reason to hate the "other" than did people in most parts of the country—which is not to say that they never did so. This is the essence of my argument. The class-specific nature of the cosmopolitanism must also be acknowledged, since in the early stages of the region's development it seems to have been primarily a value attractive to the upper and mercantile classes, who began to conceive of its commercial possibilities.

THE LONG REACH OF THE GOLD RUSH

In assessing the impact of the gold rush, one can distinguish analytically between the material and the cultural legacy. In real life, of course, the two are intertwined. For example, the huge fortunes made in the very early days of northern California by the Hearsts and the Stanfords laid the foundation for the region's cultural vitality in the 1990s: the University of California at Berkeley, blessed by Hearst dollars, and Stanford University, founded by the beneficence of Leland and Jane Stanford, are generally regarded as two of the top universities in the world. These two institutions have been of inestimable value in promoting the intellectual life throughout much of northern California.

One can also distinguish analytically between the region's major metropolis and its hinterland in the northern half of the state. We begin with the city by the Bay. In 1848, San Francisco was a village containing a few hundred souls. By the end of 1849, an additional 39,000 people, mostly men, had disembarked in the port. In 1852, a census reported a San Francisco population of 36,000.[8] By 1865, the city's population had reached 100,000. So rapid a growth led the historian Gunther Barth to use the term "instant city" to characterize San Francisco.[9]

But what was even more remarkable than the city's rapid growth was its ethnic diversity. Men and a few women came from every continent, some en route to the goldfields and some who made San Francisco their permanent home. From Canton, men came east to Gold Mountain. From Chile, men came north to work in the quicksilver mines south of San Jose, as well as to look for gold. Men came west from the "states" and from Europe. There was also a small population of African-Americans, some of whom came west to seek opportunity.

Very early in the city's history, observers began to remark about the cosmopolitan air created by this immense influx as well as about the cultural manifestations of such diversity. One of the major areas of impact noted at the time lay in gastronomy. Said Frank Soulé and his co-authors in 1855: "There were the American *dining-rooms,* the English *lunch houses,* the French *cabarets,* the Spanish *fondas,* the German *Wirtschafts,* the Italian *osterie,* the Chinese *chow-chows,* and so on to the end of a very long chapter."[10] After a return visit in 1859 to the area he had first visited during the trip described in *Two Years Before the Mast,* Richard Henry Dana effused about the quality of San Francisco's cuisine, comparing it favorably with the food he had eaten in Paris.[11] And so on. The city directory of 1854 listed dozens of restaurants, including La Estrella de Chile, the William Tell, and Au Rendezvous des Ouvriers.[12]

If we turn to the press, we note a similar phenomenon. In his book about the first five decades of San Francisco's history, Philip Ethington says,: "During the 1850s an average of seven English-language newspapers were started *every year*, and no fewer than thirty-six foreign-language papers—published in Chinese, French, German, Spanish, Hebrew, and Italian—enjoyed at least a brief life."[13] He goes on to note that as of 1880 the city had twenty-one daily newspapers. The abundance of newspapers in a profusion of languages meant that the city had an exceptionally lively and diverse public sphere from the very earliest period.

People came from all over, and they quickly transplanted the institutions that were most important to them—as is especially clear if one examines the city's religious history. Most American cities have been born Protestant, with a few notable exceptions such as Baltimore, Los Angeles, New Orleans, St. Louis, and the cities of the Southwest. San Francisco also was born Catholic, as a result of the activities of the Franciscan fathers who launched the California mission system. But unlike that of most other cities, San Francisco's religious pluralism was enhanced by the fact that its first synagogues were founded more or less simultaneously with its first Protestant churches: St. John's Methodist Church came into being in 1847, and the first Jewish services were held on Yom Kippur in 1849. Two years later, pioneers founded two synagogues. The Chinese established temples for the practice of their syncretic religion, and also attended Christian services; Richard Henry Dana, for example, reported that he visited a Chinese mission chapel in 1859. In 1852, the year that *Uncle Tom's Cabin* created a national sensation and the California state legislature passed its own version of the Fugitive Slave Act, members of San Francisco's small African-American community founded three churches.[14] And in the late nineteenth century, as the Issei population began to take shape, Buddhist missionaries came over from Japan and started what would become the Buddhist Churches of America.

The 1850s were an extraordinary time in San Francisco. Besides the founding of so many religious institutions, the decade saw outbreaks of vigilantism on two occasions, as well as numerous other acts of violence. Men came into town with money and a yen for action, and they could usually find plenty of the latter—which created abundant problems for those charged with keeping the social order. But San Franciscans also craved beauty; hence they provided a remarkably avid audience for culture. Remote and isolated as the city was before the completion of the transcontinental railroad in 1869, its wealth nonetheless drew opera companies from many lands. According to George Martin, "despite the isolation, in the years 1851–60, as Verdi ultimately became the city's favorite composer, San Francisco's taste for opera swelled into such a passion that if today's citizens of New York took to opera with equal exuberance—numbers of tickets sold relative to the population—the Metropolitan Opera Company would have to build twenty additional houses (cap. 3800) and play them every night."[15]

Rambunctious and violent, yet filled with good restaurants and glorious music—out of this past came the legend of "Only in San Francisco." Although San Franciscans can display an annoying (to others) narcissism on occasion, there is undeniably some truth to the legend. For example, San Francisco was born at the precise moment when the anti-Catholic and nativist American Party, or Know-Nothings, flourished in the "states." "Only in San Francisco" did the Know-Nothings nominate a German Catholic immigrant for mayor in 1854; but he was removed from the ticket at the last moment because of the anger of the anti-Catholic Know-Nothings.[16] In other words, the city *did* have a nativist party, but it was more moderate in its views than were such parties in the rest of the country.

As anyone with more than a passing acquaintance with California history knows, one cannot confine a discussion of the city's diversity to the celebratory mode. In particular, the treatment of immigrants from Asia constitutes a shameful chapter in San Francisco's history. The Chinese were the first to arrive, and they faced a multitude of barriers, formal and informal, culminating in the passage of the Chinese Exclusion Act (which excluded all but merchants) by the United States Congress in 1882. Workingmen organized around the slogan "The Chinese must go!" Politicians curried favor with the electorate by their willingness to pass further discriminatory legislation. Prevented from becoming citizens, harassed in the work place, residentially segregated, and discouraged from forming families by the difficulties of bringing over numbers of women equal to those of men—and then scapegoated for being "immoral"—the Chinese paid a terrible price for trying to improve their lives by coming to Gold Mountain. One man recalled: "I myself rarely left Chinatown, only when I had to buy American things downtown. The area around Union Square was a dangerous place for us, you see, especially at nighttime before the quake. Chinese were often attacked by thugs there and all of us had to have a police whistle with us at all times. . . . [O]nce we were inside Chinatown, the thugs didn't bother us."[17] When the Japanese began to arrive in significant numbers in the late nineteenth century, they, too, faced grave difficulties. They were denied access to public schools, forbidden by state law from owning property, and prevented by federal law from becoming citizens. In 1905, members of the San Francisco labor movement formed the Asiatic Exclusion League, directed at both the Chinese and the Japanese.

What we encounter when we examine the history of San Francisco, and California more generally, is a situation whereby Euro-Americans "racialized" non-European residents, creating an invidious category for these "others" in an attempt to arrogate to themselves the better part of the material goods to be found in the newly developing region. A good example of how this worked was the state legislature's passing the foreign miners' license tax in 1850, which mandated that Mexicans and Chinese, but not Euro-Americans, had to pay a premium to mine gold. Concludes sociologist Tomás Almaguer, "What stands out most clearly from this comparative history [of racial ethnic groups in California] is that European Americans at every class level sought to create, maintain, or extend their privileged access to racial entitlements in California."[18]

Given this sorry history, how can it be argued that being born so diverse had a significant positive impact on San Francisco? It is impossible in the compass of a chapter article to do justice to this question, clearly worthy of a book, but I will attempt to sketch the lineaments of an answer. On the one hand, the evidence is clear for the presence of systematic and endemic racism. On the other, I believe that certain peculiarities of the social structure in San Francisco and the larger region, precipitated by the gold rush but not confined to those years, served to erode racial hierarchies. In the first place, this city, with its compact size, continued to be a major port and to attract people from all over the world. Indeed, by 1880 San Francisco, with its population of 233,959, was the ninth largest city in the country and the one with the largest percentage of foreign-born residents, 44.6 percent.[19] Inevitably, there was contact among diverse groups, despite the patterns of residential segregation, despite the fact that members of the first generation of Chinese-American women, for example, rarely if ever left Chinatown. Many good books could be written on the social geography of this city. One would like to know, for example, precisely when people began to eat one another's ethnic cuisine, thus breaking bread together.[20] In any event, we can safely conclude that because of geography, San Franciscans could not easily ignore one another.

In the second place, many groups arrived in numbers that, in effect, constituted a critical mass capable of founding institutions, staging cultural events, and fighting back. In the 1850s, for example, residents of the city could enjoy not only Verdi, but also Chinese opera. Thus the Chinese, who suffered from the most virulent discrimination, had lost little time in securing an economic toehold and then in building lives for themselves. Perhaps most significant of what they created, members of their merchant class founded what we know as the Six Companies. With this community infrastructure in place, the Chinese were able to use an unfriendly court system to defend their interests to what one scholar calls "an extraordinary degree," hiring Euro-American lawyers to prosecute their cases.[21]

Suffering from less discrimination than the Asian immigrants, though it would be a mistake to argue that they faced none, Jews and Irish and Italian Catholics have had a history in San Francisco that resembles that in no other American city. They came with the gold rush, some made substantial sums of money, and by the time of the earthquake and fire of 1906, Jews, Irish, and Italians were part of the ruling elite that helped put the city back together again. Adolph Sutro, James Phelan, A. P. Giannini, Angelo Rossi, and Abraham Ruef exemplified the relative openness of the city by the Bay to endeavors by people who were sorely marginalized in many other American cities. Say William Issel and Robert Cherny in their authoritative history of the city between 1865 and 1932: "Unlike [in] eastern cities, no white group found itself excluded from the ladder of economic and social mobility."[22] This phenomenon, it should be noted, gave the local labor movement a source of strength missing in areas where white workers fought among themselves across ethnic lines. Above all, because of the gold rush and the plethora of diverse groups that often prospered from the beginning, there was never a thorough-going Protestant hegemony in San Francisco, as there was at the founding of most other American cities. San Francisco was not born enlightened— far from it—but it was born in such a way that many groups could contend in its public sphere.

Heterogeneous and culturally pluralistic, San Francisco's cosmopolitanism was enhanced by the allure of its many bohemian residents and environs, dating from the gold rush. Although the vice district known as the Barbary Coast, to cite one example, had its sordid and crime-ridden aspect, it and its denizens also manifested an undoubted glamour and attraction. Such people and places served as a magnet for like-minded newcomers, who might well have been in rebellion against any type of hierarchy, including those based on race. As a consequence of these patterns, according to Issel, the city possessed "a combination of elements common to international port cities throughout the world: a world-famous retail market in sex, drugs, and alcohol; a renowned array of tourist-oriented exoticism; social enclaves comprising dissenters and outsiders of various kinds whose expressions in literature, arts, and politics have put them in opposition to—and sometimes in conflict with—the dominant conventional resident population."[23] That the city was home to so many single men—it was still 55 percent male as late as 1900—no doubt contributed to its tolerance where sexuality was concerned, since nineteenth-century gender ideology regarded women as the chief upholders of sexual morality.

What is especially clear is that San Francisco quickly developed into one of the major centers for the arts in the country outside Boston and New York. Theater and opera flourished—with one of the leading impresarios, Tom Maguire, also playing a role in Democratic Party politics. From the time of Bret Harte and Mark Twain to Gertrude Atherton and Frank Norris to the Beats and beyond, the literary tradition has been powerful. And the artistic tradition has been multicultural as well as bohemian. In the 1860s, the African-American writer J. Madison Bell wrote poetry. Later in the century, the Chinese-American artist Mary Tape (who with her husband, Joseph, sued the city in 1884 to desegregate the schools) created oil paintings of flowers. In the early twentieth century, there were two Japanese-American poets: Yone Noguchi and Sadakichi Hartmann. Another prominent local bohemian of that period was the Mexican-born painter Xavier Martínez. The list could go on and on. These men and women helped create cosmopolitan San Francisco in the fullest sense of the term.[24]

If the arts represented cosmopolitanism in action, so did local politics—though in this realm people of color did not have the same opportunities that they created for themselves in the arts and in religion. The mix of people and the rise and demise of a variety of political parties, such as the People's Party (which came out of the vigilante episodes of the 1850s) and the Workingmen's Party of the 1870s, helped to create a very lively public sphere featuring an enormous variety of newspapers, as we have seen. This, in turn, allowed many men and a few women to make their impact and/or to serve as leaders in the decades following the gold rush and into the twentieth century. As a consequence, San Francisco was the first big city in the country with an Irish-American mayor, the first with a Jewish mayor, the first with a labor leader as mayor, the first with an Italian-American mayor, the first to send an Irish-American woman to Congress, the first to send a Jewish woman to Congress, all the way forward in time to the pathbreaking role of Harvey Milk, the first gay supervisor in the 1970s.[25]

Finally, the presence of a cosmopolitan ideal—though mythical for many decades in the sense connoting urbanity—created an image against which the city could measure itself. A number of historians have argued that such a legacy of idealism can have a powerful material impact, and I believe that San Francisco is a good example of this phenomenon.[26] Certainly, it is easy to find invocations of the word "cosmopolitan" to document the presence of the ideal. From the 1850s on, San Francisco's gastronomy warranted and received that adjective, as old menus and cookbooks in the collection of the San Francisco Public Library can attest. In the 1860s, school superintendent John Pelton launched instruction in German, French, and Spanish at certain schools designated "cosmopolitan."[27] We find in the September 20, 1899, issue of the *California Architect and Building News* this generalization: "San Francisco is notoriously cosmopolitan. Her architects are of varied nationality, varied tongue, and varied training." And moving forward in time to the early twentieth century, we encounter the founding of the Cosmos Club in 1919, an interracial organization composed of well-to-do members of both black and white families. Every year, the club staged an elegant interracial ball, strictly formal in dress.[28]

Ineluctably, cosmopolitanism found its way into the civic culture with so much to substantiate its presence. Moreover, as time went on, more and more San Franciscans began to comprehend the commercial and tourist value of their fabled cosmopolitanism and to act accordingly. For the World's Fair of 1939, for example, planners self-consciously used the city's cosmopolitan image to position San Francisco as the logical candidate to be queen of the Pacific Rim.[29] At the same time, it should be pointed out that there were members of the civic elite, such as the wealthy Irish-Catholic James Duval Phelan, who was elected mayor in 1896, who openly espoused an ideology of white supremacy. Until well into the twentieth century, the racist reality for people of color and the cosmopolitan ideal espoused by a portion of the Euro-American citizenry contradicted each other.

I would not argue that the cosmopolitan ideal had the same impact on the rest of northern California that it had on San Francisco, though the city's elite was bound to have a regional impact because of ties between its capitalists and their fellow ethnics or co-religionists in greater northern California.[30] I would argue, however, that the mix of people who came during the gold rush created a most unusual environment throughout much of the region, cosmopolitan in the sense of "composed of elements gathered from all or various parts of the world," if not necessarily in more integrative meanings of the word. No less an observer than Josiah Royce—who was born in Grass Valley in 1855, attended high school in San Francisco, and then wrote a history of his native state when he was a Harvard philosophy professor—spoke of the drama set in motion by the encounter among such diverse groups. Deploring the treatment accorded to foreigners, he nonetheless contended that the social situation in early California possessed an elemental significance: "But whoever knows that the struggle for the best things of man is a struggle against the basest passions of man, and that every significant historical process is full of such struggles, is ready to understand the true interest of scenes amid which civilization sometimes seemed to have lapsed into semi-barbarism."[31] He believed that the necessity to forge a community in so harsh a set of circumstances as gold-rush northern California brought out the noble as well as the base in Californians.

The Central Valley was one of the portions of California north of the Tehachapis, in addition to San Francisco and the greater Bay Area, in which this drama played itself out. Sally Miller points out that "ever since the Gold Rush, California's Central Valley has attracted people from across the face of the globe. . . . What lured the French and Swiss, Danes and Basques, Swedes and Hungarians, Canadians and Serbs, and Jews, Arabs, and Asians, as well as many others from a variety of lands, was the valley's non-bullion 'gold,' that is, the rich potential of its agriculture."[32]

As in San Francisco, this cosmopolitan mix of people in the larger region precluded the establishment of a Protestant hegemony. Laurie Maffly-Kipp has studied the spiritual consequences of the world having rushed into northern California: "Indeed, what was special about religion in California was not simply the *fact* of pluralism, but the placement of a wide variety of beliefs on a relatively equal organizational footing. Unlike the situation in southern California, where a slower immigration and a stronger Catholic church impeded the Protestantization well into the 1870s, the rapid influx of settlers to the north quickly overwhelmed an already weakened Catholic structure, producing a free market of religious beliefs."[33]

This free market of beliefs in conjunction with the dearth of women— the carriers and enforcers of middle-class norms—to say nothing of the risk taking that was central to what brought men to the region in the first place, combined to foster a remarkable spirit of openness. This legacy is arguably still present in northern California's regional consciousness. Born cosmopolitan in the sense of being ethnically diverse, the region has retained and even increased its diversity in the twentieth century while evolving into one of the globe's more intriguing and occasionally infuriating locales, because of its propensity for social experimentation. Diversity, which started out as a demographic fact, has been transformed into the inspiration for a set of values.

NORTHERN CALIFORNIA IN THE TWENTIETH CENTURY

In 1903, San Franciscan Charles Warren Stoddard published *The Pleasure of His Company,* the first gay autobiography to be written in a city now internationally known for its large and vibrant gay and lesbian community. This book is clear evidence that not only did the city have a gay population by the early twentieth century, but it was of sufficient size and confidence to produce literary representations. What the book does *not* mean, however, is that it was possible to come out of the closet with impunity. Quite the contrary. Gays and lesbians faced most of the difficulties in San Francisco that they faced elsewhere: they might be beaten up by young toughs, they might be fired if their sexual orientation became known, their clubs and nightspots might be singled out for hostile attention by the local police. It would take many decades and much civil-rights organizing before today's relatively open climate could be achieved.[34]

The subject of gay and lesbian San Francisco not only is important for its own sake, but offers insight into the tension between the cosmopolitan-bohemian ideal—which clearly attracted a gay and lesbian population to

San Francisco—and the ugly social realities for many San Franciscans of the "wrong" color or sexual orientation. To say either that San Francisco and northern California were, by the dawn of the twentieth century, oases of enlightenment toward all or that they were no different than any-place else would be a mistake. Indeed, the cosmopolitan ideal was begin-ning to make its impact. But we will need far more scholarly work on the region than we now possess before we understand these dynamics adequately.

Empirical work that has been done on other Bay Area communities has revealed ethnic patterns resembling those of San Francisco, patterns that substantiate the notion of northern California exceptionalism begin-ning in the nineteenth century and persisting into the twentieth. For example, a sample of San Jose heads of household drawn from the manu-script census of 1860 and then linked with the census of 1870 to see who was still there and how they had fared has established that there was no statistically significant relationship between ethnicity among Euro-Americans and either occupational or property mobility.[35] The published United States census of 1930 shows that several decades later there was no statistically significant difference between the rate of high-school at-tendance for native-born youngsters and the rate for those from first- or second-generation European immigrant households—this at a time when Italian immigrants (the largest single group in the San Jose area) were attending school at a much lower rate than native-born young people in eastern cities.

Even more remarkable was the situation of Japanese-American stu-dents at San Jose High School (the city's only public secondary school until 1952) in the 1930s. San Jose High yearbooks for the Depression decade reveal that these students, whose numbers ran into several dozen, not only were members of various honor societies, but also were playing on sports teams, some of which they captained, and were even getting elected to student body office.[36]

The point is not that Japanese students faced no discrimination in the 1930s—that would be a preposterous argument to make—but that some of them were able to enjoy real success in high school despite the un-doubted presence of racist attitudes. Like the autobiography of Charles Warren Stoddard, the high level of their extracurricular activities, includ-ing those that would have required the votes of non-Japanese fellow stu-dents, suggests something about the long-term legacy of northern California's having been "born cosmopolitan." One can also speculate about the relationship between the yearbook findings and the election in 1971 of Norman Mineta as mayor of San Jose, the first Japanese-American mayor of a big city in the continental United States.[37]

It is impossible in the compass of a brief chapter to make a systematic canvass of all that has transpired in San Francisco and the rest of northern California during the twentieth century. With the vigilantism and anti-Chinese demagoguery of the nineteenth century, there is plenty in the history of San Francisco and the rest of northern California to make one cringe: vigilantism directed against workers, with the actual breakdown of civil government in a few instances; widespread discrimination against African-Americans as their numbers began to increase; deportation of Mexican-Americans, including some United States citizens, during the Great Depression; inhumane treatment of the Okies during the same period; continuing maltreatment of workers of color by most of organized labor through World War II; massive violation of the civil rights of Japanese-Americans, who were sent to internment camps during the war; brutal treatment of farm workers when, led by César Chávez and Dolores Huerta, they tried to organize a union. A common theme is inhumanity directed against the "other," with employers and other propertied interests frequently standing to benefit from the expressions of hatred.

Yet that is not the whole story. People found various strategies for defending themselves against the forces of intolerance and discrimination even during the worst of times.[38] And then in the 1930s, members of some ethnic groups began to join progressive unions, and labor leaders such as Harry Bridges of the International Longshoremen and Warehouses Union staked their unions' success on overcoming racism in the ranks.[39] During the Great Depression, in other words, the first glimmerings of real progress in race relations began to occur.

Valerie Matsumoto has traced the progress of Japanese-Americans in the Central Valley. The story turns not on the relationship with progressive unions but on the power of a self-created community.[40] Facing the legal restrictions against becoming either American citizens or landowners in California, groups of first-generation Issei formed colonies in the valley in the years immediately following World War I, in order to eventually obtain land. They then weathered the anti-Japanese hostility emanating from some of their neighbors and prospered during the 1920s while surviving during the difficult Depression years. In Cortez, the subject of Matsumoto's study, they established both Buddhist temples and Christian churches, and the second-generation Nisei went to an integrated high school in nearby Livingston. When war came and they faced internment, they were able to find trustworthy Anglos to whom they could turn over stewardship of their precious land. Following the war, the Issei and their children began to enjoy more opportunity—after the initial phase of anti-Japanese feeling had dissipated.

Many scholars have suggested that World War II constituted a watershed for American attitudes about race and ethnicity. For example, Philip Gleason argues that the war experience forged a version of American identity predicated on values such as "democracy, freedom, equality, respect for individual dignity and so on. Since these values were abstract and universal, American identity could not be linked exclusively with any single ethnic derivation."[41] He further contends that in the postwar world, "what might be called a cosmopolitan version of cultural pluralism appeals to persons relatively detached from any specific ethnic tradition as a general vision of a society made up of diverse groups, all interacting harmoniously without losing their distinctiveness."[42] In other words, during the 1940s a significant number of educated Americans began to embrace the same cosmopolitan ideal to which at least some San Franciscans had long subscribed. Along with the attitudinal changes came such epochal developments as the establishment of the Fair Employment Practices Commission by presidential executive order in 1941, the repeal of Chinese exclusion in 1943, the desegregation of the armed forces in 1948 (preceded by the desegregation of major-league baseball in 1947), and the passage of the McCarran-Walter Immigration Act of 1952, which permitted the naturalization of Asian immigrants.

I mention these changes to stress that to some extent the increasingly tolerant racial and ethnic climate in San Francisco and northern California in the years since 1945 has been part of a larger national pattern. But it is also important to point out that few places were so profoundly transformed by the war as the Bay Area. Indeed, Marilynn Johnson calls her book about the impact of the war on the East Bay, *The Second Gold Rush*.[43] Once again, the world rushed in, this time because the shipbuilding industry, with its vast labor needs, constituted so powerful a draw. An already diverse region became much more diverse because of the influx of African-Americans in search of war work and because Chicanos from the Southwest moved to the Santa Clara Valley to work in the food industry. Says Charles Wollenberg of the African-American migration to the Bay Area: "The region became a new black frontier, the Afro-American population growing from less than 20,000 in 1940 to over 60,000 in 1945. The number of blacks in San Francisco more than quadrupled during the war, while that in Richmond and Vallejo grew by ten times."[44]

What the black newcomers found was frequently disdain at worst and indifference at best. Facing discrimination in housing and from organized labor, they also had to contend with the attitude of longtime black residents of the area, who "saw the new as crude, rough, and boisterous."[45] In displaying this attitude, we should parenthetically note, old-timers in the African-American community were repeating earlier patterns of behavior whereby pioneer German Jews had viewed East European Jewish immigrants with alarm, and San Francisco's Italian American *prominenti* had acted to suppress the folk rituals of later-arriving peasants. But eventually, with the vast growth of the African-American community, came new leaders and a new willingness to challenge the status quo.

As an increasing number of fine books appear about the social history of the region, we are better able to understand the dynamics of change in the postwar years. In *Black San Francisco,* for example, Albert Broussard demonstrates that there was a massive gap between the city's image of itself as a liberal bastion and the actual social reality for African-Americans until well into the 1960s. Changes during World War II laid the groundwork for progress, but a new generation of leaders would have to mount a vigorous civil-rights campaign in order to get rid of de jure residential segregation and to open up employment.[46]

Another recent book focuses on Chinese immigrants. In *Unbound Feet,* Judy Yung tells the fascinating tale of several generations of Chinese-American women. The early arrivals were either young women forced into prostitution or merchant wives with bound feet who lived socially restricted lives in Chinatown. Reform and the nationalist impulse in China produced a new-style woman in San Francisco as early as 1902, when Sieh King King, "an eighteen-year-old student from China and an ardent reformer, stood before a Chinatown theater full of men and women and 'boldly condemned the slave girl system, raged at the horrors of footbinding and, with all the vehemence of aroused youth, declared that men and women were equal and should enjoy the privileges of equals.'"[47] Over the course of the twentieth century, Chinatown women began to organize voluntary associations, gained access to education, and then threw themselves into the war effort during the 1930s and 1940s, as patriotic Americans and as loyal daughters of China, a homeland that had been brutally attacked by Japan. During the war, moreover, Chinese-Americans worked in Bay Area shipyards, a brand-new employment opportunity for a population ghettoized occupationally as well as residentially.

The war produced massive disruption in old ways of life because of the millions of men going overseas, the millions of women going into the workforce, and the strain on overburdened institutions—with the impact felt nowhere any more than in the Bay Area. After the war, with existing ideas of racial hierarchy undergoing questioning, with unprecedented levels of prosperity, and with the new demographic mix in northern California, there unfolded several decades of explosive social change in the region, a familiar story in its rough outline, but one that will require much research and analysis before it is fully understood. A major reason that the region spawned or perfected so many cultural and social movements from the 1950s through the 1970s was as a latter-day consequence of the "free market of beliefs" produced by the gold rush and the ensuing cosmopolitan mix 100 years earlier. That regional identity attracted Robert Louis Stevenson in the 1870s, Allen Ginsberg in the 1950s, and Tom Hayden in the 1960s—plus many other folks less well known—and it has sustained many native daughters and sons of northern California in their quest to better their society.

The 1960s saw enormous change in the racial and ethnic climate nationally as well as locally. Once again, following heroic efforts by the civil-rights movement to alter public opinion, Congress passed epochal legislation—most important, the Civil Rights Act of 1964, the Voting Rights Act of 1965, and the Immigration Act of 1965, which abolished discriminatory quotas based on national origins (established by Congress in 1924) and opened the door to the legal entry of hundreds of thousands of newcomers from Mexico, other Latin American countries, and Asia. Tens of thousands of new immigrants flocked to northern California, creating a colony of Hmong in Fresno, of Vietnamese in Silicon Valley, and of Russians in San Francisco, and refashioning San Francisco's Mission District into a diverse Latino community within the larger city.

The region's economic health may nurture its cosmopolitanism. It seems clear that such a relationship exists, and the analysis offered by Annalee Saxenian is compelling. She points out that "Silicon Valley is now home to one-third of the 100 largest technology companies created in the United States since 1965." In contrast to the area around Boston, the high-tech capital of California has continued to flourish despite vicissitudes. Why the difference? "Silicon Valley has a regional network-based industrial system that promotes collective learning and flexible adjustment among specialist producers of a complex of related technologies. The region's dense social networks and open labor markets encourage experimentation and entrepreneurship."[48] This suggests that the openness of the Bay Area has had a benign economic impact as well as a benign sociopolitical one. It also suggests that the openness and the region's economic vitality have had a reciprocal relationship. As jobs are shipped overseas, will the cosmopolitan ideal survive and flourish? This is an open question that others besides a historian should be considering.

Shirley Ann Moore, historian of the African-American community in Richmond, tells a story that perfectly captures the spirit of northern California at its best. Interviewing long-time residents about their experiences before the war, she found some who remembered going to bullfights in the old days. Richmond's Mexican-Americans staged them, and Richmond's blacks were welcome attendees.[49] Maybe there were other places where so multicultural an event could have taken place in those years, but surely there were not many of them.

This chapter began and ends with Willie Brown. Whether or not he will be an effective mayor of San Francisco is unknown as of this writing. What is certain is that his inauguration on January 8, 1996, was a community ritual of inclusion. People came from all over the Bay Area, not just San Francisco itself, to be part of the festivities, and the newspaper coverage made it clear that the celebrants were as diverse as the region. The cosmopolitan ideal was being realized as fully as it ever has been in the history of the area—Brown's announcing his appointment of the city's first Chinese-American police chief and its first African-American fire chief during his inaugural speech underlined this—and many of the people for whom the ideal is a precious part of their lives wanted to publicly affirm it. That Brown chose to stage the inauguration in front of the city's beautiful memorial to Martin Luther King, Jr., heightened the emotional wallop of the event. Only in San Francisco.

But the difficulties Brown is confronting are massive, as they are for all big-city mayors: homelessness on a vast scale, deteriorating social services, political gamesmanship in Sacramento and Washington that undercuts much needed sources of revenue for cities. Sadly, the list of difficulties could be a very long one. I do not want to sentimentalize the city or the region by suggesting that either is immune from the problems that beset all Americans.[50] I do want to suggest that in grappling with these problems, the politicians and the citizens of San Francisco are well served by a vision of inclusivness as generous as exists in the United States, a vision that draws on the legacy of the cosmopolitanism that initially developed in the nineteenth century.

NOTES

A first draft of this essay was presented to the "California Studies Seminar" at the University of California, Berkeley. The author wishes to thank the members of the seminar for their generous and helpful comments, especially Dick Walker, whose collegial support has been invaluable. Later drafts were read by Robert Cherny, Phil Ethington, Estelle Freedman, David Igler, Sherry Katz, Michael Steiner, Jim Van Buskirk, David Wrobel, and Judy Yung, to all of whom she is similarly indebted. The author is solely responsible for any errors.

1. Carey McWilliams, *California: The Great Exception* (New York: Current Books, 1949).

2. Richard White, *"It's Your Misfortune and None of My Own": A New History of the American West* (Norman: University of Oklahoma Press, 1991).

3. McWilliams, *California*, 51.

4. Ibid., chap. 6. David Igler is currently completing a dissertation at the University of California, Berkeley, in which he is exploring the extent to which the land was monopolized.

5. Michael Bradshaw, *Regions and Regionalism in the United States* (Houndmills, Eng.: Macmillan, 1988), 53. See also Michael C. Steiner, "Frederick Jackson Turner and Western Regionalism," in *Writing Western History: Essays on Major Western Historians,* ed. Richard W. Etulain (Albuquerque: University of New Mexico Press, 1991), 103–35.

6. *Webster's New Collegiate Dictionary* (Springfield, Mass.: Merriam, 1956), 188, defines cosmopolitan as follows: "1. Belonging to all the world; not local. 2. At home in any country; without local national attachments or prejudices. 3. Characteristic of a cosmopolite; as *cosmopolitan* traits; 4. Composed of elements gathered from all or various parts of the world."

7. For a discussion of the emergence of a cosmopolitan ideal among American intellectuals in general, see David Hollinger, "Ethnic Diversity, Cosmopolitanism, and the Emergence of the American Liberal Intelligentsia," in *In the American Province,* ed. David Hollinger (Bloomington: Indiana University Press, 1985), 56–73. Says Hollinger, "The [cosmopolitan] ideal is

decidedly counter to the eradication of cultural differences, but counter also to their preservation in parochial form" (59). This, it seems to me, would be a good way to characterize the "Only in San Francisco" ideal as it developed over the decades.

8. Philip J. Ethington, *The Public City: The Political Construction of Urban Life in San Francisco, 1850–1900* (Cambridge: Cambridge University Press, 1994), 2.

9. Gunther Barth, *Instant Cities: Urbanization and the Rise of San Francisco and Denver* (New York: Oxford University Press, 1975).

10. Frank Soulé, John H. Gihon, and James Nisbet, *The Annals of San Francisco* (New York: Appleton, 1855), 640.

11. Richard Henry Dana, *Two Years Before the Mast,* 2nd ed. (Boston: Osgood, 1873), 438.

12. I co-curated with William Issel of San Francisco State University an exhibition, "San Francisco: The Dimension of Diversity," for the opening of the new public library in 1996. Much of the information for this chapter, including the early city directories, was gathered in the course of my curatorial duties.

13. Ethington, *Public City,* 20.

14. I am indebted to a conversation with the Reverend Dr. Amos Brown, current pastor of Third Baptist, for the insight about the three churches being founded in the year of *Uncle Tom's Cabin.*

15. George Martin, *Verdi at the Golden Gate: Opera and San Francisco in the Gold Rush Years* (Berkeley: University of California Press, 1993), 4.

16. Ethington, *Public City,* 113–14.

17. Quoted in William Issel and Robert Cherny, *San Francisco, 1865–1932: Politics, Power, and Urban Development* (Berkeley: University of California Press, 1986), 73.

18. Tomás Almaguer, *Racial Fault Lines: The Historical Origins of White Supremacy in California* (Berkeley: University of California Press, 1994), 210. See also Alexander Saxton, *The Indispensable Enemy: Labor and the Anti-Chinese Movement in California* (Berkeley: University of California Press, 1971).

19. Olivier Zunz, *The Changing Face of Inequality: Urbanization, Industrial Development, and Immigrants in Detroit, 1880–1920* (Chicago: University of Chicago Press, 1982), 19.

20. On the necessity of cleaning up Chinatowns in order to attract tourists to restaurants, see Ivan Light, "From Vice District to Tourist Attraction: The Moral Career of American Chinatowns, 1880–1940," *Pacific Historical Review* 43 (1974): 367–94.

21. Roger Daniels, "Ah Sin and His Lawyers," review of *In Search of Equality: The Chinese Struggle Against Discrimination in Nineteenth-Century America,* by Charles J. McClain (Berkeley: University of California Press, 1994), *Reviews in American History* 23 (1995): 472–77.

22. Issel and Cherny, *San Francisco*, 206.

23. From the theme statement for the exhibition "San Francisco: Dimensions of Diversity," manuscript in my possession.

24. For a discussion of this subject, see Kevin Starr, *Americans and the California Dream, 1850–1915* (New York: Oxford University Press, 1973), Chapter 8. See also Franklin Walker, *San Francisco's Literary Frontier* (New York: Knopf, 1939); and Lawrence Ferlinghetti, *Literary San Francisco* (San Francisco: City Lights Books, Harper & Row, 1980). An exhibition mounted at San Francisco State University in the fall of 1995, entitled "With New Eyes: Toward an Asian American Art History in the West," featured the work of not only Mary Tape but of many other superb visual artists in San Francisco and the greater Bay Area.

25. The Irish-American mayor was Frank McCoppin, elected in 1867. The Jewish mayor was Adolph Sutro, elected in 1894. The labor leader was Eugene Schmitz, elected in 1901. The Italian-American mayor was Angelo Rossi, who was appointed to the office when James Rolph became governor of California in 1930. The Irish-American woman was Mae Ella Nolan, who served from January 1923 to March 1925. The Jewish woman was Florence Prag Kahn, who served from March 1925 to January 1937. Both of the women were widows of congressmen who had died in office.

26. See, for example, the argument made by George Fredrickson in *White Supremacy: A Comparative Study in American and South African History* (New York: Oxford University Press, 1981): "The abolition of slavery in the United States carried with it a certain heritage of moral idealism that might be violated in practice but could not be breached in principle without a catastrophic effect on the national self-image" (38).

27. Issel and Cherny, *San Francisco*, 104. Gray Brechin has shared with me a number of clippings from San Francisco newspapers of the early twentieth century, clippings in which the cosmopolitan ideal is celebrated particularly but not exclusively with respect to cuisine.

28. Albert S. Broussard, *Black San Francisco: The Struggle for Racial Equality in the West, 1900–1954* (Lawrence: University Press of Kansas, 1993), 65.

29. Lisa Rubens, "Competing Visions: American Identity and the 1939 San Francisco World's Fair" (Ph.D. diss., University of California, Berkeley, 1997).

30. It is well known, for example, that the city's Italian-American bankers lent money to *paesani* in the surrounding area.

31. Josiah Royce, *California: From the Conquest in 1846 to the Second Vigilance Committee in San Francisco* (Santa Barbara, Calif.: Peregrine, 1970), 175.

32. Sally M. Miller, "Changing Faces of the Central Valley: The Ethnic Presence," *California History* 74 (1995): 175. See also Gerald Haslam, *The Other California: The Great Central Valley in Life and Letters* (Santa Barbara, Calif.: Capra Press, 1990). Says Haslam about his native region: "In 1863

Brewer noted, 'The hotel where we stopped showed a truly Californian mixture of races—the landlord a Scotchman, Chinese cooks, Negro waiter, and a Digger Indian stable boy.' The population in the Valley remains decidedly multiethnic, because this region has attracted the determined and desperate, willing to toil in its fields . . . over one hundred distinct groups" (24). Haslam goes on to note that all the diversity does not necessarily mean brotherhood. For a discussion of the Central Valley with respect to its Okie population, a possible explanation for the ways in which the valley is so much more conservative than the rest of northern California, see James N. Gregory, *American Exodus: The Dust Bowl Migration and Okie Culture in California* (New York: Oxford University Press, 1989). Gregory argues that the Okies created a culture predicated on what he calls "plain folk Americanism."

33. Laurie Maffly-Kipp, *Religion and Society in Frontier California* (New Haven, Conn.: Yale University Press, 1994), 117.

34. Susan Stryker and Jim Van Buskirk, *Gay by the Bay: A History of Queer Culture in the San Francisco Bay Area* (San Francisco: Chronicle Books, 1996).

35. Glenna Matthews, "Ethnicity and Success in San Jose," *Journal of Interdisciplinary History* 7 (1976): 305–18. The sample also contained a number of Californios and other Latinos, whose success was distinctly less than that of the Euro-Americans. Asian-Americans and African-Americans were too few to analyze.

36. Glenna Matthews, "A California Middletown: The Social History of San Jose During the Great Depression" (Ph.D. diss., Stanford University, 1977). The information about the yearbooks comes from research I have conducted more recently.

37. For more on the Japanese-American community in San Jose, see Timothy J. Lukes and Gary Y. Okihiro, *Japanese Legacy: Farming and Community Life in California's Santa Clara Valley* (Cupertino: California History Center, 1985). I should point out that Janet Gray Hayes, who became mayor of San Jose in the mid-1970s, was the country's first woman mayor of a city over 500,000 in population. On western cities and political innovation, see Carl Abbott, *The Metropolitan Frontier: Cities in the Modern American West* (Tucson: University of Arizona Press, 1993).

38. Miller, "Changing Faces of the Central Valley"; Sucheng Chan, *This Bittersweet Soil: The Chinese in California Agriculture, 1860–1910* (Berkeley: University of California Press, 1986).

39. I attended the memorial service for Harry Bridges at the ILWU Hall in San Francisco in 1991. Over and over, the men and women who spoke brought up the subject of Bridges's leadership in the fight against racism. Robert Cherny of San Francisco State University is currently working on a biography of Bridges.

40. Valerie Matsumoto, *Farming the Home Place: A Japanese-American Community in California, 1919–1982* (Ithaca, N.Y.: Cornell University Press, 1993).

41. Philip Gleason, *Speaking of Diversity: Language and Ethnicity in Twentieth-Century America* (Baltimore: Johns Hopkins University Press, 1992), 172.

42. Ibid., 177.

43. Marilynn S. Johnson, *The Second Gold Rush: Oakland and the East Bay in World War II* (Berkeley: University of California Press, 1993).

44. Charles Wollenberg, "James v. Marinship: Trouble on the New Black Frontier," in *Working People of California,* ed. Daniel Cornford (Berkeley: University of California Press, 1995), 160.

45. Ibid.

46. Broussard, *Black San Francisco.*

47. Judy Yung, *Unbound Feet: A Social History of Chinese Women in San Francisco* (Berkeley: University of California Press, 1995), 52.

48. Annalee Saxenian, *Regional Advantage: Culture and Competition in Silicon Valley and Route 128* (Cambridge, Mass.: Harvard University Press, 1994), 2. See also Richard Walker, "The Playground of U.S. Capitalism: The Political Economy of the San Francisco Bay Area in the 1980s," in *Fire in the Hearth: The Radical Politics of Place in America,* ed. Mike Davis, Steven Hiatt, Marie Kennedy, Susan Ruddick, and Michael Sprinker (London: Verso, 1990).

49. Shirley Moore, conversations with the author.

50. For the argument that politics in San Francisco suffers from "hyperpluralism," or a fragmented left, see Richard Edward DeLeon, *Left Coast City: Progressive Politics in San Francisco, 1975–1991* (Lawrence: University Press of Kansas, 1992). I believe that while DeLeon overstates his argument, he correctly delineates the downside of the openness. The thunderous criticism that greeted the splendid new library after the initial euphoria wore off, for example, helped convince me of this.

10

Privileging the Mission over the Mexican:

The Rise of Regional Identity

in Southern California

William Deverell

This chapter must begin at the desk of Carey McWilliams, southern California's preeminent journalist, activist, reformer, writer, and historian of the twentieth century. McWilliams is that rarest of chroniclers of a time and place who gets more, rather than less, important with each passing decade. It is tempting to be remarkably brief in this chapter, to write simply "read Carey McWilliams," and leave well enough alone. McWilliams has left us with a powerful and lasting legacy about understanding southern California. In his masterpiece, *Southern California Country,* McWilliams gave hard covers and hundreds of pages to a set of enduring ideas about southern California and regional consciousness.

Carey McWilliams knew his history, and he knew how to tease meaning out of what he called "the light peculiar irrelevance of life in Southern California."[1] He knew that for the region to embrace anything as coherent as an identity, narrative sense had to be forged out of the passage of time, brutal ethnic and national conflicts, and the transfers of power and influence that ensued. This was done in large part through the production of images and stories. In interpreting these representations of the past, McWilliams offered two especially important observations: southern California's culture is distinctive ("an island"), and the cloak that wraps and thereby shapes much of that culture is the comforting "Spanish Fantasy Past."[2]

McWilliams reminds us that regional identity in southern California (he marked the geography as "south of the Tehachapi") has everything to do with ethnic relations and ethnic history. Flowing from the script laid out in countless journalistic, booster, and historical narratives in the years following the Mexican War, the Spanish Fantasy Past took the form of a societywide history lesson. Its purpose was to explain the nineteenth century *to* the nineteenth century. At its most simple (where it worked best), the story went like this: Spanish people, including those cast unfortunately by the whims of nationalism as Mexicans, once lived in a southern California of, if not plenty, at least plenty of happiness, music, and beauty. Then Americans came, both landing at the water's edge and drifting over the San Bernardino Mountains. The resulting proximity and intimacy changed this world forever. As the story goes, the Spaniards-Mexicans resisted valiantly (nobly, gracefully, calmly) the inevitable fate already befallen the region's Native Americans. Anglo-Saxons would *naturally* triumph, through genetic and racial primacy, Yankee entrepreneurialism, and the master plan of Manifest Destiny.

For their part, Americans welcomed the exotic closeness to Mexico and "the Latin race," according to the way the story worked, if only because they, too, recognized that racial progression had a great inevitability to it. As one turn-of-the-century visitor explained matter-of-factly, the non-Anglos of southern California simply melted away in the face of conquest, "as if a blight had fallen upon them."[3] In the meantime, proximity invited Americans to play Latins, to take part in a kind of brownface social theater, especially emulating those they deemed Spanish enough to invite imitation. As requiem to the fading culture, Anglos laced the streets with parades and fiestas and their own bodies with silver conchas and, every now and then, rosary beads and heavy silver crosses. The sheer and essential Whigishness of the narrative and its physical expressions made it easy to explain recent warfare as progress, to turn a blind eye as Manifest Destiny's consequences continued to bloody the streets of Los Angeles well after the signing of the Treaty of Guadalupe Hidalgo. The Spanish Fantasy Past acted as a screen to block the memories of such late unpleasantness.

The story not only helped to orient the world. Before long, Anglos, especially Anglos with power, discovered that this very usable past could be as profitable as it was soothing. Vibrant fiestas and crumbling missions attracted tourists and settlers alike. These people spent money, money made the region grow, and growth meant more money and, consequently, more opportunities to create or massage ideals of regional meaning and explanation. Before long, the twin strands of historical interpretation and capitalist ambition had been woven so tightly together as to make them virtually indistinguishable: out of such cloth are regional identities made, if not born.

McWilliams's ideas and conceptions about regional culture and regional identity have influenced two generations of scholars, none more important than two of the most recent. In his impressive treatment of the state's history, California State Librarian Kevin Starr has devoted most of the chapters in his four-volume history to southern California. Like McWilliams, Starr thinks that there is a lesson beneath so much of southern California's confusing veneer. Unlike McWilliams, whose prose is often laced with profoundly depressing and pessimistic analyses, even prophesies, Starr's work is unapologetically about possibilities, often pregnant with the promise of regional redemption through mutual understanding (no mean feat in the late 1990s). Starr does not ignore the insights of McWilliams; on the contrary, he has done more than any scholar to further the interpretive project begun by *Southern California Country*. But at heart, Starr's southern California is about drive, vision, and ambition; about the maintenance of community amid impossible stresses; and about the ability of people to contemplate projects and ideas bigger than themselves. Critics have wrinkled their faces, but Starr has told one version of southern California's story and has found historical matches for his own, often unbridled, belief in southern California's sheer promise.

Mike Davis is a different story altogether, much closer to the second coming of Louis Adamic than Carey McWilliams. Davis has wrung McWilliams of any romance about the place. His southern California is less about soaring ambition than about searing pain, dislocation, degradation, wider and wider divisions between the haves and the have-nots. It has devolved to a militarized region of hatred, mistrust, and only the tiniest pockets of hope, activism, and redemption. If McWilliams warned of trouble in *Ill Fares the Land,* Davis predicted worse in *City of Quartz.*[4]

Even if described through just the work of these two scholars, the legacy of Carey McWilliams has been magnificent. We are all his students. He spent a lifetime producing a veritable Rosetta stone for deciphering regional history; as eyewitness to much of what he analyzed, McWilliams was, in that classic phrase used by California writers from Frank Norris through John Steinbeck and on to Paul Taylor, "on the ground." The body of his work has become required reading for scholar and nonscholar alike. Yet despite his unquestioned, and I think growing, impact on regional understanding, there has been a kind of fork in the path that McWilliams blazed. He was at his best, analytically and stylistically, when he wrote about the ways in which an Anglo elite in southern California shaped a regional consciousness and culture around this thing called the Spanish Fantasy Past in the years before World War II. This was simply his way of saying that the dominant culture kept alive one compelling version of the past because it paid certain kinds of dividends (psychic as well as commercial). That creation, nurtured and sustained by the most powerful people and institutions in southern California, had everything to do with ethnicity, everything to do with the complicated relationship between Anglos and Mexicans.

There can be little doubt that some of the most talented historians of the past twenty years have poked large and important holes in the veracity of the Spanish Fantasy Past, which, of course, McWilliams had always characterized as myth, albeit a kind of necessary one. The fantasy required that Latinos either exit the stage once the twentieth century arrived or lurk conveniently amid the darkness of those "obscure corners" on "the edges of the displacing civilization," as one true believer saw it in 1907.[5] Yet whole populations did not fade away, nor did they loiter in history's off stages. Historians have made the twentieth-century Mexican communities of Los Angeles and southern California among the most studied ethnic communities in all the United States, and we have an extraordinarily rich portrait of the complexity, diversity, and continuity of Mexican and Mexican-American life in the modern region.

That work takes up one of the directions that McWilliams helped to pioneer. But there has been a road not taken. The clues McWilliams left about the activities of that dominant Anglo culture, about the ways in which it understood, manipulated, or commodified "things Mexican," have largely been left sitting within the pages of his most important books as intriguing vignettes. And that has meant that analysis of the complicated choreography between, for instance, the ethnic past and present, the Mexican and the Anglo, has remained curiously circumscribed, even one-sided. We are left in a bit of a cultural or historical vacuum, less prepared to contextualize modern events or entire patterns of cultural activity, discrimination, racism, exclusion, or violence, themselves doubtless part of a recognizable regional consciousness in late-twentieth-century southern California.

To be sure, exploration of Anglo–Mexican relations in southern California is only one of countless ways in which an analysis of something as broad and as murky as regional consciousness could be organized and pursued. And my argument is not that this prism is the most critical or the most important or even necessarily the most telling. Rather, my sense is that within the orbit of ethnic relations, one can discern a rising regional identity that, because it is so rich in images, documents, and ramifications, can and should be submitted to historical scrutiny. The Anglo project of creating a category occupied by "the Mexican" and assigning Mexican space on the landscape provided the outlines of a specific regional consciousness in that it, at the very least, established cultural perimeters and parameters (for Anglos) of "what we aren't." Such are the advantages of sketching the silhouettes of "others."

We can discern patterns of exclusion and appropriation that allowed the dominant society to "freeze" Mexicans in place and in space. This cultural cryogenics inevitably helped shape a regional identity, at least for those Anglos inevitably complicit in the project. In excavating some of this history (and history making), we should pay particular attention to appeals to teaching, lessons, and morals. For if anything can tell us about a southern California identity, it is the way in which pedagogical lessons were inevitably built around regional history and regional culture. How did southern California "teach" about ethnicity, and how do those lessons help us to understand the rise of regional consciousness?

Think of some of the most common ways in which life in southern California is imagined, or has been imagined, in popular culture and the ways in which these images and associations are themselves informed by ethnic attitudes. Think of even just the myriad catchphrases used to lure investment, tourists, and settlers (the latter two often modified by "Anglo-Saxon") from the 1880s forward. Climatological exclamations are impossible to miss: southern California is the "land of sunshine," the "sunny southland," the "semi-tropic land of tomorrow." Beyond mere sunshine, Los Angeles is "nature's workshop," the city of the future, the jewel in the open-shop crown, even the "magic city." Southern California is the dream factory, the promised land, the Pacific coast paradise; it is the land of homes, the land of farms, the land of business, the land of oranges, the land of vegetables, the land of honey. Los Angeles is the "city of balanced prosperity," the "climatic capital of the New World," the "metropolis of the Southwest."

These descriptions are clearly important in terms of relaying a slice of regional sense of self. To excavate ideas about ethnicity imbedded in them, I think we must try to analyze the ways in which such regional descriptions tend to seek out a mean, to classify institutions, landscapes, and people as "typical."[6] Reliance on the descriptive power of "the typical" became, during the first decades of the twentieth century, a cultural reflex in southern California, a kind of adjectival default. What did it mean? It meant simply that elites in southern California—that constellation of business, public-relations, and political organizations and those individuals who composed them—evinced an irrepressible desire to describe individual things on the southern California landscape as representative of some greater whole.

The examples are legion. First (always) there was the weather: a "typical" day in southern California as depicted on an orange-crate label or a postcard or a captioned photograph would be bright, clear, sunny. A vista could, most often was, captured: foregrounded by citrus fruit bursting with ripe goodness, backgrounded by either big homes or big, snow-capped mountains. The sheer attractiveness of the images is still telling these decades later.

Homegrown maps, which are at heart ways to represent landscape at its "most typical," tended in the late nineteenth century to depict certain aspects of that landscape in very particular ways. The best known of these is probably the series of bird's-eye views done of Los Angeles from the 1880s that tend to depict the Los Angeles River as a kind of California Seine—thick, wide, running full. It isn't that this wasn't exactly true: the Los Angeles River did, after all, provide most of the city's water needs until the early part of this century. It is, however, important to note that the Los Angeles River could run both dry and wild, and these mapped depictions of it tended not to raise that issue.

A better example of the "typical reflex," a kind of culturewide return to an often-fictional mean, can be found in the descriptions of the built environment in southern California. Sprawling luxury hotels become "typical tourist hotels." Palm- or oak-lined roadways in elite neighborhoods become "typical southern California boulevards." A postcard map of homes stretching from Santa Barbara to San Diego, from the earliest years of the 1880s booms until well into the 1920s, would suggest to non-natives that southern California was either the land of millionaires or the land where everyone lived like a millionaire. Postcard after postcard depict gigantic homes: soaring Tudors, rambling ranch houses, stately Mission Revivals. And many of the photos are captioned with such phrases as "typical Southern California home" or "typical Santa Barbara residence." And for each of these typical houses there exists an equally, apparently prosaic, "typical California garden": ambitiously landscaped acres adorned with all variety of succulents or fruit trees or Japanese touches.

Woven all together, this tapestry tells an important story: southern California is not only a paradise, but a paradise in which everyone could apparently have workers working for them. At first postcard glance, typical southern California looks classless, even raceless. Postcards never depicted gardeners; tourist images rarely show off anyone but Anglos. But the project is, of course, all about class and ethnicity. Even those images that stooped to depict "a typical workingman's home" or "the typical workingman's bungalow" (which meant, almost by definition, those homes in a white neighborhood) urge a kind of dissonance, as though the region had no industrial districts, company towns, substandard housing, deadends.[7]

Captions, then, became not only the word additions to images, but a kind of interpretive lesson all by themselves. Although it would be difficult to call this captioning project a highly organized endeavor, and would consequently be hard to discover its origins, it is possible to speculate on its purposes. The association of "the typical" with "the wealthy" or, at least, "the beautiful" is certainly an attractive marketing scheme. But we cannot forget the racial and ethnic specificity of these images, designed to go east into the parlors of white America.

We can assume that the reflex had domestic, local impacts. The famed booster campaigns of emergent southern California can never be viewed as simply external projects designed to attract and appeal to non-Californians; after all, those doing the boosting and the campaigning had local agendas, circumstances, and individuals to contend with as well.[8] In other words, it probably did not take a great conceptual leap to move from thinking of "a typical workingman's home" to imagining "a typical workingman." Such a characterization certainly operated in the world of southern California's extremely powerful anti-union organizations and campaigns; a typical workingman, by definition, had to be an open-shop man. Otherwise, the paradigm and appeals for greater industrial investment made little sense. The mere fact that many workingmen (and -women) obviously felt otherwise was only proof to open-shop stalwarts that the gospel had been corrupted. We know far too little about the local circumstances that produced those booster ideas and ideals designed to be flung worldwide.

For our purposes, the typical reflex is best scrutinized as the way in which members of the dominant society thought about the Mexicans in their midst who chose not to fade away with the coming of the twentieth century. If the litany of references to Mexicans in both popular and official pronouncements is any indication, they too were rendered in a kind of typically classless southern California space. But in the case of Mexicans, the "typical" classlessness did not equate wealth and beauty with ordinary life in southern California; on the contrary, the pyramid was simply inverted. Mexican classlessness existed solely because the dominant society tended to view Mexicans as naturally existing within the boundaries of a sole identity: workers, veritable beasts of necessary burden. There was no ladder for them to climb; "they" (as necessarily opposed to "we") were Mexicans.

This perception is what made the phrase "the Mexican" so commonplace in southern California, an unexamined assumption of supposed essential ethnic traits. And it was accompanied by enough descriptions of Mexican character and Mexican characteristics to render the stereotypical portrait all the more full. Before moving to further examination of some of these specific constructions, it makes sense to briefly broaden the view momentarily because ideas about ethnic essentialism in southern California were linked to ideas about regional geography. If we take an aerial view of the landscape, much as McWilliams would have us do, we very soon encounter Mexico. So, too, did turn-of-the-century southern Californians, so much so that I think there existed a profound set of connections between how Anglos thought about Mexico and how they thought about Mexicans.

It is a simple truism that southern California is informed, in all the subtle and profound senses of that word, by proximity to Mexico. As *Los Angeles Times* journalist Harry Carr stated matter-of-factly, "Los Angeles has always been conscious of the fact that it is next door to Mexico."[9] But *what* constituted that "door"—not to mention *where* it was placed—have rarely been items of passive acceptance or unexamined consciousness. What is compelling about southern California's regard of Mexico is a recurring territorial tension. This is heir to the "all Mexico" rallying cries that made it possible to imagine United States marines and soldiers capturing the whole of Mexico's territory—instead of the nearly half that the United States ended up with by the gold-rush era. We should not forget that Los Angeles acted as a staging and recruitment depot for the various ill-fated attempts to continue fighting the Mexican War well after the ink had dried on the documents of peace and territorial transfer.[10]

This adolescent bluster about wild territorial expansion matured into something else by the end of the nineteenth century. In what can be described as the cultural backing and filling to crude military action and land grabbing, southern California (as well as elsewhere in the greater Southwest) embarked on a usually much more subtle, though corollary, enterprise. This project, imperialism of a different stripe, was complex and far-reaching, and it involved attempts by the dominant society to gain control (both physical and interpretive control) over "things Mexican" on either side of the border.

It is too easy to delineate southernmost California in the post–Mexican War period by reference to the international border south of San Diego. It may be technically correct and yet simultaneously misleading to argue that there is California on one side and Mexico on the other. The blunt dichotomy obscures the fact that southern California regional consciousness is in large part forged by the *sin fronteras* reality of transborder identities. And while this chapter discusses only one facet of such a world, that of Los Angeles elites who consciously thought of Mexico in their backyard, it is critical to point out that regional consciousness in this place is in so many ways a product, and a continuing product, of both the proximity and the permeability of the international border. But the complexity is not new: southern Californians have long believed in muddying the distinctions between here and there, not to mention between "ours" and "yours."[11]

The turn of the century marks southern California's startling geographic discovery of "our Mexico." Nurtured in tandem by parlor writings and sophisticated entrepreneurial appraisal of Mexico's raw land, raw minerals, and raw goods, this diplomatic fiction became a commonplace assumption, a sort of corollary to the conceit that semitropical southern California was "our Italy." Perhaps it was simply a more mature version of mid-century filibustering. In any event, southern California had become an important center for the launching of books as well as adventurers and tourists, all of which embraced the idea that Mexico existed as a virtual possession of or an adjunct territory to southern California.

The semantic and possessive construction connoted by "our Mexico" continued through the violent cycles of the Mexican Revolution, when many a southern Californian thought little of the hubris (not to mention danger) of ignoring the border in trying to protect investments. By the late 1910s and early 1920s, southern California businessmen and business organizations firmed up the notion that what was south, at least as far as raw goods and raw labor were concerned, might just as well be considered American territory. "Western Mexico is in reality a hinterland to California," stated one representative Los Angeles business publication.[12] Not to be outdone, another group heard one of its spokesmen tell of his south-of-the-border efforts to "solidify still further the supremacy of Los Angeles in the upbuilding of Mexico. . . . [T]hey know that Los Angeles is anxious to grasp their hand."[13] But if Mexico was "ours," where did that leave Mexicans, especially those in the United States? Were they "ours," too?

Southern Californians responded to the human dimensions of "our Mexico" with an ambitious program of trying to understand Mexicans— explicitly, "our Mexicans."[14] But it was a program without flexibility, already bounded at the start by stereotype. It was a static project, reinforced by the expressions (and convictions) of the ethnic typicality and representativeness. Examples abound.

Mexicans, read one state report on labor and housing conditions, were "quick to learn as children but slow when grown up. They are with us to stay; we can mold them as we will, and if we groom our horses, feed them, give them shelter and a bed when they have toiled hard for us at work which we could not do for ourselves—-shall we do less for the hard-working stranger within our gates whose sons and daughters will soon be our American citizens?"[15]

Surely the sentiment is as coercive as it is wishful: hope expressed as the establishment of a bounded place, itself within "our gates." And just as there were "Mexicans" who were disallowed mobility or the ability to transcend cultural barriers, there were literal urban spaces for these Mexicans. *Colonias* outside farming lands; *barrios* nestled against hillsides or pressed hard against the banks (or in the beds) of the Rio Hondo, San Gabriel, or Los Angeles Rivers; shacks squished together in the middle of the industrial railyards skirting downtown Los Angeles. These were Mexican spaces, and they held.

We should not forget that this manner of figurative and literal placement had blunt political ramifications, in part because it could effectively screen out so much. In other words (as McWilliams pointed out), the Spanish Fantasy Past offered a version of history as determined as it was nostalgic. As the state report illustrates, reserving specific sites and behaviors for Mexicans was hardly the preoccupation of just history books or history teachers depicting a hazy view of a romantic past. On the contrary, the reflex was so commonplace that it could just as easily be found in public discourse, where historical means served political ends. For instance, sometime in the 1920s, a hack writer for the Better America Federation, a Los Angeles political organization of "superpatriotic" form, wrote a short essay that addressed, in large part, California history. Although the essay sounds and reads like a speech, it is probably right to assume that it was designed solely for publication, most likely as a kind of propaganda piece placed in Los Angeles Spanish-language newspapers.[16] The narrative is admirably succinct. The writer renders two generations of California history into a tale of successful ethnic assimilation, which is, whether in 3 or 300 pages, no mean feat of historical interpretation. Listen for the reflexive categorizations.

Once (upon a time), beneath California's bright skies and "among its fields of poppies and hills of mesquite, sage brush, buckthorn and manzanita bush," there lived a large population of natives of Mexican descent, people who knew "no other country but California." But times changed, and "a new order of things came to pass. Old traditions were swept aside. New habits were formed." The pace of life quickened: "Different codes of honor were established. . . . Customs of old were abolished and new ones came into vogue. The wheels of industrial life were started in many new channels. Social activities of a new character were indulged in as the march of progress and Americanism swept over valley and hillside— over former cactus covered deserts, profitable ranchos and cattle grazing lands."

Environmental, social, and demographic change all went together, so much so that it was hard to say which caused which: "Cities sprang up almost over night, where herds of sheep and cattle formerly grazed. Large deciduous and citrus orchards began to dot the former plains and hills and the picturesque haciendas, where the beautiful Mexican Señoritas were wont to entertain in their well known hospitable style, became the homes and ranch houses of the newer generation. The former barbecues, fiestas and other gala day gatherings soon faded into an almost forgotten past."

Despite the revolutionary sweep of such transitions, these were apparently changes determined by natural progression, or so it seemed. In other words, this "new order of things" was less a world turned upside down than a world turned right side up. America, Americans, and Americanism had come to the Far West in fulfillment of ordained destiny: that "march of progress" and that "march of . . . Americanism" were exactly the same thing. Now, naturally, twentieth-century Mexicans wanted to be twentieth-century Americans, too; they wanted to push back even farther those memories, those ways, of that "almost forgotten past." After all, "they are all a part of our American life, living day by day, under our constitution and under the protection of our flag." The Better America Federation could help; in fact, the organization saw it as a duty to help. Through, especially, its "Racial Council," the federation offered the institutional setting by which to prepare "all Mexicans to become better American citizens, to be better able to adopt American methods and standards in their dealings and life work."[17]

A University of Southern California instructor wrote in 1916 that "the burden of Americanization falls directly upon Los Angeles."[18] Excavating the ideological underpinnings of just this simple declaration could keep historians busy for years. We know too little about Americanization, especially how this supposedly national ideal was refracted through local political and cultural settings. For Americanization was often shaped into a regional idiom: it had to vary from place to place and setting to setting depending on the specificity of local conditions, demographics, circumstances, and politics. At least in the case of the activist Better America Federation, Americanization loosely gathered the various strains that made up a particular stripe of southern California right-wing patriotism. Rhetoric becomes a kind of thin icing atop, among other things, wishfulness, fearfulness, and self-righteousness. Listen to the closing words of this little speech: "Surely our Mexican citizens should be appreciative of the Americanization work being accomplished, and become a full-fledged American citizen who believes in and is ready to defend this Republic and its form of government."[19] As intriguing as the operation of the entire Americanization drive are some of these profoundly local assumptions that undergird it: highly particularized, regional conceptions of what is or isn't "a Mexican," what is or isn't "a Mexican citizen," or, for that matter, what and who constitute "our Mexican citizens."

If descriptions were not enough to create identifiable boundaries, local southern California institutions (like the Better America Federation itself) could *always* be counted on. For instance, segregation's tag-team duo of local custom and real-estate restrictions made Mexican space (as well as the spaces of other "others") sharply etched on the landscape. "Race segregation is not a serious problem with us," a Whittier real-estate agent proudly declared in the mid-1920s. "Our realtors do not sell [to] Mexicans or Japanese outside certain sections where it is agreed by community custom they shall reside." A fellow realtor not far away in Glendale mixed patriotism with exclusion, without even the slightest indication that he recognized the heavy irony in his words. Through enforcement of "suitable race restrictions, we can maintain our high standard of American citizenship," he wrote, all the more appropriate, apparently, in an "American town like Glendale."[20]

Should the crudeness of ethnic and racial restriction present any moral dilemmas to the community (of realtors or of Anglos), one could always fall back on the supposedly essential behavioral characteristics of "the Mexican." "The Mexicans can be well handled," wrote Charles Stewart of the Monrovia realty board, "and are quite reliable." Apparently, one could even count on the ethnic populations of the various southern California communities to do the work of segregation themselves. "The Japanese, Mexican and colored population have segregated themselves in groups largely according to their own wishes," stated a realtor from Riverside. Such blindness to the reality of ugly patterns of segregation and exclusion must be examined not simply as indications of dissonance, but as examples of the dominant society's assurance that there was such a static social and ethnic category as "the Mexican" and that membership within that group entailed certain and specific behaviors. It must have been easier to explain away *barrios* and *colonias* as "a Mexican habit" than as a response, culturally as well as geographically, to firm segregation.

"We have provided a section [of Ontario] expressly for Mexicans and Negroes," wrote realtor R. P. Garbutt, as though the action were an example of community pride or progress, which, of course, it was.[21]

My sense is that the project was all about cultural pedagogy, teaching Anglos about Mexican places and spaces, and teaching Mexicans themselves by segregationist example.[22] And if we consider this world as one in which lessons and pedagogy were critical cultural tools, then it does not take much imagination to see the other ways in which southern California created stock images, stock texts, and stock characters to portray life because literal "Mexican space" had its figurative counterparts, especially as related to temporal dimensions.

The Spanish Fantasy Past could work as a regional identifier and as a commodity to lure tourists and consumers precisely because it was about the past. It negated the present. Elite Anglos had embarked on a vision about southern California that was emphatically a racial vision; theirs was a fundamentally Anglo-Saxon plan. Nonwhites had their roles to play: they built things, they worked, and they stayed not exactly out of sight (invisibility would be dangerous), but certainly out of the way in well-established places and spaces. In other words, Anglos found Mexicans where they expected to: in "our Mexico," in poverty-stricken *colonias,* in *barrios,* and in the laboring hundreds working for the railroad, the citrus firms, or the brickyards. They also found them in the past, where they could be cloaked in the stage directions of fantasy. The present, what with the Mexican Revolution, was a bit too unsettling: best to keep Mexicans out of sight in segregated communities as well as create fictions about what was or was not this social-ethnic-occupational category known as "the Mexican," held fast in place and in space.

Staging the past makes for great instruction about the present, particularly if such theater is self-consciously advertised as the medium by which to learn history. Such was the case, I think, of *The Mission Play,* southern California's "great" theatrical phenomenon of the twentieth century. Written by journalist and historian John Steven McGroarty, *The Mission Play* was apparently seen by as many as 2.5 million people from 1912, when it was first staged, to the coming of the Depression. This epic saga, focusing mostly on the missionizing efforts of Friar Junípero Serra, captured nineteenth-century California as a kind of moral play, a linear tableau that presented cultural and ethnic progressions (read progress) as inevitable, as natural. To top it off, the play was staged on the grounds of the San Gabriel Mission itself, a relic of the early nineteenth century in the center of the rapidly expanding San Gabriel Valley, a tangible reminder of what was.

To our eyes and ears today, *The Mission Play* is hopelessly romantic, unidimensional, and a whitewash of an extremely complicated and troubling era in the region's history. Sun-splashed California natives try to follow the path blazed by sturdy, tough-loving Franciscans; simple Mexican peasants live in harmony with the rhythms of the land and its seasons. Our response in the late twentieth century is irrelevant; what is important to keep in mind is that *The Mission Play* worked at several different levels in the audience.

Most important, perhaps, is that McGroarty knew what he was doing. To be sure (and to be fair), McGroarty's dedication to Catholicism and the traditions of the Church explain much of the play's setting and plot. But *The Mission Play*'s dialogue, characterizations, sets, and costumes (sewn by McGroarty's wife) matched, and I think furthered, the era's need to explain the past in certain ways. Audiences wept as they watched the play, as they saw the Franciscan tenderness toward Native neophytes, as they saw the grandeur of Spain fade from the landscape like the waning light of a bright sun at dusk. Dignitaries, ranging from Mary Austin to important historians and scholars, congratulated McGroarty on his ability to touch his audience and "get the story right." Already in 1912, one critic could hardly restrain his enthusiasm for the play's truthfulness: "Without losing the essence of the historical and educational pageant . . . 'The Mission Play' adds the molding and vitalizing force of chronological narrative and the individualizing of historical personages. Herein lies its great significance."[23]

McGroarty was, in the words of one theater reviewer, "the living saint of Missionland."[24] His characterizations of Mexicans, as trustworthy, simple people, struck members of the audience as on the money, and they told him so. Ella Rebard, a former resident of Los Angeles, felt a kindred regard for McGroarty. She had moved to Mexico City to, as she put it in a letter to the playwright, "study the traits of the people" in order to "convince the world" that "the virtues of the Mexican far exceed his faults." She believed that both she and McGroarty recognized Mexicans for their "friendships, kindness of heart, patience and fortitude in the petty ills of life."[25]

There is no doubt that McGroarty's tale struck a nerve. It could even be epiphanal: "I saw the Mission Play this evening," Los Angeles reform crusader Bromley Oxnam wrote in his diary in the spring of 1913. "The play is good, very good. . . . I had learned to love Junipero Serra and his faithful fathers thru the pages of history." But seeing them come to life offered greater rewards: "I have learned what sacrifice means and truly these men were inspired with a gospel of service. . . . [M]ay I serve as truly as they served."[26] Another viewer had a simpler, though similar, reaction: "It makes people want to go to Mass," wrote one man.[27]

Sentimental regard for a mythic past soaked in romance had existed in southern California for decades. McGroarty simply packaged it within the pages of script and stage directions. But *The Mission Play* was far more than a theatrical extravaganza. It is important to remember that it not only made people cry, but made them think that they understood the past. It was a history text, acted out in front of audiences (hence students) day in and day out. Right, wrong, sentimental, or otherwise, it must be stressed that *The Mission Play* existed as an ersatz history lesson for thousands and thousands of Californians. It represented a form and an understanding of regional consciousness so commonly understood, so popular, that it could literally be taught, theatrically or otherwise.

Carey McWilliams wrote that "a tourist who went to California and failed to see Catalina Island, Mt. Wilson, and *The Mission Play* was considered to have something wrong with his head."[28] But the play also attracted busload after busload of local schoolchildren, from grade schoolers on up. "I enjoyed it very much," schoolgirl Maisie Marjenhoff wrote to McGroarty, "and I never will forget it as long as I live."[29]

Nor were adults and nontourists immune from the lessons. "Your efforts to instill in the minds and hearts of our people a love for the history and traditions of our glorious state, through the medium of your Mission Play, have certainly borne fruit," wrote one enraptured peace officer. Local insurance man James Going stated simply that he and his guests loved the play: "the performance was inspirational, as well as educational."[30] Theater as history: *The Mission Play* was everything a usable past was meant to be. McGroarty "has rendered a great service to California by this visualization of the Franciscan mission and the interpretation of their ideals," wrote critic Willard Huntington Wright. "For the first time in drama their romance has been adequately caught and transmitted to the present-day people of El Camino Real."[31] Its admixture of Christian morality, ethnic hierarchies, sentimentalism, and historical staging made *The Mission Play* southern California's most important example of the intersection of boosterism and history in the years prior to World War II. The Rose Bowl might "teach" about southern California's climate each January 1, but it cannot hold a candle to the lessons imbedded in *The Mission Play*.

Another critical component to bear in mind when considering *The Mission Play* is that the combination of a successful theatrical vehicle with an accessible and popular history lesson helped to create an immensely viable (not to mention valuable) cultural commodity. By the mid-1920s, the play was literally owned by a wing of the Los Angeles Chamber of Commerce, which smartly hired impresario L. E. Behymer to run the show. Commodification of the past had reached a peculiar apogee in southern California. *The Mission Play*'s exuberant declaration of regional identity produced amazing results: tears, lessons, tourists, dollars. "There has been no pageant in American history that means more to the ear, the eye, the religion or the history of this country than that produced by the Mission Play," wrote L. E. Behymer in 1926.[32]

Adjunct to *The Mission Play* itself was a related pursuit. The stock corporation formed to take over the play from author McGroarty in the mid-1920s pledged a portion of gate proceeds (after profit percentages had been guaranteed to investors) toward restoration work of the state's numerous coastal missions. Previous generations had seemed content to see mission adobe literally melt away with the passage of time. As journalist William Wallace wrote from Los Angeles in 1855, "these old Missions, with their Alladin-like legends, become more interesting as they fade into dim obscurity; and as their adobe walls, like the superstitions upon which they were built, melt away, the romance of history will envelop them."[33] But late-nineteenth-century Anglo entrepreneurs and civic-minded preservationists were far less passive. By then, the missions had achieved cultural status as true relics, dignified ruins on the landscape, postcard reminders of a pastoral (and quaintly Catholic) past, graceful and harmless icons, potential tourist destinations.

The restoration juggernaut undoubtedly had been spurred by the astounding success of Helen Hunt Jackson's writings, especially her novel *Ramona* (1885). Interest in the missions only increased through the close of the century. From parlor discussions, to photographic pilgrimages, and, eventually, to establishment of various preservation associations, mission mania became an institutionalized phenomenon in southern California. Critical to the movement was Charles Fletcher Lummis. Best known as a writer and editor, Lummis is often dismissed, as he was in his own time, as an eccentric bohemian. But he was far more complicated than easy adjectives or descriptions allow; in the words of one group of turn-of-the-century tourists, he was "certainly a good deal of a crank and more or less of a genius." For our purposes, however, it is perhaps enough to acknowledge two apparently contradictory sentiments in the man's make-up. For one, Lummis was an avowed "Anglo-Saxonist." As Kevin Starr has pointed out, Lummis believed wholeheartedly that southern California would mark the perfection of the race.[34] At the same time, Lummis worked exhaustively to protect and preserve artifacts of the region's non-Anglo peoples, native Californios and Native Americans especially. And one of Lummis's chief preoccupations was saving the missions.

Despite the apparent contradictions, the preservation pursuits fit the man, the region, the region's sense of self, and the era. Missions were, by definition, ancient. They marked an older culture's imprint on the landscape, California's version of Roman roads or aqueducts. Starr rightly points out that Lummis appreciated the missions mostly because they stood as reminders of the rigor and vigor of frontier life. The favored view of the region exchanged Lummis's regard for ruggedness for one of romance. Preservationists under his leadership were more apt to see the missions as through the paintings of southern California's Impressionists and plein-air artists: hazy, nostalgic, pastel meeting the pastoral in booster heaven. An example, culled from a representative railroad advertisement of around 1920, printed the following over images of Gatsbyesque golfing tourists: "Old Spanish Missions, reflecting the zeal and courage of the Padres of three centuries ago! Mexican towns and gay suburbs, adobe homes, foreign customs and costumes, gay young Carmens in picture-book clothes, wrinkled old Juans and Miguels, recounting feats of their favorite Toreadors!"[35]

The supposed regional irony placed a triumphal Anglo-Saxon version of the future atop a foundation of preserved non-Anglo myths and structures. But it holds up to scrutiny, or at least to cynicism. If the past could be captured, preserved, and interpreted, it could have power. It could be used to teach, to lure, to create categories and hierarchies, to make money, and to create places to "put" entire subsets of the population.

Surely there was some profound connection, and not just a temporal coincidence, between the rise of the Mexican Revolution, the resulting influx of tens, if not hundreds, of thousands of Mexicans into southern California, and the simultaneous flowering of *The Mission Play* and its cousins: the mission-preservationist movement and Mission architectural boom. The Spanish Fantasy Past was reinvigorated precisely when the Anglo present needed the comfort of myth, the soothing sense that the world worked the way it was meant to. Coincidence?

The dissonance remained obvious. If Mexicans were part of the past, and were consigned to out-of-mind, out-of-sight places in the present, what does that say about the ability of these cultural productions to help shore up a regional identity based in large part on ethnic privilege? It was as though, in David Gutierrez's provocative phrasing, the dominant Anglo society had figured out a turn-of-the-century way to set off a cultural neutron bomb, in that the "ersatz Spanish revival" allowed elite Anglos "to celebrate quaint monuments of a past sanitized of the people who had built them and afforded them the luxury of believing that the last remnants of that conquered race had disappeared."[36] Missions remained on the landscape as important components of regional identity. But their iconographic presence alone, gracefully aged and empty, signaled the southern California tendency to compartmentalize an entire people into spaces of "typical" behavior and separate neighborhoods, less critical to the present than hopelessly identified with a lovely past.[37]

Of course, it was not always so neat or so airtight. This regional cultural phenomenon that I have attempted to describe, which tended to fix Mexicans on the various real and imagined landscapes of southern California, and did so with a clear aim toward instruction, cannot be said to be exactly hegemonic. All manner of individuals and institutions resisted the boxes of ethnic categorization. Carey McWilliams himself resisted simply by taking his books and his ideas off his desk and into the wider world.

This chapter is meant only to suggest that a broad cultural project underlay so much of southern California's rise in the late nineteenth century. It was an enterprise that at every step seemed designed to racially rationalize and explain away the inevitable connectedness between warfare and further, if cultural, imperialistic expansion. It is the ethnic lessons at work in southern California, at work on all levels of society, that seem to mark the coalescence of an entire set of ideas about regional identity and regional consciousness.

Beneath it all—the appeals to sunshine, the hollow celebrations of "industrial freedom," and the promises of new beginnings and sure fortunes—an extraordinarily diverse society was being forged in southern California. This was accompanied by a curious blend of images and lessons that were explicitly designed to help form a regional consciousness riven by inequities. In both the short and the long run, what was privileged was missions over Mexicans, and southern California seems as enmeshed in that decision, and ever the poorer for it, today as much as it was eighty years ago.

Things will change, if only by the sureties embedded in demographic projection. Southern California never used to have a Mexican future. By definition, the dominant Anglo culture expected Mexicans to be in the past, barely in the present, surely not an important feature of the future. But there is most certainly a Mexican future to California now. This region, the state, and the nation would be better off if equally important transitions—built around engaged awareness of regional historical legacies—occur simultaneously with that demographic reckoning, lest that reckoning coincide with something more fervent than regional redemption.

NOTES

I would like to thank co-editors Michael Steiner and David Wrobel both for inviting me to participate in this innovative project and for their valuable aid in helping me with this essay. My thanks to Albert Camarillo and David Gutierrez, who, by personal and professional example, first encouraged me to think seriously about the historical issues under study here. I am grateful to the anonymous reader for the University Press of Kansas who helped strengthen this piece.

1. Carey McWilliams, *Louis Adamic and Shadow-America* (Los Angeles: Whipple, 1935), 28. For more on McWilliams, see Lee Ann Meyer, "Great Exception: Carey McWilliams' Path to Activism," (Ph.D. diss., Claremont Graduate School, 1996).

2. Carey McWilliams, *Southern California Country: An Island on the Land* (New York: Duell, Sloan & Pearce, 1946). The dust jacket on my copy of the book lists the subtitle as "An Island in the Land," a typographical mistake that serves to further McWilliams's argument about the region's distinctiveness.

3. C. A. Higgins, *To California over the Santa Fe Trail* (Chicago: Passenger Department, Santa Fe Railroad, 1907), p. 124.

4. Carey McWilliams, *Ill Fares the Land: Migrants and Migratory Labor in the United States* (Boston: Little, Brown, 1942); Mike Davis, *City of Quartz: Excavating the Future in Los Angeles* (London: Verso Press, 1992).

5. Higgins, *To California*, 127, 130.

6. In an essay that explores, especially, the outbreak of infectious disease in Los Angeles in about 1924, I have begun to discuss typicality as a way to think about elites in Los Angeles and their conceptions of the material, social, and ethnic world around them. My discussion here is drawn from that piece: "Plague in Los Angeles, 1924: Ethnicity and Typicality," in *Over the Edge: Mapping Western Experiences,* ed. Valerie Matsumoto and Blake Allmendinger (Berkeley: University of California Press, 1997).

7. I am grateful to my colleague Doug Flamming for his invaluable help with interpreting these images of southern California life.

8. For an introduction to some of the ways in which boosterism may have operated on a local level, as an internal versus external phenomenon, see Doug Flamming and William Deverell, "Race, Rhetoric, and Regional Identity: Boosting Los Angeles, 1880–1930," in *Power and Place in the American West,* ed. John Findlay (Seattle: University of Washington Press, forthcoming). See also Kevin Starr, *Material Dreams: Southern California Through the 1920s* (New York: Oxford University Press, 1990), esp. chap. 5; Clark Davis, "From Oasis to Metropolis: Southern California and the Changing Context of American Leisure," *Pacific Historical Review* 61 (1992): 357–86; Robert Fogelson, *The Fragmented Metropolis: Los Angeles, 1850–1930* (Berkeley: University of California Press, 1993), esp. chap. 4; and Davis, *City of Quartz,* chaps. 1, 2.

9. Harry Carr, *Los Angeles: City of Dreams* (New York: Grosset & Dunlap, 1935), 327.

10. Los Angeles was a popular jumping-off point for soldiers of fortune out to claim southern territory. These groups included the cartoonish and tragic filibustering adventures of the self-styled "emigrants" under the leadership of Henry Crabb. Crabb and his soldiers, out to take Sonora, ended up instead standing before Mexican firing squads in 1857.

11. For an introduction to these realities, see David G. Gutierrez, *Walls and Mirrors: Mexican Americans, Mexican Immigrants, and the Politics of Ethnicity* (Berkeley: University of California Press, 1995).

12. Commercial Federation of California, *Weekly Letter 25,* 10 December 1919.

13. Los Angeles Chamber of Commerce, Minutes, 27 September 1923, board of directors stenographic reports, Los Angeles Chamber of Commerce, Regional History Center, University of Southern California. At the close of his remarks, chamber of commerce director Sylvester L. Weaver suggested a different meaning for the Los Angeles grasp. Lapsing into a tried-and-true

reference to the exoticism of Mexican women, Weaver confessed that he "was sorry that I had four children and a wife."

14. For instance, the impressive legacy of the University of Southern California's social work and sociology students, dating from the first decade of this century, stand as examples of the region's attempts to understand ethnic Mexican life in southern California. Yet they were often handicapped by precisely this return to some essential cultural mean as described by "the Mexican." For an interesting quasi-fictional example of this tendency (written by a settlement-house worker), see Amanda Mathews, *The Hieroglyphics of Love: Stories of Sonoratown and Old Mexico* (Los Angeles: Artemisia Bindery, 1906).

15. Clipping, California Commission of Immigration and Housing [ca. 1915]; author's files. Again, the pronounal hubris is fascinating.

16. The typewritten essay is annotated marginally, in pencil, with a note reading "Spanish & Mexican papers." Better America Federation, Untitled document, Margaret Kerr Papers, Hoover Institution Archives, Hoover Institution on War, Revolution, and Peace, Stanford University.

17. For a brief analysis of the Better American Federation, see Edwin Layton, "The Better America Federation: A Case Study of Superpatriotism," *Pacific Historical Review* 30 (1961): 137–47.

18. Gladys Patric, *A Study of the Housing and Social Conditions in the Ann Street District of Los Angeles, California* (Los Angeles: Los Angeles Society for the Study and Prevention of Tuberculosis, [1916]), 7.

19. Better America Federation, untitled document, Margaret Kerr Papers.

20. Whittier and Glendale real-estate survey forms, "Race Relations" collection, Hoover Institution.

21. Ibid. Remarkably, the results of this real-estate survey were published in *California Real Estate,* July 1927. As McWilliams wrote about towns in southern California, they "deny that they practice segregation, nevertheless, segregation is the rule" (*Southern California Country,* 219).

22. We know virtually nothing about the ways in which Anglo elites may have constructed such cultural containers as the Spanish Fantasy Past as a way to self-consciously build barriers against outside, also Anglo, competition for, for instance, investment. In other words, could the creation of this "island on the land," be in part designed to demonstrate that southern California was simply too exotic to be understood by those from the outside who wished to profit by the region's growth juggernaut?

23. See, for instance, Mary Austin to John S. McGroarty, 8 January 1913, in John Steven McGroarty "Happy Book" scrapbook, vol. 1, Archival Center, Archdiocese of Los Angeles. Austin stated further that McGroarty could utilize her appreciation of the play to good advertising use. My thanks to Monsignor Francis Weber for permission to cite from the McGroarty materials. The critic was Willard Huntington Wright, "The Mission Play: A Pageant-Drama of the History of the Franciscan Missions in California," *Sunset,* July 1912, 92.

24. G. F. Rinehart, in *Covina Citizen*, undated newspaper clipping [March 1922], "Happy Book," vol. 1.

25. Ella Rebard to John Steven McGroarty, 26 March 1922, "Happy Book," vol. 1.

26. Bromley Oxnam, Diary entry, 25 April 1913 [with tipped-in photographic reproduction of Benjamin Horning as Father Serra], Bromley Oxnam Papers, Library of Congress, Washington, D.C.

27. Robert Graham to John Steven McGroarty, 4 April 1922, "Happy Book," vol. 1.

28. McWilliams, *Southern California Country*, 79.

29. Maisie Marjenhoff to John Steven McGroarty, 4 May 1922, "Happy Book," vol. 1.

30. Deputy Robert Hanley to John Steven McGroarty, 18 January 1923; James Going to McGroarty, 4 August 1922, "Happy Book," vol. 1.

31. Wright, "Mission Play," 100.

32. L. E. Behymer to "Mr. Pyke," 13 January 1926, L. E. Behymer Papers, Huntington Library, San Marino, Calif. The play also operated at a curious intersection of patriotism and commercialism. After the Chamber of Commerce took the play over and built the Mission Playhouse, the men responsible invariably received regional congratulations for their patriotism: "Patriotic business men of Los Angeles, at the instance of their Chamber of Commerce, are responsible for this magnificent monument in California which houses the romantic conditions as well as the history of the State the builders love." See John Steven McGroarty, *The Mission Play* [ca. 1930] (souvenir pamphlet), Huntington Library.

33. William Wallace, "Letter from California," undated newspaper clipping [likely published in the *Alta California*], William Wallace journal, Beinecke Rare Book and Manuscript Library, Yale University, New Haven, Conn.

34. In this, Lummis shared a vision of southern California as the city of Anglo-Saxon triumph with (among countless others) physician-writer Joseph Pomeroy Widney. For a discussion of racial attitudes and behavior in the region from around 1900 to 1910, see Kevin Starr, *Inventing the Dream: California Through the Progressive Era* (New York: Oxford University Press, 1985), 89–93. See also Mike Davis, *City of Quartz*, 28. The "crank" quote is from Frank Doubleday, Edward Boks, and Coit Johnson, *On the New Santa Fe Trail* (New York: World's Work Press, 1903).

35. *The Garden of Allah: Arizona [and] California*, (Chicago: Rock Island Railroad, [ca. 1920]).

36. David G. Gutierrez, "Myth and Myopia: Hispanic Peoples and the History of the West," in Geoffrey Ward, *The West* (Boston: Little Brown, 1996). See also David Hurst Thomas's excellent "Harvesting Ramona's Garden: Life in California's Mythical Mission Past," in *Columbian Consequences*, vol. 3, *The Spanish Borderlands in Pan-American Perspective*,

ed. David Hurst Thomas (Washington, D.C.: Smithsonian Institution Press, 1991), 119–57.

37. See for instance, the novel [by Z.Z.], *A Business Venture in Los Angeles, or, a Christian Optimist* (Cincinnati: Clarke, 1899), which despite its missionless plot, utilizes missions as icons on the cover and to open each chapter.

11

Region and Ethnicity:

Topographical Identities in Texas

Arnoldo De León

Hollywood films, western novels, television programs, billboards, and various other media present an exaggerated (sometimes stereotypical) image of Texans. Most residents of Texas, of course, do not own mammoth ranch estates, make millions from oil wells, drive new Cadillacs, or belong to powerful political cliques that wield influence as far as Washington. But the sense of "Texanism" (a peculiar consciousness or frame of mind that Texans are better than most other Americans) as portrayed in popular fiction does seem to have its believers. Texas citizens tend to display an exclusivity and an attachment to place—the Lone Star State. They claim a historical tradition and feel something about themselves that they contend differentiates them from their fellow citizens.[1]

This chapter argues that, in truth, Texans hold several perceptions of themselves. Those self-images may be attributed to a variety of reasons, with regions and the events happening in them ranking as among the most salient agents molding such understandings. Identity among African-Americans, Mexican-Americans, and Anglo-Texans has been determined by what has transpired in eastern Texas, border Texas, and western Texas, respectively.

ORIGINS OF A MYTH

What forces nourish the sentiment that Texans belong to a grand community, one sharing a homogeneous past and having common passions and beliefs? At the most elemental level, many Texans bask in the general knowledge that their state stands as the largest (Texans discount Alaska) in the nation. More significantly, the public-school curriculum seeks to inculcate this idea in impressionable youngsters. Seventh-grade Texas history, a required course, stresses the Texas war for independence (1836); the majesty of the Republic of Texas (Texas is the only state ever to have been an independent nation, from 1836 to 1845); the lost cause of the Confederacy; and the frontier of cowboys, cattle, Indians, and outlaws. From this rather brief, traditional, and largely triumphalist presentation of Texas history—one having all the ingredients of a great epic, including the forces of good (Anglo-Texans) against the overwhelming forces of evil (Santa Anna, the North, or Indians)—students deduce the lesson that the Lone Star State is special and that its history distinguishes its inhabitants from other Americans.[2] Manifesting Texas nationalism are a string of patriotic celebrations, observed on a yearly basis, that reinforce people's high esteem for their state's uniqueness and grandiloquence. All Texas, for example, commemorates Confederate Heroes Day (January 17), Sam Houston and Texas Independence Day (both March 2), and San Jacinto Day (April 21). At the community or county level, civic groups arrange festivals dedicated to perpetuating the memory of the fallen heroes of the Alamo (March 6) or of specific defenders of the "shrine of Texas liberty" (Menard County hosts a Jim Bowie Fair every September). In 1986, the state observed for 365 days the sesquicentennial of its independence from Mexico and, in 1995, its sesquicentennial as a state in the union.

Such ethnocentric displays emanate from an Anglo-American perspective of the state's past. That interpretation is in reality an Anglo construct, invented by contemporaries who participated in the Texas independence movement in 1836 and in the subsequent adventures of the nineteenth century. Such ways of seeing the Texas saga received credence from early Texas scholars writing under the influence of historians such as Frederick Jackson Turner. Walter Prescott Webb, who stated that he had not read Turner but certainly subscribed to his premises, portrayed the Texas Rangers as larger-than-life western characters. In a now famous passage from *The Texas Rangers,* Webb observed that this peerless peace officer was "a man standing alone between a society and its enemies. It was his duty to meet the outlaw breed of three races, the Indian warrior, Mexican bandit, and American desperado, on the enemy's ground and deliver each safely within the jail or the cemetery gate. [A ranger] could calmly gaze into the eye of a murderer, divine his thoughts, and anticipate his action, a man who could ride straight up to death."[3]

Such a paragon of the Texan and the imputed prowess that accompanied the taming of the wilderness went hand-in-hand with the thought that a superior United States civilization had been divinely guided from Atlantic to Pacific and even to other parts of the globe. Until the 1960s, few questioned the explanation of the typical Texas chronicle and the identity that evolved from it.[4] Today, society often keeps the so-called Texas myth alive in a form that resurrects the image of a cowboy-stomping West: the names of professional sports teams include the Texas Rangers, Dallas Cowboys, and Dallas Mavericks. Individually, men try to display a bravado once associated with the Texas western tradition by donning Stetson hats and cowboy boots and driving around in pickups (a vicarious substitute for the horse).

In fact, a variety of identities exist—and have existed through time— and they diverge from the one just described. Not all Texans accept the romance that enthralls the popular imagination. There live in the state ethnic groups—generally people of color—whose experiences actually run counter to those of most white Texans, and they are not complete converts to the fantasy. This discrepancy in experiences may be due to assorted forces, among them events that transpired within particular regions.

Stated another way, the convergence of diverse peoples in different regional settings explains the miscellaneous images that Texans have of themselves. On the one hand, the meeting of Anglos, Native Americans, African-Americans, and Mexican-Americans engendered an identity that became a mix of South and West. On the other hand, the encounter produced a mosaic of ethnic populations and even ambivalent feelings about the relevance of the state's history to those ethnic groups involved. Historically speaking, the intersection of peoples with dissimilar cultural backgrounds involved separate time periods and occurred in different physical settings. Often fractious, the contact had as its backdrop racist attitudes and opposing economic expectations. All groups involved used violence either as a form of domination and control or as defense and retaliation. In the twentieth century, such discordance evolved into a rapprochement, but the people involved by then had developed an identity that reflected the experiences of their respective regions. The result is disparate guideposts for self-reference.

MIGRATION AND ANTAGONISM

The occupation of Texas by humans actually entailed various frontier movements. Some people came from the north, others from the south, still others from the east. The first occupants were Native Americans who many aeons ago arrived from Asia. After the 1850s, however, the Comanches emerged as the most formidable band and, until the 1870s, retained a tenacious hold on the area west of a line beginning near modern-day Fort Worth and extending to the Texas Hill Country. They sought to ward off nonindigenous people moving into their territorial orbit.

The settlement of the "border country" of Texas—that section extending from below San Antonio down toward the Nueces River and into Corpus Christi, south from there to the Rio Grande, thence west through a transitional geographical zone around Del Rio, and past it beyond the Pecos River all the way to El Paso—may be traced to Spanish colonizing efforts undertaken during the eighteenth and first half of the nineteenth centuries. Fending off Indian attacks, Tejano settlers by the mid-nineteenth century had managed to transform the trans-Nueces area into a viable ranching section that conducted a modest amount of commerce with Mexico. All the while, surges of migration persisted from Coahuila, Nuevo León, and Tamaulipas toward southern Texas and from Chihuahua to western Texas.[5] This thrust north represented a frontier movement of its own, for the pioneers in the Mexican north brought with them accouterments that would give border Texas a Hispanic cultural aura. *Vaqueros* applied their knowledge of the range to a landscape that did not differ markedly from that in Mexico's north. Settlers also imported an ethos generally associated with

Mexico's northern rim: fair governance, independence, self-reliance, and bravery.[6]

The cultural violation of Texas by the United States began in the 1820s, when Anglo-Americans from the lower and upper South arrived in the eastern parts of Mexican Texas. Immigrants from Louisiana, Mississippi, Alabama, Georgia, and other plantation states gravitated toward the southeastern perimeters of this region, and there established a Deep South ambiance. Southerners from Kentucky, Missouri, Arkansas, and Tennessee, along with descendants of European immigrant groups who had earlier settled in the Middle Atlantic colonies, began migrating into northeastern Texas during the 1830s. In that geographical area of what became the Republic of Texas, each implanted a culture that extended the boundaries of the slave South. In fact, both had brought African-American bondspeople along.[7]

From the eastern portions of Texas, but primarily from North Texas, settlers from the upper South during the 1840s and 1850s trekked in a westwardly course, past the ninety-eighth meridian, as well as into the Upper Hill Country. Most of them came without slaves, as the western reaches (at that time) of the state did not physiographically support the peculiar institution. This pattern of white migration continued after 1865, so that by the 1880s Upper South–origin settlers had closed in on the New Mexico border.[8]

These migratory patterns necessarily cast different peoples into common physical settings, each group with its own ideas about how to use the land for basic survival. The migrants distrusted and disliked one another not only because of racial and cultural aversions, but also because they pursued conflicting economic goals.

The southern Anglos who crossed the Sabine River into Texas believed that African-Americans were biologically inferior to whites. Commenting on miscegenation, for instance, the *Texas Almanac* of 1858 warned that mixture between blacks and whites could not occur "without producing disease and death to the offspring. The Mulatto of the fourth degree, unless bred back into pure white or black cannot reproduce himself." The majority of whites also held that a higher being had ordained black people to their station in society, that, in fact, they would even be rewarded spiritually for their kindness in guiding a less advanced race.[9] Not surprisingly, slavery flourished; by mid-century, the rich soils of eastern Texas bolstered what one modern historian has called a "virtual empire for slavery."[10] The slave community surely must have entertained different notions about exploiting those lands for community and individual well-being. Whites, however, hardly extended them such an option.

Once the Civil War abolished slavery, racial readjustments occurred as white society sought ways to continue oppressing and exploiting blacks. Conflicts between the two groups inevitably erupted, much of it in the eastern half of the state. Deep into the twentieth century, disputes occurred over racial policies regulating segregation and sexual relations, the need for political control, and less significant issues such as "impudent" behavior. Violence often manifested itself in cold-blooded murders, lynchings, burnings at the stake, and race riots.

As Anglo-Americans pushed into Native American lands, they did so with a hatred traceable to early contacts with Indians on the Atlantic seaboard. While Texans such as Sam Houston maintained tolerant attitudes toward Native Americans, most believed Indians to be savages, nonhumans, heathens, primitive and unkempt people who represented obstacles to civilization that should be pursued in the struggle for the continent. Houston's political adversary, Mirabeau B. Lamar, put that intention succinctly in late 1838:

> Nothing short of this [expulsion] will bring us peace or safety. . . . The white man and the red man cannot dwell in harmony together. Nature forbids it. . . . Knowing these things, I experience no difficulty in deciding on the proper policy to be pursued towards them. It is to push a rigorous war against them; pursuing them to their hiding places without mitigation or compassion, until they shall be made to feel that flight from our borders without hope of return, is preferable to the scourges of war.[11]

Contention between Texans and Native Americans revolved around mutually antagonistic racial attitudes and the desire to control West Texas beyond the ninety-eighth meridian. Texans wanted the expanse to stop Indian attacks on the farmsteads and ranchsteads along the line of settlement and to raise sheep, goats, and cattle; Native Americans needed the same space for tribal survival through time-proven ancestral traditions. In this struggle for domination of the region, both sides waged vicious war. Indians committed horrible atrocities, while the bloody campaigns against the Comanches proved equally gruesome. The scorched-earth policy that Texans employed in the panhandle plains between 1871 until 1875 occasioned the killing of horses, the burning of villages, the destruction of household utensils and home supplies, the decimation of the buffalo, and, of course, the massacre of women and children.

Once capitalism triumphed in West Texas by the mid-1870s, Anglos transformed the region into a cattle-ranching entity, though by the 1920s, agriculture had joined livestock marketing as the section's other major enterprise. Today, no discernible Indian population remains in western Texas, save perhaps for small enclaves in the El Paso region.

Anglo-Americans showed no more tolerance for Mexicans in Texas than they had toward the other two peoples of color. To them, Mexicans represented one more inferior race in the march of civilization. Although negative sentiments toward Tejanos surfaced during the 1820s, they erupted with abandon when Anglos arrived in the border country of southern and western Texas during the 1840s. Thereafter, Anglos pressed for old Tejano lands and initiated a sometimes subtle, often vicious campaign for domination of the area. Some Tejanos adjusted to the imposed arrangement, but others resisted. The tenuous occupation during the nineteenth century produced resentment: Tejanos abhorred the arrogance of the newcomers, lamented relegation to menial occupations, and bemoaned the use of their labor to transform old ranch lands into new productive farms from Brownsville to El Paso. Whites unhesitatingly used a number of stratagems to keep Tejanos under submission, not the least of them being violence, a tactic that has been chronicled by numerous students of Mexican-American history. Within Mexican-American communities today there survive folkloric tales recalling terrible deeds of injury and even death that Anglos inflicted on Mexicans even into the 1950s.[12]

ETHNOREGIONAL IDENTITIES

The multipronged structure of migration, and the ensuing wariness and conflicts, begot ethnic heterogeneity in Texas over the course of time. Many African-Americans and Mexican-Americans opted for biculturation, for two very significant reasons. Primarily, black Texans and Tejanos preferred a loyalty to their mother (or in-group) culture, and elected to practice it in an equilibrium with mainstream American culture. In black neighborhoods and in *barrios,* these two minorities molded a sense of self-identification based on their selective acceptance of Anglo culture and their attachment to African and Mexican traditions, respectively. The syncretic lifestyle of African-Americans and Mexican-Americans, however, also owes much to racism in those areas where they have historically been heavily concentrated. Until the early 1960s, prejudice in eastern Texas and border Texas relegated both groups to a segregated status, so that bicultural ethnicity has also been a way of dealing with patterns of oppression.

African-American culture certainly has been molded by the course of events in eastern Texas and the section's ties to the South. That region of Texas historically has had the greatest concentration of African-Americans. Following the demise of slavery, African-Americans continued to be the main laboring force that worked the cotton fields, as either pickers or tenant farmers. Southern attitudes governed interracial customs, for despite Anglo-Texans' fixation with the West, their attitudes toward blacks have traditionally been grounded on southern habits. After all, most Anglos had entered Texas from the upper and lower South. Whites expected deference and respect from African-Americans, and certain taboos endured. Black men were not to mix with white women or to assault white people. For such a transgression, the penalty could be physical retaliation, if not lynchings. Conversely, society generally overlooked such outrages upon blacks.

"Southern techniques" for dominating blacks politically—the poll tax, the white man's primary, the Ku Klux Klan, and other devices—found their warmest reception in eastern Texas, and society used them to stifle African-American political power. Jim Crow laws were more specific to that section—though, of course, the entire state enforced segregation. Race riots, lynchings, violent acts, mass demonstrations, and 1960s-style sit-ins all had their broadest expressions in eastern Texas.

Consequently, the experience in the eastern Texas cultural milieu has shaped the nature of black culture in the Lone Star State. The African-American personality there (and, of course, in other parts of the state into which blacks have dispersed) naturally embraces the two cultural worlds, African and mainstream American. The most obvious manifestations of mainstream American conventions among blacks include language, foods, fashions, and belief in the democratic system. A more telling example may be the way African-American folkloric tradition in East Texas integrates the white, black, and Mexican-American presence in the state. Some jokes, for one, incorporate known stereotypical traits of the three groups to elicit laughter.[13]

But southern-style prejudice has also influenced cultural responses. In reaction to attitudes that discouraged them from participation in mainstream institutions, African-Americans established their own businesses and cultural institutions (funeral parlors and churches), present in inner-city neighborhoods such as those in Dallas and Houston. Such institutions that tend to African-Americans' needs in what may amount to a sub-city are duplicated in small communities throughout the region where de facto segregation survives as in other racially divided regions of the country, among them the modern-day South.

The poverty, travail, and injustice that have typified black life in eastern Texas inspired a Texas version of African-American music. The blues, borrowed for the most part from the Deep South and popularized in Texas by such 1950s luminaries as Blind Lemon Jefferson, Mance Lipscomb, and T-Bone Walker, made a significant contribution to mainstream white musicians, influencing the innovative style of white pop singers like Buddy Holly and Roy Orbison. Music found dissemination through black radio programming, which appeared in the 1930s when black radio's audience consistently predominantly of African-Americans. By the 1950s, however, most of the larger cities in the state featured black radio stations that played the influential music of the best African-American stars of the era, among them Little Richard and Chuck Berry.[14]

African-Americans still commemorate events that bear a connection to a southern past. Some communities celebrate a special day in the African-American calendar, such as the annual Juneteenth, which commemorates the day (June 19) on which General Gordan Granger arrived in Texas in 1865 and announced the slaves' freedom. The long history of discrimination also played a hand in determining the tradition of ethnic dances, church functions, sports activities, and the like.[15]

Mexican-American culture, in contrast to that of African-Americans, is more closely tied to the history of the border country and to Mexico. The Tejano experience in that region of the state is complex and has been defined by several factors. Field work and a migrant pattern of life stamped South Texas particularly, while ranching and sheep herding came to be more familiar to Tejanos living in the areas west of Eagle Pass. Laws and traditions molded on southern Jim Crow regulations took root against Mexicans along the border, and whites applied them as strictly to Mexicans here as they did to blacks in eastern Texas. Whites came to despise "dirty" Mexicans, and they struggled to control the same people they exploited by establishing separate schools and sections of towns. Social codes governing black and white matters hardly differed in that section.

When interacting with Anglos, according to a team of ethnographers, Mexicans were to assume

> a deferential body posture and respectful voice tone. One also used the best polite forms of speech one could muster in English or Spanish. One laughed with Anglos but never at them. One never showed extreme anger or aggression towards an Anglo in public. Of course, the reverse of this was that Anglos could be informal with Mexicanos. Anglos could slap Mexicanos on the back, joke with them at their expense, curse them out, in short, do all the things people usually do only among relatively familiar and equal people.[16]

From Brownsville to Corpus Christi, thence to San Antonio, and from there to El Paso, one finds a region that to some degree is an extension of Mexico in terms of its Catholic religion, folklore, architectural styles, medium of communications, and cuisine. There remain such strong "Mexican" beliefs as *curanderismo* (folk healing). Among other folkloric beliefs still vibrant in border Texas is the story that the devil appears at dance halls—decked out in fine threads and looking seductively handsome—to keep an eye on women engaged in any wayward behavior, or perhaps to tantalize them with the prospects of escape from the drudgery of their working-class experience.[17]

But the conditions to which the majority of Mexican-Americans have been exposed along the border country have also influenced their ethnicity. The Tejano way of life there (and elsewhere that Tejanos have relocated) displays the cultural syncretism cited already. Mainstream ingredients evident in the Tejano lifestyle include standard English, fads and trendy clothing styles, children's names, and, of course, the ethic of buying now and paying later.

For the most part, Mexican-American culture in border Texas represents a conciliation with Anglo traditions. Mexican-Americans speak Spanish and English fluently, though they employ numerous linguistic codes. Since opportunities for learning formal Spanish are not easily available in the state, the Spanish used in Mexican-American neighborhoods comes in vernacular varieties. These include "nonstandard" Spanish, which may incorporate numerous English loan words; code-switching, which involves conversations moving alternately from one language to the other; and even *pachuco* argot, an in-group street idiom.[18]

Mexican-Americans throughout the state, but more so along the border, stage ethnic entertainment that further indicates how they fused their Mexican background with mainstream cultural elements. Leisure-time festivities include the observation of the national holidays of Mexico—*Cinco de Mayo* and *Diez y Seis de Septiembre*—and local community commemorations of a particular patron saint. Grand spectacles for popular enjoyment include the *pan de campo* fiesta (in which contestants bake bread on an iron pan over mesquite coals, just as did *vaqueros* in the open range) held in San Diego, Duval County, each summer. Mexican (and Tejano) motifs, themes, entertainment, decorations, and fellowship invariably permeate such gatherings.

Anglo-American identity, in contrast to that of African- and Mexican-Americans, was largely determined by the culture imported from east of the Mississippi River, but events that transpired beyond the ninety-eighth meridian modified it. Western Texas, after all, hosted much of the Texas drama after the war for independence: this was the sphere of Native Americans, Texas Rangers, intrepid pioneers, and macho gunfighters, and a setting featuring open space, sparse settlement, and topography associated with the Far West. Indeed, much of the "Texas myth" rests on such adventures, even if most Texans today are clustered in geographical areas outside western Texas.

Some Texas scholars have made the case that the state has closer ties to the South than to the West. Southernness does endure in attitudes toward race relations; literary themes, which include a pastoral past of corn and cotton lands, and of sharecropping farmers in overalls; the popularity of country-and-western music, which, of course, borrows from the blues of the black South; the use of the "southern drawl"; and the kinship to the fundamentalist South. Texans have also given support to southern-style traditionalism and provincialism, as evidenced in the predominance of the Democratic Party until the 1970s and its faithfulness to states' rights.[19] It is also apparent in a lingering attachment Texans have to the Civil War. Until rather recent times, the Confederate flag waved during some of the Friday-night football games, and teams still go by such names as the Rebels.

But more than a century ago, possibly during the last three decades of the nineteenth century, many Anglo-Texans made a conscious decision to break with the South both culturally and ideologically. Several factors weakened ties with the erstwhile motherland, while other influences strengthened people's identification with the region to the west of a line from Fort Worth to the Hill Country. The Civil War and Reconstruction did not influence Texas as they had the rest of the South. More immediately, the Confederacy's loss in 1865 hardly measured up to the high drama against Native Americans and Mexicans, two formidable opponents not present in southern history.[20]

Buttressing the Texas preference for a western historical heritage, the educational system at all levels has fed the public huge doses of the western myth. As already noted, most Texas historians until the last quarter of the twentieth century regarded nineteenth-century Texas history as part of a divine plan of westward settlement that culminated in the rescue of the frontier from backward Indians and Mexicans. The emphasis that many professional scholars placed on the state's frontier heritage filtered down to the public-school level, where students learned about the bravery of frontier settlers (assisted by Texas Rangers) who had won the West by building huge cattle estates and burgeoning cities where Indians had once roamed.[21] Texas literature also emphasizes a western connection, as seen in the writings of Larry McMurtry, but more prominently in the works of Elmer Kelton, the acknowledged dean of western authors in the state. The ambient of "westernness" has seduced Texans into imitating the cowboy tradition, manifested in the wearing of popular western apparel and, as of 1996, the right to carry concealed weapons.

TEXANISM AND THE AMERICAN WEST

In the minds of most Anglo-Texans, therefore, West Texas represents the quintessential place and identity. What has happened in regions such as East Texas and border Texas is conveniently subsumed in history and lore to the frontier adventure that unfolded beyond the ninety-eighth meridan, where Anglo-Texans found heroism, romance, and exemplars that made Texas preeminent among other states. Such ideals appeared only tangentially in eastern and border Texas. For instance, southern traits—among them chivalry, honor, hospitality, romanticized womanhood, and Christian righteousness—have not been integrated into the Texan persona to the same degree as have western values.

Coincidentally, the image that many Anglo people have of West Texas evokes a vision that others hold of the larger American West. The saga includes individuals with a penchant for independence, intrepid pioneers bringing civilization to savage lands, cowboys building ranches, or law officers taming unruly Natives. The scenario involves males displaying streaks of machismo, with women playing only supportive roles. Even to this day, both West Texas and the larger American West contain geo-demographic features that make them alike: vast open spaces, more areas where nature thrives undisturbed, comparatively (to other sections) fewer peoples of color, and a contagious neighborliness.

  Ethnic minorities in Texas have long recognized that such a state of mind represents something foreign to their own experiences. For one thing, African- and Mexican-American youngsters learned in the public schools that the discussion of the Texas narrative did not integrate them or, if it did, depicted them only as villains or victims in the West Texas drama. What most grown-ups faced until very recent times in everyday actions ran counter to the prerogatives that Anglo-Americans took for granted. Experiences compelled minorities to form a more realistic out-look of Texas exceptionalism. That judgment has been evident in the academic works published by ethnic historians since the 1960s. Their revisionism has taken issue with the Texas myth and has portrayed Texas as Elliott West describes the New Western History: a "longer, grimmer, and more interesting story" that is more ethnically diverse than the West Texas–frontier interpretation presented in the older scholarship.[22]

  Despite any uneasy views that African-Americans and Mexican-Americans may hold toward Anglo-Saxon "Texanism" and the larger West, both minorities owe unquestionable loyalty to the state and the nation. Such an ambivalence derives from a rapprochement reached decades ago. Certainly, the lessons taught in civics classes, mass information dissemi-nated through various media, positive day-to-day encounters, and the accommodationist philosophy advanced by some minority activists, among others forces, have satisfied minorities that American democratic insti-tutions have no equal. Submergence in mainstream culture (while re-taining in-group ways) is testimony to this allegiance.

  Even ethnoregional pride does not blunt identification with the larger state. To this day, eastern Texas and border Texas remain the strongholds of black and Tejano populations, respectively, and this concentration rein-forces minority distinctiveness. But just as faith and trust bind Anglo-Texans to the greater West, so they link minority groups to the larger Lone Star State and, of course, the nation. Mexican-Americans, for instance, display an acknowledged haughtiness in being "Tejano." Many Tejanos consider themselves to be somehow superior to Mexican-Americans in California and the Midwest, even as these groups associate Tejanos with rural backwardness. Texas Hispanics boast of their homegrown "Tejano music," literature, vocabulary, and foods (fajitas, burritos, *menudo,* and *tripas*). Some even display the fashions and symbols that smack of the very culture that has historically persecuted them: tight-fitting blue jeans, cowboy boots, Stetson hats, belts (with name monogrammed), and the ubiquitous pickup truck.

Texas history, as we have seen, has been more ethnically diverse than the West Texas–frontier story has acknowledged. Instead of the Anglo-unicultural Lone Star account, a variety of ethnic groups have contributed to the settlement and development of Texas. Among the many things that occurred when people of different racial and ethnic backgrounds met one another was syncretic exchange. All added in-group components through cultural interaction. Even Anglos, while disdaining the African- and Mexican-American cultures and generally rejecting intermarriage, have borrowed words, customs, and music from those otherwise scorned people.

Given such cross-cultural mixing, the feared breakup of the nation along cultural lines, manifested in such campaigns as the English-only movement, may well be unfounded. What has been demonstrated in Texas regarding ethnicity and region over the years appears more or less a duplication of those complex processes—fragmentation coexisting with cooperation—evident throughout the trans-Mississippi West. As elsewhere, Texans of all ethnicities may heed the uniqueness of their local group, next the community, then the region, but ultimately they concede allegiance to the state and finally the nation. If, as in the nineteenth century, the meeting of peoples in frontier regions caused conflict, colonization, and economic exploitation of the less powerful, the encounter also involved a zone where, as in the present day, creative interaction involving both cultural resistance and accommodation takes place as people with diverse outlooks and ways of life pursue not so different life ambitions.

Texas, then, may be compared with other areas in the trans-Mississippi West where regional consciousness also took root partly as a result of historical conflicts, but ultimately led to the acceptance of a mainstream ethos by those involved. Ethnicity, race, culture, day-to-day experiences, and other factors, however, begot not one type of Westerner, but many.

Certainly, such an observation reflects still another facet of the historically contested nature of the West and its diverse peoples.

NOTES

1. George N. Green, *The Establishment in Texas Politics: The Primitive
Years, 1938–1957* (Norman: University of Oklahoma Press, 1979), 3–4; Terry
G. Jordan, "The Anglo-Texan Homeland," *Journal of Cultural Geography* 13
(1993): 76–77.

2. David G. McComb, "Texas History Textbooks in Texas Schools,"
Southwestern Historical Quarterly 93 (1989): 191, 192–94; Jordan, "Anglo-
Texan Homeland," 77. See also Margaret Swett Henson, "Texas History in
the Public Schools: An Appraisal," *Southwestern Historical Quarterly* 82
(1979): 408.

3. Walter Prescott Webb, *The Texas Rangers: A Century of Frontier
Defense* (Boston: Houghton Mifflin, 1935), ix. See also Stephen Stagner,
"Epics, Science, and the Lost Frontier: Texas Historical Writing, 1836–1936,"
Western Historical Quarterly 12 (1981): 179–81; and Michael P. Malone,
"Beyond the Last Frontier: Toward a New Approach to Western American
History," *Western Historical Quarterly* 20 (1989): 411–13.

4. Walter L. Buenger and Robert A. Calvert, *Texas Through Time:
Evolving Interpretations* (College Station: Texas A&M University Press,
1990), xviii.

5. Daniel D. Arreola, "The Texas Mexican Homeland," *Journal of Cultural
Geography* 13 (1993): 62; Terry G. Jordan, "A Century and a Half of Ethnic
Change in Texas, 1836–1986," *Southwestern Historical Quarterly* 89 (1986):
398.

6. Miguel León-Portilla, "The Norteño Variety of Mexican Culture: An
Ethnohistorical Approach," in *Plural Society in the Southwest,* ed. Edward H.
Spicer and Raymond H. Thompson (Albuquerque: University of New Mexico
Press, 1972), 112–13.

7. Terry G. Jordan, with John L. Bean, Jr., and William M. Holmes, *Texas:
A Geography* (Boulder, Colo.: Westview Press, 1984), 73–74, 77, 91.

8. Ibid., 74, 77.

9. Billy D. Ledbetter, "White over Black in Texas: Racial Attitudes in the
Antebellum Period," *Phylon* 34 (1973): 411.

10. Randolph B. Campbell, *An Empire for Slavery: The Peculiar Institution
in Texas, 1821–1865* (Baton Rouge: Lousiana State University Press, 1989),
2, 78.

11. Quoted in T. R. Fehrenbach, *Lone Star: A History of Texas and Texans*
(New York: Macmillan, 1968), 453.

12. Arnoldo De León, *They Called Them Greasers: Anglo Attitudes Toward
Mexicans in Texas, 1821–1900* (Austin: University of Texas Press, 1983), 104–5.

13. Roger D. Abrahams, *Positively Black* (Englewood Cliffs, N.J.: Prentice-Hall, 1970), 69, 37–39.

14. Robert A. Calvert and Arnoldo De León, *The History of Texas,* 2nd ed. (Wheeling, Ill.: Harlan Davidson, 1996), 369.

15. Alwyn Barr, *Black Texans: A History of Negroes in Texas, 1528–1971* (Austin: Pemberton Press, 1973), 167–68.

16. Douglas E. Foley, Clarice Mota, Donald E. Post, and Ignacio Lozano, *From Peones to Politicos: Ethnic Relations in a South Texas Town, 1900–1977* (Austin: Center for Mexican American Studies, University of Texas, 1977), 43–44.

17. José E. Limón, *Dancing with the Devil: Society and Cultural Poetics in Mexican American South Texas* (Madison: University of Wisconsin Press, 1994), chap. 8.

18. Rosaura Sánchez, "Spanish Codes in the Southwest," in *Modern Chicano Writers,* ed. Joseph Sommers and Tomás Ybarra-Frausto (Englewood Cliffs, N.J.: Prentice-Hall, 1989), 44–45, 48–51.

19. Green, *Establishment in Texas Politics,* 4–7.

20. Jordan, "A Century and a Half of Ethnic Change in Texas," 388; Jordan, "The Anglo-Texan Homeland," 78–80.

21. Buenger and Calvert, *Texas Through Time,* xiv–xv.

22. Elliott West, "A Longer, Grimmer, and More Interesting Story," in *Trails: Toward a New Western History,* ed. Patricia Nelson Limerick, Clyde A. Milner II, and Charles E. Rankin (Lawrence: University Press of Kansas, 1991), 103–11.

Part Four:

EXTENDED WESTS

In contemplating western boundaries, there has been more uncertainty about where the West begins than where it ends. The eastern boundary of the West has been a matter of much discussion among western historians. The Mississippi River, the second tier of states west of the Mississippi (from North Dakota to Texas), the ninety-eighth and hundredth meridians (which run through those states), the Missouri River, and the Rocky Mountains—all have been deemed contenders for the title "eastern boundary of the West." There has been less debate over the West's western, northern, and southern boundaries. The Pacific Ocean, it is generally assumed, marks the western end of the West, and the Canadian and Mexican borders, respectively, mark the northern and southern limits. For most observers, then, the West is bounded by an ocean to the west, geopolitical borders to the north and south, and a mountain chain, rivers, a meridian, or state lines, to the east (depending on whom one asks).

The eastern boundary of the West has been the focus of so much of the discussion about "where the West is" because "westernness" is generally perceived in direct contrast to "easternness." Indeed, New Western Historians who view the West as a geographically bounded place or region, share with frontier, or process-centered, historians an emphasis on contrast between East and West. The presence of an ocean at the western end of the West and national borders to the north and south help explain the comparative absence of discussion over the West's "noneastern" borders. It is difficult to imagine a more substantive marker, concrete or symbolic, for the border of a region than the edge of a continent. Furthermore, ideas of American uniqueness or exceptionalism, coupled with notions of the West as the "most American part of America," have made it difficult for many Americans to imagine parts of Canada or Mexico as "western."

Still, difficult as it may be, it is worth considering areas that lie outside the contiguous western United States as part of the West or, at least, in relation to the West. The chapters in this section help extend or enlarge our sense of the West and its boundaries. Whether one concludes that the American West is defined by national borders (to the north and south) and continental limits (to the west) or that western boundaries are more fluid and extensive, consideration of "extended Wests" enhances our understanding of western regional identity.

In "The Other Northwest," Richard Maxwell Brown examines similarities and differences between British Columbia and the United States Northwest. While physiographically and climatically connected, the two Northwests are divided, Brown suggests, by more than an international border. While striking cultural, economic, and political parallels exist between British Columbia and Oregon and Washington, the contrasts seem more pronounced. Yet the parallels are fascinating. Brown notes, for example, that British Columbia is to Canada what California is to the United States—both are sunny promised lands of sorts, and both are situated (symbolically, as well as geographically), in the estimation of some observers, "west of the West."

In drawing a plethora of comparisons and contrasts between these two Northwests, Brown illuminates the subtleties that underlie relationships between regions and subregions, regions and nations, metropolises and hinterlands, different cultures within regions, and, more broadly, the Canadian and American Wests. He demonstrates the benefits of comparative analysis of nations and of regions within nations. Indeed, Brown's comparative analysis of British Columbia and Oregon/Washington should prove to be a catalyst to comparative studies of other Canadian and American borderlands—for example, Alberta and/or Saskatchewan and Montana, or Manitoba and the Dakotas.

In "Noncontiguous Wests," John Whitehead examines both the forces that drew Alaska and Hawai'i into the American West and those that bound the mainland Wests together, to the exclusion of these "noncontiguous Wests." He questions whether noncontiguity is a sufficient reason for the exclusion of the forty-ninth and fiftieth states from "the West." Whitehead emphasizes that Hawai'i, Alaska, and the northwest coast of North America were very much interconnected in the "maritime mind" of the early- to mid-nineteenth century; indeed, they were reckoned to be a "contiguous Pacific area," bound by the "maritime, cultural, and commercial influence of New England." By 1900, Alaska and Hawai'i were even more fully integrated into the "gold rush West." However, the urban–industrial growth of the Pacific Slope in the early twentieth century was not mirrored in Alaska, where the population remained sparse and the image of an untransformable frontier developed. Similarly, in Hawai'i, a comparatively slow rate of urban–industrial growth, coupled with images of an untransformed paradise, have, in the decades since statehood, nurtured a sense of separateness among both the islands' inhabitants and most mainland Americans.

Whitehead paints a picture of Alaska and Hawai'i as places that were once most definitely "western," but now no longer are, though they may become so again. In doing this, he demonstrates the essential fluidity of western borders over time. Interestingly, the development of regional identity in Alaska and Hawai'i, and the changing perceptions of those places among residents of the contiguous United States, constitute a curious inversion of Frederick Jackson Turner's frontier thesis. In Turner's estimation, the forces of industrialization and urbanization were what made the West increasingly and inevitably less "western" (or less "frontier-like") over time. For Whitehead, though, it is the comparative absence of industrialization and urbanization in Alaska and Hawai'i that places them outside "the West" in the twentieth century. He concludes, essentially, that the noncontiguous Wests are (or, at least, are reckoned to be) too frontier-like, too untransformed, to be part of the modern West. Alaska and Hawai'i are, in a sense, what the West once was.

While Brown and Whitehead enlarge our sense of the West north and west of the national border, Paula Gunn Allen in *"Cuentos de la Tierra Encantada"* looks to the south. She perceives the Southwest as a transnational region, embracing Mexico and portions of Central America as well as New Mexico and Arizona, along with southern California and western Texas—all shaped by the confluence of Indian, Spanish, and Anglo cultures. For Allen, the highly porous and glaringly artificial line between the United States and Mexico is overshadowed by the geospiritual reality of the Southwest. For all its technological and military might centered in the Southwest, Allen suggests, the Anglo-dominated culture of the United States may ultimately be transformed by the indigenous cultures it set out to conquer.

Allen emphasizes the power of stories, food, architecture, film, and other creative expressions as wellsprings of southwestern identity. The region's deep-seated tradition of "magical realism" engenders a poignant sense of place; its many "wondrous, wild, and deeply satisifying" narratives permeate a vast region artificially (and officially) separated by the Rio Grande. While magical realism may seem to historians a less tangible commodity than, for example, political or economic development, Allen's driving theme illuminates the significance of the subconscious, spiritual, and supernatural in creating regional identity. Thus in addition to stretching our geographical sense of this "magical, multiple borderland," Allen expands, through her telling of stories that have been cradled in the land, our understanding of the forces that shape sense of place.

The Other Northwest: The Regional Identity

of a Canadian Province

Richard Maxwell Brown

A land of spectacular beauty, British Columbia has yet to be much discovered by American tourists, and one hopes that it never will be. A leading Canadian writer, Stephen Leacock, is said to have declared while visiting British Columbia that if he had known how beautiful it was, "I wouldn't have been content with a mere visit, I'd have been born here." A character in an esteemed British Columbia novel said upon coming to the province in middle age, "It is so lovely . . . that I feel I've wasted my life in not living here before." If British Columbia is virtually unknown to American tourists, it is little known, as well, to American historians and regionalists. Not many studies comparing British Columbia with the American Northwest or West have been published, but American scholars have much to learn from a closer look at British Columbia.[1]

Two scholars have defined the Canadian–American borderlands as "a region jointly shared by" the United States and Canada "with common social characteristics in spite of the political boundary between them." They further define the borderlands to suggest the way in which British Columbia at times opposes the dominance of Canada.[2] In British Columbia, for example, there is during our age of nationalism a strong sense of separation from Canada. This and a number of other related themes are explored in this chapter, including the physical environment and artistic culture of British Columbia as a part of the Great Raincoast of North America; a neglected episode of decades-long radical religious violence in a generally peaceable province; the strong left–right dichotomy and the polarity of individualistic and moralistic values in a distinctive political history and culture; British Columbia as an intriguing venue for exploring questions of exceptionalism (within Canada, within western North America, and "why there is no socialism" in the United States and Canada); the transition in British Columbia consciousness from a nineteenth-century Britannic frontier perspective to a late-twentieth-century regional perspective shaped by metropolitanism and ethnic pluralism; British Columbia as "Canada's California," counterpointed by the recent rise of the great subregion of northern British Columbia; and, in historiography, the parallel between the New British Columbia History and the New Western History of the United States. Although this chapter will focus on British Columbia, there will be comparative attention to Oregon and Washington and, more broadly, to western America.

BRITISH COLUMBIA AS PART OF THE GREAT RAINCOAST OF NORTH AMERICA

The similarities between British Columbia and its Pacific Northwest neighbors to the south, Washington and Oregon, are evident. In climate and topography, the Canadian province is simply a northward extension of Oregon and Washington or vice versa. Peculiar to the Great Raincoast of North America, British Columbia shares with the two states the long rainy season from fall to spring that releases heavy precipitation from the Pacific shore to the Cascade Mountains in the states and to the Coast Mountains in British Columbia. Beyond the Coast Mountains, the depleted clouds of British Columbia float above a semiarid central interior before rising over a rugged eastern expanse to drop huge snowfalls on the province's Monashee, Selkirk, Purcell, and Rocky Mountains. Common to this Great Raincoast of North America on both sides of the international boundary is a medley of natural resources on which British Columbians, Washingtonians, and Oregonians have historically been dependent: forests, salmon, minerals, and hydroelectric power.

Headed by Grand Coulee, the chain of enormous hydroelectric dams along the Columbia and its tributaries in Oregon, Washington, and Idaho are well known. Seldom seen even by British Columbians is the gigantic Peace River project of the public agency BC Hydro, in the distant northeast of the province. The cornerstone of the project is the stupendous W.A.C. Bennett Dam on the mighty Peace River. Physically larger than Grand Coulee, it measures 600 feet in height, 1.2 miles along its top, and 0.5 mile thick at its base, in contrast to the dimensions of the American dam: 300 feet high, 1 mile long at its crest, and 500 feet thick at its base. Construction of the W.A.C. Bennett Dam created Williston Reservoir, whose 406,727 acres make it the largest lake in British Columbia and five times as big as the 81,000–acre Franklin D. Roosevelt Lake created by Grand Coulee Dam.[3] Downstream from the W.A.C. Bennett Dam is the smaller but still impressive Peace Canyon Dam. And there is more, for BC Hydro also operates two other huge hydroelectric dams—Mica and Revelstoke—along the provincial stretch of the Columbia River.[4] Relative to the comparatively small population of British Columbia, BC Hydro is one of the greatest power-generating agencies on earth.

A region in its own right, British Columbia's 366,000 square miles dwarf the 162,000 square miles of Oregon and Washington and even make the 268,000 square miles of Texas look smallish. Only the 656,000 square miles of Alaska exceed the area of British Columbia. Yet British Columbia's 1991 population of 3,282,061 is only a bit more than Oregon's 3,086,188 (1994) and only about three-fifths as big as Washington's 5,343,090 (1994). Even more concentrated than that of Washington and Oregon, the majority of British Columbia's population is crowded into the extreme southwestern corner of the province, where nearly 57 percent of the province's population is absorbed by Greater Vancouver (1,602,502) and Greater Victoria (299,550).

Like so much of the American West, British Columbia is highly urbanized. Even the vastly underpopulated interior of British Columbia finds many of the inhabitants spread among a host of towns of over 1,000 all the way up to the biggest of them—the three cities of Kamloops (67,000),

Prince George (70,000), and Kelowna (76,000). Graced with grand and almost limitless mountains flanked by beautiful but often highly constricted valleys (many of them limited by poor soil), British Columbia has long had a shortage of arable land and, consequently, a scanty farm population. About half of British Columbia lies above the fifty-fourth parallel, a huge area so thinly populated as to be—with the exception of the Peace River section (whose biggest town, Fort St. John, has only 14,000 residents)—almost uninhabited. Outside the Peace River country, the only two towns north of the fifty-fourth parallel with over 1,000 inhabitants are Mackenzie, with 5,700, and Fort Nelson, with 3,800.

VIOLENCE

One of the settled truths of United States–Canadian comparative scholarship is that the dominion has been much less violent than the republic. In recent years, however, Canadian violence has become much more Americanized—as has worldwide violence—with serial killings, assaults, robbery, and horrible murders ever more prevalent. British Columbia exemplifies the rising tide of Canadian violence, though the dominion's homicide rate still lags far behind that of the United States.

For three-quarters of a century, one scholarly comparison between British Columbia and the American West and Northwest has been in the realm of violence. The common scholarly wisdom has been that western Canadians in the frontier era were much more peaceable than western Americans. While this generalization still stands, recent research has significantly modified it at least in regard to British Columbia, where historians have found more frontier and local violence than had been previously recognized. Conversely, scholars have found in the American West a more pervasive law-minded mentality than had usually been acknowledged.[5]

Virtually ignored by historians, however, is that twentieth-century British Columbia is the locale of the longest sustained epsiode of violence in the history of the United States and Canada. From 1923 to 1962, the radical, nihilistic Sons of Freedom faction of the religious Doukhobors of British Columbia engaged in a campaign of arson and dynamite in their home country of the Kootenays. The Sons of Freedom dramatized their dissidence with widely reported nude parades featuring nubile maidens, hefty matrons, stripling boys, and strapping farmers. The religious rebels were motivated by passionate principles in opposition to governmental authority, especially in regard to military conscription, taxation, and education. Sharing the same religious beliefs as the Sons of Freedom were the peaceful majority of Tolstoyan-pacifistic British Columbia Doukhobors, who, however, resorted to neither violence nor nudity. In 1961 and 1962, acts of terrorism carried out by the Sons of Freedom climaxed and concluded with nearly 400 bombings and burnings, including the torching of an entire small town. It all quickly ended, however, when in the following year 600 Freedomites formed a protest caravan from the Kootenays to Vancouver that exposed the zealots to the outside world and eroded their paranoia. This, along with effective legal proceedings against hardcore violent activists, terminated the nearly half-century vendetta of violence and nihilism.[6]

As George Woodcock and Ivan Avakumovic have noted, Sons of Freedom insurgency was above all a long-term struggle against assimilation into the modern, secular society of British Columbia and Canada.[7] Premodern in ethos, the Freedomite dissidence combined the "primitive rebellion" of violence with the defiance of nude parades akin to "social banditry" in their daring rebuke of the established order.[8] Like all such uprisings in Europe and North America, it failed.

COLONY, PROVINCE, AND REGION

British Columbia was founded in 1866 as a crown colony uniting two previous colonies: Vancouver Island (1849) and, on the mainland, British Columbia (1856).[9] In 1871 British Columbia reluctantly agreed to join the new Dominion of Canada, which had been launched in 1867. British Columbians thought they had little to gain from membership in the new confederation. Only the dominion's promise of a transcontinental railroad linking British Columbia to Canada persuaded the erstwhile colony to join. During the 1870s, when the dominion dragged its feet on building the railroad, British Columbia threatened secession several times.[10] The railroad eventually was completed in 1886, but the pattern of British Columbia antagonism toward the federal tie with Canada had been set and, to a significant extent, continues to this day.

Despite its status as a Canadian province, British Columbia continued to be more oriented to Britain than to the North American republic. The Anglophilia of British Columbia was especially strong during the late nineteenth and early twentieth centuries. Heavy migration to the province from Albion bred a distinctive British Columbia accent that was strongly English and was even spoken by those who had never been to Britain.[11] Victoria, the provincial capital, was well known as the most British city in Canada.[12] On a per capita basis, British Columbians exceeded all other Canadian provinces in volunteering for military service as they patriotically rushed to the defense of Britain in World War I.[13]

By World War II, British Columbian's pride in its connection with the United Kingdom was scarcely diminished.[14] As a region and not just a province of Canada, British Columbia early on triangulated itself, as it does today, in regard to three powers: Britain, the United States, and Canada itself. The Anglophile ethos of British Columbia faded following World War II, but "elements of it" are even today "subsumed within the British Columbia identity."[15]

Never as wary of the United States (to which by 1950 it sent 84 percent of its lumber exports) as most of Canada, the British Columbia attitude to the giant to its south has been, in contrast to the resentment often felt elsewhere in Canada, occasionally hostile but on the whole one of "good natured tolerance" of American qualities.[16] A revealing example of the attitudes of British Columbians and Pacific Northwesterners to each other's societies appears in Norbert MacDonald's outstanding comparative history of Seattle and Vancouver. The work includes an intriguing contrast between the attitudes of University of British Columbia students to Seattle and of University of Washington students to Vancouver. The University of Washington students praised the "cosmopolitan" flavor of Vancouver, the congeniality of its people, and the harmony of its races, while deploring its high prices and its, at times, irritating anti-Americanism. The University of British Columbia students found Seattle ugly overall, but beautiful in spots, and its people "friendly, open, and courteous," though, in contrast to their experience in Vancouver, they were often uneasy about their personal safety. With the British Columbia students being much more negative about Seattle than their Washington peers were about Vancouver, the former usually reacted with "shocked disbelief" when they learned that Seattle was "rightfully regarded as one of America's most liveable cities." For his own part, MacDonald, a Canadian who had lived and worked in both Seattle and Vancouver, noted the common features of the two cities—"superb coastal settings, rainy climate, lush vegetation, and comfortable, prosperous residential neighborhoods"—but condemned the indifference of Americans to "things Canadian" and the "condescension" of Canadians to the United States.[17]

Going back to its entrance into the dominion, British Columbia has been remarkably "ambivalent" about Canada. As a proudly "self-conscious community," British Columbia "hardened" its attitude against the central government. The province has characteristically denounced Ottawa for giving the Pacific province less than its due and imposing (or attempting to impose) unwanted policies on it. Conscious of British Columbia's bountiful natural resources and outstanding Pacific port of Vancouver, Premier W.A.C. Bennett asserted in 1967 that "we're the only part of Canada that really could go it alone" as a separate dominion.[18] Current British Columbia leaders of both left and right continue the tradition of skepticism toward the central government. Federal policies and intitiatives to appease Quebec have, for example, been roundly opposed in British Columbia.

In political and economic matters, the full Canadianization of British Columbia has never been achieved. It would be wrong to say, however, that the British Columbia attitude to Canada is one of *separatism,* for it has been more than a century since threats of secession were voiced. But there is a deeply engrained British Columbia psychology of *separation* that is close in spirit to separatism without really being it. The American state most closely resembling British Columbia in this regard is Texas— perhaps because both Texas and British Columbia came into their respective federal unions independently and on their own terms.

POLITICS AND POLITICAL CULTURE

In internal politics, British Columbia shares with its southern neighbor, Washington, a heritage of left radicalism and militant labor unionism, often accompanied in both places (and in Oregon) by a vicious anti-Asian prejudice that lasted through World War II.[19] In British Columbia, however, there is a huge difference in governmental structure with its adherence to the British and Canadian system of parliamentary government, in contrast to the separation-of-powers structure of the United States. In British Columbia, the Legislative Assembly elects the head of the government, the premier. The premier heads the leading party in the Legislative Assembly. The need to marshal the votes to install and then maintain a government puts a much higher premium on party unity

and discipline than is the case in the state legislatures of the United
States.

Yet political parties in British Columbia have not been the strong,
comparatively stable entities found in the United Kingdom. It was not until
1903—over thirty years after it entered the dominon—that British Columbia adopted the system of political parties in emulation of the two-
party rivalry of Conservatives and Liberals long dominant in the rest of
Canada and in Britain.[20] While British Columbia provincial political parties are more disciplined in particular sessions of the Legislative Assembly than are American parties in their state legislatures, the party system
in British Columbia has during most of the twentieth century been more
unstable and complex than that in the states. Since the 1930s, British
Columbia has had over the long run not just third parties but also significant fourth (and sometimes fifth) parties—the situation, for example, at
this writing.

The bumptious quality of British Columbia politics (something of a by-
word in Canada) has been transcended by strong premiers who dominated
their eras: Sir Richard McBride for the Conservatives (1903–1915), Duff
Pattullo for the Liberals (1933–1941), and W.A.C. Bennett for the Social
Credit Party (1952–1972). All three were astute politicians and charismatic
leaders whose appeal was greater than that of their own parties.[21]

Since the beginning of the Great Depression of the 1930s, there has,
however, been a theme of great consistency in British Columbia politics:
"a sharper left–right focus than in any other part of English-speaking
North America." The economic disaster and human suffering of the Great
Depression was every bit as severe in British Columbia as it was in
Oregon and Washington (perhaps more so, for it seems to have been the
worst in Canada), but the British Columbia response was more radical.
In the 1933 election, an outright radical socialist party, the Co-operative
Commonwealth Federation (CCF), appeared on the scene to challenge
the long hegemony of the two-party Liberal and Conservative adherents
of capitalism. Strong left–right polarization continued in the 1950s, but
in a complicated and startling development in 1952 the hitherto far-fringe
Social Credit Party shot up behind its unheralded but brilliant and canny
leader, W.A.C. Bennett, to supplant the Liberal and Conservative Parties as the defender of capitalism in the continuing conflict with the CCF.
Becoming premier in 1952, Bennett headed the British Columbia government for twenty years and became "undoubtedly the most effective

political leader in British Columbia history."[22] A migrant to British Columbia from the maritime province of New Brunswick by way of Alberta, Bennett became a prosperous hardware merchant in the growing interior city of Kelowna. In his ardent espousal of free enterprise and his successful campaign to cut back reformist welfare-state programs undertaken by the previous Liberal–Conservative coalition and Liberal governments, Bennett as premier was a high-profile embodiment of "Thatcherism" and "Reaganism" long before there was a Margaret Thatcher and a Ronald Reagan to lead their respective governments.

Yet there was another entirely different side to the protean Bennett, for he was also a throwback to the dynamic spearhead of big government, Franklin D. Roosevelt. In exploiting British Columbia's enormous hydroelectric potential and other notable policies, Bennett resembled FDR in using the power of government to achieve for his province the goals of natural resources–based development that were the cornerstone of New Deal policy in the American West and Northwest. When BC Electric (the private-power colossus in the province) resisted Bennett's vision of a mammoth Peace River hydroelectric project, the premier sponsored a breathtaking governmental takeover of BC Electric. Using the new publicly owned BC Hydro to supplant BC Electric, Bennett went ahead with his audacious Peace River project—which was supplemented in the 1960s and 1970s, at Bennett's behest, by the construction of two more giant hydroelectric dams along the province's stretch of the Columbia River.[23]

As a natural impressario of big-government operations, Bennett also revitalized a long moribund provincially owned "streak of rust" into a modern railroad rechristened BC Rail and running the length of British Columbia from Vancouver to the Peace River country. Meanwhile, Bennett's huge highway-construction program blessed the vast interior of British Columbia with, at last, an adequate system of paved roads—a policy that was capped by the Bennett regime's provision of the bulk of the funds that made possible in 1962 the completion of the Trans-Canada Highway across the mountains, finally giving the province an all-weather, all-seasons paved highway link to Alberta and beyond.[24] Bennett rounded out his transportation program with the government's acquisition of the province's privately owned oceanic ferry lines. This new agency, BC Ferries—the largest ferry system in the world—especially benefited the raincoast, with its heavy dependence on seagoing service from Vancouver and Victoria to Prince Rupert and the Queen Charlotte Islands.[25]

It was a favorite pastime of commentators to point out the paradox of Bennett, the almost fanatical proponent of free enterprise and enemy of CCF socialism, hugely expanding the sway of the provincial government in British Columbia affairs. Neither Bennett nor the electorate was bothered by the paradox, however, because BC Hydro, BC Rail, BC Ferries, and the road-building program more than paid off by pacing the dynamic economic growth and booming prosperity of the 1950s and 1960s. The boom was at the core of what Bennett repeatedly referred to as "the good life" of British Columbia.[26]

Partly in an attempt to escape the burdensome stigma of its socialist tradition, the CCF in 1961 changed its name to the New Democratic Party (NDP). By the time of the provincial election of 1966, the NDP was moving away from its socialist origins and, with strong support from the labor-union movement in British Columbia, was playing down its collectivism in favor of a welfare-state, pro-labor stance that had more in common, for example, with the liberalism of the Democratic Party of Oregon and Washington than the CCF of old.

Yet the NDP retains a minority socialist faction that, however, realizes the futility of promoting a full-fledged collectivist program. As recently as 1996, Canada's weekly national news magazine, *Maclean's,* referred to the NDP government in British Columbia as one by "ruling socialists."[27] The term referred more to the lingering socialist mythos of the NDP than to contemporary political reality. But with both the British Columbia left and right having to appeal to a large middle portion of the electorate that swings, often abruptly, from one side to the other, there is much truth in the statement by Premier William Bennett, who succeeded his father in the leadership of the conservative Social Credit Party, that "we are a populist party slightly to the right of centre" and "the NDP is a populist party slightly to the left."[28]

Even before the CCF bolted onto the scene in 1933 with a collectivism that was the nightmare of the capitalist-oriented majority in British Columbia, there had long been a tradition of socialist activism and radical-labor militancy. Going back to 1909, socialist and/or labor parties in British Columbia had often won the votes of more than 10 percent of the electorate, but to this day neither they nor the CCF and NDP have ever attracted more than 46 percent of the popular vote. Of the CCF or NDP on the left, only the NDP has ever governed British Columbia, and since the rise to power of W.A.C. Bennett in 1952 the NDP has governed for a total of only nine years (1972–1975, 1991–1996) compared with the thirty-six-year sway of the right (1952–1972, 1975–1991).

All of this is, however, to neglect the real power of the left in British Columbia politics. It has been perceptively said that the great (but entirely unintended) achievement of the left has not been one of governing, but of galvanizing conservatives to unite in successful opposition to it.[29] Scholars who focus on the issue of "American exceptionalism" often address the classic question of why socialism has never thrived in the United States.[30] They might well ponder the case of British Columbia. There the longstanding polarization of politics has much more often than not witnessed the defeat of socialism and the left. Is this a case of "British Columbia exceptionalism"?

American scholars have approached the United States as a test case of exceptionalism, but, with the exception of Seymour Martin Lipset, they have shied away from the comparative example of Canada. Lipset believes in American exceptionalism—an exceptionalism of a sort that he also finds to a significant but lesser degree in Canada. If Lipset is right about Canadian exceptionalism, a case might be made that in Canadian terms British Columbia is an exception within an exception in much the same way that Carey McWilliams proclaimed California as "the great exception."[31] It may be that the American scholarly tendency to view the United States—but not Canada—as a test case of exceptionalism has had an intangible but significant spillover effect in steering American historians away from much comparative interest in British Columbia and western Canada or even in the noncontiguous American states of Alaska and Hawai'i.

Aside from electoral politics and governmental regimes, how does British Columbia compare with Oregon and Washington in the broader realm of political culture? The political scientist Daniel J. Elazar has used historical research to formulate three types of political culture in the American states of the twentieth century: traditionalistic, individualistic, and moralistic. Elazar classifies Oregon's political culture as moralistic. He sees Washington's as moralistic-individualistic, with moralistic values dominant but coexisting with a strong individualistic strain. In these terms, British Columbia's political culture before, at least, 1910 was traditionalistic—a reflection of the strong Anglophilia that suffused British Columbia into the twentieth century. By the 1930s (if not before) and certainly today, the political culture of British Columbia is best understood, like that of Washington, as a blend of the moralistic and the individualistic. The combination of the moralistic and the individualistic seems to be neatly balanced in British Columbia, with the leading provincial right-of-center political party (until five years ago the Social Credit Party but now the Liberal Party) most successfully invoking the individualistic strain and, on the left, the New Democratic Party playing most successfully to moralistic values.[32]

CULTURE

British Columbia culture much resembles that of Oregon and Washington, but in its own unique way represents cultural themes common to all three. As is the case with Oregon and Washington, British Columbia is part of the Great Raincoast of North America. Intertwined with the raincoast climate is the blend of mountains, valleys, forests, rivers, lakes, and sea that have nurtured British Columbia's version of the raincoast culture in art and literature.[33] Although she died a half-century ago, Emily Carr towers over the culture of British Columbia in a way that is rare in North America. Carr is remarkable in being both the greatest painter and the greatest writer produced by the province. Whether in art or literature, Carr's highly original talent is redolent with the ecology and culture of the British Columbia raincoast.

It was only late in her life that Carr turned to publishing to complement her immense achievement as a painter, and, in truth, it is as a painter that Carr most brilliantly and powerfully represents the raincoast.[34] Born of British parents in Victoria in 1871, Carr first cultivated her skill in painting. Training in Europe resulted in early work that was promising but derivative. Yet Carr had British Columbia deeply in her bones. Not, however, until she was in her early fifties did she find her métier in her unrivaled depiction of the deep forests, Indian villages, and coastal scenes of British Columbia. For years, she had struggled to gain self-confidence in the face of the indifference of her fellow British Columbians to painting that they rejected as being strange and unfashionable in both subject and style.

Recognized in the Canadian art world by the late 1920s, Carr's work was much slower to win over the British Columbia public. Since her death in 1945, admiration for Carr's painting by British Columbians has risen steadily and strongly and has not yet peaked.[35] Carr's strong and thickly textured greens and browns and the haunting, mystical quality of her scenes of isolated or abandoned Indian villages, totem poles, and thick forests run riot are unforgettable. In her portrayal, especially, of deserted Indian villages and fallen totem poles, Carr powerfully conveys the searing beauty and profound tragedy of such scenes.

As a writer, Carr was a diarist, memoirist, and essayist of great talent. Much of her writing—notably, the classic *Klee Wyck*—was published before her death and caught the public fancy more quickly than her painting. In autobiographical sketches, journal entries, and essays, she wrote about the places she had visited and the people she had known: among the former were the Indian villages and totem poles of Vancouver Island, the raincoast, the wild shores of the Queen Charlotte Islands, and lonely mainland sites.[36] One of the latter was the most militantly antiwhite community of Indians in British Columbia: Kitwancool, with its incomparable array of totem poles, which Carr desperately wanted to paint. She finally got to Kitwancool in 1928, justifiably fearful of what her reception by the villagers would be. Blessed by a natural rapport with Indians (her best friend was Sophie Frank, an Indian woman of Vancouver), Carr won over the Kitwancoolians and produced some of her greatest paintings, including *Kitwancool* and *Totem Mother, Kitwancool*.[37] In the early twentieth century, many of the Indians still spoke little or no English, but as an old-time British Columbian reared decades earlier Carr conversed fluently with them in Chinook jargon—the century-old lingua franca of the Great Raincoast of North America in which many whites and Indians of the older generation were adept.[38]

In the last two decades of the twentieth century, two Haida woodcarvers, Bill Reid and Robert Davidson, are the greatest artists of British Columbia. Using modern techniques to carve totem poles and Indian statuary, Reid and Davidson have revitalized "the only form of art" that, with a nearly 1,000-year heritage, is truly Canadian.[39] Reid, the senior of the two, came out of a thoroughly assimilated British Columbia background but was drawn to his cultural roots in the "sacred groves" of "Haida Gwai," the Queen Charlotte Islands. From these ancient ancestral lands, Reid drew inspiration for the art epitomized in his marvelous sculptural tableau *The Spirit of Haida Gwai*, a striking combination of realism and abstraction.[40] Davidson, in contrast, was reared in a traditional woodcarving family, learned about tribal rituals and totem poles from his grandfather, and grew up to carve the first totem pole in his native Haida village, Masset, in almost fifty years.[41] The artistic revival under way among the Indians of the province, who are often spoken of by themselves and others as "First Nations" people, has spread far into the interior. Just one example of talent flourishing at the grassroots is the impassioned, graphic painting by the Gitxan artist 'Wii Muk'wilixw (Art Wilson) of the upper Skeena River country, with his denunciatory theme of the historic oppression of the First Nations by white British Columbians.[42]

Like those of Oregon and Washington, the writers of British Columbia have characteristically focused on typical subjects of the Great Raincoast: the region's physical environment, Native people, natural resource–based industries, loggers, and embattled labor militants.[43] The classic work, *Woodsmen of the West,* by Martin Allerdale Grainger; the fiction and non-fiction works of the distinguished naturalist Roderick Haig-Brown; and the treatment of Indians in *Mist on the River,* a novel by Hubert Evans, are just a few of many examples. Ethel Wilson is often regarded as British Columbia's greatest writer of fiction. The characters in Wilson's novels and stories are all British Columbians. Although her forte is psychological realism, resulting in comparisons with Virginia Woolf and E. M. Forster, the atmosphere of Wilson's fiction is strongly oriented to the raincoast climate and fascinating beauty of the province.[44]

A special case is Malcolm Lowry, an alcoholic, whose autobiographical novel of Mexico, *Under the Volcano,* is highly acclaimed by critics worldwide as a tour de force of literary modernism. An Englishman, Lowry resided in British Columbia during the most productive years of his life, 1939 to 1954. Although he wrote only one novel set in the province, Lowry loved the beauty of his shoreline locale near Vancouver and was both at his most creative and least alcoholic when he lived there. Lowry found balm for his deeply troubled soul in the spectacular scenery he could see from his Burrard Inlet house.[45]

FRONTIER, REGION, AND SUBREGION

Much of the history of British Columbia has been a transition from frontier to region. With the establishment of British colonies in the mid-nineteenth century, the future province was regarded much more as a frontier of British settlement than as a frontier of Canada. The creation of the province of British Columbia, given its huge size, resulted in a jurisdiction that was, in its political and other aspects, much more than the equivalent of all but a few American states (California, for example) but, of course, much less than a nation.

There is a conundrum about British Columbia as a region. It is easy to see the province in terms of climate, physiography, economy, and culture as an integral part of what Americans call the "Pacific Northwest." But in Canadian terms, it is a geographical absurdity to refer to British Columbia as a Pacific northwestern province. Canada's Northwest is, instead, Yukon Territory and the western edge of the Northwest Territories. For Canada, British Columbia is the Pacific Southwest. The conundrum is resolved when British Columbia is viewed, as indeed it is, as part of the North American region of the Great Raincoast: Oregon, Washington, and British Columbia. Even the eastern semiarid country of British Columbia, Washington, and Oregon is climatologically linked to the Great Raincoast by the rain-shadow effect of the Coast Mountains (British Columbia) and the Cascades (Oregon and Washington) in inflicting semiaridity on the eastern lands. By definition, the Great Raincoast of North America knows no international boundary.[46]

The comparative regionalist Robin Winks once suggested that the key to regionalism is understanding the significance of regions and regional consciousness within different nations.[47] The concept of "Pacific Southwest" has no meaning for Canadians and is a term not used by them, whereas in the United States the Pacific Southwest is a proper regional label for California. Actually, comparing British Columbia with California helps clarify the regional identity of the province in the Canadian context. Because the reputation and lure of British Columbia to Canadians focuses on the province's California-type features—Pacific location, mild coastal climate (no small appeal to other Canadians, with their frigid, snowy winters), and booming prosperity (typically having the highest per capita income in Canada)—British Columbia has much the same standing in Canada as California does in the United States. In short, British Columbia is Canada's California.

In both the United States and Canada, respectively, California and British Columbia are often viewed as not being really "western." Instead, the prairies, Plains, and Rocky Mountains are seen as the true West of the "cowboys and Indians" of myth and reality. Yet the indubitably western geographical locations of British California and California cannot be ignored. Thus Jean Barman entitled her general treatment of British Columbia history *The West Beyond the West*.[48] In this view of "the West beyond the West," the Far Wests of British Columbia and California are seen in their respective nations as the ultimate promised lands of new beginnings.

Compared with the "California Dream" treated by Kevin Starr,[49] Canadian scholars do not speak of the "British Columbia dream." There does, however, seem to be such a concept at the grassroots of Canada. One of the leading historians of British Columbia began her history of the province with the following words: "Growing up on a farm south of Winnipeg, I *dreamt* of British Columbia. Totem poles and snow-capped mountains symbolized the west coast province. I fell in love sight unseen" with British Columbia.[50] The role of Vancouver in British Columbia and Canada is analogous to that of Los Angeles in California and the United States, for the same historian, Jean Barman, wrote with great accuracy that Vancouver seems "destined to become an international city, almost a city-state unto itself"[51]—a status already achieved by Los Angeles.[52]

It appears that British Columbia has for Canadians something of the same significance as a trendsetter that is embodied in the American saying that "California is where it happens first." In the United States, that was true of the counterculture of the 1960s, which first emerged in full flower in the San Francisco Bay Area. By the same token, Vancouver quickly emerged as the countercultural capital of 1960s Canada. Not only did many young antiwar Americans flee to Vancouver to avoid military service, but Vancouver's Fourth Avenue was soon regarded as the equivalent of the Haight–Ashbury district in San Francisco.[53] One Mark Vonnegut found his way to British Columbia and with other young middle-class American countercultural and environmentalist expatriates settled down on a solitary raincoast farm north of Powell River. The literary result was Vonnegut's memoir, *The Eden Express* (1974). Of this phase of his life, Vonnegut wrote: "We hadn't taken to the woods just for a change of scenery and a different way of life. The physical and psychical aspects of our adventure were inextricably intertwined, but the head changes were what we were really after. We expected to get closer to nature, to each other and our feelings."[54]

Getting "closer to nature" reminds one that in his regional typology of North America, Joel Garreau described a domain that he called "Ecotopia," which hugs the Pacific Ocean from northern California to southern Alaska.[55] British Columbia is in the heart of Garreau's Ecotopia, and, certainly, the province has a vital environmental movement, as do Washington and Oregon.

Thus British Columbia has a number of regional identities: as the Canadian counterpart to the American Pacific Northwest, as part of the Great Raincoast of North America and of Ecotopia, and as the California of Canada.[56] Further, as a gigantic Canadian province, British Columbia is a region in its own right. This was the outcome of its development in the twentieth century, when from the 1920s to the 1940s it completed the transition from British frontier outpost to a fully fledged region with its own rich and extensive variety of subregions. Among British Columbia subregions are Vancouver Island, the lower mainland (including Greater Vancouver), the Okanagan orchard area, the East and West Kootenays, and the old gold-mining and ranching Cariboo country.

The many subregions of British Columbia are transcended by three grand divisions: West, East, and North. The West is the raincoast country beyond the Coast Mountains all the way north to Prince Rupert as well as the offshore Vancouver Island and Queen Charlotte Islands. The East stretches across a succession of mountains, valleys, plateaus, and rivers down from the Coast Mountains to the Continental Divide atop the Rockies, which coincides with the Alberta border. Northern British Columbia is a daunting area of roughly half the province.

Although it has long fully participated in its political affairs, the North is truly British Columbia's "last frontier."[57] At its southern edge, Prince George is the metropolis of northern British Columbia. Climbing toward 100,000 in population, Prince George, a transportation hub for highways, railroads, and jet and propeller aircraft, is a thoroughly modern city with an attractive civic center as well as a university. An infant computer industry is growing alongside the city's well-established and huge wood-products plants, which process the output of the almost endless spruce forests surrounding Prince George. On the streets of the city, Indians in traditional or modern garb from the great northern hinterland are to be seen along with whites and Asians from all walks of life.

Along Highway 16 from Prince George west to the seaport of Prince Rupert is a chain of small towns ranging in population from a few hundred to Terrace, with 11,000. Should one venture north of Highway 16 or north of the Peace River–area towns of Fort St. John and Dawson Creek, it is all frontier country crossed only by the paved Alaska and Cassiar Highways, which lead northward to Yukon Territory and eventually Alaska. There are no urban nodes to speak of, except for occasional small way stations located along the two highways.

Away from the two north–south highways, the northern British Columbia frontier is hardly penetrated by roads, even of the unimproved sort. For transportation across this enormous northern wilderness, the main dependence is on the bush pilots and their small planes, which are capable of plummeting out of the clouds to alight on lakes or in rough clearings. Except for the huge area's mainly Indian local inhabitants, few British Columbians or anyone else have seen the off-highway wilderness. Among the small band who regularly ride in on bush planes are government employees, geologists, mining engineers, and sportsmen avid for fish and game. Mineral development is in the wind as a branch line of BC Rail and a gravel road have probed into the promising Omineca country, the scene of an old mining boom.[58]

The northern British Columbia wilderness has some of the most spectacular scenery in North America, though, as noted, few have seen it. The best way to view it in the mind's eye is to read a little-known classic of North American regionalism, *Notes from the Century Before* (1969) by Edward Hoagland, a leading American author. Taking to the air to visit remote areas reachable in no other way, Hoagland flew over a "gigantic ocean of heaped-up land" with "uncountable vivid valleys" and "wild-looking" lakes amid mountain peaks in "a tumult of rock and snow." On the ground, he interviewed white and Indian old-timers to preserve for his readers the graphic history, lore, and mystique of this fascinating last frontier.[59]

The new spirit and aspirations of the North are on display at the provincially founded University of Northern British Columbia. Since 1994, the university has enjoyed its striking mountaintop campus on the outskirts of Prince George. Blending wood, concrete, pleasing angles, and high, wide cathedral skylights in an ingenious version of the Northwest architectural style, the campus is a unique cluster of linked buildings well adapted to the climatic extremes of the Far North. The campus allows its users to stroll aboveground in summer sunshine or, for winter warmth, to enter spacious enclosed passages with floor-to-ceiling glass that lets in the precious light of the short northern days and keeps out the freezing cold and snow.

The academically and socially idealistic University of Northern British Columbia is dedicated to a new pluralistic regionalism in which the races, classes, and sexes meet equally on common scholastic ground.[60] The university is especially committed to its First Nations (Indian) interdisciplinary-studies program. In the interest of racial understanding, such an initiative is timely, for in recent years there have been troubling outbreaks of violence and intimidation between whites and Indians in regard to the unresolved and highly contentious issue of First Nations' land claims in British Columbia.

On the American Pacific Northwest frontier, Indians yielded land to whites in return for treaties whose provisions have been upheld and rigorously enforced in federal courts and legislation in recent decades. Thus in the United States, the issue of Indian land claims has long since been settled with federally recognized tribes acknowledged as sovereign entities. But not so in British Columbia, where few treaties were ever signed.[61] In British Columbia, overlapping Indian land claims cover the entire province. At times, Indians have used roadblocks to shut off white access to ranch and residential property. An explosive situation at such a roadblock flared into violence in interior British Columbia during the summer of 1995 while tangled negotiations between the First Nations and the provincial and federal governments proceeded at a glacial pace.[62]

Two landmark moments in the 1994/1995 academic year of the University of Northern British Columbia highlighted the white and Indian heritage of the North and the province as a whole. On the first occasion, August 17, 1994, Queen Elizabeth II came all the way to preside over the opening of the beautiful new campus. On the second occasion, May 26, 1995, the year was concluded with the awarding of degrees at a grand convocation. The traditional academic procession was, to beating drum, led with great panache by a delegation of First Nations people stunningly attired in the brilliant reds and blacks of their proudly worn Native regalia.

FRONTIERISM, METROPOLITANISM, AND THE NEW BRITISH COLUMBIA HISTORY

As a leading Canadian scholar, J.M.S. Careless, pointed out in an influential article, Canadian historians have resisted the application of the frontier interpretation to explain the history of their nation. Instead, their scholarship has fitted more comfortably into the historiography of "metropolitanism." Metropolitanism (in contrast to "frontierism"), in the words of Careless, "implies the emergence of a city of outstanding size to dominate not only its surrounding countryside but other cities and their countrysides, the whole area being organized by the metropolis, through control of communications, trade, and finance, into one economic and social unit that is focused on the metropolitan 'centre of dominance' and through it trades with the world."[63] Echoing Careless, the American historian William Cronon notes that in Canada "this city was Montreal; in the United States, it was New York. Beneath the central metropolis were smaller cities playing similar but less extensive roles, since 'the metropolitan relationship is a chain, almost a feudal chain of vassalage, wherein one city may stand tributary to a bigger center and yet be the metropolis of a sizable region of its own.'" The leading North American examples of the second-level metropolis are Toronto and Chicago. In British Columbia, the metropolis of this type came to be Vancouver.[64] On the American west coast, San Francisco, Portland, and, later, Seattle were metropolitan centers of dominance for their hinterlands.

British Columbia scholars writing about their province have frequently referred to the frontier, but it is mainly in the work of a leading British Columbia academic historian of the first half of this century, Walter N. Sage, that a conceptual frontierism figures.[65] Metropolitanism was especially congenial to the professional historians of eastern and central Canada, who by geographical placement were naturally interested in the relationship of Montreal and Toronto to the Canadian hinterland and by academic inclination were attracted to the theoretical "sweetness" of the metropolitan thesis. The meeting ground of both frontierism and metropolitanism in British Columbia scholarship was the element above all others that fascinated mainstream British Columbia historians down to 1960: the British factor.[66] In the view of these historians, it was the British who penetrated the *frontier* to establish their standards as the dominant ones, doing so as cultural protagonists not for Canada, but for the *metropole,* Britain.

The metropolitan interpretation works very well for British Columbia from the middle nineteenth century on. In the nineteenth century, the metropolitan chain of economic and cultural domination that stretched from Montreal to Winnipeg and westward never quite got over the Canadian Rockies to reach British Columbia, even after the transcontinental railroad was completed. British Columbia's outside metropolis was not Montreal, but a non-Canadian metropolitan quartet of London, Liverpool, New York, and San Francisco—places with which colonial British Columbia had direct seaborne connections through the entrepôt of Victoria.[67] Victoria's hegemony over interior British Columbia was, however, weak except in the realm of government.

With the completion of the transcontinental Canadian Pacific Railway across British Columbia to the Pacific in 1886, an all-encompassing metropolitan pattern began to emerge. What changed was not that London, Liverpool, New York, and San Francisco were supplanted by Montreal as the distant metropolis of British Columbia, but that the province's own brand-new metropolis, Vancouver, used the Canadian Pacific and later railroads to probe and dominate the interior's economic and cultural affairs. Vancouver was a new metropolis; it literally did not exist until it was created in 1886 to serve as the Candian Pacific coastal terminus. As the "terminal city" of the province, Vancouver soon pushed aside Victoria as British Columbia's leading port.[68] This, in turn, led to the steady deindustrialization of Victoria into the twentieth century. By the 1920s, Victoria's once flourishing factories, foundries, and mills were largely gone. Although its port and the nearby Esquimault naval base remained important, Victoria had assumed its present status as mainly a governmental center, commercial beehive, tourist destination, and mecca for retired Canadians.[69]

In the early twentieth century, two more rail lines were built to connect Vancouver to the interior, making it, at last, the great and true metropolis of the province.[70] Said Margaret A. Ormsby, the dean of British Columbia historians, writing pointedly of Vancouver in the 1920s: "To its harbour . . . it had drawn the freight cars filled with the prairie wheat which spelled prosperity. Its stockyards set the price of beef for the Cariboo cattle industry, and its Water Street jobbers determined the price of apples for the Okanagan fruit industry," while it "had the stock exchange, and the head offices of the banks and the insurance companies. Each year the lines of its commerce radiated further inland to reach the almost inexhaustible mining, forest, and agricultural wealth of the province."[71]

Premier W.A.C. Bennett's policy of building up the infrastructure and economy of interior British Columbia in the 1950s and 1960s was entirely successful, but it had the paradoxical result of increasing, not reducing, the metropolitan power of Vancouver. The booming profits of economic growth and prosperity in the revitalized interior were more than ever channeled into the corporation coffers and bank vaults of Vancouver.[72] In our own age of communication satellites and television, the impact of the print and electronic media of Vancouver provides a new, enhanced dimension to Vancouver's cultural leadership of the province.

Thus the growing nineteenth-century economic and financial power of Montreal was forestalled in British Columbia by the province's enhanced ties with England and America—ties that in British Columbia all but shut out the traditional east-to-west Canadian metropolitanism. With Vancouver in the 1990s stronger than ever as the metropolis of British Columbia, the burgeoning cities of Prince George, Kamloops, Kelowna, Nanaimo, and Victoria clearly remain satellites. Outside the province, however, the internationalization of finance and the multinationalism of corporations produce a cloudier picture than in the long-gone years when London, Liverpool, New York, and San Francisco exerted direct metropolitan influence on British Columbia.

Yet recent British Columbia historians have turned away from emphasizing the frontier, metropolitan, and British factors to produce what I should like to call the "New British Columbia History"—a historiographic innovation that, in terms of American scholarly conceptualization, combines the approaches, especially, of the New Social History and the New Western History. Indeed, the similarities between the New Western History and the New British Columbia History are striking, but the New British Columbia History and the New Western History arose independently of each other. While British Columbia historians have been much more aware of new developments in western American historiography than the reverse, it is undeniable that the New British Columbia History has been a response to an internal social and intellectual dynamic of some thirty-five years.

As a leading British Columbia scholar, Allan Smith, has written, a new "conceptual shift" in British Columbia historiography began in the 1960s. It diverted the academic historians of British Columbia from the traditional emphasis on Briticism to a focus on the non-British element of the provincial population. Monographs and articles dwelled anew and in new ways on Indians and other non-Britons in "the interest [of] articulating" the pluralistic character of British Columbia in order "to build a strong and integrated community making all its members feel that they had a place in it." This instrumental stance of the New British Columbia History closely resembles the ethnic and racial inclusiveness and motivations of the New Western History.[73] It is also a response by British Columbia historians to the post–World War II ethnic transition from a strongly British province to a much more pluralistic one—a demographic revolution similar to that occurring in the same period in the American West.

Thus the British Columbia population in 1941 was by ethnic origin 69.9 percent British, 21.5 percent continental European, 5.2 percent Asian, and 3 percent Native American. By the most recent census in 1991, the percentages with one exception were dramatically altered: British, way down to 43.2 percent; continental European and Asian, way up to 39.2 percent and 12 percent, respectively; and Native American, up only to 3.6 percent. Yet the Indian population had strikingly increased from only 24,882 in 1941 to almost five times more in 1991: 118,731.[74] This increase accords with the situation today in which the Indian presence in British Columbia is many times more prominent and aggressive than it was in 1941.

As syntheses of the New Western History and the New British Columbia History, respectively, *"It's Your Misfortune and None of My Own"* by Richard White and *The West Beyond the West* by Jean Barman, both published in 1991, are similar in approach and outlook.[75] Two leading historians of British Columbia have, however, noted that the protagonists of the New Western History have been more aggressive and successful in reaching the public than their academic counterparts in British Columbia.[76]

WESTERN CANADA AND WESTERN AMERICA COMPARED

Just as the New Western History of the United States may be compared with the New British Columbia History, so may western Canadian history be compared with western American history. This is most meaningful when the provinces of British Columbia, Alberta, and Saskatchewan are compared with the northern tier of western states: Oregon, Washington, Idaho, Montana, and the Dakotas.

What is striking in this comparison is *how much* the Canadian borderland provinces and the American borderland states have in common in regard to geography, physiography, climate, and history as well as races and ethnic groups, immigration, social and economic history, agriculture, industry, commerce, labor, religion, art, and literature.[77] Only recently, however, have Hispanics become a significant element in the population of the American Pacific Northwest, while their presence is still small in western Canada. Although the recent Speaker of the British Columbia Legislative Assembly, Emery Barnes, is black, the black population of western Canada is small, in contrast to that of the American Pacific North-west.[78] Conversely, the French-speaking element of the population was sparse in the old Oregon Country south of the forty-ninth parallel, but was of great importance in the Canadian prairie provinces of the nine-teenth century.[79]

A big difference between the Canadian West and the American West is in the realm of myth. Frontier and western mythology has been a per-vasive and potent presence in American cultural history.[80] Significant but weaker in their impact on the Canadian side of the border are combina-tions of myth and reality in regard to the famous Northwest Mounted Police and the building of the Canadian Pacific Railway in the early 1880s.[81] The absence of an overall mythic Canadian West reflects a pro-found cultural difference between the Canadian and American nations, for, as William G. Robbins has noted "no grand mythologies about the Canadian nation-state" have arisen.[82] In the United States, the national identity and the national mythology form a seamless web, while in the Canadian West and Canada generally, the national identity focuses more on the national political culture, stressing "moderation, compromise, and accommodation"[83]—qualities that, though under great pressure, have managed to hold Canada together in the years of national and constitu-tional trauma going back to the late 1980s.

As yet to be assessed fully in western Canadian history is "dream" thought. Kevin Starr's *Americans and the California Dream* stands out among many such studies of the American West, but Canadian scholar-ship is skimpy on the lure of the West as a land of "new beginnings."[84] Yet Jean Barman touches intriguingly on her youthful dream of British Columbia, while Gerald Friesen mentions the "western Canadian dream."[85] Friesen even more broadly refers to the "North American dream,"[86] a concept that deserves study by transboundary historians of the United States and Canada.

Of all matters, the greatest gap between the Canadian and American Wests is in politics and government. Like British Columbia, Alberta and Saskatchewan (and all Canadian provinces) have parliamentary forms of government, which results in greater intraparty discipline in the pro-vincial assemblies than in the American state legislatures. Resembling that in British Columbia is the strength of third parties in Alberta and Saskatchewan. In the United States, the Democratic and Republican Parties have ruled the roost nationally since the 1860s, and no third party has ever controlled the presidency or either house of Congress. In the western United States, third parties have only occasionally and briefly headed state governments. Similar to the experience of the United States is the national history of Canada, in which the dominion government has always been in the control of one of the two major national parties: the Liberal and the Conservative.[87]

At the provincial level, however, the experience of western Canada has been very different from that of the western United States. In all three of the far western provinces of Canada, third parties have flourished. For nearly half a century (since 1951), the British Columbia government has been held by one or the other of the two organizations that in national Canadian terms are third parties: the Social Credit Party and the New Democratic Party. By the same token, Alberta was continuously governed by third parties for half a century: the United Farmers (1921–1935), and the Social Credit Party (1935–1971).[88] Saskatchewan has also been a bastion of third-party power, with the Co-operative Commonwealth Federation/New Democratic Party governing from 1944 to 1964, 1971 to 1982, and since 1993.[89]

The provinces of Alberta and Saskatchewan were not formed until 1905. As in the case of British Columbia, however, separationism (as opposed to separatism) has been strong in Alberta and Saskatchewan during the twentieth century. The thinking that the dominion government has been neglectful when not actually oppressive has been very strong in the two prairie provinces and even stronger in British Columbia. Western alienation in Canada has been even deeper and more persistent than similar sentiment in the western United States.[90] With much evidence to support them, the three far western provinces have believed their national government to be antiwestern more often than not. From this far western viewpoint, the Canadian government has been continually biased in favor of the two most populous and economically powerful central Canadian provinces: Ontario and Quebec. Thus bitter distrust of the Ottawa government has often been the mood of the peoples and politics of Alberta and Saskatchewan as well as British Columbia—a distrust usually shared by all parties in the three provinces.[91] Many Canadians fear that the nation is being pulled apart by Quebec, on the one hand, and the three provinces of the Far West, on the other.[92]

Among the modern, technologically advanced democracies of western and central Europe, North America, Australia, and Japan, Canada is the one country whose national existence seems to be jeopardized by political, economic, and cultural regionalism. It is difficult, however, to see British Columbia escalating its endemic separationism to secessionism because, for all the heat of its provincial politics, the mild personal temperament of the typical British Columbian is entirely lacking in the zealotry of which secessionists are made.

NOTES

1. Leacock (1937) and Ethel Wilson, *The Innocent Traveller* (1982), quoted in Jean Barman, *The West Beyond the West: A History of British Columbia* (Toronto: University of Toronto Press, 1991), 3. Standing out in comparing British Columbia to the American West and Northwest are Kenneth Coates, "Border Crossings: Pattern and Process in the History of the Pacific Northwest" (Keynote address presented at the "Symposium on Canadian–American Relations West of the Rockies," University of Washington, 12–14 September 1996); William G. Robbins, *Colony and Empire: The Capitalist Transformation of the American West* (Lawrence: University Press of Kansas, 1994), chap. 3 (a chapter on the Canadian and American Wests that does not neglect British Columbia); Carlos A. Schwantes, *Radical Heritage: Labor, Socialism, and Reform in Washington and British Columbia, 1885–1917* (Seattle: University of Washington Press, 1979); John McLaren, Hamar Foster, and Chet Orloff, eds., *Law for the Elephant, Law for the Beaver: Essays in the Legal History of the North American West* (Pasadena, Calif., and Regina: Ninth Judicial District Historical Society and Canadian Plains Research Centre, University of Regina); and William J. Trimble, *The Mining Advance into the Inland Empire: A Comparative Study of the Beginnings of the Mining Industry in Idaho and Montana, and Eastern Washington and Oregon, and the Southern Interior of British Columbia and of the Institutions and Laws Based upon that Industry* (Madison: University of Wisconsin, 1914). For a Seattle–Vancouver comparison, see Norbert MacDonald, *Distant Neighbours: A Comparative History of Seattle and Vancouver* (Lincoln: University of Nebraska Press, 1987); and Robert A. J. McDonald, *Making Vancouver: Class, Status, and Social Boundaries* (Vancouver: University of British Columbia Press, 1996). F. W. Howay, W. N. Sage, and H. F. Angus, *British Columbia and the United States: The North Pacific Slope from the Fur Trade to Aviation* (Toronto and New Haven, Conn.: Ryerson Press and Yale University Press, 1942) is less a comparative study than one of the link between British Columbia and the United States. John M. Findlay cites many leading works of scholarship on the American Pacific Northwest in "A Fishy Proposition: Regional Identity in the Pacific Northwest" (this volume); the leading general work is Carlos A.

Schwantes, *The Pacific Northwest: An Interpretive History*, 2nd ed., rev. (Lincoln: University of Nebraska Press, 1996).

2. Lauren McKinney and Victor Konrad, quoted in Coates, "Border Crossings," 5.

3. For the dimensions of Bennett Dam, see American Automobile Association, *Western Canada and Alaska Tour Book* (Heathrow, Fla.: American Automobile Association, 1995), 92. See Paul C. Pitzer, *Grand Coulee: Harnessing a Dream* (Pullman: Washington State University Press, 1994). When it was completed, Williston Lake was the largest human-made lake in the world.

4. William Dietrich, *Northwest Passage: The Great Columbia River* (New York: Simon and Schuster, 1995), 102–5, 279, 310–19, 410–11.

5. John Phillip Reid leads the scholarship that finds widespread law-mindedness in the West; see, for example, *Law for the Elephant: Property and Social Behavior on the Overland Trail* (San Marino, Calif.: Huntington Library, 1980) and "The Layers of Western Legal History," in *Law for the Elephant*, ed. McLaren, Foster, and Orloff, 23–73. For the growing revisionist scholarship focusing on more-than-generally-recognized frontier and local violence in British Columbia, see, among other works, Roderick C. Macleod, "Law and Order on the Western-Canadian Frontier," in *Law for the Elephant*, ed. McLaren, Foster, and Orloff, 90–91; and Robin Fisher, "Indian Warfare and Two Frontiers: A Comparison of British Columbia and Washington Territory During the Early Years of Settlement," *Pacific Historical Review* 50 (1981): 31–51.

6. George Woodcock and Ivan Avakumovic, *The Doukhobors* (Toronto: Oxford University Press, 1968); Simma Holt, *Terror in the Name of God: The Story of the Sons of Freedom Doukhobors* (New York: Crown, 1965).

7. Woodcock and Avakumovic, *Doukhobors*, chap. 14.

8. On primitive rebellion and social banditry, see E. J. Hobsbawm, *Primitive Rebels: Studies in Archaic Forms of Social Movement in the 19th and 20th Centuries* (1959; New York: Norton, 1965).

9. Outstanding general treatments of British Columbia history are Barman, *West Beyond West;* and Margaret A. Ormsby, *British Columbia: A History* (Toronto: Macmillan, 1958).

10. Barman, *West Beyond West*, 105.

11. Patrick A. Dunae, *Gentlemen Emigrants: From the British Public Schools to the Canadian Frontier* (Vancouver: Douglas & McIntyre, 1981), 106–7, 243.

12. Ibid.

13. Barman, *West Beyond West*, 198–99.

14. Ormsby, *British Columbia*, 469.

15. Barman, *West Beyond West*, 345.

16. Howay, Sage, and Angus, *British Columbia and United States*, 408. At the beginning of the 1930s, about half of British Columbia's lumber exports

went to Britain, and only about one-fourth to the United States. By 1950, this had been more than reversed, with 84 percent going to the United States and only about 8 percent to Britain. See Barman, *West Beyond West,* 281.

17. MacDonald, *Distant Neighbours,* xv, 184–87; on Vancouver itself, see McDonald, *Making Vancouver.*

18. H. Keith Ralston, "Theme and Pattern in British Columbia History," in *British Columbia: Patterns in Economic, Political, and Cultural Development,* ed. Dickson M. Falconer (Victoria: Camosun College, 1982), 4; Bennett, quoted in David J. Mitchell, *W.A.C. Bennett and the Rise of British Columbia* (Vancouver: Douglas & McIntyre, 1983), 351–52.

19. Schwantes, *Radical Heritage;* Patricia E. Roy, *A White Man's Province: British Columbia Politicians and Chinese and Japanese Immigrants, 1858–1914* (Vancouver: University of British Columbia Press, 1989); W. Peter Ward, *White Canada Forever: Popular Attitudes and Public Policy Toward Orientals in British Columbia* (Montreal: McGill-Queens University Press, 1978).

20. Three outstanding studies of twentieth-century British Columbia politics and political culture and history are Donald E. Blake, David J. Elkins, and Richard Johnston, *Two Political Worlds: Parties and Voting in British Columbia* (Vancouver: University of British Columbia Press, 1985); Donald E. Blake, R. K. Carty, and Lynda Erickson, *Grassroots Politicians: Party Activists in British Columbia* (Vancouver: University of British Columbia Press, 1991); and Michael Howlett and Keith Brownsey, "British Columbia: Public Sector Politics in a Rentier Economy," in *The Provincial State: Politics in Canada's Province and Territories,* ed. Keith Brownsey and Michael Howlett (Mississauga, Ont.: Copp Clark Pitman, 1992), 265–95.

21. On McBride, see Ormsby, *British Columbia,* chap. 12, 375–91; on Pattullo, see Robin Fisher, *Duff Pattullo of British Columbia* (Vancouver: Douglas & McIntyre, 1983); on Bennett, see Mitchell, *W.A.C. Bennett.* In addition to these sources and Blake, Elkins, and Johnson, *Two Political Worlds;* Blake, Carty, and Erickson, *Grassroots Politicians;* and Howlett and Brownsey, "British Columbia," my treatment of British Columbia politics depends for continuity on Ormsby, *British Columbia;* and Barman, *West Beyond West.* A major source is the monumental *Electoral History of British Columbia, 1871–1986* (Victoria: Elections British Columbia, 1988); based on it and conveniently listed in Barman, *West Beyond West,* 355–62, are the premiers of British Columbia and summaries of the votes in the British Columbia provincial elections from 1903 to 1986. A spirited, provocative study of British Columbia political history that stresses corporation control is Martin Robin, *The Company Province,* 2 vols. (Toronto: McClelland & Stewart, 1972, 1973). For events of the 1990s, I depend on British Columbia's leading newspaper, the *Vancouver Sun,* and the weekly Canadian national news magazine, *Maclean's.*

22. Hugh Keenleyside, a British Columbia historian, diplomat, and government official, quoted in Barman, *West Beyond West,* 296.

23. Mitchell, *W.A.C. Bennett,* 74, 77, 285–91, 302–13, 317, 320–22, 352, 371.

24. Ibid., 259–63, 350–51.

25. Ibid., 269–72.

26. Ibid., 384. Three leading historians of the American Pacific Northwest also emphasized the "good life" in their region: Gordon B. Dodds, *Oregon* (New York: Norton, 1977), 42; Norman H. Clark, *Washington* (New York: Norton, 1976), 61; and Oscar Osburn Winther, *The Great Northwest: A History,* 2nd ed., rev. (New York: Knopf, 1952), dedication.

27. Chris Wood, with Scott Steele, "The Battle for B.C.," *Maclean's,* 26 May 1996, 20–27.

28. Quoted in Barman, *West Beyond West,* 351. On William (Bill) Bennett, see Allen Garr, *Tough Guy: Bill Bennett and the Taking of British Columbia* (Toronto: Key Porter, 1985).

29. Barman, *West Beyond West,* 343.

30. Werner Sombart, *Why Is There No Socialism in the United States?* (1906; White Plains, N.Y.: International Arts and Sciences Press, 1976); Ian Tyrrell and Michael McGerr, "American Exceptionalism in an Age of International History," *American Historical Review* 96 (1991): 1031–72; Seymour Martin Lipset, *American Exceptionalism: A Double-Edged Sword* (New York: Norton, 1996). Emphasizing the frontier issue is David M. Wrobel, *The End of American Exceptionalism: Frontier Anxiety from the Old West to the New Deal* (Lawrence: University Press of Kansas, 1993).

31. Lipset, *American Exceptionalism,* chap. 3; Carey McWilliams, *California: The Great Exception* (New York: Current Books, 1949). See also Seymour Martin Lipset, *Continental Divide: The Values and Institutions of the United States and Canada* (New York: Routledge, 1990).

32. Daniel J. Elazar, *American Federalism: The View from the States,* 2nd ed. (New York: Crowell, 1972), 94–102, 118; Blake, Elkins, and Johnston, *Two Political Worlds,* 73. The notion that British Columbia's pre-1910 political culture was traditonalistic is my own. The complexity of British Columbia politics is heightened by the fact that partisan alignments and provincial and national alignments do not always match up in ideological terms. For example, currently in provincial politics the right-of-center party is the Liberal Party, while in national elections in British Columbia the Liberals are, as elsewhere in Canada, the left-of-center party. A typical situation in British Columbia today is to find a nonsocialist British Columbian voting for the NDP in provincial elections and the Liberal Party in national elections. Conversely, a conservative British Columbian might typically vote for the Liberal Party in a provincial election and either the Reform Party or the Conservative Party in a national election. On the success of the Liberal Party in the British Columbia provincial elections of 1991 and 1996, see Norman J. Ruff, "An Ambivalent Electorate: A Review of the British Columbia General Election of 1996," *BC Studies* 110 (1996): 5–23.

33. On art and literature, see Richard Maxwell Brown, "The Great Raincoast of North America," in *The Changing Pacific Northwest:*

Interpreting Its Past, ed. David H. Stratton and George A. Frykman (Pullman: Washington State University Press, 1988), 46, 49, 52–53, 159–60, 162–63.

34. In addition to reading her books and viewing her paintings in the art galleries of Victoria and, especially, Vancouver, the following treatment of Emily Carr is based on three outstanding books: Maria Tippett, *Emily Carr: A Biography* (New York: Oxford University Press, 1979); Paula Blanshard, *The Life of Emily Carr* (Seattle: University of Washington Press, 1987); and Doris Shadbolt, *The Art of Emily Carr* (1979; reprint, Vancouver: Douglas & McIntyre, 1987), a critical study lavishly illustrated with color reproductions.

35. Almost a cult, Carr is now a cultural icon in British Columbia and Canada, where the number of her admirers is growing. See, for example, the *Emily Carr Calendar, 1996* (Vancouver and Toronto: Douglas & McIntyre, 1995), with its beautiful 10- × 6½-inch reproductions in color of some of her best paintings. A striking exhibiton was "The Art of Emily Carr: Deep Forest," Art Gallery of Greater Victoria, November 1995. Permanently on exhibit in the Vancouver Art Gallery is the largest and best collection of Carr paintings.

36. *Klee Wyck* (1942), *The Book of Small* (1942), *Growing Pains* (1946), *Hundreds and Thousands: The Journals of Emily Carr* (1966), and *The Heart of a Peacock* (1986) are conveniently reprinted in *The Emily Carr Omnibus,* introduction by Doris Shadbolt (Vancouver and Seattle: Douglas & McIntyre and University of Washington Press, 1993).

37. Carr, *Klee Wyck,* 97–107. On Kitwancool, see Robin Fisher, *Contact and Conflict: Indian–European Relations in British Columbia, 1774–1890,* 2nd ed. (Vancouver: University of British Columbia Press, 1992), 208; and Wilson Duff, ed., *Histories, Territories, and Laws of Kitwancool* (Victoria: Royal British Columbia Museum, 1989).

38. Richard Maxwell Brown, "Language and Exploration: The Role of Chinook Jargon," in *Encounters with a Distant Land: Exploration and the Great Northwest,* ed. Carlos A. Schwantes, assisted by Evelyne S. Pickett (Moscow: University of Idaho Press, 1994), 93–94, 100.

39. Doris Shadbolt, *Bill Reid* (Seattle: University of Washington Press, 1986); Robert Bringhurst, *The Black Canoe: Bill Reid and the Spirit of Haida Gwai* (Seattle: University of Washington Press, 1991); Ian M. Thom, ed., *Robert Davidson: Eagle of the Dawn* (Seattle: University of Washington Press, 1993). On "the only form of art," see Charles C. Hill, *The Group of Seven: Art for a Nation* (Toronto: National Gallery of Canada and McClelland & Stewart, 1995), 192.

40. Shadbolt, *Bill Reid,* 167, 178; Bringhurst, *Black Canoe.*

41. Ian M. Thom, "The Evolution of an Artist," in *Robert Davidson,* ed. Thom, 65, 70.

42. Exhibition of his paintings at 'Ksan Indian Museum, Hazelton, British Columbia, July 1995.

43. Brown, "Great Raincoast," 52, 162–63. Its founding editor, Howard White, dedicated the British Columbia periodical *Raincoast Chronicles,* vols.

1–10 (reprint, Madeira Park, British Columbia: Harbour, 1976–1983), to preserving the historical and cultural heritage of the British Columbia raincoast. An intriguing geographical and historical overview of the raincoast is Kenneth Campbell, *North Coast Odyssey: The Inside Passage from Port Hardy to Prince Rupert* (Victoria: Sono Nis Press, 1993). A unique British Columbia raincoast diary was by the keeper of the Pointer Island inside-passage lighthouse, Ben Codville, from 1891 to 1964; from 1898 to 1917, Codville included a freehand drawing of one event for each day. See ibid., 92–99. A social history of the British Columbia raincoast in artful photographs is Ulli Steltzer and Catherine Kerr, *Coast of Many Faces* (Seattle: University of Washington Press, 1979).

44. Martin Allerdale Grainger, *Woodsmen of the West* (1908; reprint, Toronto: McClelland & Stewart, 1964); Hubert Evans, *Mist on the River* (Toronto: Copp Clark, 1954); E. Bennett Metcalfe, *A Man of Some Importance: The Life of Roderick Langmere Haig-Brown* (West Vancouver: Wood, 1985). Among Ethel Wilson's novels is *Hettie Dorval* (Toronto: Macmillan, 1947). On Wilson, see Desmond Pacey, *Ethel Wilson* (New York: Twayne, 1968).

45. Malcolm Lowry, *Under the Volcano* (New York: Reynal & Hitchcock, 1947). On Lowry in British Columbia see Gordon Bowker, *Pursued by Furies: A Life of Malcolm Lowry* (New York: St. Martin's Press, 1995),   . chaps. 15–16, xx, 343, 453, 465, 497, 547 and passim. Beautifully evoking the raincoast climate, land, and seascapes of British Columbia is Lowry's autobiographically inspired and unfinished but impressive posthumous novel, *October Ferry to Gabriola*, ed. Margerie Lowry (New York: World, 1970). The main collection of Lowry manuscripts is at the University of British Columbia, Vancouver.

46. On the Great Raincoast climate and the rain-shadow effect, see Brown, "Great Raincoast," 51, 162.

47. Robin W. Winks, "Regionalism in Comparative Perspective," in *Regionalism and the Pacific Northwest,* ed. William G. Robbins, Robert J. Frank, and Richard E. Ross (Corvallis: Oregon State University Press, 1983), 32–33.

48. Barman, *West Beyond West.* For the view of a minority of American scholars and regionalists that California is not truly a part of the West, see Walter Nugent, "Where Is the American West? Report on a Survey," *Montana: The Magazine of Western History* 42 (1992): 6–7 and passim.

49. Kevin Starr, *Americans and the California Dream, 1850–1915* (New York: Oxford University Press, 1973).

50. Barman, *West Beyond West,* vii (emphasis added).

51. Prevalent in British Columbia is the Northwest architectural style treated in a monumental work of scholarship: Thomas Vaughan and Virginia Guest Ferriday, eds., *Space, Style, and Structure: Building in Northwest America,* 2 vols. (Portland: Oregon Historical Society, 1974).

52. Barman, *West Beyond West,* 338. On Los Angeles as an international city, see Mike Davis, *City of Quartz: Excavating the Future in Los Angeles* (New York: Random House, 1992). The comparison of Vancouver with Los Angeles is mine, but has probably been made by others.

53. Barman, *West Beyond West,* 314–15.

54. Mark Vonnegut, *The Eden Express* (1975; New York: Dell, 1988), 60; Barman, *West Beyond West,* 315.

55. Joel Garreau, *The Nine Nations of North America* (Boston: Houghton Mifflin, 1981).

56. Recently two concepts of "Cascadia" have emerged, but they are quite different. One version of Cascadia focuses especially on the urban corridor from Vancouver, British Columbia, to Eugene, Oregon, and is oriented mainly to commerce and north–south transportation. The other version of Cascadia is a conceptualization of riverine-focused bioregionalism for Oregon, Washington, and British Columbia.

57. Barman, *West Beyond West,* vii.

58. The lines of BC Rail that extend into northern British Columbia are listed in *BC Rail Time Table 5* (n.p.: BC Rail, 1994).

59. Edward Hoagland, *Notes from the Century Before: A Journal of British Columbia* (1969; reprint, San Francisco: North Point Press, 1982), 61, 64, 154–56, and passim.

60. *A Northern Vision: UNBC* (Prince George: Prince George Citizen and University of Northern British Columbia, 1994); *University of Northern British Columbia: 1995–1996 Calendar* (Prince George: University of Northern British Columbia, 1995), 5 and passim. What is the university calendar in British Columbia is known as the university catalogue in the United States.

61. Paul Tennant, *Aboriginal People and Politics: The Indian Land Question in British Columbia, 1849–1989* (Vancouver: University of British Columbia Press, 1990); Fisher, *Contact and Conflict,* 151–53. Fisher's critique of Tennant and other scholars on particular points is on xvi–xix; but Fisher, Tennant, and all scholars agree that few land treaties were signed in British Columbia. On overlapping Indian land claims, see Chris Wood, with Scott Steele, "A Standoff Moves in the Courts," *Maclean's,* 29 July 1996, 13. On British Columbia, see also Tennant, "Aboriginal Rights and the Canadian Legal System: The West Coast Anomaly," in *Law for the Elephant,* ed. McLaren, Foster, and Orloff, 106–26. The huge Nisga'a land claim in northern British Columbia was recently settled in principle by negotiation between tribal and provincial authorities. Both sides hope that it will be a prototype for a peaceful solution to the issue of First Nations land claims in British Columbia.

62. On violent outbreaks in 1995, see *Maclean's,* 7 August 1995, 10–11; *Maclean's,* Sept. 18, pp. 22–23; *Maclean's,* Sept. 25, pp. 13, 15, 17; Nicholas Blomley, "'Shut the Province Down': First Nations Blockades in British Columbia, 1984–1995," *BC Studies* III (1996): 5–35.

63. J.M.S. Careless, "Frontierism, Metropolitanism, and Canadian History," *Canadian Historical Review* 35 (1954): 1–21; Careless, *Frontier and Metropolis: Regions, Cities, and Identities in Canada Before 1914* (Toronto: University of Toronto Press, 1989). The metropolitan interpretation owes much to the pioneering scholarship of Canada's greatest historian, the late Harold A. Innis, on such basic staples of Canada as the fur trade, mining, and cod fishing. On Innis's "staples theory," a convenient reference is Robbins, *Colony and Empire,* 55–56, 214–15.

64. William Cronon, *Nature's Metropolis: Chicago and the Great West* (New York: Norton, 1991), 400–401; in this book, Cronon successfully applies the metropolitan thesis to the history of Chicago. Careless found that Vancouver had extended its metropolitan sway eastward into the prairie provinces. See "Frontierism, Metropolitanism," 20.

65. Allan Smith, "The Writing of British Columbia History," *BC Studies* 45 (1980): 84–85.

66. The attraction of pre-1960 mainstream British Columbia historians to the British factor is epitomized by the final sentence of Ormsby, *British Columbia,* published in 1958: "[in 1958] 'British Columbia' still suggests more aptly than any other name could do, the sentiment and the outlook of the Canadian people who live in the furthest west" (495). In her magisterial history, Ormsby gave due treatment to frontier and metropolitan factors but, adopting neither as conceptual keynotes, stressed the British theme.

67. J.M.S. Careless, "The Business Community in the Early Development of Victoria, British Columbia," in *Historical Essays on British Columbia,* ed. J. Friesen and H. K. Ralston (Toronto: Gage, 1980), 183.

68. MacDonald, *Distant Neighbours,* 26–29; Ormsby, *British Columbia,* 296–302.

69. Barman, *West Beyond West,* 111–12, 239.

70. What became in 1923 the transcontinental Canadian National Railway line was completed from central Alberta into British Columbia and along the Thompson and Fraser Rivers to Vancouver in 1915. The secondary line of the Canadian Pacific to Vancouver from southernmost Alberta into British Columbia and through the Kootenays and along the U.S. boundary was completed in 1916. See Howay, Sage, and Angus, *British Columbia and United States,* 253–56; Barman, *West Beyond West,* 195–96.

71. Ormsby, *British Columbia,* 439.

72. Barman, *West Beyond West,* 348–49.

73. Smith, "Writing of British Columbia History," 88, 95. In addition to Barman, *West Beyond West;* Roy, *White Man's Province;* Ward, *White Canada Forever;* Fisher, *Contact and Conflict;* and Tennant, *Aboriginal People and Politics,* among many important books in the New British Columbia History are Patricia Marchak, *Green Gold: The Forest Industry in British Columbia* (Vancouver: University of British Columbia Press, 1983); Douglas Cole and Ira Chaikin, *An Iron Hand upon the People: The Law*

Against the Potlatch on the Northwest Coast (Vancouver: Douglas & McIntyre, 1990); and Tina Loo, *Making Law, Order, and Authority in British Columbia, 1821–1871* (Toronto: University of Toronto Press, 1994). The first edition of Fisher's *Contact and Conflict,* published in 1977, was in its approach as well as its meticulous scholarship and innovative interpretation a model and, as it were, a keynote for the New British Columbia History. Allan Smith's entirely accurate emphasis on pluralism as the great theme of contemporary British Columbia historians ("Writing of British Columbia History," 88, 95) has been intellectually escalated by him to the intriguing thesis that the Canadian national identity increasingly stresses post-modern linguistic, cultural, and racial pluralism. See Allan Smith, *Canada: An American Nation? Essays on Continentalism, Identity, and the Canadian Frame of Mind* (Montreal: McGill-Queen's University Press, 1994), 225–27 and passim.

74. Jean Barman, *The West Beyond the West: A History of British Columbia,* 2nd ed., rev. (Toronto: University of Toronto Press, 1996), 379. The total British Columbia population in 1941 was only 817,861, compared with the 3,282,061 of 1991. Thus the greatly increased Indian population of 1991 is only a scanty 3.6 percent of the provincial population that has quadrupled since 1941. Barman's ethnic percentages add up to 99.6 percent for 1941 and 98 percent for 1991.

75. Richard White, *"It's Your Misfortune and None of My Own": A History of the American West* (Norman: University of Oklahoma Press, 1991); Barman, *West Beyond West.* Although some highly significant books were published as early as 1979, the acclaimed prototype for the New Western History was Patricia Nelson Limerick, *The Legacy of Conquest: The Unbroken Past of the American West* (New York: Norton, 1987).

76. Robin Fisher and Kenneth Coates, comments at the Conference on New Directions in British Columbia History, University of Northern British Columbia, 27–28 May 1995. Under the titles of his publications, Coates's first name often appears only as Ken. There is no journal of New British Columbia History, but the outstanding interdisciplinary journal *B C Studies* publishes important articles and book reviews on the province's history.

77. For the Canadian prairie provinces, one of the classics of the regional history of North America: Gerald Friesen, *The Canadian Prairies: A History* (Lincoln: University of Nebraska Press; Toronto: University of Toronto Press, 1984). For Idaho, Montana, and the Dakotas, see Carlos A. Schwantes, *In Mountain Shadows: A History of Idaho* (Lincoln: University of Nebraska Press, 1991); Michael P. Malone, Richard B. Roeder, and William L. Lang, *Montana: A History of Two Centuries,* 2nd ed., rev. (Seattle: University of Washington Press, 1991); Elwyn W. Robinson, *History of North Dakota* (Lincoln: University of Nebraska Press, 1961); and Herbert S. Schell, *History of South Dakota* (Lincoln: University of Nebraska Press, 1961). For Montana and the Dakotas, see John R. Borchert, *America's Northern Heartland: An Economic and Historical Geography of*

the Upper Midwest (Minneapolis: University of Minnesota Press, 1987), a classic work of historical geography.

78. On African-Americans, see Quintard Taylor, *The Forging of a Black Community: Seattle's Central District from 1870 to the Civil Rights Era* (Seattle: University of Washington Press, 1994). On Hispanics, see Erasmo Gamboa, *Mexican Labor and World War II : Braceros in the Pacific Northwest, 1942–1947* (Austin: University of Texas Press, 1990).

79. Friesen, *Canadian Prairies*, chaps. 5–6, 10.

80. Since Henry Nash Smith's classic *Virgin Land: The American West as Symbol and Myth* (Cambridge, Mass.: Harvard University Press, 1950), the scholarship is nearly as outstanding as it is prolific. Recent examples include John G. Cawelti, *The Six-Gun Mystique* (Bowling Green, Ohio: Bowling Green University Popular Press, 1975); Brian Dippie, *Custer's Last Stand: The Anatomy of an American Myth* (Missoula: University of Montana Press, 1976); William H. Goetzmann and William N. Goetzmann, *The West of the Imagination* (New York: Norton, 1986); Richard Slotkin, *Gunfighter Nation: The Myth of the Frontier in Twentieth-Century America* (New York: Atheneum, 1992); and Richard White and Patricia Nelson Limerick, *The Frontier in American Culture*, ed. James R. Grossman (Berkeley: University of California Press, 1994).

81. Friesen, *Canadian Prairies*, 163–86.

82. Robbins, *Colony and Empire*, 55.

83. Roger Gibbins and Sonia Arrison, *Western Visions: Perspectives on the West in Canada* (Peterborough, Ont.: Broadview Press, 1995), 76.

84. Starr, *Americans and the California Dream;* Friesen, *Canadian Prairies*, 304–5, 340, 355, mentions the lure of the West.

85. Barman, *West Beyond West*, vii; Friesen, *Canadian Prairies*, 361.

86. Friesen, *Canadian Prairies*, 300.

87. In 1942 the Conservative Party changed its name to Progressive Conservative. It is well understood in Canada that the Progressive Conservatives—the "Tories"—are the conservative party in contrast to their rivals, the Liberals—often referred to as the "Grits" (the term "Grit" arose in the nineteenth century as the Canadian equivalent of the British term "Whig"). Throughout this chapter in order to avoid confusion, I have referred to the Progressive Conservatives as, simply, the Conservatives, as does, for example, the *Canadian Encyclopedia* (1988).

88. Friesen, *Canadian Prairies*, chaps. 14–16; Peter J. Smith, "Alberta: A Province Just Like Any Other?" 243–64, *Provincial State*, ed. Brownsey and Howlett, 251, 254, 256–57. Third-party sentiment remains strong in Alberta: although the Conservatives won the provincial election of 1993, in the national election of the same year the new Reform Party captured twenty-three of twenty-five Alberta seats in the Canadian House of Commons. The Reform Party was also very strong in British Columbia, where it won twenty-four of thirty-two House of Commons seats. Saskatchewan's seats were

divided almost equally among the Reform, New Democratic, and Liberal Parties. See "Appendix: The Election Results," 161–205, in *The Canadian General Election of 1993,* ed. Alan Frizzell, Jon H. Pammett, and Anthony Westell (Ottawa: Carleton University Press, 1994), 193–204. A study of the meteoric rise of the Reform Party in the 1990s is Trevor Harrison, *The Passionate Intensity: Right-Wing Populism and the Reform Party of Canada* (Toronto: University of Toronto Press).

89. Friesen, *Canadian Prairies,* chaps. 14–16; Christopher Dunn and David Laycock, "Saskatchewan: Innovation and Competition in the Agricultural Heartland," 207–42, Brownsey and Howlett, eds., *Provincial State,* 231.

90. On the alienation of western Americans against outside control of their region, the latest study is Robbins, *Colony and Empire,* which, in addition to its own viewpoint, copiously cites a large literature on the subject going back to the classic statements of Western grievances in Bernard DeVoto, "The West: A Plundered Province," *Harper's Magazine,* August 1934, 355–64; and Walter Prescott Webb, *Divided We Stand: The Crisis of a Frontierless Democracy* (New York: Farrar and Rinehart, 1937).

91. Barman, *West Beyond West;* Ormsby, *British Columbia;* Friesen, *Canadian Prairies;* Gibbins and Arrison, *Western Visions.*

92. In *Western Visions,* Gibbins and Arrison ingeniously argue that the western provinces are actually extremely nationalistic and that their ire against the Ottawa government in recent decades stems from their belief that it has pursued pro-Quebec and other policies that undermine the nation. Whatever its basic cause, western alienation from the national regime, all authorities agree, has been deep in recent years.

Noncontiguous Wests: Alaska and Hawai'i

John S. Whitehead

Are Alaska and Hawai'i a part of the American West? Do Westerners consider them as such? And do the residents of those two outlying, or "noncontiguous," states consider themselves a part or even a subset of the western region? Questions such as these constantly confound our ability to place Alaska and Hawai'i in the context of the other "mainland" or "lower forty-eight" states. Mapmakers have not helped the situation by placing the two in little boxes, dubbed by one of my students as "halaskas," that are then arbitrarily placed at spots ranging from Puget Sound to the Gulf of Mexico. Geographic journalists such as Joel Garreau have muddied the waters by calling Hawai'i "schizophrenic" and Alaska "the nation's most endearing aberration."[1]

Politicians have also muddied the waters. When both territories tried to enter the union after World War II, some western senators opposed their entry and cited noncontiguity as a major problem. In 1955, Senator Mike Monroney of Oklahoma warned that if Congress admitted Alaska and Hawai'i, "We will be leaving our concept of a closely knit union, every state contiguous to others, bonded by common heritages, common ideals, common standards of democracy, law and customs." Proponents of admission dismissed Monroney's claim and countered that California was not contiguous to another state when it was admitted in 1850. Certainly California had always been an American and a western state. Both Alaska and Hawai'i were finally admitted to the nation in 1959. Did that make them an integral part of the American West and lay the "noncontiguity" argument to rest?[2]

To bring some closure to the debate in the current day, "inclusionists" could quickly assert that they are clearly "in" the West because both belong to the Ninth United States Circuit Court of Appeals and the Federal Reserve Bank of San Francisco. And their governors belong to the Western Governors Association. However, this definition of inclusion may be as unsatisfactory to some as the "exclusionist" argument of western historians Michael Malone and Richard Etulain, who claim that Alaska and Hawai'i are not part of the region because they are not "arid." Alas, both Alaska and Hawai'i are among the wettest and driest of the fifty states. To make matters even more confusing, Alaskans frequently refer to themselves as "Northerners" (circumpolar rather than Yankee), and the peoples of Hawai'i seem happiest with the appellation of "islanders." "Western" or "Westerner" are not designations that are widely voiced in either state.[3]

There may be no clear-cut answer either way. Both "inclusion" and "exclusion" stand on questionable ground. Rather than continue the debate, it may be more helpful to examine the historical forces that first drew the two into the western region—even before the region itself existed—and then to see how other westernizing historical forces tended to bind the contiguous mainland region and leave Alaska and Hawai'i out—or, from another perspective, leave them alone. The combination of these "inclusionary and "exclusionary" forces may tell us not only more about Alaska and Hawai'i, but more about the nature of the western region itself.

THE MARITIME WEST OF NEW ENGLAND

Hawai'i and Russian America, as modern-day Alaska was universally called before the American Purchase of 1867, became the first extended or noncontiguous "Wests" of the new United States, virtually coincident with the drafting and signing of the constitution. The Northwest–Hawai'i–China fur trade, which was inaugurated in the late 1770s by the British with the third voyage of Captain James Cook, attracted the first American ships a decade later. Departing from Boston in September 1787, the frigates *Columbia* and the *Lady Washington* successfully navigated the treacherous waters around Cape Horn and entered the Pacific bound for Nootka Sound on modern-day Vancouver Island. After lingering a year along the Northwest Coast and collecting a modest cargo of sea-otter pelts, the *Columbia,* captained by Robert Gray, continued on to Hawai'i in August 1789 and became the first American vessel to dock in the islands. Gray added to his ship's roster two Hawaiian cabin boys, Attoo and Opie, who continued on the journey to Canton and back to Boston, becoming the first islanders to visit the United States. Gray's arrival in Boston in August 1790 caused quite a sensation. Although the voyage was not a financial success, the simple fact that it had succeeded in circumnavigating the globe aroused enough commercial enthusiasm, as well as popular interest in Hawai'i, to back the captain on a repeat voyage. On his second voyage along the Northwest Coast, Gray successfully entered the river that he named the Columbia in 1792, thus laying the nation's first claim by discovery to the Oregon Country.[4]

Over the next two decades, the Northwest–China fur trade became dominated by the "Boston Men," as British trading ships were called home in response to the Napoleonic Wars of the 1790s. By 1800, some twenty American vessels annually plied the waters from Nootka to Hawai'i and Canton, and then back to Boston. The Boston Men used the mid-Pacific islands not only as a way station between the Northwest and China, but also as a venue to collect additional cargo items. The Chinese showed little interest in American manufactured goods, but Hawaiians readily accepted the Boston articles in exchange for sandalwood, which was favored in China. King Kamehameha I, who had united the islands politically by 1795, gave American merchants a monopoly on the sandalwood trade in 1810. In the first two decades of the nineteenth century, the value of the furs and sandalwood carried by American vessels to Canton ranged from $300,000 to $1 million annually. Overharvesting of the Hawaiian wood, a result of both merchant and royal greed, led to one of the West's first environmental disasters, with the virtual depletion of the sandalwood forests by the 1820s.[5]

Hawai'i was a source not only of products in the fur trade, but also of labor. The young Hawaiians, whom Gray carried home, were not the first he met on his voyage. When Gray arrived in Nootka Sound in 1788, he found Hawaiians working on the British ships that were already there. Hawaiians readily joined the crews of both British and American ships. The "Kanakas" became a mainstay of labor in the Pacific Northwest for both American and British-Canadian interests in the first decades of the nineteenth century, particularly as the fur trade pushed inland. In modern day Idaho, the Owyhee River and Owyhee County (using an older spelling for Hawai'i) are lingering reminders of the Kanaka presence.[6]

The search for labor and products in the fur trade by the Boston Men also extended to Russian America. American ships gradually pushed both northward and southward from Nootka Sound in search of more furs. Although Russian America, like Spanish California, was technically closed to trade, Alexander Baranov, the governor of the Russian-American Company, had reasons to circumvent these restrictions. The Chinese did not allow the Russians to trade at Canton, but only at the inland Russian–Chinese border post of Kiakhta. Also the company was chronically under-capitalized and lacked a fleet of ships to carry its furs even back to Siberia. Added to these problems was the difficulty of obtaining food and other supplies in the agriculturally deficient colony. American merchants could offer food supplies as well as ships to transport and sell Russian furs into the more lucrative port of Canton.

Joe O'Cain, a Bostoner who had first visited Russian America as a sailor in 1792, returned as captain of his own ship in 1803. At the time, Baranov was particularly willing to make a deal with him. In 1802 the fierce Tlingit Indians burned the new capital of the Russian-American Company at New Archangel, or Sitka. Baranov was forced to retreat to his previous head-quarters on Kodiak Island. In exchange for American firearms to help retake Sitka as well as ships to transport Russian furs, Baranov offered O'Cain something the Bostoner needed—labor to harvest sea-otter and seal pelts off the coast of California. As Spanish California was closed to American interests, O'Cain had to find his labor elsewhere. Baranov agreed to send Aleut hunters under the control of the Russian-American Company on the Bostoner's ship. O'Cain could now increase his supply of furs north of Nootka Sound as well as south of Nootka with Aleut labor. Both the cargo and the labor arrangements with O'Cain and other Yankee captains set the pattern for American relations with the Russians for the next two decades.[7]

By 1820, the Maritime West of New England, bordering on the triangle from the Northwest Coast up to Russian America and over to Hawai'i, was emerging. American vessels carried New England goods to the Northwest and Russian America in exchange for furs. The Yankees and their cargoes then proceeded to Hawai'i for yet more trade in sandalwood and provisions before heading on to Canton. Hawaiians labored on American ships and on land in the Northwest; Aleut hunters helped American captains garner seal and otter pelts off the California coast. The Russians in their constant quest for agricultural provisions extended the boundaries of the emerging region and helped weave it together by establishing an agricultural colony in 1812 at Fort Ross in northern California, just above the last Spanish mission and presidio at San Francisco. They also reached westward in the mid-1810s in an abortive attempt to create another agricultural outpost in Hawai'i. In all of this movement, Hawai'i, and particularly the port of Honolulu, emerged as the center of this new West. Although settlement was not yet a driving motive of the Americans or even permitted on a permanent basis by the Hawaiian monarchy, there were almost 200 Europeans, mainly Americans, living in Honolulu by 1819.

With this continual flow of people and products, we can well call the Maritime West of New England a definite region, not just a set of noncontiguous trading areas. In the maritime mind of the early nineteenth century, these ports were contiguous; they were connected to and by the Pacific Ocean. Although the distances between Nootka Sound, Sitka, and Honolulu make the area look disjointed to the land-oriented mind, such distances did not create barriers to the maritime mind. The arduous journey "west" was the year-long voyage from Boston around the dangerous Cape Horn—the maritime equivalent of Donner Pass—and up to the Northwest Coast. Once safely in the northern Pacific, the Yankee argonauts saw themselves in an "American lake." The voyage north from Nootka Sound to Russian America or west to Honolulu took a matter of weeks, not months. The interconnectedness of the Maritime West of New England was not unlike the interconnectedness of the European and North African ports of the Mediterranean. In maritime terms, it was a contiguous Pacific area. The only noncontiguity was with New England— of which the Maritime West was an extension.

After 1820, the Maritime West of New England blossomed, and its different parts became even more interwoven. In addition to New England sea captains and merchants, New England missionaries entered the area. Their first departure to the Maritime West in 1819 was triggered by the growing presence in New England of young Hawaiians who had been returning with Yankee ship masters since the arrival of Attoo and Opie in 1790. One young man, 'Opukaha'ia (Henry Obookiah to the Yankees), had converted to Christianity at the Cornwall Foreign Mission School in Connecticut, but died there before he could return to his homeland. 'Opukaha'ia's example prompted the newly founded American Board of Commissioners for Foreign Missions (ABCFM) to send a mission of seven couples to Hawai'i. The missionaries were accompanied on their journey by two Hawaiian princes who encouraged the new king, Kamehameha II (Liholiho), to allow the group to land and start its mission on a provisional basis in 1820. Over the next three decades, succeeding waves of ABCFM missionaries came to the islands, established schools and churches for the Hawaiian people, and designed the political foundations for the constitutional monarchy established in the 1830s under Lilholiho's successor, King Kamehameha III.[8]

The extension of New England missionaries in the Maritime West was not limited to Hawai'i. It was the same ABCFM that dispatched Marcus and Narcissa Whitman to the Oregon Country in the mid-1830s. The Whitmans were met upon their arrival in Oregon by Kanaka laborers, who turned out to be the only successful conversions made by the couple! From Oregon to Hawai'i, the Maritime West in the 1830s was being connected and "Americanized" by similar processes in its widely spread parts.[9]

The boundaries and ports of the Maritime West expanded southward along the eastern Pacific coast after 1821 with the opening of Mexican California to American trade. Ships sponsored by the same Boston merchant firms that engaged in the Northwest–China fur trade began to call regularly—rather than under the guise of being in distress and needing repairs—at Monterey and Santa Barbara. With the flourishing of the hide and tallow trade in the 1830s, Kanaka laborers joined with Hispanics and Yankees in California. Gradually, American representatives of Boston firms established permanent residences in California, as they had in Honolulu. The travels of entrepreneurs who were lured to newly opened Mexican California illustrated the growing interconnectedness of the Maritime West. Before establishing his farming estate at New Helvetia,

Johan Sutter visited Honolulu and Sitka to establish credit and supply lines with the mercantile companies there.[10]

The Maritime West continued to grow with the expansion of the whaling trade to the Pacific in the late 1830s and 1840s. New England vessels in vastly greater numbers than those engaged in the fur trade plied the coastal waters of California, Russian America, Hawai'i, Japan, and the South Pacific in search of the wealth derived from whale oil, ambergris, spermaceti, and baleen. Again, Honolulu emerged as the center of this trade, with some 300 to 400 whaling vessels annually visiting there and at the port of Lahaina on Maui. The whaling trade stimulated agricultural and mercantile enterprises on the islands to service the ships. As in the days of the fur trade, American merchants were in the lead, but by no means had a monopoly on the trade. They were joined by British and German merchants. To protect the native population from the hordes of sailors leaving the whaling ships for shore, American missionaries created a set of blue laws to regulate alcohol, prostitution, and other vices.[11]

The extent of whaling activity off the coast of Russian America so upset Russian authorities that they momentarily tried to limit American mercantile and shipping influence. In 1838 the Russian-American Company ended its contracts with the visiting merchant ships of New England and made what it thought would be a permanent arrangement with the British Hudson's Bay Company in Oregon to supply the colony. The Russian-American Company sold its Fort Ross agricultural outpost in California to Johan Sutter. Despite the action of the Russians, Yankee maritime influence still remained pervasive, with whaling ships roaming and despoiling the waters of the northern colony.

As the Maritime West expanded in the 1830s and 1840s, Hawai'i, and particularly Honolulu, strengthened its role as the commercial and cultural center of the region. It should not be surprising that a number of American "firsts west of the Rockies" took place there. The printing press brought by ABCFM missionaries to print the Bible in the Hawaiian language was the "first printing press west of the Rockies." The schools established by the American missionaries and other teachers for both Hawaiian and Caucasian children assumed an importance that was felt across the region. Thomas O. Larkin, the leading Yankee merchant in California, sent his children to Honolulu to the missionary-run O'ahu Charity School. The Punahou School, started in 1840 for the children of ABCFM missionaries, still thrives in the 1990s and is one of the oldest secondary schools "west of the Rockies." Celebrating its 170th anniversary in 1996, Honolulu-based C. Brewer and Company, founded in 1826 as J. Hunnewell & Company, is the "oldest American business firm operating west of the Rockies."[12]

Although Yankee influence was dominant in the Maritime West, the actual settlement of Americans in the region was still slight by the mid-1840s. In Hawai'i about 700 non-natives, predominantly but not exclusively American, resided with 100,000 native Hawaiians. A similar number of Americans were resident in Mexican California. In Russian America, no Yankees had been allowed to settle permanently. Only in the Oregon Country did American settlement reach into the thousands by the mid-1840s.[13]

In 1845 the Maritime West of New England was not the exclusive political region of any nation. It was an international region with varying patterns of political stability. Hawai'i was the most politically well-organized and stable government in the region. The Hawaiian monarchy, with its missionary-inspired constitution, far surpassed the unstable Mexican regime in northern California, the quasi-governmental power of the Russian-American Company, or the politically unorganized base for the jointly occupied Oregon Country. Nonetheless, the maritime, cultural, and commercial influence of New England had connected Russian America, Hawai'i, Oregon, and California into a definite region—the first of "many Wests" in which those geographic entities would interact.

THE GOLD RUSH WEST OF CALIFORNIA

The international Maritime West of New England began to change in 1846 with the end of joint United States–British occupation of Oregon. By the treaty of 1846, the lower half of the old Oregon Country was now under the American flag. Over the next two years, the flag extended south to California, following the American conquest in the Mexican War. Despite these political changes, the commercial and cultural operation of the region continued as before. President James K. Polk initially intended to leave California the distant, sparsely settled region it had been before the Mexican War. In early 1848, the great interconnected maritime triangle from California to Russian America to Hawai'i was much the same as it had been in 1845.

The discovery of gold at Johan Sutter's New Helvetia soon spelled the transformation of the entire region. The story of the California gold rush, resulting in the sudden influx of over 100,000 miners and settlers by the end of 1849 and the admission of California as the first Pacific state in 1850, is well known and need not be retold here. Our concern is the impact of that event on the Maritime West. At first, the gold rush highlighted and enhanced the interconnectedness of the region. News of the findings at New Helvetia leaked to other areas of the region in the summer of 1848. Both Caucasian merchants and Hawaiian laborers from the islands arrived that summer with Yankee migrants lured south from Oregon. For the next two years, Hawai'i was the major agricultural supplier for California's booming mining population. The islands also became a popular recreation station for California miners in the winter. Commerce between California and Hawai'i boomed as never before.[14]

The emergence of San Francisco as the commercial center of gold-rush California in the early 1850s had a profound effect on the Maritime West. It quickly became the new metropolis of the region, replacing Honolulu as the West's major port. It also became Hawai'i's principal market. For the next fifty years, exports from the islands, particularly of sugar, would be permanently tied to the port of San Francisco.

The impact of San Francisco quickly reached north to Russian America. Although the Russian-American Company had tried to resist Yankee maritime influence with its contract with the Hudson's Bay Company, there was no way to resist the influence of San Francisco. Merchants from the new metropolis were eager to supply the colony. A new San Francisco company founded in 1851, the American-Russian Company, soon became the principal supplier to the north. In exchange for agricultural and mercantile provisions from the San Francisco firm, the Russian-American Company exported ice to the south. California politicians, principally United States Senator William Gwin, advocated the purchase of Russian America in 1854 as an integral extension of California's commercial empire.[15]

The commercial dominance of California was not the principal alarm to either Hawai'i or Russian America. Both areas had dealt with Yankee ships and commercial influence before. What truly alarmed the two was the vast influx of people to California. The influence of small numbers of Yankees could be dealt with; the influx of large numbers could not. Hispanic California had been so transformed by the gold-rush onslaught that

Richard Henry Dana, who had worked alongside Hispanics and Kanakas in the hide and tallow trade, could find little of that old California when he returned in 1859. Even before Dana surveyed the results of the gold rush in California, observers in both Hawai'i and Russian America feared a similar fate. If 100,000 Yankees could come to California in a year, they could come to Hawai'i or Russian America. Fully half of the forty-niners arrived in California by ship around Cape Horn; they could just as easily continue west or north. In the maritime mind of the 1850s, water connected areas and made them contiguous, not noncontiguous. Mountains and deserts were what truly separated regions.[16]

At first, it appeared that Hawai'i might capitulate to the feared onslaught. In 1854 King Kamehameha III initiated overtures for annexation to the United States. A treaty was negotiated and debated in the Senate, but Kamehameha died before a final decision could be made. His royal successors withdrew the treaty and quickly tried to eschew American political and missionary influence. Instead, they sought an alliance with the British monarchy over the next fifty years to combat American influence, much as the Russians had tried to ally with the Hudson's Bay Company.[17]

In Russian America, there appeared to be no new protectors or potential allies who could turn the gold-rush tide. The Crimean War between Russia and England broke out in 1853, though both countries declared their holdings in North America "neutral." The extension of the Pacific mining boom from California to British Columbia in the late 1850s led Russian authorities to fear that it was only a matter of time until a Yankee mining invasion hit their colony. The overtures of purchase from Senator Gwin were taken seriously. Before a decision could be made, the American Civil War erupted.

Rather than disrupting the burgeoning influence of the Gold Rush West in Hawai'i and Russian America, the Civil War firmly cemented it. The secession of the sugar-producing state of Louisiana forced the Union to look for new sources of sugar. Sugar exports from Hawai'i boomed during the war, with San Francisco further solidifying its hold as the port of entry for the island product. American, as well as British and German, merchants in Honolulu realized that their future prosperity required either a reciprocity treaty with the United States or annexation to prevent discriminatory tariff treatment of their product. King David Kalākaua, who ascended to the throne in 1874, successfully steered his country in the path of reciprocity and negotiated the needed treaty in 1875.[18]

The amicable relations between the Union and imperial Russia during the Civil War produced a base of goodwill that eased the way for a continuation of the diplomatic negotiations for the purchase of Russian America begun a decade earlier. The Russians agreed to an American purchase for $7.2 million; the Alaska Purchase Treaty was negotiated and ratified in April 1867. In October of that year, the formal transfer took place in Sitka. The American flag flew over the former Russian colony now called Alaska, a name with Aleut origins proposed in the treaty by Secretary of State William Seward. Almost everyone assumed that the long anticipated mining boom would extend northward overnight. San Francisco positioned itself to maintain its hold over the northern outpost. Yet another new company headquartered in San Francisco, the Alaska Commercial Company, bought out the Russian-American Company and assumed its operations.[19]

In the decade after the Civil War, both Alaska and Hawai'i were, if anything, more integrated in the new Gold Rush West than they had been in the Maritime West. And the Gold Rush West was even more a "western" region than the Maritime West had been. Boston merchants and investors lost their interest in Pacific commerce after the Civil War and turned their attentions and dollars elsewhere. San Francisco was now the undisputed capital of the region.

Over the last quarter of the nineteenth century, the ties grew even stronger. With the ratification of the reciprocity treaty in 1875, commerce between California and Hawai'i skyrocketed. Sugar exports to California surged from 25 million pounds in 1875 to 250 million pounds in 1890. And the nature of those exports further cemented the bond. Only raw sugar could be exported. The Hawaiian crop had to be processed in San Francisco refineries, principally those owned by California sugar magnate Claus Spreckels. Hoping to control both production and processing, Spreckels headed west in 1876 to Hawai'i, allied with King Kalākaua to gain much needed water rights, and brought thousands of acres of land into production. By 1890, the Californian controlled one-third of Hawai'i's sugar production.[20]

The growth in Hawai'i's sugar empire led to other dramatic transformations in the islands. The rush of westward-moving Americans to

Hawai'i never materialized. To find labor for the sugar fields, the Caucasian plantation owners looked to Asia and recruited contract laborers from China and Japan, along with a smaller number of Portuguese and other European workers. By 1890, a demographic revolution had occurred that seriously undermined the status of native Hawaiians in their own kingdom. The percentage of native Hawaiians in the total population dropped from 97 percent in 1853 to 45 percent in 1890. The Asian component grew from less than 1 percent in 1853 to 32 percent in 1890. As a counterweight to the decreasing influence of their people, King Kalākaua and his successor, Queen Lili'uokalani, attempted to enhance the power of the monarchy and to strengthen the role of Hawaiians in the political structure—with a corresponding decrease in the power of Caucasian merchants and missionaries who had played prominent roles in the government since the 1830s.[21]

The ramifications of these economic, demographic, and political changes were the Revolution of 1893 and the annexation of 1898. Both events are complex and controversial and continue to be debated in Hawai'i 100 years after they occurred. The Revolution was staged by a group of local Caucasians, or *haoles*, led by Lorrin Thurston, a grandson of ABCFM missionary Asa Thurston. The revolutionaries were more concerned with the conduct of the monarchy than the financial interests of the sugar planters. They were moved to action in January 1893 when Lili'uokalani announced that she would proclaim a new constitution. The Revolution succeeded with the aid of United States Consul John Stevens, who ordered a contingent of marines to land in Honolulu. Despite the intervention of American troops, the Hawaiian Revolution was staged by competing groups (*haoles* versus monarchy) within the islands; it was not imposed on the kingdom by the United States.[22]

In addition to toppling the monarchy, Thurston and his followers desired annexation to the United States. President Grover Cleveland repudiated the Revolution, disavowed annexation, and favored the restoration of the monarchy. Thurston and his annexationists held firm. They refused to restore Lili'uokalani and in 1894 formed the Republic of Hawai'i. Four years later, President William McKinley accepted the continuing overtures of annexation from the islands. Although anti-imperial sentiment was still strong in Washington, expansionist euphoria generated by the Spanish-American War swayed Congress to approve annexation through a joint resolution in July 1898.

Regardless of the particular precipitating motives for the Revolution and succeeding annexation, the increasing links between Hawai'i and California since 1848 and the dramatic internal changes these had wrought on the islands set the overall stage. The Gold Rush West had now integrated the international Maritime West into one geographic and political union under the American flag.

The year 1898 was as important in Alaska as Hawai'i for uniting the Gold Rush West. The long anticipated mining boom to Alaska simply did not blossom in the three decades following the purchase in 1867. By 1880, fewer than 500 Americans had settled in Alaska. Although some mining activity occurred over the next decade, there was still a non-Native population of only 4,000 to 6,500 by 1890. Relative harmony prevailed between these newcomers and the 25,000 Natives in Alaska.[23]

As miners increasingly explored the tributaries and creeks of the Yukon River, which had been extensively explored by the United States Army in the 1880s, the odds for an eventual boom mounted. In August 1896, Yukon Valley miners found their long anticipated El Dorado at Bonanza Creek on the Klondike River. Although the Klondike was in Canada, passage into and out of it was through Alaska—either the southeastern route through the Chilkoot Pass or the trans–Yukon River route across Alaska. In the summer of 1897, two ships laden with gold arrived in San Francisco and the newer Pacific coast port city of Seattle. Within two weeks pandemonium reigned. The Klondike gold rush—the last great gold rush—erupted and rivaled the California event of a half-century earlier. In 1897 and 1898, an estimated 60,000 to 100,000 people left for the Klondike via the ports of San Francisco and Seattle. As miners filled the Yukon Valley, they rushed to new strikes in Alaska at Nome in 1899 and then at Barnette's Landing, later Fairbanks, in 1901.[24]

By 1900, Alaska's population had expanded to 63,000, now equally split between Natives and non-Natives. Would the boom continue and fully integrate Alaska into the Gold Rush West? Boosters and boomers answered in the affirmative, particularly as Alaska's population held firm over the next decade. When Seattle and Alaska businessmen sponsored the Alaska-Yukon-Pacific Exposition in 1909, Alaska's name seemed fully incorporated into the Gold Rush West.

The Gold Rush West of 1900, stretching from San Diego to Alaska and then westward to Honolulu, certainly seemed more integrated than the old Maritime West of 1845. If this was so, one may well ask why the image of Alaska and Hawai'i as noncontiguous, disconnected extensions gained such credence in the ensuing century. To solve this perplexing riddle, we must now look at Alaska, Hawai'i and the mainland Pacific coast in the twentieth century to understand why the once unified region drifted apart into those "halaskas" of the mapmakers' design.

TWENTIETH-CENTURY ALASKA AND HAWAI'I: THE UNTRANSFORMED WEST?

The annexation of Hawai'i and the "last great gold rush" in 1898 signaled a closer bond between the old triangular points of the Pacific region. The new unity of the region would be short-lived, lasting little more than a decade.

By 1910, changes in the mainland Pacific coast began to sever it from any memory of or connection to the earlier Maritime and Gold Rush Wests. As the twentieth century progressed, Americans, both western and eastern, who had never known those earlier Wests no longer regarded Alaska and Hawai'i as part of any American West. By 1910, the Pacific Slope from San Diego to Puget Sound had been transformed into an urban–industrial society tied to national markets and transportation systems. The transformation was not sudden, but had been evolving over the half century from 1860 to 1910. The rush of westward-moving miners and settlers that first overran Hispanic California in the 1850s—and was so feared in Hawai'i and Russian America—kept coming to the Golden State. California's population reached 1 million between 1880 and 1890, and then soared to 2.4 million by 1910, concentrated in the major cities of the state. Even more important than the sheer numbers was their mode of arrival. The gold-rush argonauts arrived both by ship and by land. With the completion of the transcontinental Central Pacific and Union Pacific Railroads in 1869 and the Southern Pacific in 1883, California's new settlers increasingly arrived by land routes. The economy and trade of California turned eastward via the railroad to the overland routes of the continental United States rather than westward to the Pacific sea routes. It became more and more the west coast of the United States rather than the eastern shore of the Pacific. In the process, the whole concept of contiguity and noncontiguity changed. Landmasses were contiguous, regardless of mountains and deserts, and hence connected. Trade connections, as well as settlement, by sea routes came to be seen as noncontiguous to land-minded Americans—both western and eastern.[25]

The flood of settlement by land and railroad that overtook California swept northward up the Pacific coast. Washington Territory was inundated by settlers arriving via the newly completed Northern Pacific and Great Northern Railroads in the mid-1880s and 1890s. The territory's population swelled from 75,000 in 1880 to 357,000 a decade later. Washington's admission to the union in 1889 was thus propelled by a wagon-trail and railroad invasion rather than by the maritime onslaught that put California's star on the American flag in 1850. The growth of Washington continued into the twentieth century and stood at 1.1 million in 1910. Seattle, now a major metropolis with a 1910 population of 237,000, owed its urban growth more to its railroad depots than to its ports or its role as the jumping-off spot for the "last great gold rush."[26]

While California and Puget Sound rushed forward into urban–industrial America, Alaska and Hawai'i retained their links to those older Wests and did not experience the same transformation as the mainland. In Alaska, the population simply did not grow after 1910, despite the hopes of northern boosters at the Alaska-Yukon-Pacific Exposition. The granting of a territorial legislature in 1912 and the federal construction of the Alaska Railroad between 1915 and 1923 pointed the way to future development. But the population boom and economic transformation never came. World War I interrupted mining activity and drew away labor. Alaska's population fell from 64,000 in 1910 to 55,000 in 1920. Its economy rested on the seasonal fishing industry, primarily salmon. By 1940, the territory had grown to only 73,000 people—a net gain of 9,000 since the turn of the century. This was hardly the kind of transforming boom that had modernized Washington a half century earlier. Alaska's politicians, particularly territorial governor Ernest Gruening (1939–1953), continually lamented the small population and absence of industrialization. They sought scapegoats for Alaska's failure to be like the rest of the West, repeatedly blaming the federal government and absentee economic interests. Seattle-based shipping and salmon-canning companies were excoriated for holding Alaska in a "colonial" vise grip.[27]

Alaska's stalemate was not all negative. In the absence of population and industrial growth, Alaska was spared another of the transformations that marked the lower Pacific coast. The territory's Native population was not devastated. As late as 1940, Natives still constituted roughly half of

Alaska's population. The actual number of Natives in 1940 was 32,000, the same as in 1880. Virtually no federal reservation, removal, or Native land policies extended north until the Alaska Native Claims Settlement Act of 1971. With the organization of the territorial legislature, Natives in southeastern Alaska voted, even though federal Indian policy did not legally confirm the franchise until 1924. The Alaska Native Brotherhood, organized in 1912, sought continued acculturation with the Caucasian population that had long characterized the economic interdependence of Alaska's Native and non-Native populations, even back to Russian times.[28]

While Alaska stood still before World War II and receded from the urban–industrial West, mainland Americans became wedded to images of those earlier Wests in the North. Jack London created the most memorable gold-rush image in his *Call of the Wild,* published in 1903. Although London was a San Francisco maritime figure who caught the first boat north after the arrival of the gold-laden ships in July 1897, his portrait of the Yukon and Alaska did not reinforce the longstanding San Francisco–Alaska maritime connection dating to the 1850s. Instead he portrayed a distant, often cruel, land unconnected to any past or region he had known—and one to which he never returned. In some ways, London's story of his snowbound Klondike winter of 1897/1898 resembled the snowbound-saga of California's Donner Party in 1846/1847. But even as London wrote, the Donner Party saga no longer provided a usable past for residents of urban–industrial California. It belonged to a bygone era. However, the "Call of the Wild" image would continue to define an untransformed Alaska for the rest of the twentieth century. The Yukon Quest and Iditarod sled-dog races, which consciously re-create the frozen travails of that earlier time, continue to grow in popularity in the late 1990s. Even some teachers recruited from the "lower forty-eight" states for Alaska's rural schools in 1996 revealed that one of the chief lures to the North was the desire to answer that primeval "call."[29]

Alaska was rescued from its years of arrested growth by international events. World War II and the ensuing Cold War led to a major military build-up in the territory during the 1940s and 1950s, pushing Alaska's population to 220,000 in the mid-1950s. The military growth finally brought a limited urban–industrial society to Alaska. Anchorage, founded as the headquarters for the Alaska Railroad in 1915, became the military headquarters of the territory and grew to over 50,000 in its metropolitan area by the late 1950s. Fairbanks shared a similar, but more limited, military growth. This new population and economic stability provided the needed supports for statehood; Alaska joined the union as the forty-ninth state in 1959.[30]

The discovery of oil on Alaska's North Slope in 1968 by the Los Angeles–based Atlantic Richfield Company (ARCO) continued to push the new state toward the urban–industrial norm. Unprecedented economic wealth flowed to Alaska with the completion of the Trans-Alaska Oil Pipeline in 1977. Oil also tied the state more closely to the Pacific coast. Alaskan oil, like Hawaiian sugar, was refined almost exclusively in Puget Sound and California refineries. But even this industrial transformation did not have the impact on Alaska that the transcontinental railroads had had on the Pacific coast a century earlier. The oil boom brought no real "onslaught" of people. By 1980, Alaska's population reached only 400,000, less than California in 1870 or Washington in 1900. Metropolitan Anchorage, however, could claim about half of the total, making it similar in size to Seattle in the decade after the Klondike gold rush.[31]

In the last decade of the twentieth century, the vast state still retains much of its distant, untransformed aura. This has given a strange sense of place to the state's residents, and one that varies with different groups within the population. The sense of place for Alaska Natives is clearly Alaska, the land to which they have always belonged. There is virtually no sense of belonging to a region beyond Alaska. In fact, it has been only in the years since statehood that the different Native groups have seen themselves as "Alaska Natives" rather than Arctic Slope Eskimos, interior Athabascans, or southeastern Tlingits. The transient military population, about 15 percent of the overall population in the 1990s, clearly regard themselves as sojourners from various parts of the United States, temporarily dropped in a northern land. They do not see themselves as Westerners either in origin or in temporary location. The old-time white pioneers, or "sourdoughs," might have the most ready claim to call themselves Westerners. Many trace their ancestry to Klondike pioneers or to other migrants from the Pacific coast. And in the present day, many continue to be tied to Seattle for medical and educational, as well as commercial, reasons. However, in the years since statehood few have trumpeted their western heritage. The prestatehood connection to Seattle carried connotations of colonial exploitation and dependence. With statehood and the ensuing oil wealth, sourdoughs have tended to forgo any connection to a broader western region while severing the old colonial tie. Instead, they proudly see themselves as Alaskans, inhabitants of a unique land who at times advocate political independence from the United States. In a mellower mood for the purpose of attracting tourists, they often present themselves as unique proprietors of a "last" or "lost" frontier. To call themselves "Westerners" might seem a demeaning or diminutive stance.[32]

In Hawai'i, a variation on the "untransformed" theme that has characterized Alaska in the twentieth century also distanced the islands from the mainland West. By 1910, urban Honolulu, with a population of 52,000 out of an island total of 154,000, and the highly developed plantation sugar industry placed Hawai'i closer to the western urban–industrial norm than Alaska. Hawai'i's sugar exports to San Francisco and the Spreckels refineries had been an important part of California's climb to agricultural prominence in the latter part of the nineteenth century. The tie grew even stronger in the twentieth century when canned pineapple joined sugar as an export to the mainland. Mainland canners moved to the islands and joined local firms to produce and process the crop. Sugar and canned pineapple were the cornerstones of Hawai'i's economy before World War II. But as the twentieth century progressed, California's domestic production of wheat, cotton, and citrus fruit grew dramatically and dwarfed the importance of sugar and pineapple in the consciousness of the mainland West.[33]

The "labor" tie between California and Hawai'i also remained strong in the new century. From 1900 to 1920, the flow of workers from Hawai'i to California was greater than it had been in the days of the Maritime and Gold Rush Wests. Asian and European workers who went to Hawai'i in the late nineteenth and early twentieth centuries often continued on to California. In fact, the least likely permanent option for a Hawaiian plantation worker was to remain on the islands. The more likely options were to return home or migrate to California. The figures are quite astounding. Of the 62,000 Japanese who immigrated to Hawai'i between 1905 and 1916, 30,000 returned home and 28,000 continued to the west coast. The anti-Japanese xenophobia of white Californians in the twentieth century was directed as much against Hawai'i as Japan. President Theodore Roosevelt halted Japanese migration from Hawai'i to the mainland in 1907—a full year before implementation of his Gentlemen's Agreement. In the first decades of the twentieth century, Hawai'i was the direct source of much of California's Asian population. But this migration was no longer regarded as a connecting bond between the two. California's hostility to Asian immigrants and the fact that the flow of settlers from Hawai'i to California was now so much smaller than the population flow from the eastern United States to the Pacific coast distanced rather than united the two old Pacific partners.[34]

The status of native Hawaiians, like the status of Alaska Natives, linked Hawai'i more to its past than to the western industrial norm—or to the western pattern of Native annihilation. Although much has been written about the impact of Americans and other foreigners on Hawaiians and the dramatic population decline from 1778 to 1900, most of that impact and decline occurred in the era of the Maritime and Gold Rush Wests. After 1910, their number began to increase. Native Hawaiians, unlike Natives in the mainland West, were an important part of territorial political life. Hawaiians, though not Asians, were immediately enfranchised upon annexation and constituted a majority of the electorate. Hawaiians were elected to the territorial legislature, and Prince Jonah Kūhiō Kalaniana'ole, an heir to the Hawaiian throne, was Hawai'i's territorial delegate to Congress from 1902 until his death in 1922. In the years since statehood, native Hawaiian John Waihee served as governor from 1986 to 1994, and Daniel Akaka is currently one of the state's two United States senators.[35]

Native political issues maintain bridges to the past. The overthrow of the monarchy is still a controversial issue 100 years after the Revolution. In 1993 the Revolution was not a quaint reminder of a bygone era in a transformed Hawai'i, but a source of continuing contention that resulted in an official apology from the United States (PL103-150) for its role in the overthrow of Queen Lili'uokalani. Writings by modern Hawaiian authors such as John Dominis Holt and Haunani-Kay Trask constantly reexamine the heritage of the monarchy and the Hawaiian people. These authors seek to revive and enrich Hawaiian cultural values as well as pursue political objectives. The diacritical marks on Hawaiian words in this chapter are the result of a movement over the past decade to restore traditional orthography as the standard style in Hawai'i.[36]

As in Alaska, the military importance of Hawai'i to American national security had a transforming impact on the territory, particularly in the migration of mainlanders to the islands. By 1940, some 20,000 military personnel were stationed at Pearl Harbor, Schofield Barracks, Fort

Shafter, and other installations near Honolulu. The territory's overall population had risen to 422,000. With the bombing of Pearl Harbor in December 1941, Hawai'i became the center of operations for the Pacific War. Population from the mainland flowed to the islands as never before. In the peak war year of 1944, Hawai'i's population soared to 859,000. More than 1 million troops passed through Hawai'i over the course of the war.[37]

Hawai'i's population declined in the decade after World War II to about 500,000 in the mid-1950s. But the continued military importance of Hawai'i during the Cold War maintained the prominence of the islands in the national consciousness. This, along with the superb World War II and Korean War record of Hawai'i's military veterans, the embarrassing label of "colonialism" that Hawai'i gave the nation, and the constant reminder by Hawai'i statehooders that the islands were "normal" in terms of economic development and political maturity, finally convinced Congress to admit Hawai'i, after Alaska, as the fiftieth state in 1959.[38]

In the years after statehood, one might have expected Hawai'i to become an extended version of the mainland West, particularly as its military importance in the Pacific Rim increased. There have been definite trends in that direction, but other forces have worked to maintain at least the image of an "untransformed West." The advent of jet aircraft in 1959 led to a poststatehood boom in tourism that supplanted military spending and agriculture as the mainstay of the state's economy by the early 1970s. With tourism, as with sugar, the link to California and the Pacific coast has been dominant. In 1981, 47 percent of all westbound tourists to Hawai'i were from the Pacific and Mountain states—with a full 30 percent or 785,000, from California alone. But this substantial westward population flow, transient as it may be, has not fused a new, western consciousness on either California or Hawai'i. Californians do not flock to Hawai'i as just another Pacific beach that they could find within a short ride from their homes. Instead, the image of an exotic, Polynesian paradise and escape has been carefully cultivated and maintained to sustain the islands' economy. The lure of the "old Hawai'i"—or at least what tourists think is the old Hawai'i—can be seen in the longevity of the Kodak hula show, performed continually in Honolulu from the 1930s to the present day.[39]

With tourists clinging to the hula show and islanders continually debating the implications of the Revolution of 1893, an untransformed

Hawai'i, like Alaska, still lives in the shadows of its not so distant pasts and produces a unique sense of place for islanders. As in Alaska, that sense varies with groups within the population. Native Hawaiians, like their northern counterparts, see Hawai'i alone as their home. If they are connected to a broader region by history or common cause, it is to a wider Polynesia. Hawai'i's military population, as in Alaska, has a sojourner consciousness.

Other groups might have a feel for being western. Hawai'i's Asian-Americans do have a sense of belonging to a broader Asian-American population, many of whom are located in the western United States. In recent years, an increasing number of Asian-American islanders have moved to the mainland in search of better jobs. However, these mainland migrants often see themselves as exiles from Hawai'i. There is a yearning to return home rather than to be freely moving members of a wider western Asian-America. And what of the Caucasian settlers whose ancestors date to the nineteenth century, the so-called *kama'ainas* who owned the plantations, who created the California sugar connection, and whose ships plied constantly between Honolulu and the mainland coast? Are they the islands' "Westerners" who feel just as home in San Francisco as in Honolulu? While some *kama'ainas* could claim such an identity, there would be little reason to do so. The "lure of paradise" is now the mainstay of the Hawaiian economy. The *kama'ainas,* even those who trumpeted Hawai'i's economic and political "normalness" in the days before statehood, now have a vested interest in maintaining the "legend that sells."[40]

Noncontiguous or untransformed? If history is to be our guide, it is not physical space or geography that has distanced Hawai'i and Alaska from the mainland Pacific West. Alaska and Hawai'i were integral parts of that West in the nineteenth century. Instead, the distance has come from the relatively slower transformation of Alaska and Hawai'i to the urban–industrial norm that had overtaken the Pacific coast by the first decade of the twentieth century. Despite nineteenth-century fears that a Yankee onslaught was imminent in both Alaska and Hawai'i, the surges of westward-moving American settlers that came to the mainland Pacific coast did not continue west or north, except in the war years. With the boom on the mainland coast, the relative importance of trade with Alaska and Hawai'i diminished, but in no way vanished. The political survival and importance of the Native populations of Alaska and Hawai'i also marked a difference between these less transformed areas and the main-land coast. Cultural images of the past, whether the "call of the wild" or the "lure of paradise," lingered in both areas and were not totally over-whelmed by the trappings of urban–industrial society.

As the twentieth century progressed, these untransformed Wests seemed more and more distant to some mainlanders. By mid-century, a growing number insisted that no connection had ever existed or could exist with these areas they now called "noncontiguous." The noncon-tiguous label was resented in Alaska and Hawai'i as long as it was a po-litical liability to statehood. But once in the union, residents of the forty-ninth and fiftieth states seemed happy with a sense of place that set them apart from the mainland coast. It gave them a unique or special identity, rather than a sense of being lesser or extended parts of the dominant West. Mainland tourists responded to this special identity; the differentness of both Alaska and Hawai'i became a highly marketable tourist commodity.

If the issue is transformation rather than proximity, one may ask if Hawai'i and Alaska will remain "untransformed Wests." Or is it simply a matter of time before the forty-ninth and fiftieth states blend into the San Diego to Seattle norm. On the one hand, a drift toward the norm is possible. Both Anchorage and Honolulu are clearly modern metropoli-tan areas. A visitor to the former might confuse its mountain-bowl set-ting with that of Salt Lake City; someone standing in Honolulu's Finan-cial Plaza of the Pacific might well see a duplicate of Newport Beach, California. On the other hand, there is little indication that the phenom-enal westward-moving population surges that transformed the west coast will overwhelm Hawai'i or Alaska.

It is also possible that the old Pacific triangle of Alaska, Hawai'i, and the Pacific coast will regain its former unity as a military defense perim-eter. The military buildup of Alaska and Hawai'i since World War II has been the single most important factor in transforming the two areas to the western norm. And it has been a lasting transformation. The troop con-centrations and defense installations in Alaska and Hawai'i are not mere extensions of those in California and Puget Sound, but vital, coequal part-ners in the defense of the Pacific Rim. In fact, with the end of the Cold War, Alaska and Hawai'i have experienced substantially fewer base closures than has the mainland coast. We may well see a Pacific Military West in the twenty-first century that rivals the old Maritime and Gold Rush Wests.

There is, however, an alternative scenario. Must Hawai'i and Alaska become more like California and Puget Sound to regain their historic place in the Pacific West? It is also possible that the urban–industrial West may look to Alaska and Hawai'i in the twenty-first century as the future norm to preserve and aspire to. Hawai'i, the only state in which there is not a Caucasian majority, may well become the social model for other western states as the longstanding white majorities on the mainland give way to multiethnic societies. Patricia Limerick has called this possibility the "Hawaiianization of the nation." And the vital political role of Natives in both Hawai'i and Alaska may well be the model for the political future of Native Americans in western, as well as eastern, American states.[41]

The transformation of the American Pacific coast permanently destroyed much that existed in the past. That Pacific past and the many Wests to which it once belonged may still be found only in Alaska and Hawai'i. The transformed coast may well have a vested interest in drawing closer to Alaska and Hawai'i as the only surviving link to its past and the chart to its future.

NOTES

1. Joel Garreau, *The Nine Nations of North America* (Boston: Houghton Mifflin, 1981), 107, 118. My student at the University of Alaska, Fairbanks, geography major Michael Wilson, used the term "halaska," claiming he found it in a "Sniglet."

2. Mike Monroney, "Let's Keep It 48," *Colliers*, 4 March 1955, 32. For a visualization of the noncontiguity of California and later Oregon, readers may want to refer to the classic textbook map of the election of 1860 in which California and Oregon appear to be floating in a distant and noncontiguous western, Pacific hinterland.

3. Michael P. Malone and Richard Etulain, *The American West: A Twentieth-Century History* (Lincoln: University of Nebraska Press, 1989), 9.

4. For the best account of Gray's voyages, see John Scofield, *Hail, Columbia* (Portland: Oregon Historical Society, 1993).

5. For general descriptions of the Boston-based Northwest–China fur trade, see Samuel Eliot Morison, *The Maritime History of Massachusetts* (Boston: Houghton Mifflin,1921); Richard Batman, *The Outer Coast* (New York: Harcourt Brace Jovanovich, 1985); Arrell Morgan Gibson, *Yankees in Paradise* (Albuquerque: University of New Mexico Press, 1993); and John Whitehead, "Hawai'i: The First and Last Far West?" *Western Historical Quarterly* 23 (1992): 153–77. Kamehameha I unified the Hawaiian kingdom in 1795 with the exception of the island of Kauai, which did not submit to his rule until 1810.

6. For the use of Hawaiian labor on ships and in the Northwest, see Tom Koppel, *Kanaka: The Untold Story of Hawaiian Pioneers in British Columbia and the Pacific Northwest* (Vancouver: Whitecap Books, 1995).

7. For the story of Joe O'Cain, see Batman, *Outer Coast,* 135–52.

8. For the often controversial story of the ABCFM missionaries to Hawai'i, see as a standard source Ralph Kuykendall, *The Hawaiian Kingdom,* vol. 1, *1778–1854, Foundation and Transformation* (Honolulu: University of Hawaii, Press 1938), 100–116. For a recent source favorable to the missionaries, see Nancy Zwiep, *Pilgrim Path: The First Company of Women Missionaries to Hawaii* (Madison: University of Wisconsin Press, 1991). For a highly critical account by a native Hawaiian, see Lilikala Kame'eleihiwa, *Native Land and Foreign Desires* (Honolulu: Bishop Museum Press, 1992). For the latest account of the story of Opukaha'ia, see Albert J. Schutz, *The Voices of Eden* (Honolulu: University of Hawaii Press, 1994), 85–97.

9. For the story of the Whitmans and their Hawaiian converts, see Julie Roy Jeffrey, *Converting the West: A Biography of Narcissa and Marcus Whitman* (Norman: University of Oklahoma Press, 1991), 126–27.

10. Sutter's travels between California, Hawai'i and Russian America are well presented in Howard Lamar, "John Augustus Sutter, Wilderness Entrepreneur," in *John Sutter and a Wider West,* ed. Kenneth Owens (Lincoln: University of Nebraska Press, 1994), 26–50.

11. For a background on the whaling industry and its impact on the region, see Gibson, *Yankees in Paradise,* 131–54.

12. For Larkin's educational connection to Hawai'i, see Harlan Hague and David J. Langum, *Thomas O. Larkin* (Norman: University of Oklahoma Press, 1990), 50–53. For the story of C. Brewer and Company, see Scott C. S. Stone, *The Story of C. Brewer and Co., Ltd* (Honolulu: Island Heritage, 1991).

13. For Hawai'i population statistics, I have used Robert C. Schmitt, *Historical Statistics of Hawaii* (Honolulu: University of Hawaii Press, 1977). The decline of the native population of Hawai'i was a major issue in the nineteenth century. The mid-1840 population of 100,000 was down from an estimated 300,000 (some estimates go as high as 1 million) at the time of Cook's arrival in 1778. The native population continued to decline to a low of 40,000 by 1900.

14. For the initial effects of the gold rush on Hawai'i, see Edward Joesting, *Hawaii: An Uncommon History* (New York: Norton, 1972), 111–26.

15. For the best background to the impact of San Francisco on Russian America and the early purchase overtures, see Ronald J. Jensen, *The Alaska Purchase and Russian–American Relations* (Seattle: University of Washington Press, 1975); and Howard I. Kushner, *Conflict on the Northwest Coast: American-Russian Rivalry in the Pacific Northwest, 1790–1867* (Westport, Conn.: Greenwood Press, 1975). These books are the prime secondary works for all ensuing aspects of the purchase of Alaska by the United States.

16. For Dana's account of his return to California in 1859 and 1860, see "Twenty Four Years After," an appendix to his *Two Years Before the Mast* (1840) that was first added to the 1869 revised edition of *Two Years.*

17. For the annexation attempt of 1854, see Kuykendall, *Hawaiian Kingdom,* 1:383–428.

18. For the road to reciprocity, see Merze Tate, *Hawaii: Reciprocity or Annexation* (East Lansing: Michigan State University Press, 1968); and Ralph Kuykendall, *The Hawaiian Kingdom,* vol. 3, *The Kalakaua Dynasty* (Honolulu: University of Hawaii Press, 1967).

19. Although ridiculed by a few newspapers as "Seward's Folly," the purchase enjoyed broad support in Congress. The Alaska Purchase Treaty of 1867 was one of the most quickly written and ratified treaties in American history. Less than two weeks elapsed from the assurance of the Russian ambassador on March 29, 1867, that his government was willing to sell to the final Senate ratification of the treaty on April 9, 1867. See Jensen, *Alaska Purchase;* and Kushner, *Conflict on the Northwest Coast.*

20. The best source on the role of Claus Spreckels and the rise of sugar in Hawai'i is Jacob Adler, *Claus Spreckels: The Sugar King in Hawaii* (Honolulu: University of Hawaii Press, 1966).

21. The actual number—as well as the percentage—of Hawaiians had dropped from the mid-1840s figure of 100,000 to 71,000 in 1853 to 41,000 in 1890. In addition to the increase of Asians, the percentage of Portuguese in Hawai'i rose from less than 1 percent in 1853 to 14 percent in 1890. "Caucasian" and *haole* are the standard terms for referring to Europeans in Hawai'i. The Portuguese, who are included in the Caucasian designation, were not members of the dominant merchant-plantation faction. The dominant Caucasian group—referred to as "other Caucasians"—in population had increased from 1,600 (2 percent of total) in 1853 to 6,200 (7 percent of total) in 1890. The total population of 90,000 in 1890 was actually less than in the mid-1840s.

22. For the standard accounts of the Revolution of 1893, see Kuykendall, *Hawaiian Kingdom,* vol. 3; Merze Tate, *The United States and the Hawaiian Kingdom* (New Haven, Conn.: Yale University Press, 1965); and William Adam Russ, Jr., *The Hawaiian Revolution, 1893–94* (Selingrove, Pa.: Susquehanna University Press, 1959). For Lili'uokalani's contemporary account, see *Hawaii's Story by Hawaii's Queen* (Rutland, Vt.: Tuttle, 1964). For examples of recent accounts critical of the Revolution, see Michael Dougherty, *To Steal a Kingdom: Probing Hawaiian History* (Waimanola: Island Style Press, 1992); Rich Budnick, *Stolen Kingdom: An American Conspiracy* (Honolulu: Aloha Press, 1992); and Michael Kioni Dudley and Keoni Kealoha Agard, *A Call for Hawaiian Sovereignty* (Honolulu: Na Kane Oka Malo Press, 1990).

23. For the best account of Alaska's early years under American rule, see Ted C. Hinckley, *The Americanization of Alaska* (Palo Alto, Calif.: Pacific Books, 1972).

24. For the best description of the Yukon Valley gold rushes in Alaska and Canada, see Melody Webb, *Yukon* (Lincoln: University of Nebraska Press, 1993).

25. For the urban–industrial growth of the Pacific coast, see Earl Pomeroy, *The Pacific Slope: A History of California, Washington, Oregon, Nevada, and Utah* (Lincoln: University of Nebraska Press, 1991); and Carlos A. Schwantes, *The Pacific Northwest: An Interpretive History* (Lincoln: University of Nebraska Press, 1989).

26. For the argument that Seattle's growth was not dependent on the gold rush, see Roger Sales, *Seattle: Past to Present* (Seattle: University of Washington Press, 1976), 51–53. The impact of the gold rush on Seattle also faded as the business section of the city shifted away from the Skid Road section, which was prominent in the Klondike era. Not until the 1960s and 1970s would this older, dilapidated area be revitalized as Pioneer Square, with a unit of the National Park Service's Klondike National Historic Monument.

27. For the lament over the stagnation of Alaska's population and lag in industrial growth, see Ernest Gruening, *The State of Alaska* (New York: Random House, 1954). The Alaska Railroad, running from the port of Seward to interior Fairbanks, did not connect Alaska with the mainland western states. Sea transportation from Seattle or San Francisco was still necessary to tie Alaska with the mainland Pacific coast.

28. For early Native voting, see Stephen Haycox, "William Paul and the Alaska Voters' Literacy Act of 1925," *Alaska History* 2 (Winter): 17–37. As in Hawai'i, "Caucasian" is the preferred racial term; "Anglo" and "white" are rarely used.

29. For the lure of the "Call of the Wild," see my comments on London in the chapter "Writers as Pioneers," in Gibson, *Yankees In Paradise*, 379–409. My comments on the lure of school teachers and the popularity of the Yukon Quest and Iditarod dog sled races are drawn from articles in the *Fairbanks Daily News Miner*, January–March 1996.

30. For the impact of World War II and the Cold War on Alaska, see John S. Whitehead, "Alaska and Hawai'i: The Cold War States," in *The Cold War West*, ed. Kevin Fernlund (Albuquerque: University of New Mexico Press, forthcoming).

31. For a general overview of Alaska's oil era, see Claus M. Naske, *A History of the 49th State* (Norman: University of Oklahoma Press, 1987).

32. Alaska Natives divide into six major groups: Eskimo, Athabascan, Tlingit, Aleut, Haida, and Tsimshian. Prior to statehood each group tended to pursue its political goals separately. In 1962, the groups founded the Alaska Federation of Natives to present a united political front.

33. For the best economic history of Hawai'i and a description of the sugar and pineapple industries, see Thomas Kemper Hitch, *Islands in Transition: The Past, Present, and Future of Hawaii's Economy* (Honolulu: First Hawaiian Bank, 1992).

34. For the flow of Japanese workers from Hawai'i to California, see Edward D. Beechert, *Working in Hawaii: A Labor History* (Honolulu: University of Hawaii Press, 1985), 122–23, 131–32.

35. For the most recent writing on the impact of foreigners on Hawai'i and the native population decline, see David Stannard, *Before the Honor: The Population of Hawai'i on the Eve of Western Contact* (Honolulu: University of Hawaii Social Science Research Institute, 1989); and O. A. Bushnell, *The Gifts of Civilization: Germs and Genocide in Hawai'i* (Honolulu: University of Hawaii Press, 1993). The Hawaiian and part-Hawaiian population bottomed from 1896 to1910 at roughly 39,000. By 1920, the number recovered to 42,000 and rose to 64,000 by 1940.

36. For centennial writings on the Revolution of 1893, see Dougherty, *To Steal a Kingdom;* Budnick, *Stolen Kingdom;* and Dudley and Agard, *Call for Hawaiian Sovereignty.* PL 103-150 signed on November 23, 1993, formally apologized to native Hawaiians for the role of "agents and citizens" of the United States in the 1893 overthrow and "urges the President of the United States . . . to support reconciliation efforts between the United States and the Native Hawaiian People." The resolution makes no specific formal proposals for reconciliation. For examples of modern Hawaiian writing, see Haunani-Kay Trask, *From a Native Daughter: Colonialism and Sovereignty in Hawai'i* (Monroe, Maine: Common Courage Press, 1993); John Dominis Holt, *On Being Hawaiian* (Honolulu: Topgallant, 1964); and Holt, *Monarchy in Hawaii* (Honolulu: Topgallant, 1971).

37. For the impact of World War II on Hawai'i, see Gwenfread Allen, *Hawaii's War Years* (Honolulu: University of Hawaii Press, 1950).

38. For the impact of the Cold War and its role in bringing statehood to Hawai'i, see Whitehead, "Alaska and Hawai'i."

39. For statistics on the origins of tourists to Hawai'i, see *Atlas of Hawaii,* 2nd ed. (Honolulu: University of Hawaii Press, 1993), 173–77. For the best general background to the development of tourism in Hawai'i, see Bryan H. Farrell, *Hawaii: The Legend that Sells* (Honolulu: University of Hawaii Press, 1982). For criticism of the manipulation of the tourist image of "old Hawai'i," see Elizabeth Buck, *Paradise Remade: The Politics of Culture and History in Hawaii* (Philadelphia: Temple University Press, 1993).

40. The number of Hawaiian-born persons living on the mainland has risen dramatically since World War II. The figure rose from 19,437 in 1930 to 115,010 in 1960 and to 250,000 by 1980. See *Atlas of Hawaii,* 124. My conclusion that many island-born Asian-Americans yearn to return to Hawai'i is anecdotal and based on conversations with Asian-American colleagues at professional meetings. For a discussion of the term "Asian-American" in the context of Hawai'i, see Jonathon Y. Okamora, "Why There Are No Asian-Americans in Hawaii: The Continuing Significance of Local Indentities," *Judicial Process in Hawaii* 35 (1994): 161–78.

41. Patricia Nelson Limerick, "The Multicultural Islands, Review Article," *American Historical Review* 97 (1992):121–35.

14

Cuentos de la Tierra Encantada:

Magic and Realism in the

Southwest Borderlands

Paula Gunn Allen

For the most part, people of the United States have but a general idea of what makes the American Southwest culturally and politically as well as geographically a distinct entity within the greater American landscape. Some no doubt see it as depicted in films such as *Tombstone* or earlier movies such as *Stagecoach* and *True Grit*. In these depictions, the Southwest is the West, a land of buttes, mesas, wide-open spaces, chaparral, mesquite, redskins, gunslingers, desperados, and Frito bandidos. The language is not necessarily American, and what defines the region is its primal struggle to emerge into the full light of Anglo-American identity after more than a century as frontier. So pervasive and powerful is this media-inspired image of the Southwest that tourists routinely call the state tourism bureau of New Mexico, Arizona, Utah, and parts of Texas to inquire about the monetary rate of exchange, the frequency of Indian raids, and the availability of accommodations with plumbing and electricity.

The Southwest is identified as the source of Native American silver and turquoise jewelry, neocolonial Spanish-American furniture and architecture, fashions based on Navajo women's dress, Pueblo pottery, Navajo rugs, and green chili everything—including vodka and foccacio. Architecture, fashions, and cuisine are promoted under the "ethnic" sobriquet "Santa Fe," reflecting the artsy and culturally aware tastes of the Anglo-American privileged. A subset of this segment of the population, New Age spiritual trekkers, flock to the region, visiting all the spots deemed "sacred": the Garden of the Gods outside Colorado Springs and Rancho de Taos—renowned for its artsy ambience as much as for its Hispanic character and the nearby Pueblo.[1] They visit the church at Chimayo to secure some dirt that possesses supernatural healing power, and perhaps leave an offering to the small statue of St. Anthony, which, according to decades of local testimony, walks about at night to save people in dire need. His tiny footprints have been left in mud or snow. The visitors take the baths or just fish and hang loose at Jemez Springs in northern New Mexico, and make their way through a variety of "vortexes" that surround Sedona, in northern Arizona.[2] Attendence at the Girl's Puberty Ceremony at Mescalero in July has become de rigeur for those who know the location of this most happening scene.

Favored sites variously feature restorative mineral baths, adobe houses floored in saltillo tile, bent junipers, and cliff dwellings in exotic locales, where one can soak up spiritual vibrations in a vortex, chase UFOs, make offerings to Native gods, and wait to hear spirits sing and weep among the magnificent ruins of Chaco Canyon, Mesa Verde, Bandelier, and Canyon de Chelly. Nor are these versions without merit. They are as accurate as one-dimensional portraits usually are, hinting at the reality of southwestern identity: it is magical, a place where mystery and myth are as factual and everyday as any other aspect of contemporary life in the United States. Just think: the hump-backed flute player Kokopelli, Old Man Coyote, other supernaturals and spirits unnamed, and myriad kachinas grace walls, doorways, and towel racks in businesses and homes, while santos, tin sculpture, and icons of La Virgin de Guadalupe ornament plazas, patios, and gardens across the region, taking their place alongside old wagon wheels and yellowing skulls of dead cows. All over the region, UFOs routinely emerge from buttes and lakes, and the old gods still walk the wilderness.

But miracles in the region are not confined to the exotic Other. While the Southwest is filled with the quaint, the curious, and the paranormal, it is also home to more high-tech innovations and installations, military and civilian, than any other region in the United States. Along with consumer goods such as turquoise and silver jewelry; Pueblo pottery; "Santa Fe" furniture, architecture, and art; Navajo and Chimayo rugs; a wealth of fine sculpture and painting; and a rich, multilingual and many-cultured body of literature produced by Native, Hispanic, and "Anglo" artists and writers, the region provides gas, oil, coal, copper, silver, and uranium for the nation. It was the birthplace of the nuclear age at Los Alamos, outside Santa Fe, and of space age medicine—as Lovelace Medical Center and Kirtland and Manzano Air Force Bases and the Atomic Energy Commission collaborated on support and health systems for astronauts and associated workers. The region also made significant contributions to the electronic era. Microsoft developers Bill Gates and Paul Allen lived in Albuquerque while they designed the interpreter program for BASIC, used in conjunction with the first personal computer, the Altair, designed by Edward Roberts and two assistants. Roberts, whose Altair was nearly as revolutionary as the wheel, was employed as a research engineer in the Weapons Lab at Kirtland Air Force Base in Albuquerque in the early 1970s.

The contributions of the Southwest to contemporary America's lifestyle are indeed great: most of the foodstuffs Americans consume are raised in the Southwest; many of the most American of them originate there, and from there comes the fastest-growing "ethnic" American food craze, chili. Chili, of course, comes in many presentations, among them Tex-Mex chili, salsa, chili stew, posole, tamales, rellenos, and burritos. These American favorites are composed of combinations of chili, corn, tomatoes, and/or pinto beans, which have long been staple foods of the Native American peoples of the transborder region, which includes major portions of Central America and Mexico. It must be remembered, of course, that a large portion of Mexico only recently came within United States political boundaries; most of what was northern Mexico has been the American Southwest for only one and a half centuries, an area that stretches from western Texas through southern California. And while Anglo culture and its accompanying system of government have taken root in the region, the permeability of its borders combined with the Indio-Hispanic nature of its present non-Anglo population make the region as much Indio-Latino as Norte Americano.

Because of its recent status as northern Mexico, the cultural identity of the Southwest is confluential. For while there are three major contributing groups to its cultural distinctiveness, they do not fuse into one, nor do they remain entirely separate. Rather, each retains its separate and unique identity while engaging in a variety of modes of interchange. These three major cultural strands give the Southwest its other major distinguishing characteristic: in a nation that is all but history-less and mono-cultural at public levels, the Southwest provides a profound connection with the ancientness of human culture in its widely placed ruins and presently occupied villages. It also provides a sharp sense of the multi-cultural nature of American life in general in the widespread public use of several languages, chiefly Spanish and American English, seasoned with splashes of Dinetah and various Pueblo expressions, place names, phenomena, and events.

A region's particular identity is established by its characteristic sounds, smells, colors, textures, and flavors. In the Southwest, these aspects are shaped by the highly visible presence of American Indian communities and cultures to an extent far greater than in the rest of the nation. In the Southwest, the very brief history of Anglo-America is of far less moment than that of the ancients, whose presence is recorded in the very rocks, canyons, mesas, and mountain ranges, and maintained in contemporary American Indian communities in New Mexico. Along with the highly visible American Indian presence, the centuries-old Hispanic presence has left its own indelible imprint, and it is these three factors that cause the American Southwest to bear a greater likeness to Mexico, Guatemala, Belize, El Salvador, and Nicaragua than to the rest of the United States.

The unique, almost non-Anglo character of the Southwest, particularly in the less accessible areas, leads to the impression that the Southwest borderlands are not part of the greater United States—except in the convenience of its language, highways, post offices, and monetary and legal system. A "Third World" groupie can wander and even settle there without need for hassles with immigration authorities. The majority of Anglo-Americans who relocate to the borderlands take on Southwest customs, costumes, and outlook to one degree or another. Quite a few "go native," while others limit their acculturation to eating chili, beans, and tortillas or sopapaillas and occasionally sporting Indian jewelry.

In this way, residing in the area is in many ways similar to entering a new country, one much like and yet palpably distinct from the one left behind. Much of the reason behind the sense of living in another country stems from cultural factors: the culture complex that deeply and anciently informs the region is closely related to Maya and Aztec cultures farther south; this relationship predates the Hispanic presence, to be sure, but the Hispanic–Native American civilization that emerged after the Spanish conquest served to heighten the similarities already in place over the region. Present-day Pueblo peoples of New Mexico and Arizona, their cousins the Tohono Oodam (Pima and Papago) of Mexico and Arizona, the recently arrived Apache, and their closely related but Pueblo-influenced Diné (Navajo) make up a coherent cultural complex. In many respects, the worldview of this complex is shared by all the Native peoples in the Southwest, particularly in the sedentary, horticulture-based lifestyle, though the coastal and desert people do not depend on corn, squash, and beans as basic foodstuffs. Nevertheless, the worldview that the peoples of the Southwest share profoundly influenced the Hispanic peoples, giving present-day Mexico and nearby regions and the American Southwest their particular flavor: a relaxed, warm, otherworldly outlook that so intrinsically expects miracles that they are seen as part of everyday life. Thus arose the idea of "magic realism," by which was originally meant "the magic is factual, real, everyday."

The third cultural group contributing to the cultural climate of the Southwest is, of course, the Anglo-American, the one least affected by the civilizations to the south.[3] The cultural pattern of Anglo-America privileges a northern European worldview, which for historic reasons deprecates contributions to regional (or national) culture emanating from southern European countries such as Italy, Spain, Portugal, and France. Nevertheless, the larger commonality of Anglo-European and other Old World cultures is highly visible in the Southwest, where it remains somewhat outside the basic matrix of southwestern civilization.

The oldest and greatest formative influence of the Anglo-American establishment in the area has been the military. Many, if not most, of the Anglos who would obtain great power in the region arrived with the military as soldiers, support staff, or merchants devoted to supplying military personnel with whiskey, women, and gambling. First assigned to a variety of forts to fight Native and Hispanic peoples, the United States military presence continued to grow over two centuries. The installation in Albuquerque ensured the routing of the railroad through that city rather than through the old capitol, Santa Fe, and its routing through the rest of New Mexico Territory and southern California was determined primarily by the needs of military supply and, secondarily, by the needs of Anglo mining interests. Fully one-half of Arizona and at least one-third of New Mexico is in the hands of the armed forces. For over a century, Anglo-American culture's most powerful contribution has been through the military. Among the many lasting imprints this cultural complex has made on the region, granting it the dubious distinction of being the first place in the world to be nuked must rank among the most definitive.

Among my earliest history lessons was that we had been invaded and colonized not once but three times in recent memory: first by the Diné, about 1,000 years ago; then by the Spanish, around 500 years ago; and finally by the Americans, less than a century before I was born.[4] Another lesson was that American history didn't begin on the Atlantic coast in the early seventeenth century; it began when Estebanito, the Moorish explorer from Spain, came north from Mexico to Acoma, very near my birthplace, in the early sixteenth century. That was before the defeat of the Spanish Armada, at a time when the Holy Roman Empire, with its allies the Spanish Inquisition and the Spanish–Portuguese monarchy, ruled western Europe and wielded considerable influence in the Levant and Mediterranean, all of which, of course, had a decisive effect on southwestern American culture as well as on the course of Western civilization over the ensuing centuries.

A region's flavor is inscribed in its every cultural form, and none is more definitive than its cuisine. Corn, of course, is pure American. It has been the grain staple of choice in this hemisphere for several thousand years. One of the earliest cultivated crops—chili is said to have been the first—its status as a fundamental source of nourishment and prosperity runs so deep that it enjoys hemisphere-wide status as a major archetype in sacred narrative. When Jesus came, the Corn Mothers did not disappear; they just took in another son. They are always associated with the divine twins; it's just that the twins got a brother, a third divine son of the sun Oshrats. But the mother(s), the clans, the kin, the people, retained their feminine-valued sense of identity, and as surely as the southwestern sun grooves European skin, the idea that nurturing is superior to battling gains sturdy hold in the minds and hearts of southwestern Americans.

Corn, our dear mother, nurtures us in a variety of mythic ways, but for now let us consider the most delicious: dinner. Take a ride up toward Taos from Santa Fe. Take the old High Road, and head for Chimayo. There's a restaurant in Chimayo that is a confluential wonder—Restaurante Rancho de Chimayo. You go into a building that looks like an old mountain hacienda, which it is. Somebody greets you, and if you're lucky, you get seated with no wait. It's best to do this midweek, somewhat after peak mealtime. You open the menu, and as you read from item to item you realize you died and went to heaven. Someone brings out a basket of corn chips and salsa—a relish made of chopped tomatoes, onions, garlic, green chili, or jalapeños, and dressed in a bit of oil and vinegar in which you dip your chip, take a bite, and start to sweat, swear, and praise all the saints.

But that's only the beginning: as they say, the proof of the pudding is in the eating, and there's plenty of proof to be had when your order is before you. There are the tamales, which are stuffed corn cakes, made of corn flour, filled with meat and thick red chili, wrapped and tied in corn husks and steamed. For those who prefer vegetarian tamales, no problem. The filling might be whole kernels of corn slathered with thick red chili, but the result's the same: sweet corn, spicy-hot chili, flavoring and texture of boiled and then twice-roasted beef or pork that would be falling off the bone if the bone was included. Or you can have a bowl of posole, a fiery corn soup laden with tamal, a kind of firm hominy, red chili, pork, perhaps a bit of oregano, cumin, some salt and pepper, and, of course, plenty of chopped onion and garlic. With this a taco, an enchilada or two, a basket of sopapillas—which in Indian country is bigger and called fry bread—honey or salt to sprinkle on it, or maybe one prefers a fragrant, fresh pile of white flour tortillas. Spread with real butter, this incredible version of bread is a sterling example of what can be achieved when two hemispheres combine in savory harmony. Your entrée includes calabasitas—a fresh vegetable dish composed of zucchini and sweet corn, and spiced with bits of fresh roasted green chili, all sautéed in olive oil just long enough to gain full flavor. Musn't forget the frijoles, pinto beans of distinct flavor. At this exemplary grazing place, they are prepared just as they should be: slowly simmered until plump, brown, juicy—no additives but salt.

Most of the ingredients are indigenous, but they are not ethnic. Corn tortillas and corn-based foods are as American as turkey, tomatoes, Coca-Cola, chocolate, and coffee. All are native to this hemisphere—as are some 60 percent of the world's foods—and in the Southwest they achieve their culinary glory. One can end the feast by lingering over a lovely serving of natillas, a custard pudding that is Spanish-Mexican in style. Like its cousins—crème brûleé, custard pudding, and flan—natillas is flavored with cinnamon lavishly sprinkled on top. A rich cup of coffee, almost as good as what we called "sheep-camp" coffee—the kind that stood by the coals all day and had grounds and water added periodically so that, at its best, you could stand a spoon upright in a cup of it—ahh. No need to eat again for a couple of days.

Besides food, stories provide a deep sense of continuity within a psychospace. A region is bounded and shaped by its climate and geography, but these features take on a human and spiritual dimension when rendered significant in narrative. The smells, sounds, and tactile sensations that go with a locale are as central to its human significance as the sights, and it is within the stories that all the dimensions of human sensation, perception, conception, and experience come together, providing a clear notion of where we are, who we are, and why.

Each of the three cultures that form the cultural basis of the Southwest possesses a particular narrative tradition. The Native American tradition invariably interweaves the worlds of the supernatural and the mundane. Supernatural beings and their human counterparts interact, sometimes in mortal realms, sometimes in realms where physical laws follow very different principles.

The Hispanic tradition is very like the Native American one; the main difference lies in its close relationship to western European narrative. Because of this connection, Hispanic narratives are likely to feature a single hero; a lot of interaction with the dead as well as gods, goddesses, and the like; and almost as much romance. In many ways, Hispanic narratives, including ballads known as *corridos,* resemble a fusion of *Don Quixote de la Mancha* and the *Popol Vuh.*[5] While Spain and the rest of Europe followed Miguel de Cervantes into modernism, Spanish-language writers of the New World, true to a literary heritage honored on both sides of the Atlantic for millennia, blended the arcane and the mundane, the magical and the mysterious, with a modernist view. This fusion, this interpenetration of one narrative tradition with another quite foreign to it, yields stories that are wondrous, wild, and deeply satisfying. Among the multitude of wonderful works by Americans of Spanish-speaking persuasion, Mexican writer Laura Esquivel's *Like Water for Chocolate* (1991) springs to mind. The idea of "magical realism," like "surrealism"—an earlier attempt to encapsulate the worldview of writers from non-English-speaking American climes—represents the attempt of rationalist-oriented critics to hew out an approach to contemporary literature that is neither "modernist" nor "postmodernist," but is altogether something else.[6]

Recognizing the power of this kind of narrative and poetic in contemporary literature, critics have aptly dubbed as "magical realism" the kind of text that articulates a worldview that does not erect unbridgable dichotomies of history and myth, dream and waking, science and magic, logical and irrational. It is a term to which most Spanish- and Portuguese-language writers object, but which itself provides a bridge between two worlds officially separated by the Rio Grande.

Anglo-American southwestern narrative is drawn almost entirely from the Western epic-heroic tradition. In it, brave cowboys take part in the old cattle drives along the Chisum Trail; steely-eyed, gentle-spoken heroes ride the mesas, brave the canyons, ford the rivers, and wade the mesquite, cactus, and chaparral, meeting up with eerie, uncanny, or downright evil adversaries. A kind of Ulysses on horseback, the cowboy never marries, never settles down, just goes from event to event, crisis to crisis, triumphing over obstacles against all odds as he goes. In Anglo-American narrative, true heroes ride to the rescue of powerless, law-abiding citizens who suffer from the depredations of avaricious landowners, cupidinous industrialists, corrupt power brokers, outlaw gangs, and assorted other stock western European villains.[7]

For Laguna Pueblo and other southwestern Native peoples, the stories are as old as the land, and as new as one's most recent sojourn to *tierra encantada,* the enchanted land. These are the original southwestern magical mystery tales, and those for children's ears fostered a sense of the immediate reality of the miraculous that not even the Church could compete with or override. One of my favorites—loved because it tells as much about the mysterious significances of place as it tells me about the meaning of myself within the matrix of my people—is the one about the wicked giantess that my great-grandmother Meta Atseye Gunn told me. When I was about five or six, we went to Albuquerque. My mother drove, and Grandma Gunn and I rode together in the back seat. Driving east on old Highway 66, we passed old Laguna, and Grandma Gunn pointed to a couple of very large sandstone rocks—one roughly round, and the other rectangular, almost cylindrical. The round one may have been five or six feet in diameter, and the rectangular one was the size of a small sandstone house. "That's the head and body of the wicked giantess," my great-grandmother notified me, pointing to the great boulders with her lips. At Laguna, it's very rude to point with your finger.

I gazed out the rear window, turning in the seat and kneeling to face backward to eye the petrified monster. She continued, "You know the old giantess that almost killed the little girl," as though I had heard the story countless times. As Grandma Gunn had many grandchildren and great-grandchildren from her own seven offspring, I imagine she told the story often. But it was my first time. Not at all certain that I had seen the exact rocks she meant, I sat back down beside her, saying nothing. I guess that meant she should go on, and she did.

"Once upon a time," she began. She always began stories about the supernatural that way, it was part of her Carlisle Indian School heritage. She used to tell us stories adapted from Spenser and Tennyson, beginning them "Once upon a time" as well.[8] It was the proper opening, as I imagine this very proper old Laguna woman, to whom propriety was the secure guiding principle of human conduct, believed, for a children's story. So.

"Once upon a time there was a young girl who went out to hunt rabbits. She had her rabbit hunting stick, and she went all over the low hills near the village, searching out rabbit holes. Finding one, she would shove the long stick in after licking it carefully, and turn it around and around. If there was a rabbit in the hole, the wet stick would get all stuck in its hair. Then the girl could pull out the stick with a rabbit stuck on it, bash it over the head to kill it, and take it home for dinner." Grandma vigorously demonstrated the actions with her hands, glancing sidelong to ascertain my reaction. "Then, as the little girl was bending over one hole she heard a terrible laughing, and a big shadow fell over her. She looked up, and there was the giantess, huge, huge, looking down at her. She was very frightened, and she ducked, very quick, under the huge old woman's skirt and ran away.

"The little girl kept running until she found a cave with a small opening that she could barely fit in, and then she stayed there, being very quiet. She could hear the giantess, her footsteps booming and her voice calling 'Little girl! Little girl! Come here! You have my rabbits! Give them here!'

she called. Of course, the little girl was even more quiet. She was afraid to breathe.

"She was crouched in the little cave, pulled as far back against the back wall as she could get, barely breathing, when the giantess found her cave. The huge woman had a long stick too, and she shoved it into the cave and began to turn it around and around. The little girl draw farther back, keeping out of the stick's reach, but she was even more frightened. Suddenly, in spite of her fear, she saw a small spider on the wall near the cave entrance. And she remembered what she was supposed to do. 'Please, Grandmother Spider,' she whispered, 'please, please help me!' As she called out to the old fairy woman for help, the little rabbit girl was twisting this way and that to stay out of the stick's reach. But she kept up her prayer. Soon she heard some more noises outside the cave. It was the voices of two young men, and she heard them call out to the giantess. 'You get away from that hole,' they cried. 'There's nothing in there for you!'

"But the giantess didn't heed them. She redoubled her twisting and poking with her rabbit stick, and she was hitting the poor little girl with it. But the little girl was brave, and she didn't cry or make a sound. She just kept on dodging the stick as best she could. Soon she saw the shadow fall away from the cave, and she poked her head out cautiously. There she saw the young twins, the ones who always helped Grandmother Spider. They were fighting the giantess in a terrible battle. They were very small, and she was so large; but they had special magic, and soon they defeated her. When the giantess was dead, they split her head from her body, and threw them both in separate directions. It's those rocks I showed you that are the evil giantess's body, or what remains of it," Grandma Gunn concluded.

She didn't say anymore about it, then or ever, but every time I pass that spot I recall the little rabbit huntress and how Grandmother Spider and the Little Twins saved her when they killed the giantess. The proof of the story is right there, lying along the now vanished old road that led from Old Laguna north to Paguate, and then on to the eastern spur of Tse'pina, or Veiled-in-Clouds, the old woman mountain. That's the one the Anglo maps identify as Mount Taylor, named after the old Indian fighter and president of the United States, Zachary Taylor, changing meaning, gender, and our relationship to that mysterious, beautiful place. For 200 or so years, the mountain was known as Cerro Pelone, or Bald

Peak, to the local Natives because its 14,000-foot peak is above the timberline.

Over thirty years after Grandma Gunn told me the story of rabbit girl and the giantess, I learned that the uranium used in the first nuclear bombs was dug up from a spot near the giantess's stony remains just off the old Paguate road. Perhaps the old woman was getting her revenge on rabbit girl, the Laguna people, the Little Twins (Little Boy and Fat Man?), and the old supernatural, Grandmother Spider, She-Who-Thinks.

Eventually, throughout the 1950s and 1960s, the uranium-mining industry circumscribed the mountain, and tons of yellowcake were heaped into a bizarre echo of the flat-topped mesas that edge the valleys of the sacred lands. Jackpile Mine, located just outside the Laguna Pueblo village of Paguate, was the foremost supplier of uranium in the world for a long time. Yellowcake blew everywhere during those years of terrible drought. Our dust storms were radioactive, and our death rate from cancer has skyrocketed since that time. But one wonders since whatever is on, in, or around was dreamed up by the old Keresan deity Spider Woman, why she would conjure such terrible deadliness, making it the sacred color of woman—yellow?

Imagine: it was about the time that Grandma Gunn told me the story of Spider Woman and the little rabbit girl, give or take a year, that the bomb was detonated at Stallion Gate about seventy or so miles southeast of Laguna. It was sunrise that day, July 16, 1945, a sunrise that came earlier than the rising sun itself. It was the day the fourth world ended and the fifth world began. That was the time one of the Old Spider's sister-nieces came home. Her name was Sun Woman, and she had gone away long ago, heading east, but they always said she would come back. Some Pueblos say that in July 1945 she did.

My dad has always called New Mexico "God's Country." When out-of-staters would come by, he'd greet them, "Welcome to God's country." For him, I suppose, the Southwest is western New Mexico. Most of my sense of the region as a neverending tale comes from him, for he is an inveterate storyteller. My dad is the son of immigrants. His grandfather, grandmother, and father, who was then a young boy, came to the United States from Lebanon. They were Maronite Catholic (as distinct from Roman Catholic), and he always bragged that Lebanon was the first nation to accept Christianity. I say this because Americans in general perceive Lebanon as Muslim, but that is erroneous. In any event, much of my sense of place, my understanding that I am of the Southwest, comes from his stories and those of his father. They never went anywhere that was not an occasion for a tale. And there are so many that it's difficult to find just one or two, the most telling, the most place-revealing. For it is in the nature of the oral tradition to make significance from story piled on story, without benefit (dubious) of abstraction, theory, and linguistic and intellectual alienation.

For storytellers like my father, place is more personal than almost anything. Sense of place is about an ongoing relationship not only of self, but of others who have touched one's life. And all those events are cradled in the land: "On that mesa, that's Enchanted Mesa, you know, there used to be thick wooden stakes stuck in the sides. You can't get up there now." Listening, I contemplate the sheer-sided mesa that rises off the flatland not far from Acoma Pueblo: "When I was young, oh, maybe fifteen or sixteen, we climbed up it." Years later, I read a thriller novel in which the hero was stuck on Enchanted Mesa, with the bad guys all around, and his buddy flew in, landed on the mesa top, and rescued him. Reading, I imagined the hero, my youthful dad, atop Enchanted Mesa, adventuring.

One story he always used to tell when we went on the annual family picnic to Portales, just above Seboyeta, concerned the sharp incline just before one reached Bibo: "When it would rain you couldn't drive up it. Your mother used to bring the horses down from Seboyeta and meet me, and we'd ride home." Of course, the road doesn't steeply rise out of the plain at that place any more. Paved, it takes a genteel sloping journey inward, toward the sacred spring sheltered beneath the great white sandstone overhang at Portales. The last few miles are about as rough, though, and during the rainy season that last stretch of road is probably washed out. Perhaps my favorite of his stories related to that site is about the wild stallion. The hero of the tale is my father, a young family man, who saw a beautiful stallion he longed to own: "I heard that if you shot them, just barely creasing their head, you could catch them when they dropped. But they wouldn't really be hurt, just stunned. So one day old Benino and I went out there. I had my rifle, and finally we found the stallion. We stopped far enough away not to scare him off, and walked close enough to get off a shot. I raised the rifle and took careful aim—I was a good shot in those days—and squeezed the trigger. The horse turned to look at me just then, and the shot got him between the eyes." After all these years, my dad's eyes still get moist with tears, and he shakes his head, sorrowful, full of regret. We are bathed with "both a sense of sorrow and pride," left reflecting on "fragility and permanence."⁹ This is what it means to know the land, to be personally bonded with it, for richer or poorer, in sickness and in health, till death do you part—and probably not even then. And it is this exactly personal relationship to place that for me defines *mi país,* the Southwest, land of enchantment, where for the most part reality is magical.

This is probably why I fail to connect with the "new" Southwesterners, those transplants who move to God's country and pave it, develop it, merchandise it, commodify it, and, entirely unaware of the land and its actively intelligent presence, attempt to transplant that oddity of spiritual deadness, American culture, to our sacred and hardy land. I know people who have resided in our *tierra encantada* for two or more generations and yet see themselves as though in Wisconsin, Massachusetts, or anywhere other than this magical, multiple borderland. It's as though they brought the concept of franchise hotels with them, before there was such a thing: stay at HoJo's, and you could be anywhere.

But what's the use of being able to imagine you're anywhere, when you are there, here, where there is and I passionately hope will always be a here, there? Such emigrants have never attended a dance at one of the pueblos. Nor do they learn a word of Spanish other than Spanish place and street names or the names of a few local foods—and those they mostly mispronounce. They never listen to *corridos* or popular *músicos,* never recount a *chiste*—possess nary a *dicho* among them. Many, though not all, eat chili almost ritually, and that's that. Imagine! Their children go here and there trying to find their own souls, as though a soul were a commodity, a consumer good, buyable, sellable, mutually interchangeable with anything at all. Reminds an academic of the Raj; makes one long for postcolonialism along the borderlands. These usually WASPish (but this category includes a number of Roman Catholic, Middle Eastern, Asian, and African-American immigrants), generations-long tourists have, largely superciliously, given birth to the idea that we invent ourselves. And perhaps they do, perhaps they must, because they seem bereft of that profoundly human capacity to be created in relationship to place—to the smells, the sounds, the tastes, the language, the rhythm that makes one region clearly different from another. *¡Que lástima!*

Another story my dad repeats with gusto: one Sunday at Mass in the Spanish-Mexican village of Barelas, which is near Albuquerque, one of the old men, a heavy drinker—especially on Saturday nights—had taken his place in the tiny balcony at the back of church. When the Mass was over, he attempted to descend the steep, narrow stairs and he fell. He landed with a loud thwack. *La gente* gathered around, to see if he was badly hurt, to offer him a hand up. He gathered himself up, and standing as tall as he could regarded the excited crowd indignantly. "*¡Cada quien se 'pea como el quiere!*" he snorted. "Everyone gets down the way he chooses!" Plopping his hat firmly on his balding head, he stomped—staggering only a little—out the church door.

These little *chistes,* or humorous anecdotes, are narrative companions to larger narratives, the magical stories. Since narratives, like geographic and climatic features, are no respecters of political boundaries, most of them are transborder, funneling up from regions south of the border along the Rio Grande, the Colorado River, the Old Cattle Trail, and, recently, superhighways. One of the most widespread concerns *La Llorana,* the wailing woman. I have heard several versions of the tale, and have traced its origin to the court of Moctezuma, on the eve of the arrival of the conquistadors in the land of the Aztec people. There the voice of the Aztec goddess Coatlique was heard wailing, her voice ringing through the streets of the Aztec barrios, "Oh, my children, where can I hide you?" signifying the prophesied end of the Aztec Empire at the hands of the blond aliens who came out of the sea. The text of her wails changed somewhat, as the circumstances of her people changed, and the reasons given for her *grita,* her wail of rage, changed as well.

The story went north with the Christianized, Spanish-speaking Mexicans sent to colonize the vast regions north of the outposts of the Spanish Empire in Maya–Aztec country. They followed the Rio Grande into the northern reaches of New Spain. After the Mexican Revolution, New Spain became New Mexico (Nuevo México), and a portion of its northernmost reaches retains the name. As the story of *La Llorana* goes in New Mexico, the Texas borderlands, Arizona, and parts of southern Colorado, she is the ghost of a woman who murdered her *hijos,* her babies. She had them by a Spaniard, an upper-class *don,* aristocrat, who abandoned her to marry a Spanish lady of his class. Thus she is known to stalk philandering husbands returning home late from romantic trysts, and she is often seen standing on a sandbar in the Rio Grande, near the Bridge Street bridge in southeast Albuquerque. She travels railways and highways and, for all I know, hangs around airports by now, yet her favorite haunts are waterways. Children are cautioned to avoid arroyos, *acequias* (irrigation ditches), and river banks. Often you can hear her wailing. "*Aiii, mis hijos!*" she wails, lamenting. "*¿A dónde va? ¿A dónde va?* Oh, my children! Where are you?" Sometimes she visits someone's house, and she is terrible to behold, with her long fingernails and silvery eyes, which stare empty of all but eerie rage. She often steals children, and when she succeeds, their bodies are found floating in a ditch, an arroyo, or the river.

One imagines that we impose our sense of place on the land, but given the oddly similar lines of these narrative strands as they work themselves out in the Southwest and elsewhere, one wonders: Is it we who invent the stories and thus inform the land, or does the land give us the stories, thus inventing us?

Contributions to the cultural matrix such as amazing stories, great food, exotic fashions, rugs, arts and crafts, horticulture, along with varieties of Puebloan and Spanish colonial-outpost architecture and music are not limited to Native or Hispanic denizens of the Southwest. Anglo-European, African-American, and myriad other groups who have moved into the region in the past century or so have brought their own complement of cultural and environmental goodies, blending them with those already there. In its contemporary mode, the cultural, linguistic, and environmental features of the region are unique to itself while displaying the texture and layered significance that have characterized the region for more than 1,000 years. The newcomers have introduced their own kinds of music, literature, law, and government; they mandated the English language and spread Protestantism, mercantilism, industrialism, and allied modes of business and financing; they have developed architectural modes that make artful use of the best features of earlier forms indigenous to the area. These early designs were energy-efficient and land-friendly, a plus in an area that experiences extremes of temperature in an era devoted to ecological consciousness.

While trading, mining, and livestock have been major sources of investment and employment in the region for over fifty years and all sorts of service industries have long played a crucial economic role there, tourism probably bears most of the credit for drawing intellectuals and artists from over the world into the region, indelibly imprinting their vision of place on the Southwest: writers, artists, journalists, photographers, intelligence agents, paranormal and occult researchers and writers, and ethnographers the likes of D. H. Lawrence, Frank Lloyd Wright, Mabel Dodge

Lujan, Ambrose Bierce, Lew Wallace, Laura Gilpin, Mary Austin, Willa Cather, Georgia O'Keeffe, Bronislaw Malinowski, and Elsie Clews Parsons, along with contemporaries such as John Nichols, Barbara Kingsolver, and Terry McMillan—a star-studded host of generations of glitterati who have been drawn to the region by its mystery, its powerful American Indian and American Hispanic presence, its rugged beauty, and its mystique. In turn, they have produced a variety of works that have defined the region in public awareness and have, in turn, left their multilayered mark on American consciousness.

However, the most formative Anglo-American presence has been and continues to be the military, and the most amazing "borderland" stories have arisen from military installations. Santa Fe and the old Hispanic power base it nurtured were apparently shunted into the backwaters of power in the territory when after much wrangling the east coast magnates decided to lay the track of the transcontinental railroad through Albuquerque, where Sandia base, originally a frontier and Civil War outpost, was located. But the power that remained, while not visibly political, was great. It began to be clearly evident when, in more recent times, J. Robert Oppenheimer selected the high mountains above Santa Fe, a place called Los Alamos, or The Cottonwoods, near the ancient site of the Bird People (Los Pajaritos in Spanish), for the development of the bomb that ended World War II, and ushered in the Fifth World of the Pueblo and Diné, Sexto Sol of the Maya and Aztec, on July 16, 1945.

At a pasture locally known as Stallion Gate, which Oppenheimer significantly enough dubbed Trinity, in the midst of a flat area named Jornada del Muerto (Journey of Death) by early Spanish explorers, Fat Boy was detonated—a brilliant flash that culminated one of history's greatest colloquia of scientists. It was done, of course, in total (well almost total) secrecy under the auspices of the armed forces.

From the time of early incursions across the border against Pancho Villa or in pursuit of stopping German power plays in Mexico prior to World War I and over the ensuing decades, the military has continued to play a central role in the borderlands. During World Wars I and II, Fort Bliss, the large base at El Paso, was a major training and staging area, as it remained through the Gulf War of the early 1990s. Southern Colorado became the site of NORAD, the vast installation buried deep beneath the towering Rocky Mountains, and Fort Wingate, in Navajo country along the New Mexico–Arizona border, became the storage site for ordnance

left over from Vietnam. All who drove along the old Highway 66 can vividly remember the miles of airplanes lined up outside Kingman, Arizona,
for years after the war—World War II, that is.

There is an installation beneath the Manzano Mountains east of
Albuquerque's Kirtland Air Force Base and a large military reserve that
incorporates White Sands Proving Grounds and space-shuttle landing site
near Alamagordo, New Mexico, and Trinity site, sixty miles north as the
stealth bomber flies. Many of the bases in the region serve as debarkation
points for forays south of the United States–Mexican border. Missions in
support of the contras during the Nicaraguan civil war, or in support of
Guatemala and Mexico in their military actions against rebels and/or
Mayan and other Native Mexican or Guatemalan peoples, are launched
from military facilities in Texas, New Mexico, Arizona, and southern
California. Of course, the long-simmering border wars—which have
undergone a notable surge—are maintained at the border between the
English-speaking and the Spanish-speaking portions of the Western
Hemisphere.

Despite the overwhelmingly rationalist flavor of the military, the magical power of the Southwest is stronger. It is able to turn even these bas-
tions of rectitude and order into a rich store of myth that comes near to
rivaling that of the Native American tradition. Magical realism is not a
mode confined to Hispanic literature: the story of what some call "the
Roswell incident"; the rumors of otherworldly activity at a small military
installation at Dulce, bordering Jicarilla Apache country; odd sightings
near China Lake, Vandenburg, Monzano, and Kirtland; along with rumors
circling around NORAD and the underground base in the Manzanos—all
testify to the presence of the otherworldly in the very heart of the military's
Southwest. Even the making of the bomb possesses elements of magical
realism. Stories circulate about odd sightings around Los Alamos. Some
of them originate with Pueblo and Apache sources, but other accounts
come from otherwise logical-positivist-minded Anglos. According to one
of the latter, back when the Manhattan Project was the best-kept secret
in the country, one of the physicists at Los Alamos used to wander out on
the mesas at night, turning problems over in his overworked brain. More
than once he got the solution to his dilemma from a stranger he met out
there in the dark. Whether the stranger was an American, or even a
human, is not clear from the tale; the listener's imagination must fill in
the blanks.

There are a number of otherworldly incidents connected to military installations throughout the entire region, demonstrating that even an institution as fact and logic oriented as the military is subject to the mysterious interface between the ordinary and the extraordinary out there. One of the most famous—or notorious, if one prefers—is the one known as "the Roswell incident." So famous has this close encounter become that at least one major film and several documentaries have been made about it. Briefly, one night in 1947 a rancher in southeastern New Mexico, forty or so miles outside of Roswell, saw a huge explosion occur some distance from his ranch house. The next day, Mac Brazel went out to investigate and discovered the wreckage of a strange vehicle. According to Major Jesse A. Marcel, who was stationed at Roswell Army Air Base and to whom the local sheriff reported Brazel's find, chunks of material were found but no damaged or partially intact disk. However, the base reported that it had recovered a flying disk, a story later officially changed to say that it had recovered a weather balloon. In the wake of the military's official debunking of the flying-disk version, Marcel responded that the material wasn't the sort used for weather balloons. What he had seen, he said, "was thin and foil-like, but would not dent, and included something like balsa wood that would not burn when a flame was applied to it. He described indecipherable hieroglyphics printed on some of the debris."[10]

Whether or not there were alien bodies in the wreckage is hotly debated, but it is thought by many UFO researchers that three were recovered, one yet alive. They were taken first to Wright Patterson Air Force Base on orders from the commanding officer, Colonel William H. Blanchard; later they were transferred to Nellis Air Force Base, in Nevada, where, in top-secret facilities in Area 51, near Coyote Peak, they and the craft have long been under study. The Roswell incident and spin-offs have been featured in a number of books, major movies, television documentaries concerned with UFOs and government "cover-ups" of them, and *The X Files*, the cult hit television show of the 1990s. The blockbuster film *Independence Day* contains a number of references to the event.

These stories form a large body of contemporary mythic literature; what's notable about them in the context of the Southwest is how closely they parallel a variety of sacred stories of the various Native peoples and more than a few old Hispanic stories of the region.

Speaking of the Southwest as the original home of the magical mystery story, it must be said that Hollywood itself is located in the Southwest, albeit on "the coast." Southern California, long chided as the land of fruits and nuts, comes by its reputation honestly. The major cities as well as the small towns were originally Spanish settlements. The area was taken over by the United States in the mid-nineteenth century, at the same time as New Mexico Territory. One can imagine the political maneuvering that located the area under the governance of California—granted statehood in 1850. It seems likely that the decision had more to do with eastern financial and political finagling than with anything inherent to the existing cultural or geophysical features. Nevertheless, southern California's geographic and cultural connections to the rest of the Southwest are much in evidence: one has only to check out the names of the cities, towns, hamlets, and streets; take a quick look at the major tourist attractions; pay attention to the architecture; watch the weather, the sky; or sit in the hills or hike in the mountains to realize the presence, that indefinable, elusive something, that makes an area southwestern. Spanish is a major language from San Diego to Monterey, as it is in southwestern Texas, New Mexico, and southern Arizona.

Indeed, the Hispanic presence is powerful in southern California, a point that has many an Anglo up in arms. The idea that the Mexicans (and their Central American cousins) are about to retake quite a bit of the territory their government ceded nearly 150 years ago has mobilized political, financial, religions, and monolinguistic forces across the region. There already are more Spanish-speaking people residing in the Los Angeles area than English-speaking, and an exploding subculture of cooks, servers, clerks, mechanics, store managers, domestics, and gardeners is in universal evidence, spreading a growing middle-class, Spanish-speaking presence throughout the area.

In a recent piece produced by PBS for the *The NewsHour,* Chicano writer and popular philosopher Richard Rodriguez pointed out the effect this presence will have on United States culture. He noted that the large number of Spanish-speaking nannies raising children of rich and powerful Anglo-Americans is bound to have a transformative effect on American civilization. For as those children enter the work and voting force, their bicultural, bilingual consciousness will motivate them as powerfully as the bicultural, biracial consciousness of an earlier generation of Anglo-

Americans in the American South moved them: into the civil rights movement of the 1960s, and its continuation in public forums, media, and civic life.

Rodriguez argues that an analogous transformation will occur vis-à-vis the borderlands, suggesting that the cultural face of the United States in the twenty-first century will be radically different from its present one. One implication of his remarks is that Los Angeles and southern California in general will lead the nation toward the bilingualism specified by the Treaty of Guadalupe Hildago, signed between the United States and Mexico at the end of the Mexican War in 1848. That would mean that the United States could close one of the major gaps it suffers in this hemisphere, the language gap between Americans north and south of the politically imposed Mexican–American border.

Kachinas, hump-backed flute players, Old Man Coyote; extraterrestrials and UFOs; apparitions and hauntings in houses and along rivers and ditches, streets and byways—the realism of the magic that characterizes the Southwest in narrative and landscape has found a center of propagation in the heart of the biggest urban complex in the region. Thriving within the multitudinous expanse of southern California and the Hispanic-American Southwest, Hollywood has grown to become the narrative center of the United States, perhaps of the Western world. At least as much that is mythic comes out of Hollywood as out of the cultures that surround it; they enjoy an interactive dynamic that is the region's signal feature, its basic existential process.

The City of the Angels (or Lost Angels, as some would have it) features most forms of private and public architecture known to humankind, but favors Spanish mission adobe constructions or related forms over most other kinds. Long a major center of ranching and agribusiness, southern California has served as a center of American Indian mores, leading Anglo-American culture into a lifestyle characterized by a relaxed, inclusive attitude, and interest in and respect for the paranormal and non-normal, as these are defined in Eurocentric circles. A characteristic laid back, "live and let live" attitude characterized American Indian civilization at the time of the coming of the "white man," much to the dismay of many sixteenth-century boat people. Early colonists were much concerned about First Nations people's habit of bathing daily (they said it spread disease), tendency to turn economic decisions over to women, and, worst, unwillingness to hit, tie up, maim, or in any way terrorize or batter children.

But over the centuries, these habits have become characteristic of the larger American community. Americans bathe at least once a day, view battering of citizens who happen to be female or still growing as abhorrent, wear as little clothing as possible when weather and social obligation permit, and see no reason why state, county, and municipal treasuries and disbursement agencies should not be headed by women. Altruism and tolerance of difference, of multiplicity, are rapidly becoming fundamental American values.

Hollywood has played a major part in this process of Indianization; for nearly a century, it has been the major tool of cultural definition: it is from Hollywood that popular conceptions about the Southwest and the West, cowboys and Indians, Mexicans and gringos emanate, and these conceptions have played a powerful role in the value shifts that distinguish the United States from its Old World antecedents. It is significant that a growing proportion of its most popular recent output is concerned with supernatural, paranormal, or at least otherworldly events. There's something about the Southwest, even in Hollywood, that has that effect.

In 1996, Talking God and Growling God, or the Little Twins—depending on whose version you heard—came to Navajoland. They addressed a Navajo woman who had performed an old ceremonial. Soon word leaked out, but the Navajo Tribal Council quickly closed the site to all tourists and thrill-seekers. So it seems that the old gods still visit the people now and again; and whether they come as themselves or as super-high-tech instruments of an alien civilization, their appearance makes it clear that there's more magic in reality than modern techno-science dreams.

The Argentine writer Jorge Luis Borges has written that "myth is at the beginning of literature, and also at its end."[11] But it should be noted that the land, the supernatural beings that people it, and the spirits that flow over and within it precede and continuously inform both myth and literature, as well as most other dimensions of culture. The land that is the American Southwest is the abode of beings of such power that whoever lives on it sooner or later takes up their stories and sings their songs. Moderns would do well to keep in mind the notion that the geographic and the geologic are more of spirit than of rationalist mentation, for as southwestern writer Leslie Marmon Silko has old Ku'oosh, the Laguna medicine man in *Ceremony,* say, "You know, grandson, this world is *fragile.*"[12] It is an odd concept, perhaps, for the urbane mind, but one that bears deep contemplation. The land is alive—knowing, known, aware—

and humans, for all our preening, are merely (and magnificently!) one of a multitude of natural events in this geospiritual reality. Perhaps the Southwest borderlands are one place where the intricate relation between the sun and the web, the spirit and the substance, is undeniable. Maybe it is this characteristic that marks regional boundaries more truly than map, politics, or history can hope to do.

NOTES

1. The wealthy socialite Mabel Dodge Lujan, friend and benefactor to a variety of writers, artists, politicians, and other people of note (her circle included Frank Lloyd Wright and D. H. Lawrence), married a Taos Indian man named Tony Lujan. It is said that he haunts her old house, now used to host visiting writers, conferences, artists, and the like. One hears music from the 1930s and 1940s, smells whiskey and perfume, hears her laughing, and discerns ice tinkling in glasses. It is said she climbs into bed with visitors she finds attractive, rocking the bed raucously throughout the night. It's a hard place to get any sleep, visitors so honored say.

2. The Chamber of Commerce brochure I picked up there five years ago boasted that 4 million visitors had passed through Sedona the previous year! That's a lot of feet and water for as fragile an ecosystem as graces the Sedona area.

3. It might be useful to keep in mind that though Americans of the United States think of the base culture as Anglo, German—both language and culture—played a very large role in the shaping of American civilization. We speak English as our national language because a wagon broke down on the way to the meeting where the matter was decided, so English won the day by *one* vote.

4. To this day, I am vexed by American scholars' perverse insistence that American civilization comes from New England with, maybe, a small bow to the Virginia Colony. I am equally perturbed by the astonishing idea that the nations to the south of the United States are not Western nations. It is as though American intellectuals believe that Spanish is an indigenous American language!

5. *The Book of the Council,* trans. Adrian Recinos, ed. Sylvanus G. Morley and Delia Goetz (New York: Dover, 1950). *Popol Vuh* is a Quiché Mayan traditional myth compiled by Mayan scribes and translated into colonial Spanish.

6. The term "magical realism" was first applied to the work of the mixed-blood Peruvian poet César Vallejo and later extended to artists affected by his "transborder" vision such as Salvadore Dali. Vallejo was working in the same mystico-realist vein as Spanish-language writers all over the Americas, the best known of these being Jorge Luis Borges and Gabriel Gárcia Márquez.

7. Writers who excel at this form include, in order of appearance, Zane Grey, Louis L'Amour, and Tony Hillerman.

8. I was fascinated to learn that Sir Edmund Spenser was granted a fine castle (or perhaps a drafty one) in Ireland from which to oversee the lives and tithes of the "savages," as the English styled their Irish neighbors at the time. The Irish rose up and burned him out, causing him to return to England in 1599, only a few years after the Pueblo evicted the Spaniards from New Mexico. I imagine that none of the instructors at Carlisle Indian School informed Grandma Gunn of that odd synchronicity.

9. With special thanks to Michael Steiner for marginalia.

10. John Spencer, ed., *The UFO Encyclopedia* (Glasgow: Headline, 1991).

11. Eduardo Galeano, *Dreamtigers* (Austin: University of Texas Press, 1989), 42.

12. Leslie Marmon Silko, *Ceremony* (New York: Viking, 1977), 35. The passage continues, "The word he chose to express 'fragile' was filled with the intricacies of a continuing process, and with a strength inherent in spider webs woven across paths through sand hills where early in the morning the sun becomes entangled in each filament of web."

Contributors

PAULA GUNN ALLEN, of Laguna Pueblo–Sioux heritage, is professor of English at the University of California, Los Angeles. She is the author of eleven books, including the novel *The Woman Who Owned the Shadows* (1982), several collections of poetry and essays, and a volume of Native American myths and legends. She has also edited three anthologies of Native American fiction and a collection of critical essays and course designs for teaching American Indian literature. Her most recent publications are *The Voice of the Turtle: American Indian Literature, 1900–1970* (1994) and *The Song of the Turtle: American Indian Literature, 1974–1994* (1995).

PETER BOAG is associate professor of history at Idaho State University. He is the author of *Environment and Experience: Settlement Culture in Nineteenth-Century Oregon* (1992) and has published articles in the *Pacific Northwest Quarterly* and *Oregon Historical Quarterly* on environmental perception in the Northwest and the Snake River region.

RICHARD MAXWELL BROWN is Beekman Professor Emeritus of Northwest and Pacific History at the University of Oregon and a past president of the Western History Association. His books include *The South Carolina Regulators* (1963), *Strain of Violence: Historical Studies of American Violence and Vigilantism* (1975), and *No Duty to Retreat: Violence and Values in American History and Society* (1991). He has contributed chapters to many books, including William G. Robbins, Robert J. Frank, and William E. Ross, eds., *Regionalism and the Pacific Northwest* (1983), and Carlos A. Schwantes, ed., *Encounters with a Distant Land: Exploration and the Great Northwest* (1994). He is working on a book on the Pacific Northwest as "rain coast and rain shadow."

ARNOLDO DE LEÓN is the C. J. "Red" Davidson Professor of History at

San Angelo State University. He is the author of *The Tejano Community, 1836–1900* (1982), *They Called Them Greasers: Anglo Attitudes Toward Mexicans in Texas, 1821–1900* (1983), and *Ethnicity in the Sunbelt: A History of Mexican Americans in Houston, Texas* (1989), and co-author of *Mexican Americans in Texas: A Brief History* (1993), *Not Enough Room: Mexicans, Anglos, and Socio-Economic Change in Texas, 1850–1900* (1993), and *The History of Texas,* 2nd ed. (1996).

WILLIAM DEVERELL is associate professor of history at the California Institute of Technology. He is the author of *Railroad Crossing: Californians and the Railroad, 1850–1910* (1994) and the co-editor of *California Progressivism Revisited* (1994). He also has published articles in the *Western Historical Quarterly.*

JOHN M. FINDLAY is professor of history and director of the Center for the Study of the Pacific Northwest at the University of Washington and editor of the *Pacific Northwest Quarterly.* He has written *People of Chance: Gambling in American Society from Jamestown to Las Vegas* (1986), *Magic Lands: Western Cityscapes and American Culture Since 1940* (1992), and numerous articles. He is currently co-authoring the book *Technology, Community, and Culture at Hanford, 1942–1992,* and co-editing the volume *The Atomic West.*

ANNE F. HYDE is associate professor of history at Colorado College. She is the author of *An American Vision: Far Western Landscape and American Culture, 1820–1920* (1990) and of articles published in the *Western Historical Quarterly* and essays in anthologies. She is working on a book on the impact of the extractive industries in the Rocky Mountain West.

GLENNA MATTHEWS is an independent scholar who teaches periodically at Stanford University and the University of California, Berkeley, Davis, Irvine, and Los Angeles. She is the author of *"Just a Housewife": The Rise and Fall of Domesticity in America* (1987) and *The Rise of Public Women: Women's Power and Women's Place from the Colonial Period to the Present* (1992) and the co-author of *Running as a Woman: Gender and Power in American Politics* (1993). She is working on the book *Silicon Valley Women: From Fruit to Chips and Beyond.*

MARY MURPHY is associate professor of history at Montana State University. She is the co-author of *Like a Family: The Making of a Southern Cotton Mill World* (1987), has published several essays on women's history, and is the author of *Mining Cultures: Men, Women and Leisure in Butte, 1914–1941* (1997).

ELIZABETH RAYMOND is associate professor and chair of history at the University of Nevada. She is the author of *George Wingfield: Owner and Operator of Nevada* (1992) and co-author of *Stopping Time: A Rephotographic Survey of Lake Tahoe* (1992). She has written many essays and is co-editing a book on women in Nevada's Comstock Lode in the nineteenth century.

JAMES R. SHORTRIDGE is professor of geography at the University of Kansas. He has written *Kaw Valley Landscapes: A Traveler's Guide to Northeastern Kansas* (1988), *The Middle West: Its Meaning in American Culture* (1989), *Peopling the Plains: Who settled Where in Frontier Kansas* (1995), and numerous articles published in such journals as *American Studies, Geographical Review,* and *Great Plains Quarterly.*

MICHAEL C. STEINER is professor and chair of American studies at California State University, Fullerton. He is the co-author of *Region and Regionalism in the United States* (1988), the author of articles on regionalism and on the New Western History published in the *Geographical Review* and *Pacific Historical Review,* co-editor of *Mapping American Culture* (1992), and a contributor to Richard Etulain, ed., *Writing Western History* (1991).

BRET WALLACH is professor and chair of geography at the University of Oklahoma. He is the author of *At Odds with Progress: Conservation and Americans* (1991) and *Losing Asia: Modernization and the Culture of Development* (1996), has published articles in such journals as *Geographic Review* and the *Annals of the Association of American Geographers,* is a frequent contributor to *Focus,* and is a recipient of a MacArthur Foundation Fellowship.

JOHN S. WHITEHEAD is professor of history at the University of Alaska. He is co-author of *Yankees in Paradise: The Pacific Basin Frontier* (1993), and the author of articles on Hawaiian history published in the *Western Historical Quarterly* and *Hawaiian Journal of History*. He is writing a comparative history of Alaska and Hawai'i from 1789 to 1859.

DAVID M. WROBEL is assistant professor of history at Widener University. He is the author of *The End of American Exceptionalism: Frontier Anxiety from the Old West to the New Deal* (1993) and of articles published in *American Studies* and the *Pacific Historical Review*. He is working on the book *Becoming Western: Regional Identity in America's Promised Land*.

Index

Hollywood, 361–63
Holt, John Dominis, 333
Homestead Act (1862), 118
Honolulu, Hawai'i, 332
"Horizons" (Haste), 169–70
Houston, Sam, 264
Hudson Bay Company, 42, 323–24
Humboldt River, 75
Humboldt Sink, 73
Hunt, William Price, 186
Hyde, Anne F., 19, 33–34, 139, 207

Idaho
    and California water needs, 183
    historiography, 198n5
    northern and southern, 183–84
    and the Pacific Northwest, 62n4,
        177–78
    See also Pacific Northwest; Rocky
        Mountain region; Snake River
        region
Iditarod sled-dog races, 330
I Heard the Owl Call My Name
    (Craven), 178
Ill Fares the Land (McWilliams),
    238
Immigration Act of 1952
    (McCarren-Walter Act), 226
Immigration Reform Act of 1965,
    228
Independence Day (movie), 360
Independence Pass, 98–99
Indians. See Native Americans
Industrial Workers of the World
    (IWW), 159
In the Zone of Filtered Sunshine
    (Weber), 54–55
In Tragic Life (Fisher), 203n26
Irish in San Francisco, 219
Irrigation
    in the Great Basin, 76–81
    in the Pacific Northwest, 55
    See also National Reclamation
        Act; Newlands Reclamation Act

Irving, Washington, 139, 185–88,
    196
Isaacs, Harold, 8
Isern, Tom, 130
Issel, William, 219
Italians in San Francisco, 219
"It's Your Misfortune and None of
    My Own" (White), 212, 301

Jackson, Helen Hunt, 251
Jacobs, Jane, 6
James, Edwin, 117
Japanese
    in California, 224–25, 247, 332–
        33
    in Hawai'i, 332–33
    internment of, 46
    in the Pacific Northwest, 46
    in San Francisco, 218
Jefferson, Thomas, 117
Jews in San Francisco, 219
Jihad vs. McWorld (Barber), 8
Johnson, Jeremiah, 101
Johnson, Marilyn, 226
Johnson City, Kansas, 120
Johnson County War (1891/1892),
    106
Jordan, Terry, 9

Kahl, Gordon, 12
Kalākaua, David (king), 324–25,
    325–26
Kama'ainas, 335
Kamehameha, I, 317
Kamehameha, II, 320
Kamehameha, III, 324
Kanakas, 318, 320, 324
Kansas. See Northern Plains
Kelton, Elmer, 270
Kesey, Ken, 44
King, Sieh King, 227
Kingsolver, Barbara, 358
Kiowa, 152
Kittredge, William, 44